PREVENTING DOMESTIC HOMICIDES

PREVENTING DOMESTIC HOMICIDES

Lessons Learned From Tragedies

Edited by

PETER JAFFE
Centre for Research & Education on Violence against Women & Children, Faculty of Education,
Western University, London, ON, Canada

KATREENA SCOTT
Department of Applied Psychology and Human Development, University of Toronto, ON, Canada

ANNA-LEE STRAATMAN
Centre for Research & Education on Violence against Women & Children, Faculty of Education,
Western University, London, ON, Canada

ACADEMIC PRESS
An imprint of Elsevier

ELSEVIER

Academic Press is an imprint of Elsevier
125 London Wall, London EC2Y 5AS, United Kingdom
525 B Street, Suite 1650, San Diego, CA 92101, United States
50 Hampshire Street, 5th Floor, Cambridge, MA 02139, United States
The Boulevard, Langford Lane, Kidlington, Oxford OX5 1GB, United Kingdom

Notices
Knowledge and best practice in this field are constantly changing. As new research and experience broaden our understanding, changes in research methods, professional practices, or medical treatment may become necessary.

Practitioners and researchers must always rely on their own experience and knowledge in evaluating and using any information, methods, compounds, or experiments described herein. In using such information or methods they should be mindful of their own safety and the safety of others, including parties for whom they have a professional responsibility.

To the fullest extent of the law, neither the Publisher nor the authors, contributors, or editors, assume any liability for any injury and/or damage to persons or property as a matter of products liability, negligence or otherwise, or from any use or operation of any methods, products, instructions, or ideas contained in the material herein.

British Library Cataloguing-in-Publication Data
A catalogue record for this book is available from the British Library

Library of Congress Cataloging-in-Publication Data
A catalog record for this book is available from the Library of Congress

ISBN: 978-0-12-819463-8

For Information on all Academic Press publications
visit our website at https://www.elsevier.com/books-and-journals

Publisher: Stacy Masucci
Acquisitions Editor: Elizabeth Brown
Editorial Project Manager: Fernanda Oliviera
Production Project Manager: Paul Prasad Chandramohan
Cover Designer: Miles Hitchen

Typeset by MPS Limited, Chennai, India

Working together
to grow libraries in
developing countries

www.elsevier.com • www.bookaid.org

Dedication

We dedicate this book to the victims of domestic homicide as well as their surviving family members and friends who wonder what society could do differently in the future to prevent these tragedies.

Contents

7 Perpetrator mental health: depression and suicidality as risk factors for domestic homicide 137

Katreena Scott, Casey L. Oliver and Polly Cheng

8 Child homicides in the context of domestic violence: when the plight of children is overlooked 159

Katreena Scott, Laura Olszowy, Michael Saxton and Katherine Reif

List of contributors

Abir Al Jamal Muslim Resource Centre for Social Support and Integration

Victoria Banman Banman Counselling, St. Thomas, ON, Canada

Vicky Boldo L'Université de Montréal, Concordia University, Montreal, QC, Canada

Polly Cheng Centre for Research & Education on Violence Against Women & Children, Western University, London, ON, Canada

Randal David Centre for Research & Education on Violence against Women & Children, Faculty of Education, Western University, London, ON, Canada

Misha Dhillon Ending Violence Association of British Columbia, Vancouver, BC, Canada

Deborah Doherty Public Legal Education and Information Service New Brunswick, New Brunswick, Canada

Janie Dolan-Cake L'Université de Montréal, Concordia University, Montreal, QC, Canada

Jordan Fairbairn Department of Sociology, King's University College at Western University, ON, Canada

Elizabeth Fast Department of Applied Human Sciences, Concordia University, Montreal, QC, Canada

Olivia Fischer Counselling Psychology, University of British Columbia, and Ending Violence Association of British Columbia, BC, Canada

Kristina Giacobbe Faculty of Education, Western University, London, ON, Canada

Sepali Guruge Ryerson University, Daphne Cockwell School of Nursing, Victoria, Toronto, ON, Canada

Peter Jaffe Centre for Research & Education on Violence Against Women & Children, Faculty of Education, Western University, London, ON, Canada

Meineka Kulasinghe King's University College, Western University, London, ON, Canada

Alexandra Lysova School of Criminology, Simon Fraser University, BC, Canada

Margaret MacPherson Centre for Research & Education on Violence Against Women & Children, Faculty of Education, Western University, London, ON, Canada

Barbara MacQuarrie Centre for Research & Education on Violence Against Women & Children, Faculty of Education, Western University, London, ON, Canada

Casey L. Oliver Centre for Research & Education on Violence Against Women & Children, Western University, London, ON, Canada

Laura Olszowy Centre for Research & Education on Violence Against Women & Children, Faculty of Education, Western University, London, ON, Canada

Corinne Qureshi Faculty of Education, Western University, ON, Canada

Katherine Reif Centre for Research & Education on Violence Against Women & Children, Faculty of Education, Western University, London, ON, Canada

Catherine Richardson/Kinewesquao Concordia University, Montreal, QC, Canada

Katherine Rossiter FREDA Centre for Research on Violence Against Women and Children, School of Criminology, Simon Fraser University, and Ending Violence Association of British Columbia, Vancouver, BC, Canada

Jackie Salas Dr. Jeffrey Wong & Associates, CA, United States; Faculty of Education, Western University, London, ON, Canada

Michael Saxton Centre for Research & Education on Violence Against Women & Children, Faculty of Education, Western University, London, ON, Canada

Katreena Scott Department of Applied Psychology and Human Development, University of Toronto, Toronto, ON, Canada

Verona Singer Department of Criminology, Saint Mary's University, Halifax, Nova Scotia, Canada

Anna-Lee Straatman Centre for Research & Education on Violence against Women & Children, Faculty of Education, Western University, London, ON, Canada

Andrea Titterness Centre for Research & Education on Violence against Women & Children, Faculty of Education, Western University, London, ON, Canada

Sarah Yercich FREDA Centre for Research on Violence Against Women and Children, School of Criminology, Simon Fraser University, Vancouver, BC, Canada

Foreword

I was touched when Peter Jaffe and his colleagues Katreena Scott and Anna-Lee Straatman asked me to write the foreword to this fine new collection titled *Preventing Domestic Homicides: Lessons Learned From Tragedies*. I was similarly heartened at other junctures in the journey of memorializing and learning from domestic homicides, for example, when Peter and his colleagues included me in early conversations about the establishment of the Ontario Domestic Violence Death Review Committee (DVDRC) in the Office of the Chief Coroner. The DVDRC went on to blaze a trail in Canada, improving our understanding of and sharpening our responses to these disturbing cases and the deep social harm they cause, and alerting us to the political white heat of their fomentation. Their progress can be measured by the fact that there are now seven such committees in provinces across Canada and new committees continue to form across the globe.

The collection reminds us that studying tragedies to learn from them entails an appreciation of the unfolding of cases over time and an understanding of the context and meaning of interpersonal violence and abuse. Only then do we begin to develop appropriate perspective and deploy our imagination wisely. We know that phenomena such as domestic violence and abuse involve much more than a slap, a shove, hurtful words, a deep cut, an intimate intrusion, the taking of a life, or the sad seeming subjugation of a soul. Reviewing these perplexing cases takes violence and abuse as mere starting points, points of assemblage on our way to situating cases historically and socially, thus fine tuning our understanding and developing potentially preventive interventions.

Peter Jaffe and colleagues' collection, built using publicly available sources, incorporates an array of perspectives. In laying analytical track in the direction of social groups, subpopulations, and communities, the contributors break new ground. The collection therefore tilts its analytical lens at different angles so that light enters in different ways and we see different things. This kaleidoscope approach is no small task and the payoff is substantial, especially if readers pursue the directions identified and potentiated through the chapters. We learn about domestic homicides involving older women, rural women, Indigenous communities, teens and young adults, immigrant and refugee populations, those in lesbian, gay, bisexual, transgender, transsexual, queer, questioning, and 2-Spirit (LGBTQ2S) communities, those among the police and military, those with mental health disorders and addictions, those in the workplace, and those among children. The approach is not exhaustive, something the authors note as they map new frontiers, new subpopulations, and extant gaps in what is a relatively new literature on reviewing domestic homicides.

Just as contributors entice the reader into considering the plight of particular social groups, so too do they engage the reader about the many ways to review cases and explore domestic homicide. The collection reminds us of the at-times painful need to dig through multiple layers of interpretation. As a whole, it stresses the need to fashion expert review teams by drawing on the skills and wisdom of individual experts and doing so without resorting to blaming and shaming specific individuals and community organizations and stakeholders that handle cases. Creating expert teams remains a pivotal tenet of good reviewing. We have learned this fact the hard way and ought to bear in mind the price paid and lessons learned.

In the aftermath of landing an Airbus 320 in the Hudson River in New York on January 15, 2009, after a flock of geese flew into its engines, many hailed Captain Chesley Sullenberger a hero. After the so-called "Miracle on the Hudson," he eschewed such accolades, noting instead his successful emergency landing maneuvers within the space of a minute evidenced 40 or so years of careful and searching reviews of crashes in commercial aviation. When he first started flying, "Pilots were autocratic and arrogant. They didn't listen to the first officer.... You take a team of experts, and they make themselves into an expert team" (Ferguson, 2016).

The contributors to this collection help us realize that to review domestic homicides we need to build expert teams, tapping the talents of the many to detail the lives and cases of the tragically departed few. We need to listen to multiple voices, diverse insights, and perspectives, and always ask difficult questions such as "How do we know what we know?"

It is also worth bearing in mind that these teams have arisen in societies that some political scientists (e.g., Acemoglu & Robinson, 2012) refer to as functioning democracies the United States, Canada, the United Kingdom, New Zealand, Australia, and Portugal. Whatever the faults of these societies, they do permit at least some self-reflection and self-criticism, they permit and indeed invite, within their political infrastructures, the asking of difficult questions about those infrastructures, and more. The contributors evince this spirit of critical questioning in the way they propose, for example, various historical and contemporary axes of oppression as pivotal analytical frames for making sense of the deaths and developing preventive interventions. Readers will agree or disagree with what they posit but most will likely find appeal in the spirited mode of inquiry.

We might note review processes in other sectors that patently failed to identify dangers to communities. The classic example is the Chernobyl nuclear catastrophe of April 26, 1986, in the former Ukrainian Soviet Socialist Republic in what used to be the Soviet Union. It killed and harmed a relatively small number of people in and around the Chernobyl nuclear plant and a much greater number of people as time unfolded. The explosion, a product of a secretive Soviet political regime that failed to ask searching questions about the safety of its own nuclear power sector, was an important contributor to the downfall of the Soviet Union.

The stakes, then, are high, when it comes to assessing domestic homicides, phenomena that strike at the heart of how and what it means to get close to others, to build and maintain families and kinship networks (variously defined), to raise new generations, and to contribute in a thoughtful and prosocial way to broader society and to an increasingly globalized world. The contributors move us down this path, raise important questions, and, perhaps most importantly, invite our participation.

Neil Websdale
Northern Arizona University and Director of the National Domestic Violence Fatality Review Initiative (NDVFRI)

Introduction for Preventing Domestic Homicides

I'm Mariska Hargitay. You probably know me best as Captain Olivia Benson on the TV series *Law & Order: Special Victims Unit*.

Law & Order: SVU dramatizes the challenges of investigating crimes, apprehending, prosecuting criminals, and supporting victims and their families. The stories we tell are based on persistent, pervasive, and difficult realities. The subject of the book that you're about to read, domestic violence, troubles every layer of society, in every corner of the world, and demands our urgent attention.

At the extreme, domestic violence can end in deaths through homicide and homicide suicides. The number is shocking—in 2017 approximately 30,000 women were killed by an intimate partner across the globe. That's over 82 women per day.

One death is one too many. Women and girls face the greatest dangers in intimate relationships. The proportion of homicides committed by an intimate partner is six times higher for female homicide victims than male homicide victims. Women are victims in over 90% of domestic homicide suicides.

These homicides create tragedies for families and the survivors who are left behind. This type of violence, of course, also impacts people outside the relationship. One in five homicide victims are not intimate partners themselves, but family members, friends, neighbors, persons who intervened, law enforcement responders, or bystanders.

In the United States, last year there were over 2000 domestic homicides, and an estimated 3300 children were exposed to the aftermath of these murders. These children lost one parent to death and the other to a life sentence or both to a murder-suicide.

The physical and mental impacts of this type of trauma can resonate through families and communities for generations. These deaths didn't have to happen. Domestic homicides are often preceded by warning signs seen by friends, family, neighbors, coworkers, and community professionals like police or social services. Domestic homicides are in fact the most predictable and preventable of all homicides.

Often the friends, family, coworkers, and professionals who had contact with the victim and/or perpetrator didn't know what to do or didn't know what to say. They may have been hesitant to share their worries. Frontline professionals in policing and social services may have lacked awareness or training about domestic violence warning signs.

Research repeatedly points to DV homicide risk factors that include: a prior history of domestic violence, an actual or pending separation, the presence of a weapon, controlling behavior, strangulation, stalking, and mental health concerns with the perpetrator, among other factors.

In hindsight, many people wish they had taken action such as speaking to the victim or speaking to the perpetrator and encouraging them to get help. We need more public education and professional training so that we are all aware of the warning signs and have the skills and the resources to act. There is simply no excuse for ignorance.

Thirty years ago, domestic violence was considered a private matter, but we now know that it is a public safety concern and that it is criminal conduct. There is a far greater onus on professionals to respond appropriately, assess risk, and help with safety planning for the victim and risk management with the perpetrator.

The book that you're about to hear addresses all these issues. *Preventing Domestic Homicides: Lessons Learned from* Tragedies is written by an internationally renowned psychologist, Peter Jaffe, and his colleagues. Their intent is to educate both the public and professionals so they can better understand the warning signs associated with domestic homicide. Their work provides an excellent review of the current research in the field and case studies of homicides that might have been prevented with education and better training.

The book recognizes the diverse relationships, cultures, and economic realities in which domestic homicides take place. As the authors indicate, we must honor these victims by doing our best to prevent future tragedies. We each have the power to make change through knowledge, action, support, and education around this issue. Together we can help build a future without domestic violence.

About Mariska Hargitay

Mariska Hargitay plays Captain Olivia Benson on the NBC series *Law & Order: SVU*, where she is also an executive producer and has directed multiple episodes. She won an Emmy for outstanding actress in a drama, a Golden Globe Award, and earned an additional seven Emmy nominations, five SAG Award nominations, and two Gracie Allen Awards for American Women in Radio and Television.

Mariska's role on *SVU* awakened her to burdens that survivors of trauma often carry: the weight of shame, judgment, and isolation. Inspired by their courage, she founded the Joyful Heart Foundation in 2004, whose mission is to transform society's response to sexual assault, domestic violence and child abuse, support survivors' healing, and end this violence forever. At the heart of their advocacy work is the "End the Backlog" campaign, which aims to eliminate the backlog of hundreds of thousands of untested rape kits sitting in storage across America, so that survivors can get the closure they deserve She produced I AM EVIDENCE, an HBO documentary film on the topic that premiered in April 2018 and received an Emmy for "Best Documentary" at the News & Documentary Emmy Awards in September 2019.

Mariska also coproduced EMANUEL, a documentary about the Charleston church shooting which premiered in June 2019.

Mariska Hargitay

References

Acemoglu, D., & Robinson, J. (2012). *Why nations fail*. Crown Publishing.

Ferguson, M. (March 31, 2016). U.S. Airways hero talks up the values of preparation and teamwork. *Billings Gazette*. Retrieved from <https://billingsgazette.com/news>.

Preface

We were motivated to work on this book because of the number of domestic homicides we have reviewed in our work as researchers and clinicians over many years. We have experienced an ongoing sense of frustration, traumatic disbelief, and sorrow that more could not have been done to save lives in the face of so many warning signs in the vast majority of domestic homicides. The warning signs seem obvious with hindsight and the information held by friends, family, workplaces, and frontline professionals. Sometimes different people held critical information but were unable to share the pieces of the emerging picture of danger. We wanted to turn the hindsight into foresight for similar circumstances in the future.

In reflecting on domestic homicides, we saw that many cases shared a lot of common risk factors. At the same time, there were some unique factors across different subpopulations. Some populations appeared more vulnerable and victims faced a greater number of systemic barriers to access services and safety. Some populations were not even seen to be at risk like children living with domestic violence. We chose chapter authors who could dive more deeply into these different populations as well as emerging opportunities to engage workplaces in being part of the solution.

We acknowledge the dedicated and talented efforts of all the chapter authors who undertook a thorough literature review on domestic homicide in different populations as well as detailed case studies that illustrate the challenges in providing timely risk assessment and risk management strategies across different service sectors. The authors chose cases that were high profile from media coverage of trials, inquests, or death reviews across the world. Many of the surviving family members in the reported cases wanted the story shared in the hopes of helping others and several have been involved in public education and professional training initiatives in regards to domestic violence.

We hope that this book will be widely read by professionals in the justice system, health, social service, child protection, mental health, and education. We hope the book might be of interest to researchers in criminology, psychology, social work, and health sciences to consider important questions developing in the field on risk assessment and intervention strategies across different systems. We hope that we have assisted in the process of giving additional voice to homicide victims and their plight. At the Office of the Chief Coroner of Ontario, there is a motto on the wall that states "we speak for the dead to protect the living." We hope that this volume furthers that cause.

We would like to acknowledge the support of our universities and research centers. This book would not have been possible without the support of the Faculty of Education at Western University and the dedication of our colleagues at the Centre for Research & Education on Violence Against Women and Children in London, ON, Canada (P.J. & A.-L.S.) and University of Toronto and the Department of Applied Psychology and Human Development in the Ontario Institute for Studies in Education (K.S.). We would like to thank our caring spouses and children for their patience and forgive our distraction on endless nights and weekends when we were writing or editing to make our publication deadlines.

An introduction to domestic homicide: understanding the diverse nature of the problem

Peter Jaffe[1], Katreena Scott[2] and Anna-Lee Straatman[1]

[1]Centre for Research & Education on Violence against Women & Children, Faculty of Education, Western University, London, ON, Canada [2]Department of Applied Psychology and Human Development, University of Toronto, ON, Canada

Domestic violence is recognized as a major health problem across the globe (World Health Organization, 2013). At the extreme, domestic violence can end in deaths through homicide and homicide−suicides. In this book, we use the term domestic homicides to refer to homicides that happen in the context of an intimate relationship and perpetrated by a current or former intimate partner. These deaths can include the couple themselves or third parties such as children, new partners, other family members, or professionals such as police who intervened. Not included are homicides, primarily of women, perpetrated by other family members and often as a culmination of prior gender-related violence such as killings associated with a perception that a woman has violated gender norms and will bring dishonor to a family.

A distressingly high proportion of homicides around the world are perpetrated by intimate partners. Exact and comparable estimates of rates of domestic homicide can be difficult to compile for a number of reasons including disagreements about who is a victim of domestic homicide. Some definitions leave out children as victims, and there may be less consistency in the inclusion of very brief dating relationships as domestic homicides (Fairbairn, Jaffe, & Dawson, 2017). Some homicides may not be identified as domestic homicides because of uncertainty about the relationship between the victim and perpetrator, particularly if family and friends were unaware (Washington State Domestic Violence Fatality Review, 2012). Even without accounting for underestimates associated with these factors, domestic homicide accounts

Preventing Domestic Homicides. DOI: https://doi.org/10.1016/B978-0-12-819463-8.00001-0

for about 1 in 8 homicides around the world (Stöckl et al., 2013; United Nations Office on Drugs & Crime, 2018).

Women and girls bear by far the greatest burden of domestic homicide. In an analysis of data across 66 countries, Stöckl and colleagues (2013) reported that the proportion of intimate homicides committed by intimate partners is six times higher for female homicide than male homicide (38.6% vs 6.3%). Expressed in rate, between 0.7 and 3.1 women per 100,000 globally are killed by intimate partners as compared to less than 0.1−0.3 per 100,000 men. In numbers, in 2017 approximately 30,000 women were killed by an intimate partner across the globe, which is a little over 82 women per day (United Nations Office on Drugs & Crime, 2018).

Rates of domestic homicide vary by country and region. Perhaps contrary to what might be expected, in higher income countries, domestic homicides make up a *greater* proportion of all homicides than in developing countries. In Canada, between the years 2010 and 2015, there were 418 domestic homicides with women representing 79% of all victims (Dawson et al., 2018). Between 2009 and 2019 in the United Kingdom, 740 women were killed by their intimate partners (Femicide Census: 2017, 2016, 2015). In Australia, there were 152 domestic homicides between 2010 and 2014, 79.6% of them were women killed by male partners (Australian Domestic & Family Violence Death Review Network, 2018). In all of these countries, these rates are considerably lower than they were 40 years ago. Since the 1970s, intimate partner homicides have dramatically declined; however, rates across countries have levelled out in the past decade, and there is some concern that domestic homicide may be on the rise. In a recent paper on patterns and trends in US homicide, Fridel and Fox (2019) report that domestic homicide has increased each year between 2014 and 2017 from a death toll of 1875 in 2015 to 2237 deaths in 2017.

Domestic homicides appear to be most predictable and preventable of all homicides in hindsight (Adams, 2007). Friends, family, coworkers, and professionals who had contact with the victim and/or perpetrator often report warning signs that had concerned them. Often friends and family did not know what to do or say. They may have been hesitant to share their observations and worries. Frontline professionals may have lacked awareness or training about domestic violence warning signs. Many people wish they had taken action such as speaking to the victim or the perpetrator and encouraging them to get help. Some wished they had called the police.

Thirty years ago, domestic violence was considered a private matter. It is now considered a potential public matter and criminal conduct once it is reported. With this societal shift, there is a greater onus on professionals to respond appropriately, especially when the violence appears lethal. Knowledge in the field has developed from multiple sources. In terms of preventing domestic homicide, a major advancement was the development of standardized risk assessment tools to capture potential for lethality. The work of Jackie Campbell and her colleagues compared domestic homicide to domestic violence cases across 11 US cities and found a number of risk factors that were significantly associated with homicides. These risk factors included a prior history of domestic violence, separation, the presence of a weapon, controlling behavior, and strangulation, among other factors (Campbell et al., 2003). This research became the foundation of one of the most popular risk assessment tools—the danger assessment, which is now used in many jurisdictions and has been adapted for a variety of populations and professions (Messing, Amanor-Boadu, Cavanaugh, Glass, & Campbell, 2013; Messing & Campbell, 2016; Messing, Campbell, Sullivan Wilson, Brown, & Patchell, 2017).

Another major development in the domestic homicide field has been the advent of multidisciplinary review teams that examine these homicides in detail. These death review committees are now found in the majority of US states with technical support available through a national initiative (https://ndvfri. org/). Seven Canadian provinces now have death review committees (www.cdhpi.ca), and there are eight jurisdictional review committees in Australia. The United Kingdom and New Zealand operate death reviews at a national level (Bugeja, Dawson, McIntyre, & Walsh, 2015). Although each jurisdiction varies in legislation, funding, and process model for their reviews, the goals are mostly common ones. The central goal from the reviews is to identify how to prevent a homicide in similar circumstances in the future. Most reviews report patterns in risk factors across the cases that were known by the community prior to the homicide. The reviews most often make recommendations for improved training, resources, and collaboration across service sectors (Johnson, Lutz, & Websdale, 1999; Websdale, no date).

Standardized death reviews allow for a deeper exploration of family histories and missed opportunities for intervention. Existing studies in the field were traditionally limited by only looking at one source of information which provided a less than complete picture of these homicides. For example, looking at court decisions from criminal proceedings overlooks homicide—suicides which may never be part of a public hearing. Studies of homicide perpetrators in mental health facilities or correctional facilities depend on mental health diagnoses or specific court sentences. Leaving out child homicides in the context of domestic violence also limits understanding of the true nature of these cases and multiple victims. Using a broader definition and reviewing every case provides a more comprehensive picture of domestic homicide (Fairbairn et al., 2017).

The evolving research and publication of death review reports highlight the fact that domestic homicides do not happen out of the blue. Most often there is a trail of missed opportunities for interventions to find safety for victims and risk management for perpetrators. At the same time, it is obvious that domestic homicides are a heterogeneous problem to understand. Although there may be overlapping warning signs, each domestic homicide may have unique characteristics. Unique characteristics arise from the social circumstances and life context for the victim and perpetrator. Whether it is a teen dating relationship, or an aging couple married for over 50 years, urban or rural family, Indigenous or nonIndigenous victim, immigrant or refugee perpetrator, each circumstance poses a need for a different lens to understand the risks and the context for the homicide. This book explores these contexts clarifying both the similarities and difference in instances of domestic homicide.

One of the key similarities in domestic homicide concerns gender. As reviewed previously, domestic homicide is a gendered crime, with close to 80% of cases across datasets involving women victims and an even higher percentage of accused men. Accordingly this book focuses on domestic homicides of women with two exceptions: homicides of people in gay, lesbian, bisexual relationships and a chapter that focuses on women who kill. As explored in Chapter 13, Future directions on promoting domestic homicide prevention in diverse populations, self-defense and a history of domestic violence are often identified as reasons for homicide when women kill their intimate partners. One quarter of women who killed a current intimate partner were protected under Domestic Violence Protection orders against the male homicide victim (Australian Domestic & Family Violence Death Review Network, 2018).

The domestic violence field has evolved to consider the importance of understanding context through an intersectionality framework. Intersectionality recognizes that individuals have multiple social identities that could include gender, race, ethnicity, class, sexual orientation, age, and ability. These identities may reflect various dimensions of privilege or alternatively marginalization and oppression that combine to determine access to services and supports for domestic violence victims. Perspectives and definitions of domestic violence vary according to how patriarchy is conceived within these various cultures and contexts (Sokoloff & Dupont, 2005). Individuals have multiple identities that determine life outcomes such as health and education. For example, an Indigenous woman who is experiencing violence and lives in a remote community living with the long-term impact of colonization and residential schools is dealing with different circumstances than a nonindigenous woman in an urban center who is employed and has ready access to health care and social services (Brownridge, 2008; Tutty et al., 2017). In the early days of the domestic violence movement, analysis tended to focus on gender alone and the recognition that women were more likely than men to be injured or killed (Sokoloff & Dupont, 2005). Gender is now understood to be only part of the context to understand this victimization. Intersectionality provides a means of identifying conditions that are particularly advantageous or disadvantageous and critical to understanding domestic homicide (Tutty et al., 2017).

This book addresses domestic homicide in diverse populations and social locations. Different populations may experience a greater array of vulnerabilities and face multiple barriers to find safety and support. In being unable to escape the violence, they face serious consequences related to their mental and physical health. There are no one-size-fits-all responses to domestic violence. There are assessment and intervention strategies that may be more appropriate in some contexts versus other contexts. Community agencies need to tailor their strategies to recognize diverse cultures and economic realities. For example, calling 911 or going to a shelter for abuse victims may have unintended consequences for immigrant women who are dependent on the abuser for their residency and hopes of future citizenship. Abuse victims in rural communities may not get a timely police response or access to any services to deal with the dangers they face. These examples are a small sample of the diverse contexts we hope to explore in this book. This book addresses domestic homicide by examining the issues within each subpopulation according to the emerging literature and death reviews that highlight this subpopulation.

The need to contextualize and understand the experiences of different populations underlies this book's focus on lessons learned from domestic homicide in different groups of people. Focusing each chapter on a specific population is not to reinforce negative stereotypes or blame a culture or population group for the vulnerabilities or risk they experience. Simply reporting differences in prevalence rates among various groups and populations only serves to reinforce negative stereotypes about these populations (Sokoloff & Dupont, 2005). For example, research exploring mental health status of women experiencing domestic violence found negligible differences when comparing ethnic and cultural groups. Other structural oppression experiences such as disability played a more significant role in women's mental health status (Tutty et al., 2017). It is necessary to give voice to women's experiences from diverse racial, economic, socioeconomic, religious, and immigrant backgrounds. Each chapter provides case studies of domestic homicides that represent at least the focus of the chapter if not many others as well. We are exploring risk factors for domestic homicide in these populations in the context of patriarchy, oppression, and how social determinants of health are experienced among and between groups of people.

To highlight lessons learned, each of the chapters in this volume includes reviews of recent domestic homicides. Data for these cases was gathered from public sources including inquests and in-depth reviews, and when necessary, media reports. The case reviews provide only a brief summary of the events surrounding the homicide to emphasize particular points, risk factors, and missed opportunities. In many of the cases reviewed, surviving family members and friends shared the case details to prevent similar tragedies in the future. There are benefits in sharing the stories, and there are always concerns about leaving out critical information or violating privacy rights. In regards to the latter point, we only utilized public sources and information and omitted information that we judged to be sensationalized or unnecessary to illustrate the point we were trying to make. In regards to selecting some information and leaving other information out, we wish to acknowledge that behind each and every case we review is at least one life lost and that there is no way that a summary can capture the richness of their lives, the complexities of the circumstances that led to the homicide, or the depth of loss experienced by those left behind.

We preview each of these populations and the themes in the book chapters below.

In Chapter 2, Older women and domestic homicide, Margaret MacPherson and her colleagues explore the special challenges of older women killed by their partners. This sub-population represents the smallest portion of domestic homicides and one with often the least number of warning signs prior to the homicide. However, the red flags that do exist often suggest a gradual decline in the physical and mental health of one or both partners and often some significant cries for help. The cases reviewed highlight these trends and reinforce the importance of health-care professionals in better assessing the risks of homicides and homicide—suicides. The case studies they provide illustrate the need for enhanced training and awareness of risk factors and in particular of the problems of overlooking violence and homicide because they are not seen to be a problem in senior citizens.

In Chapter 3, Domestic homicides in rural communities: challenges in accessing resources, Anna-Lee Straatman, Deborah Doherty, and Victoria Banman underscore the unique challenges for women living in rural communities. Abuse victims face major barriers in separating safely from perpetrators and accessing services. Police and support services may be miles away resulting in significant problems in getting help on a timely basis, especially at points of crisis. Firearms in rural communities are the norm but represent special risks for domestic violence victims. In addition, values and beliefs in tight-knit communities may not only be a blessing for many but also a curse for victims needing to separate. The cases that are summarized underline the need for flexible and innovative programs that address domestic violence in these communities.

Kate Rossiter and her colleagues stress the unique challenges for individuals living with violence in same-sex relationships in Chapter 4, Domestic homicides with LGBTQ2S + communities: barriers in disclosing relationships and violence. Recent national data from Canada suggest that intimate partner violence in same-sex relationships is becoming less invisible. About 3% of reports to police regarding intimate partner violence involved couples in same-sex relationships over a nine-year period, which is higher than the known share of same-sex couples in Canada (1%) (Ibrahim, 2019). More than half of the same-sex intimate partner violence reported to police was between male couples. Between 2009 and 2017, there were 36 homicides in Canada involving same-sex partners, representing 5% of all intimate partner homicides over this time period (Ibrahim, 2019). Historically same-sex relationships received little attention in the academic literature. A recent review of research conducted in Australia between 2000 and 2016 found only four studies which examined domestic violence among lesbian, gay, and bisexual people (Perales, Reeves, Plage, & Baxter, 2019). The case studies in this chapter emphasize the lack of awareness about lethality in same-sex relationships and the need for both professional and public awareness.

In Chapter 5, Domestic homicides in teens and young adult dating relationships: ignoring the dangers of dangerous relationships, Jordan Fairbairn and her colleagues outline the risks often ignored in dating relationships. Dating relationships represent over half of all reported domestic violence (Burczycka, Conroy, & Savage, 2018) but tend to be minimized as less serious relationships in terms of potential lethality (Jaffe, Fairbairn, & Sapardanis, 2018). Even so, one quarter of all domestic homicide victims were killed by dating partners (Burczycka et al., 2018), and one quarter of police-reported intimate partner violence involves victims between the age of 15 and 24 years (Burczycka et al., 2018). Young women between the ages of 15 and 24 are seen to be at the highest risk of domestic homicide (Sinha, 2013), but either they or their friends and family may fail to recognize the dangers presented by their partners. The case studies presented from death review committees and public inquiries suggest that prevention efforts in schools and colleges as well as enhanced training for professionals may be the key to reducing these homicides.

Sepali Guruge and her colleagues highlight the many barriers to help seeking with immigrant and refugee victims in Chapter 6, Domestic homicide in immigrant communities: lessons learned. Research coming out of Canada suggests that immigrant and refugee families are not more likely to experience domestic violence (Ibrahim, 2018), but when they do, they face great obstacles to getting help because of language, culture, and victim dependency on the abuser. Often overlooked is the premigration and acculturation experiences that may be linked to the domestic violence (e.g., Hancock & Siu, 2009). The need for cultural competence among service providers as well as specialized services is critical with this subpopulation. The case studies provided offer glaring examples of the lack of community understanding about domestic violence with immigrant families and the need to provide more informed risk assessment and interventions.

In Chapter 7, Perpetrator mental health: depression and suicidality as risk factors for domestic homicide, Katreena Scott and her colleagues address the fact that depression and suicidality are prevalent in retrospective review of domestic homicides (Oliver & Jaffe, 2018). In fact, high rates of perpetrator suicide are a key difference between domestic and other forms of homicide. This chapter explores literature in this area, speculating on why perpetrator mental health has not been a stronger focus of past research and pointing out missed opportunities for intervention. These missed opportunities often involve mental health professionals trained to assess suicidal ideation but who failed to address homicidal ideation and risk of lethality in the face of known concerns around domestic violence. The case studies presented in the chapter feature many lessons that have been learned from these tragedies that can be readily adopted to enhance training and assessment of risk by frontline professionals in health care and social services.

Katreena Scott and her colleagues highlight children as a forgotten domestic homicide subpopulation in Chapter 8, Child homicides in the context of domestic violence: when the plight of children is overlooked. Although there is a growing body of literature on the harmful effects of growing up with domestic violence (Oliver & Jaffe, 2018), the risk of children being killed as part of a domestic homicide has often been ignored, treated as an afterthought in both the child abuse and domestic violence literatures, or relegated children to collateral or secondary victims (Dobash & Dobash, 2012; Meyer & Post, 2013). Recent literature based on death review committees and major inquests have brought this issue to light, along with lessons relevant to preventing these deaths. One of the most notable of the findings from these reviews is that cases involving children are perhaps among the *most* preventable. These cases are distinguished by having many of the same risk factors as adult homicide and by having significantly more professionals involved. The importance of multiple social services and family court finding better ways to collaborate and share information on risk assessments and safety planning are highlighted.

Barb MacQuarrie and her colleagues raise questions about how to prevent domestic homicide within the police and military communities in Chapter 9, Domestic homicides with police and military: understanding the risks enhanced by trauma and workplace culture. Investigating police and military domestic violence creates special challenges for internal investigations and prosecutions since losing access to a weapon may immediately impact employment status. There has been a growing literature about police and military cultures and the stress of the work that can exacerbate domestic violence. The case studies profiled demonstrate that there are many warning signs known to the workplace, friends, and family before the homicide, and feature the issue of posttraumatic stress disorder as a contributor to domestic homicide. There are lessons to be learned on early intervention and support that may prevent these homicides. Potential solutions include addressing the nature of these cultures and the reluctance to seek assistance.

Chapter 10, Domestic violence and homicide in the workplace, addresses the growing recognition that workplaces play a role in preventing domestic violence and homicide. Barbara MacQuarrie and her colleagues summarize the emerging literature on how violence at home follows victims to work. Increasingly domestic violence is being recognized as a workplace health and safety issue that places responsibility on employers to take appropriate action. The cases reviewed illustrate that when workplaces fail to act, domestic homicides can result. With hindsight these workplace tragedies appear preventable with the proper policies and practices in place. There are consistent themes in regard to workplace training, a supportive work culture and when needed, timely access to risk assessment and management strategies.

Catherine Richardson/Kinewesquao and her colleagues outline the vulnerability of Indigenous women in dealing with domestic violence in Chapter 11, Domestic homicide within Indigenous communities: examining violence in the context of historical oppression. There is little doubt that Indigenous communities face the highest levels of domestic violence due to a history of colonization and oppression. Within this subpopulation of homicide victims, context is everything. Government reports including the Canadian Truth and Reconciliation Commission underscore that this impact was not accidental but rather systematic—"For over a century, the central goals of Canada's Aboriginal policy were to cause Aboriginal peoples to cease to exist as distinct, legal, social, cultural, religious and racial entities in Canada. The establishment and operation of residential schools were a central element of this policy, which can best be described as "cultural genocide"" (Truth and Reconciliation Commission of Canada, 2015). Richardson/ Kinewesquao and colleagues identify the social responses that contribute to perpetration of violence and reluctance to report violence. Approaches to addressing the issue of violence against Indigenous women are examined including feminist, human services, and traditional cultural healing,

Alexandra Lysova and her colleagues address the issue of women who commit domestic homicide in Chapter 12, Domestic homicide involving female perpetrators and male victims. In some instances, women kill their male intimate partners. When these homicides occur, it is more likely to have happened in the context of a woman's prior history of victimization with severe domestic violence. There are some exceptions to this pattern. This chapter will explore both scenarios.

The book coeditors summarize the major themes in each chapter in Chapter 13, Future directions on promoting domestic homicide prevention in diverse populations. We acknowledge some of the limitations in the field such as a lack of consistent definitions of domestic homicide across jurisdictions which limits comparisons. At times there is a lack of information other than on high-profile homicides which may not be a representative sample. It is also hard to generalize some recommendation for future action because training, policies, and resources vary widely across jurisdictions. However, there are some important overarching themes. There are many commonalities in risk factors for these deaths which need to be acknowledged, though at the same time, domestic homicide is a heterogeneous problem that requires recognition of diverse subpopulations. Prevention must begin with understanding the context of risk and risk factors across different populations and community agencies and by creating systems with more multifaceted assessment and intervention strategies to recognize this reality.

References

Adams, D. (2007). *Why do they kill?: Men who murder their intimate partners.* Vanderbilt University Press.

Australian Domestic and Family Violence Death Review Network. (2018). *Data report.* Sydney, AU: Domestic Violence Death Review Team.

Brownridge, D. (2008). Understanding the elevated risk of partner violence against Aboriginal women: A comparison of two nationally representative surveys of Canada. *Journal of Family Violence, 23*, 353–367. Available from https://doi.org/10.1007/s10896-008-9160-0.

Bugeja, L., Dawson, M., McIntyre, S., & Walsh, C. (2015). Domestic/family violence death reviews: An international comparison. *Trauma, Violence, & Abuse, 16*(2), 179–187.

Burczycka, M., Conroy, S., & Savage, L. (2018). Family violence in Canada: A statistical profile, 2017. *Juristat.* Catalogue number 85-002-X. ISSN: 1209-6393.

Campbell, J. C., Webster, D., Koziol-McLain, J., Block, C. R., Campbell, D. W., Curry, M. A., Gary, F. A., et al. (2003). Risk factors for femicide in abusive relationships: Results from a multisite case control study. *American Journal of Public Health, 93*(7), 1089–1097.

Dawson, M., Sutton, D., Jaffe, P., Straatman, A. L., Poon, J., Gosse, M., ... Sandhu, G. (2018). *One is too many: Trends and patterns in domestic homicides in Canada 2010-2015.* London, ON: Canadian Domestic Homicide Prevention Initiative.

Dobash, R. P., & Dobash, R. E. (2012). Who died? The murder of collaterals related to intimate partner conflict. *Violence Against Women, 18*(6), 662–671. Available from https://doi.org/10.1177/1077801212453984.

Fairbairn, J., Jaffe, P., & Dawson, M. (2017). Challenges in defining domestic homicide: Considerations for research & practice. In M. Dawson (Ed.), *Domestic homicides and death reviews: An international perspective*. Palgrave McMillan.

Fridel, E.E., Fox, J.A. (2019). Gender differences in patterns and trends in U.S. homicide, 1976–2017. *Violence and Gender* (6). Available from https://doi.org/10.1089/vio.2019.0005

Hancock, T. U., & Siu, K. (2009). A culturally sensitive intervention with domestically violent Latino immigrant men. *Journal of Family Violence, 24*(2), 123–132.

Ibrahim, D. (2018). Violent victimization, discrimination and perceptions of safety: An immigrant perspective, Canada, 2014. *Juristat, 38*(1). Catalogue number 85-002-X. ISSN: 1209-6393.

Ibrahim, D. (2019). Police-reported violence among same-sex intimate partners in Canada, 2009 to 2017. *Juristat.* Catalogue number 85-002-X. ISSN: 1209-6393.

Jaffe, P., Fairbairn, J., & Sapardanis, K. (2018). Youth dating violence and homicide. In D. A. Wolfe, & J. Templeton (Eds.), *Adolescent dating violence: Theory, research and prevention*. London: Elsevier.

Johnson, J. A., Lutz, V. L., & Websdale, N. (1999). Death by intimacy: Risk factors or domestic violence. *Pace Law Review, 20*, 263.

Messing, J. T., Amanor-Boadu, Y., Cavanaugh, C. E., Glass, N. E., & Campbell, J. C. (2013). Culturally competent intimate partner violence risk assessment: Adapting the danger assessment for immigrant women. *Social Work Research, 37*(3), 263–275. Available from https://doi.org/10.1093/swr/svt019.

Messing, J. T., & Campbell, J. (2016). Informing collaborative interventions: Intimate partner violence risk assessment for front line police officers. *Policing: A Journal of Policy and Practice, 10*(4), 328–340. Available from https://doi.org/10.1093/police/paw013.

Messing, J. T., Campbell, J., Sullivan Wilson, J., Brown, S., & Patchell, B. (2017). The lethality screen: The predictive validity of an intimate partner violence risk assessment for use by first responders. *Journal of Interpersonal Violence, 32*(2), 205–226. Available from https://doi.org/10.1177/0886260515585540.

Meyer, E., & Post, L. (2013). Collateral intimate partner homicide. *SAGE Open.* Available from https://doi.org/10.1177/2158244013484235.

Oliver, C., & Jaffe, P. G. (2018). Comorbid depression and substance abuse in domestic homicide: Missed opportunities in the assessment and management of mental illness in perpetrators. *Journal of Interpersonal Violence.* Available from https://doi.org/10.1177/0886260518815140.

Perales, F., Reeves, L. S., Plage, S., & Baxter, J. (2019). The family lives of Australian lesbian, gay and bisexual people: A review of the literature and a research agenda. *Sexuality Research and Social Policy,* 1–18.

Sinha, M. (2013). Family violence in Canada: A statistical profile, 2011. *Juristat.* Catalogue number 85-002-X.

Sokoloff, N. J., & Dupont, I. (2005). Domestic violence at the intersections of race, class, and gender: Challenges and contributions to understanding violence against marginalized women in diverse communities. *Violence Against Women, 11*(1), 38–64. Available from https://doi.org/10.1177/1077801204271476.

Stockl, H., Devries, K., Rotstein, A., Abrahams, N., Campbell, J., Watts, C., et al. (2013). The global prevalence of intimate partner homicide: A systematic review. *The Lancet*, (382), 859–865. Available from https://doi.org/10.1016/S0140-6736(13)61030-2

Truth and Reconciliation Commission of Canada. (2015). *Truth and reconciliation commission of Canada: Calls to action*. Retrieved from <www.trc.ca>.

Tutty, L. M., Ateah, C. A., Ursel, J. E., Thurston, W. E., Hampton, M., & Nixon, K. (2017). The complexities of intimate partner violence: Mental health, disabilities, and child abuse history for white, indigenous, and other visible minority Canadian women. *Journal of Interpersonal Violence*. Available from https://doi.org/10.1177/0886260517741210.

United Nations Office on Drugs and Crime. (2018). *Global study on homicide: Gender-related killing of women and girls*. Vienna.

Washington State Domestic Violence Fatality Review. (2012). *Teen victims of domestic violence homicide in Washington state*. Washington State Coalition Against Domestic Violence.

Websdale, N. (no date). Reviewing domestic violence deaths. *NIJ Journal*, (250). Retrieved from <https://www.baylor.edu/content/services/document.php/28815.pdf>.

World Health Organization. (2013). *Global and regional estimates of violence against women: Prevalence and health effects of intimate partner violence and non-partner sexual violence*. Geneva: World Health Organization, ISBN: 978-92-4-156462-5.

Further reading

Black, M. C. (2011). Intimate partner violence and adverse health consequences: Implications for clinicians. *American Journal of Lifestyle Medicine*, 5(5), 428–439. Available from https://doi.org/10.1177/1559827611410265.

Burczycka, M., & Conroy, S. (2017). Family violence in Canada: A Statistical profile, 2015. *Juristat*, Catalogue number 85-002-X. ISSN: 1209-6393.

Chanmugam, A. (2014). Social work expertise and domestic violence fatality review teams. *Social Work*, 59(1), 73–80. Available from https://doi.org/10.1093/sw/swt048.

Gannoni, A. & Cussen, T. (2014). Same-sex intimate partner homicide in Australia. Trends & issues in crime and criminal justice No. 469. Canberra: Australian Institute of Criminology. <https://aic.gov.au/publications/tandi/tandi469>.

Nixon, J., & Humphreys, C. (2010). Marshalling the evidence: Using intersectionality in the domestic violence frame. *Social Politics: International Studies in Gender, State & Society*, 17(2), 137–158. Available from https://doi.org/10.1093/sp/jxq003.

Oudekerk, B. A., & Truman, J. L. (2017). *Repeat violent victimization, 2005–14*. U.S. Department of Justice. NCJ 250567.

Parker, K. F., & Hefner, K. (2015). Intersections of race, gender, disadvantage, and violence: Applying intersectionality to the macro-level study of female homicide. *Justice Quarterly*, 32(2), 223–254. Available from https://doi.org/10.1080/07418825.2012.761719.

Stubbs, J., & Tolmie, J. (2008). Battered women charged with homicide: Advancing the interests of indigenous women. *Australian & New Zealand Journal of Criminology*, 41(1), 138–161. Available from https://doi.org/10.1375/acri.41.1.138.

Older women and domestic homicide

Margaret MacPherson, Katherine Reif, Andrea Titterness and Barbara MacQuarrie
Centre for Research & Education on Violence against Women & Children, Faculty of Education, Western University, London, ON, Canada

The United Nations identified older women as being especially vulnerable to human rights abuses related to neglect, abuse, and violence in 2012. A UN sector brief was subsequently published in 2013 to review the state of knowledge with respect to the abuse of older women (UN, 2002; UN DESA, 2013). The report was a clear indictment that women in their senior years who experience domestic violence continue to be largely unseen in research, data, and in terminology used by academics to describe and classify violence and abuse (UN DESA, 2013).

Older women sit at the nexus of powerful forces that combine to create profound social isolation and invisibility on cohort-specific issues (UN DESA, 2013). Intersections of gender, age, ability, race, class, sexual orientation, and health combine under patriarchal social norms to form unique barriers that obstruct older women's human rights, personal safety, and social support (VAWG, 2016). In this chapter, we examine domestic homicides of older women to explore relationships between discriminatory social norms and gaps in research and practice that continue to be held in place by the pervasive social norms of ageism.

Ageism

Discrimination based on age may be the final indignity that we face individually and collectively. Dr. Robert Butler first identified "ageism" as a form of discrimination in 1969. He writes; "ageism reflects a deep-seated unease... a personal revulsion to and distaste for growing old, disease, disability and fear of powerlessness, uselessness and death" (Butler & Louis, 1973). Ageism is rooted in the industrialized worldview that

Preventing Domestic Homicides. DOI: https://doi.org/10.1016/B978-0-12-819463-8.00002-2

15

people have greater value to society while they are of working age. Although no one escapes completely, the experience of ageism is mitigated or intensified by individual circumstances such as economic means, status, education, and social location (Spencer, 2009).

Aging women in abusive relationships experience the triple threat of being a woman, being an older woman, and being an older woman who is, or has, experienced domestic violence (Penhale, 2014). In an ageist society, a woman may find herself trapped in a difficult and dangerous situation of having to meet the health-care needs of an ailing abusive partner. Or, her health deteriorates and she becomes increasingly dependent on the abusive partner. Both circumstances can lead to profound social isolation (Cohen & Molinari, 2010). The rise in homicide–suicides of older couples in recent years provides a clarion call as violent death rates are likely to increase with the aging population (Bourget, Gagne, & Whitehurst, 2010).

Gaps in research and practice

Despite international recognition, older women have yet to be "mainstreamed into ongoing research or discussion on violence against women (VAW)" (UN DESA, 2013). With the exception of nationally representative incidence studies, research data collection has predominantly focused on women of reproductive age. Consequently systems and resources are skewed to respond to domestic violence in younger populations rather than considering the dynamics of violence that occur across the life span (UN DESA, 2013; VAWG, 2016). Older women who are care dependent or cognitively incapacitated and possibly living in institutions are also undersampled (UN DESA, 2013). As a result, there is still little evidence to inform the development of targeted strategies, policies, or interventions to address and prevent violence that is committed against older women by their intimate partners present or past. The research that does exist is drawn mostly from developed countries. The abuse experiences of older women in undeveloped nations are even less visible (UN DESA, 2013; VAWG, 2016).

Overlapping research-related challenges make it difficult to grasp the full scope of older women's experience of domestic violence (UN Women, 2017). Inconsistent definitions and samples are used by researchers to qualify "older." Consequently age ranges of participants vary considerably in studies. "Seniors" are described starting from 50 or 60 (Brownell, 2015). Moreover older women are not a homogenous group. There are significant generational differences in what can be as much as a 40-year age range that are rendered invisible when reduced to a single "older" demographic. Women's lives are further shaped by unique characteristics and social identities. The concept and impact of polyvictimization (e.g., being racialized, living in poverty, and with violence) is not generally recognized in the elder abuse field (Brownell, 2015; McGarry, Simpson, & Hinchliff-Smith, 2017). There remains a great need for strategic and thoughtful research that examines the many intersections of structural disadvantage present in women's lives across the life span (Crockett, Brandl, & Dabby, 2015).

Competing research paradigms

Three competing research paradigms dominate the field of study: older adult mistreatment informed by social gerontology; older adult protection informed by geriatrics; and intimate partner violence informed by the domestic violence movement. Differing definitions have led to uneven findings, policy responses, programs, and practices that can appear contradictory and confusing as each is linked to different theoretical assumptions. The resulting confusion confounds the development of an overarching framework for older women (UN DESA, 2013).

Elder abuse is defined as a "single or repeated act, or lack of appropriate action, occurring within *any* relationship where there is an expectation of trust, which causes harm or distress to an older person" (WHO, 2008). Although current and former spouses and intimate partners are included in this definition, the focus of elder abuse research is often nonspousal/nonintimate caregivers such as children, other family members, and staff at long-term care centers. Elder abuse includes various forms of abuse such as physical, psychological, sexual, financial, and intentional or unintentional neglect but rarely considers coercive power dynamics in intimate partner relationships (Brownell, 2015; Nägele, Böhm, Görgen, & Tóth, 2010). As well, elder abuse literature typically does not single out older women as a separate study group nor recognize their unique vulnerabilities (Crockett et al., 2015; Pathak, Dhairyawan, & Tariq, 2019). The invisibility of domestic violence in elder abuse research creates a domino effect for older women as funding for services and research generally follows evidence (Dong, 2015).

Moreover the lack of evidence supports the myth that domestic violence is not a serious issue for older women.

Sector differences

Service provision by professionals working in the fields of domestic violence and elder abuse operate largely in siloes under different government funding streams. Consequently, the sectors have different priorities, mandates, and approaches (Crockett et al., 2015; Penhale & Porritt, 2010; Zink, Jacobson, Regan, & Pabst, 2004). Elder abuse has evolved out of health care and is still considered a "new" field (Dong, 2015). Domestic violence and VAW have evolved from a grassroots movement. Despite the imperative issued by World Health Organization (WHO) to address domestic violence as a public health issue, violence has not been considered a health issue for older people and therefore often sits apart from the traditional scope of health-care policy, education, and services (UN DESA, 2013; Zink et al., 2004). Funding for elder abuse frequently lags behind the longer existing VAW services (Dong, 2015). Until recently feminists and the VAW sector have not considered aging to be a factor that requires specialized knowledge or services expressly for older women (Calasanti, Slevin, & King, 2006; Crockett et al., 2015; McGarry et al., 2017; Penhale & Porritt, 2010). Consequently most services for abused women have been developed for younger women (Brownell, 2015; Crockett et al., 2015; VAWG, 2016).

The VAW sector focus on women as victims creates tension and a resistance to examining gender differences for professionals working to address older adult abuse. Older men also experience various forms of elder abuse at close to equal rates as older women, whereas domestic violence victimization rates are more influenced by gender (Dong, 2015; Nägele et al., 2010; NICE, 2015; Warmling, Lindner, & Coelho, 2017).

Acknowledgment of the intersecting relationship between gender and age has to be resolved for the breadth of specific experiences to be made visible and effectively addressed. Without resolution, the tension between the sectors plays out as a simple opposition, whereby those advocating and working in the older adult abuse field consider the gender lens a betrayal to older male victims and the lack of gender analysis for the VAW sector as a betrayal of older women. The incorporation of an intersectional lens that includes gender and age but also race, ability, class, and sexual orientation by practitioners, researchers, and policy makers in both fields is a significant step toward constructive and more informed interventions (Brownell, 2015; Calasanti et al., 2006; Crockett et al., 2015; McGarry et al., 2017; Pathak et al., 2019; UN DESA, 2013).

Structural violence—cohort exclusion

The idea that domestic violence only affects younger women is due in part to systemic ageism that operates as structural violence in excluding old-age cohorts from study samples (VAWG, 2016). Global and national surveys of intimate partner violence frequently include women only up to the age of 49 (Ellsberg & Heise, 2005). Hence, older women's experiences of domestic violence have not been visible because they have not been widely studied.

When domestic violence is defined solely by the presence or absence of physical violence, older women are considered to be less at risk (Ellsberg & Heise, 2005). While the prevalence of physical violence is lower among older women, other forms of violence are not (Luoma et al., 2011; McGarry et al., 2017; Mezey, Post, & Maxwell, 2002; Pathak et al., 2019). Psychological and financial abuse have been found to be the most common forms of violence experienced by older women (Luoma et al., 2011; Nägele et al., 2010; Warmling et al., 2017). Current validated risk assessment tools do not measure for controlling behavior or financial abuse, further obscuring two of the most common expressions of violence for older women (UN DESA, 2015; Warmling et al., 2017). Contrary to ageist stereotypes, sexual violence in relationships continues into later years (Bows, 2015). The health consequences of physical and sexual violence are more severe for older women. The impacts lead to increased use of health services, decline in overall health status, and poorer life expectancy (Stöckl & Penhale, 2015).

Domestic violence committed against women in their middle and later life occurs in two main contexts. The first is late-onset domestic violence, which begins for the first time in later life in a new or existing relationship. Many factors may precipitate this violence, with retirement being one important factor. As men retire from work, they take their place with women as less-valued members of society (Calasanti et al., 2006). Two studies documenting women's experiences of violence found that retirement could be a precipitating factor for violence (Hightower, Smith, & Hightower, 2006; Montminy, 2005).

The second is domestic violence "grown old" where women have experienced abuse throughout the relationship. The latter category is considered to be the most common and includes a range of behaviors including financial, psychological, physical, and sexual abuse (Bows, 2015). The types of violence women are subjected to in long-term abusive relationships may change over time from physical to psychological violence (Mezey et al., 2002; Pathak et al., 2019; Penhale & Porritt, 2010). Psychological violence is still seen as a less harmful form of abuse by professionals and often by the women themselves (Luoma et al., 2011; Zink et al., 2004). In interviews, older women share that non-physical violence often leaves scars more damaging than injuries from physical violence (Crockett et al., 2015). Nevertheless, they tend to minimize psychological abuse (Mezey et al., 2002). Early studies that shaped public perceptions of domestic violence focused almost exclusively on physical violence (Ellsberg & Heise, 2005). The persistence of this misperception is clearly demonstrated in a 2018 Washington Post article that listed the number one myth about domestic violence as the belief that it is defined by physical violence (Paisner, 2018).

The reluctance of senior women to report violence also contributes to the idea that domestic violence is a younger women's issue (Brownell, 2015; Crockett et al., 2015; Roberto & McCann, 2018; Zink, Regan, Jacobson, & Pabst, 2003). Only 27% of death review cases involving older adults had documented prior police contact where there was evidence to show that the perpetrator had used violence and made threats against the victim (Sutton & Dawson, 2017). A 2011 European study found similarly that less than half of older women talked with someone they knew about the most serious incident or reported it to an official agency (Luoma et al., 2011).

Older women experience a mix of internal and external barriers to reporting (Beaulaurier, Seff, & Newman, 2008). Internal barriers include self-blame, shame, and embarrassment as well as feelings of powerlessness and hopelessness (McGarry & Simpson, 2011; Pathak et al., 2019; Zink et al., 2004). Multiple studies highlight responses from others as a key influence as to whether a woman will seek help (Pathak et al., 2019). The attitudes and beliefs of professionals as well as family members, friends, and community organizations are highly influential in how senior women interpret their experiences (Pathak et al., 2019).

As a cohort, older women were raised in a period when preservation of the societal values of commitment and social stability in communities were paramount, and domestic violence was normalized by families and the women themselves (Zink et al., 2003). Theresa Zink writes:

What most differentiates the experiences of these older women from their younger counterparts is the social-historical period in which they grew up. Born before 1950, most came of age during a time when education and independence were not encouraged for women and when the feminist movement was still years away. Child, domestic, and elder abuse were not discussed or even recognized. Thus many older abused women were surprised to learn that their experiences were abnormal or worthy of any special services.

Zink et al. (2003, p. 1435)

Financial dependence on the abusive partner is another key barrier to help seeking. The impact of structural violence in the form of gender inequality disadvantages women throughout their lives. Economic barriers to women's advancement such as the wage gap, glass ceiling, precarious work without benefits or pensions, and lifelong unpaid domestic labor function to set women up to become dependents in later life. Social expectations of women as caregivers in unpaid work also trap women in abusive relationships with partners who may become dependent (Pathak et al., 2019). As women age, "their horizons for action diminish and they see themselves as having fewer life choices within the scope of decreasing power" (McGarry et al., 2017).

Domestic violence has significant health and psychosocial consequences for older women, exacerbated by prolonged exposure to violence (McGarry et al., 2017; Pathak et al., 2019). Current and lifetime domestic violence is associated with increased likelihood of physical symptoms including gastrointestinal, respiratory, pelvic, and genitourinary (reproductive and urinary) symptoms as well as being associated with frailty. Unless health-care practitioners are specifically educated on domestic violence in older populations, they can attribute physical consequences of an abusive relationship to age-related illness (McGarry et al., 2017; Pathak et al., 2019).

Professional and educational gaps

Service professionals and community members have reported that they find it difficult to recognize abusive relationships between older partners without training and intervention skills. Health professionals working most closely with seniors are not usually trained to recognize warning signs and risk factors of domestic violence (McGarry et al., 2017; Roberto & McCann, 2018). Lack of domestic violence education for professionals on what to look for in abusive relationships reinforces older women's inclinations not to seek help. When they do, too often they experience age discrimination, whereby all concerns are reduced to the "normal" aging process (McGarry et al., 2017; VAWG, 2016). Stereotypes play out, in particular, in the failure by professionals to query or consider sexual violence (NICE, 2015; Warmling et al., 2017; VAWG, 2016). Women who are raped by their partner can experience lasting trauma, physical injury, and exposure to sexually transmitted infections (Learning Network, 2016a, 2016b). Older women are uniquely at risk of not knowing whether they have HIV as they are unlikely to ask for a test without first being prompted by a doctor or service provider (VAWG, 2016). Women who experience sexual violence are also more likely to be killed by their intimate partner. Intimate partner sexual violence is a high-risk factor for domestic homicide (Learning Network, 2016a, 2016b).

The number of older women killed by their male partners is the hardest proof that domestic violence is a significant gendered issue that is growing as the population ages (VAWG, 2016). Femicide is the term that is used to describe the intentional killing of women and girls because they are female. In 2015 the United Nations Human Rights Office of the High Commissioner Special Rapporteur on VAW called on States to establish a "femicide watch," or "gender-related killing of women" watch (see http://femicide-watch.org/). In 2017 researchers at the Canadian Femicide Observatory for Justice and Accountability reviewed 452 femicide cases involving women 55 years and older over a 38-year period from 1974 to 2012 in Ontario, of which over a third were committed by intimate partners (Sutton & Dawson, 2017). In New York, researchers identified that 315, or 19% of femicides (including ones committed by intimate partners) involved women over 50 between the years of 1990 and 1997 (Brownell & Berman, 2004). Approximately 6% of all victim deaths resulting from spousal violence in Canada over a 10-year period (2006–16) involved seniors 60 years and older. Almost all of the victims were female (Burczycka & Conroy, 2018). Other studies have similarly found that homicides and homicide–suicides of older couples are almost exclusively perpetrated by male partners (Cohen, 2000; Eliason, 2009; Nägele et al., 2010; Penhale & Porritt, 2010; Roberto, McCann, & Brossoie, 2013; Salari, 2007; Warmling et al., 2017).

Learning from case reviews

Death reviews are important sources for information and learning to inform system changes that can lead to prevention.

Case reviews have shown that in 70% of domestic homicides, there are warning signs and risk factors that can alert bystanders, who are closest to the family, that the couple is in increasing trouble (DVDRC, 2018; Penhale & Porritt, 2010). Earlier intervention and prevention are predicated on being able to identify and respond to risks that are particular to senior couples (Crockett et al., 2015; Luoma et al., 2011; O'Neil, 2016; Penhale & Porritt, 2010).

In 2000 after reviewing Florida State medical examiner data, Donna Cohen provided a startling statistic that linked domestic homicide—suicide as an age-related characteristic. She found that 40% of all homicide—suicides occur in persons 55 years and older (Cohen, 2000). Prior to her study in 1999, there had been no investigation into the prevalence or clinical patterns of homicide—suicide in older persons (Cohen & Molinari, 2010). A Quebec study flagged the link again in 2010 after reviewing 27 cases of homicide—suicide of older couples. Bourget found that a homicide—suicide dynamic was found in nearly three quarters of the cases (Bourget et al., 2010). Similarly the Ontario Domestic Violence Death Review Committee (DVDRC) has seen in recent years an increase of cases of domestic homicide involving older couples with significantly higher rates of homicide—suicide in older cohorts (DVDRC, 2018; O'Neil, 2016). Unfortunately most countries do not keep homicide—suicide statistics, making it difficult to assess prevalence rates globally (Eliason, 2009).

Associated risk factors

The most frequent associated factors for domestic violence in older couples are alcohol consumption, depression, low-income created dependencies, functional impairment, and exposure to violence in childhood (Warmling et al., 2017). Alcohol, drugs, and cigarettes serve as coping mechanisms for many abused women (Lazenbatt, Devaney, & Gildea, 2013). Physical and mental health problems are common in homicide cases both for the perpetrator and the victim. Seniors have a higher risk of completed suicide than any other age group, yet the alarming statistics receive little attention and few efforts go toward prevention (O'Connell, Chin, Cunningham, & Lawlor, 2016). Potential links with domestic homicide have not been made despite increasing evidence that the rate of homicide—suicide of older adults is significant (Bourget et al., 2010; Brennan & Boyce, 2013).

Homicide risk factors for older offenders

A history of domestic violence is a major risk factor for victims of any age. Separation is another common high-risk factor (DVDRC, 2018). Spouses who face being separated through circumstances such as hospitalization or a move to a long-term care facility are particularly vulnerable (Cohen & Molinari, 2010; Malphurs, Eisdorfer, & Cohen, 2001).

Perpetrator characteristics that should trigger concern for professionals working with seniors include untreated depression or any other undiagnosed mental health issues. Older men who are caring for chronically ill or disabled spouses may be at risk, especially if they cannot adequately care for their spouses (Bourget et al., 2010). Suicidal ideation should be considered a risk factor for homicide when the male partner is the caregiver. A US study that compared cases of suicide' to cases of homicide—suicide found that men who suicided had physical health problems and were receiving care from their wives. By contrast, homicide—suicide perpetrators displayed significantly more domestic violence and/or were caregivers for their wives. Both groups of men had reported depression (Malphurs & Cohen, 2005).

The caregiver role

Older women and men differ in the caregiving characteristics and strategies that they adopt toward their intimate partners when coping with health stressors in late life. Men tasked with caregiving for their ailing wives may adopt an "occupational mindset," where they prioritize caregiving duties over their partner's feelings. As their wife's health deteriorates and care becomes less predictable or controlled, older men are more likely to rely on "rational extremes of their gender identity in order to take control of problematic situations in late life"— resulting in instances of violence that can be more situational than historical (Roberto et al., 2013). In contrast, women in similar circumstances were found to prioritize feelings so as to not threaten their husbands' autonomy (Calasanti, 2007).

Most murder—suicides are perpetrated by men who feel they have lost control over their intimate partner (Cohen, 2000). Defining and acknowledging the presence of coercive and controlling behavior in relationships therefore needs to be more carefully considered. For older women, homicide can be the culmination of a long-term violent relationship or it can happen without a history of violence, conceived by their partner as a "solution" to deteriorating health situations, such as in cases of dementia.

Dementia adds another layer to the complexity of domestic violence. Recent studies have made connections between head trauma that occurs from physical abuse and increased risk for developing dementia in later life (Stone, 2018; Weaver, 2018). Repeated head trauma that can result in chronic traumatic encephalopathy is also being explored as a risk factor for increased aggression that heightens the risk for the perpetration of domestic violence (Diamond, 2014).

For women providing care to demented husbands who are violent, in the absence of an understanding of domestic violence, his violent behavior is likely to be interpreted by health professionals as "responsive behavior," an attempt to communicate rather than to cause harm. The definition is a dangerous misnomer without an assessment. Professionals who are not trained to recognize risks associated with intimate partner homicide are not prepared to address what is happening and may actually increase the risk. A behavioral therapist interpreting violent and threatening behavior as "responsive" may encourage the woman not to "take the behavior personally" and to "set better boundaries" (Alzheimer Society of Ontario, 2019; see https://alzheimer.ca/en/on). This is the same message often conveyed to women in abusive situations by their partner—that they are the problem and the ones who need to change to stop the violence (Zink et al., 2004). In situations where there is an undetected history of violence, the label of responsive behavior can be a cruel mirroring of the abusive partner's perspective and power.

No prior history of domestic violence

Although a good deal of domestic violence against older women occurs in relationships where abuse has been ongoing over years, death reviews have also found cases where there is no prior history of domestic violence (Bourget et al., 2010; Cohen, 2000; O'Neil, 2016). This is largely unexplored territory where domestic violence and health issues overlap in ways that are quite specific to older couples. It is in these cases as well that a "mental illness, mercy killings, or suicide pacts" motive is often (problematically) proposed in official records and news reports. Roberto et al. (2013), especially when one partner can no longer provide the extensive care required by the other. The wishes of the victim are often unclear and/or unreported.

Regardless of the husband's motive, the majority of women killed did not experience a "merciful" method of death. Excessive force is used in many cases and victims were more likely to die from being beaten or the subsequent complications (Sutton & Dawson, 2017).

Applying a gender lens can provide insight into the dynamics that drive actions and responses in the relationships of many older couples (McGarry et al., 2017).

When a death review committee finds no history of violence in the relationship, the finding is based on the information that is available to the review panel. Examining gender roles and control dynamics posthumously can be difficult. If both partners accept that men are the natural authority in the home, power abuses can remain relatively invisible until something happens to challenge or disturb the status quo. Controlling coercive behavior by the male partner may have existed quietly and unchallenged throughout the relationship. Physical and cognitive decline in later life may act as a catalyst for more explicit violence that was not previously recognized as such (Montminy, 2005). More in-depth investigation of the risk factors for domestic homicide in older women is needed to appreciate the complexity of these deaths and to understand the ways that "merciful" motives may end up being attributed to violence that is experienced as unescapable.

Case studies

This section highlights two cases of domestic homicide involving older women. Information about the homicides has been in the public domain through media accounts, trials, and/ or published death reviews. Each case highlights valuable lessons learned that can help friends and family members, as well as professionals from legal, social service, and health-care sectors prevent similar deaths in the future. The first case looks at homicides in which there was a history of domestic violence. The second case reporting suggests there was not a history of violence in the relationship.

Toronto, Canada: the case of Edith Francomano

Many of the details outlined in this case can be retrieved from: https://www.thestar.com/news/2007/03/28/jealous_husband_gets_life_term.html. For additional references, see the references under Case study references.

Edith Francomano was 63 years old when her husband of 45 years, Mario Francomano, bludgeoned her to death with a baseball bat. He was 66 years old at the time. On the morning of the homicide, Mr. Francomano drove his son to work, returned home, and killed Ms. Francomano. Following the homicide, he drove to the police station and confessed. In his statement to police, he reported that Ms. Francomano had been refusing him sex, and that morning, having refused him again, he "exploded." He reported that he believed she was having an affair. He also admitted that he used to hit her but claimed that it hadn't happened in a long time.

Mr. Francomano was described as being physically, emotionally, and verbally abusive with a volatile temper. He was also jealous, controlling, and possessive. Mr. Francomano was convinced that his wife was unfaithful to him. After he retired from his job as a chef in 2003, he became more and more paranoid about her activities. Ms. Francomano's body was found on the morning of September 22, 2005, in the basement of their home after she failed to turn up for work at the small beauty salon she operated nearby. Mr. Francomano had demonstrated abusive characteristics throughout the entire marriage. At his sentencing, the judge described him as an "ill-tempered bully who alienated anyone near to him."

Ms. Francomano contacted police the month before her murder but was afraid the intervention would aggravate him and put her whole family at risk. The day before he killed her, she phoned a friend and said, "this is the end," predicting her own death. Mr. Francomano pled guilty at his trial in 2007 and was sentenced for second-degree murder, which carries a mandatory life sentence. Parole eligibility was set at 12 years.

Themes and recommendations

The phrase "domestic violence grown old" is sometimes used to reference violence in relationships of older couples (Bows, 2015). Ageist assumptions underlie the phrase and may cause people who are bystanders to the situation to look the other way when they see abusive behavior. They may rationalize that the situation has always been this way and there is no point in getting involved now. Further if the woman has been experiencing abuse for a long time then others may assume that it cannot be serious, or they may believe that she has "made her bed and has to lie in it." In these ways, older women face specific pressures imposed by society that are particular to their generation (Bows, 2015; Zink et al., 2004).

Ms. Francomano's call to the police a month before the murder is an indication of the desperation she felt. She was afraid of the consequences for herself and others in her family. That fear may have prevented her from taking further steps to protect herself. While it is often the neighbors, friends, and family members who are most likely to be aware of domestic violence situations, unless they have had education and training, they may be unsure how to respond and are unlikely to understand the risks or where to find help (DVDRC, 2015). They may also be afraid of the perpetrator. Similarly professionals, such as family doctors, are unlikely to recognize warning signs or risk factors that indicate an escalating situation unless they have training on domestic violence (Zink et al., 2004).

Ms. Francomano's contact with professionals was a missed opportunity to provide support and to do safety planning. While many women do not recognize the risk for homicide, Ms. Francomano was very aware of the danger she was in. Unfortunately her help seeking did not translate into the support she needed.

Cardiff, Wales: the case of Margaret Mayer

Many of the details outlined in this case can be retrieved from: https://www.walesonline.co.uk/news/wales-news/daughter-man-who-killed-dementia-12733307. For additional references, see the references under Case study references.

Margaret and Gus Mayer were married in 1952. They were just 19 and 20 when they met working in a lab in South Wales. They had six children and settled in Heath, Cardiff. According to their children, the couple lived a vital and happy life. There were no reports of prior violence in the relationship. "We had such a fun childhood, Mum had so much energy and was a real outdoors person. Dad loved fishing, gardening, history and archeology. They'd go to concerts, entertain their many friends and play bridge. Mum even played at an international level. Dad used to say every day was a blessing and he wanted to live to 100" (Wales News Service, 2017).

Ms. Mayer was diagnosed with Alzheimer's in 2012 and her husband became her caregiver. As her health deteriorated, the family could see that Mr. Mayer was losing weight and showing signs of exhaustion. "He found it hard that his vivacious, brilliant, active wife had become confused and disoriented. That shared history of 64 years was slowly being deleted from her memory" (Wales News Service, 2017). In the months leading up to the murder, the family saw that Mr. Mayer was losing his spark and worried that he was caring for his wife all day and then getting up two and three times through the night. In February 2012, they arranged for Ms. Mayer to attend a day center twice a week to give him a break. In July they tried to get him to accept more help from social services but he refused, telling them that he was coping. The family were starting to worry that Mr. Mayer might lose his temper out of sheer fatigue and a sense of hopelessness.

On July 28, 2016, 86-year-old Mr. Mayer attempted to smother Ms. Mayer. When he was unsuccessful, he bludgeoned her to death with a table lamp. He left the house and went to the train station to kill himself by lying on the tracks in front of an oncoming train. His leg was crushed, but he survived for 7 weeks before succumbing to his injuries. He told a police officer who came to his aid that he had killed his wife because he did not want her to suffer any longer. He was charged with murder but never left hospital.

The Mayer family was highly critical of social services in the media and indicated that the Cardiff adult services were "passive rather than proactive." In the inquest into the murder, the adult services manager told the hearing that there was nothing to suggest that Ms. Mayer was in danger and even in hindsight, nothing would have been done differently. The Coroner ruled: "There is nothing that suggests this was a foreseeable death," adding that there was "no failure" on the part of social services. He recorded a verdict of unlawful killing. The Mayer's were cremated separately, 6 weeks apart.

Themes and recommendations

Following the verdict, the Mayer family called for changes in the social care system. They spoke about the guilt of not being able to prevent the murder, frustration with the service system that did not act on the fears being expressed by the family, and the refusal of social services to include the family in care planning.

There are a number of factors that may have led Mr. Mayer to decide that murder—suicide was the best solution for this situation. Older caregivers who refuse help may do so for a variety of reasons including a sense that they are the only one who can give good care to their partner, a sense of obligation to protect the loved one from what is perceived as an uncaring system, a fear of losing control, and the interruption of having professionals coming into their homemaking decisions

(Calasanti, 2007). Ms. Mayer had told her husband that if he ever put her in a home she would kill herself.

Many seniors are afraid of long-term care homes. The pervasiveness of ageist attitudes in society is reflected in systemic problems that make older adults more vulnerable to abuse and neglect in long-term care facilities. Media focus on poor and unsafe conditions has created a generalized fear of long-term care facilities that may have contributed to Ms. Mayer's assertion that she would rather be dead than in an institution. While there are serious issues in the long-term health-care system in many jurisdictions, there are good and even excellent care facilities in every country. Public education is needed to balance the fear and assist families to make more informed decisions about available services and care options.

The WHO report, Dementia: A Public Health Priority in 2012, stated dementia is overwhelming for caregivers and that adequate support is required from the health, social, financial, and legal systems (WHO, 2012). Rather than waiting for Mr. Mayer to reach his limit, caring services should have recognized that a senior providing around-the-clock care to his ailing partner needed to be seen as a risk to both partners. The WHO report also supports the Mayer children's assertion that their input could have provided important insights in formulating the care plan for their mother (WHO, 2012). People with dementia and their caregivers have unique insights into the condition and experiences that accompany it. They should be involved in setting policies, plans, laws, and services that relate to them.

The verdict of the Coroner indicates the need for and the importance of education and training for professionals in justice and human services to be able to recognize warning signs and risk factors of domestic homicide that are particular to older couples. The decision that the murder was not "foreseeable" highlights the lack of understanding of risk factors that remain unseen, even in hindsight. Ms. Mayer required around-the-clock care that rested almost entirely on the shoulders of her 86-year-old husband. The impossibility of one person, of any age, being able to carry those demands without significant support is itself a red flag that underlines the need for a strongly proactive approach that includes the input of the family (WHO, 2012).

Summary

The United Nations has identified older women as being extremely vulnerable to human rights abuses related to neglect, abuse, and violence (UN DESA, 2013). Domestic violence is an urgent and global public health issue (WHO, 2017).

Ageism is the pervasive social context and the worldview that relegates older adults to margins of society as "unproductive" citizens once their paid working lives are completed (Spencer, 2009). For older women, a lifetime of structural violence in the form of sexism and economic gender inequality sets them up to be dependent and poorer than older men (CARP, 2011; Zink et al., 2003). They are further disadvantaged by inequities attributed to discrimination by race, class, ability, and sexual orientation (Crockett et al., 2015).

Older women who experience domestic violence remain mostly invisible in research, and by extension in society, due to competing definitions and methodologies that lack the intersection of age and gender-related analyses (UN DESA, 2013). Research findings are therefore limited by the partial perspectives. Resulting policies and practices by sectors and disciplines cannot currently or adequately capture the complexity of the many intersections of women's lives that combine to make them more vulnerable to abuse in later years.

As a cohort, older women may not recognize abuse because they have been socialized to domestic roles, often not working outside of the home at a time when gender norms that situate them as subordinate in their own households have been accepted. They were raised in a period of sweeping social, legal, and economic changes including the feminist and civil rights movement of the 1980s and 1990s. "Although they witnessed these changes, they did not always benefit from them" (Zink et al., 2003, p. 1430).

The rise in domestic homicides that involve older couples in recent years has brought attention to the specific vulnerability of older women as a cohort. Higher rates of homicide–suicide in the swiftly aging population carry a sense of urgency to develop targeted responses and interventions. Women over 50 represent nearly one-quarter of women around the world (UNGA, 2013). By the year 2030 the number of people aged 60 and older will reach 1.4 billion, with women outliving men (UN DESA, 2015). Effective strategies for intervention and prevention of domestic homicide will first need to comprehend the specific issues of older couples and older women in particular (Pathak et al., 2019).

Researchers in a number of studies promote the adoption of a life span approach in addressing VAW to incorporate experiences of discrimination, trauma, and violence over the course of a lifetime (Brownell, 2015; Crockett et al., 2015; McDonald & Thomas, 2013; McGarry et al., 2017; VAWG, 2016). One of the largest population studies in the United States finds that adverse events in childhood create risk of violence in adulthood and have demonstrable economic, social, and health impacts (Felliti et al., 1998). To develop appropriate prevention and interventions, more holistic connections need to be drawn between types of violence at different stages of the life course and set into an ecological framework (Brownell, 2015; Williams, 2003).

The ecological framework was adapted in 1998 by Lori Heise to provide a theoretical structure for considering the multidimensional factors of VAW that occur as a result of interactions between individuals in their relationships, communities, and society (Heise, 1998). The WHO promotes the ecological model for domestic violence as well as elder abuse (WHO, 2019).

Despite the challenges, the systemic exclusion of older women within advocacy for the rights of women and girls is starting to change. The United Nations Sustainable Development Goals to "leave no one behind" promises to expand data collection on violence against older women (VAWG, 2016). Comprehensive and recent systematic reviews provide opportunities to synthesize existing knowledge and recognize gaps across disciplines and countries. Resulting analyses are informing recommendations for future directions in research and practice that are specifically designed for older women who are experiencing domestic violence (McGarry et al., 2017; Meyer et al., 2019; Nägele et al., 2010; Pathak et al., 2019; Warmling et al., 2017).

Governments are also recognizing the cascade of human and economic costs that follow from unaddressed interpersonal violence. The prioritizing of gender based and intersectional analyses is increasingly apparent on government websites along with explicit acknowledgment that diversity and inclusion are key to the development of just, equitable, effective, and targeted interventions and strategies. The Canadian government has made significant investments to develop health equity-oriented curriculum to educate professionals and to acknowledge the intersections of oppression and violence as health issues that persist in relationships, systems, and society. Equity-oriented education across disciplines is a strategic direction that has the potential to bridge long-standing research and sector tensions by anchoring education in human rights. An equity orientation provides the foundation for the development of shared principles and practices using a common language that is well versed in the relationship between social location, trauma, and violence at all levels of society (Equip Health Care, 2017; Ford-Gilboe, Wathen, & Varcoe, 2018; VEGA Project, 2019).

Domestic homicide is preventable when those closest to the situation become aware of the unique life circumstances of older people who struggle under the weight of intersecting forms of discrimination. Discrimination is societal violence that propels the dynamics of risk in individual lives. Addressing the unique barriers that obstruct older women's human rights, personal safety, and social support requires long-term commitment and targeted action at all levels of society (VAWG, 2016).

References

Alzheimer Society of Ontario. (2019). *Examples of responsive behaviors*. Retrieved from: <https://alzheimer.ca/en/on/We-can-help/Resources/Shifting-Focus/Examples-of-responsive-behavior>.

Beaulaurier, R. L., Seff, L. R., & Newman, F. L. (2008). Barriers to help-seeking for older women who experience domestic violence: A descriptive model. *Journal of Women & Aging, 20*(3–4), 231–248. Available from https://doi.org/10.1080/08952840801984543.

Bows, H. (2015). Domestic violence 'grown old: The unseen victims of prolonged abuse. The conversation. Retrieved from: <https://theconversation.com/domestic-violence-grown-old-the-unseen-victims-of-prolonged-abuse-43014>.

Bourget, D., Gagne, P., & Whitehurst, L. (2010). Domestic homicide and homicide-suicide: The older offender. *Journal of the American Academy of Psychiatry and the Law Online, 38*(3), 305–311.

Brennan, S., & Boyce, J. (2013). Family-related murder-suicides. *Family violence in Canada: A statistical profile*. Statistics Canada Catalogue no. 85-002-X.

Brownell, B., & Berman, J. (2004). Homicides of older women in New York City. In A. R. Roberts, & K. R. Yeager (Eds.), *Evidence-based practice manual* (pp. 771–778). New York: Oxford University Press.

Brownell, P. (2015). Older women and intimate partner violence. *The Encyclopedia of Adulthood and Aging*, 1–5.

Butler, R. N., & Lewis, M. I. (1973). *Aging & mental health: Positive psychosocial approaches*. St. Louis, MO: Mosby.

Burczycka, M., & Conroy, S. (2018). Family violence in Canada: A statistical profile, 2016. *Juristat, Canadian Centre for Justice Statistics, Statistics Canada*. Retrieved from: <https://www.canada.ca/en/public-health/services/health-promotion/stop-family-violence/problem-canada.html>.

Calasanti, T. (2007). Taking 'women's work' 'like a man': Husband's experiences of care work. *The Gerontologist, 47*(4), 516–527. Available from https://doi.org/10.1093/geront/47.4.516.

Calasanti, T., Slevin, K., & King, N. (2006). Ageism and feminism: From "et cetera" to center. *NWSA Journal, 18*(1), 13–30.

CARP. (2011). *Ageism meets sexism: Economic issues faced by older women*. Retrieved from: <https://www.carp.ca/2011/11/18/ageism-meets-sexism-economic-issues-faced-by-older-women/>.

Cohen, D. (2000). An update on homicide-suicide in older persons: 1995-2000. *Journal of Mental Health and Aging, 6*(3), 195–200.

Cohen, D., & Molinari, V. (2010). The untold story: Caregivers who kill. In G. Maletta, & M. Agronin (Eds.), *Principles and practice of geriatric psychiatry* (2nd ed., pp. 53–56). Philadelphia, PA: Lippincott, Williams & Wilkins.

Crockett, C., Brandl, B., & Dabby, F. C. (2015). Survivors in the margins: The invisibility of violence against older women. *Journal of Elder Abuse & Neglect, 27,* 291–302.

Diamond, D. (2014). Does playing football make you violent? Examining the evidence. *Forbes.* Retrieved from: <https://www.forbes.com/sites/dandiamond/2014/09/16/does-football-make-you-violent-examining-the-evidence/#42c8fc3ffb7e>.

Domestic Violence Death Review Committee. (2015). *2013-14 annual report to the Chief Coroner.* Toronto: Office of the Chief Coroner.

Domestic Violence Death Review Committee. (2018). *2017 annual report.* Toronto: Office of the Chief Coroner.

Dong, X. Q. (2015). Elder abuse: Systematic review and implications for practice. *Journal of the American Geriatrics Society, 63*(6), 1214–1238. Available from https://doi.org/10.1111/jgs.13454.

Eliason, S. (2009). Murder-suicide: A review of the recent literature. *Journal of the American Academy of Psychiatry and the Law Online, 37*(3), 371.

Ellsberg, M., & Heise, L. (2005). *Researching violence against women: A practical guide for researchers and activists.* Washington, DC: World Health Organization, PATH.

Equip Health Care. (2017). *Trauma-and violence-informed care (TVIC): A tool for health & social service organizations and providers.* Retrieved from: <https://equiphealthcare.ca/equip/wp-content/uploads/2018/01/TVIC-tool-ONTARIO-January-12-2018.pdf>.

Felliti, V., Anda, R., Nordenberg, D., Williamson, D., Spitz, A., Edwards, V., ... Marks, J. (1998). Relationship of childhood abuse and household dysfunction to many of the leading causes of death in adults. *American Journal of Preventive Medicine, 14*(4), 245–258.

Ford-Gilboe, M., Wathen, C.N., Varcoe, C., et al. (2018). *How equity-oriented health care affects health: Key mechanisms and implications for primary health care practice and policy.* Retrieved from: <https://www.milbank.org/wp-content/uploads/mq/volume-96/december-2018/FORD-GILBOE_et_al-2018-The_Milbank_Quarterly.pdf>.

Heise, L. L. (1998). Violence against women: An integrated, ecological framework. *Violence Against Women, 4*(3), 262–290. Available from https://doi.org/10.1177/1077801298004003002.

Hightower, J., Smith, M. J., & Hightower, H. C. (2006). Hearing the voices of abused older women. *Journal of Gerontological Social Work, 46*(3–4), 205–227. Available from https://doi.org/10.1300/J083v46n03_12.

Lazenbatt, A., Devaney, J., & Gildea, A. (2013). Older women living and coping with domestic violence. *Community Practitioner, 86*(2), 28–33.

Learning Network. (2016a). *Issue 18: Violence against women who are older.* London, ON: Learning Network, Centre for Research and Education on Violence Against Women and Children.

Learning Network. (2016b). *Issue 17: Intimate partner sexual violence.* London, ON: Learning Network, Centre for Research and Education on Violence Against Women and Children.

Luoma, M.-L., Koivusilta, M., Lang, G., Enzenhofer, E., De Donder, L., Verté, D., ... Penhale, B. (2011). *Prevalence study of abuse and violence against older women. Results of a multi-cultural survey in Austria, Belgium, Finland, Lithuania, and Portugal (European report of the AVOW Project).* Helsinki, Finland: National Institute for Health and Welfare (THL).

Malphurs, J. E., & Cohen, D. (2005). A statewide case–control study of spousal homicide–suicide in older persons. *The American Journal of Geriatric Psychiatry, 13*(3), 211–217.

Malphurs, J. E., Eisdorfer, C., & Cohen, D. (2001). A comparison of antecedents of homicide–suicide and suicide in older married men. *The American Journal of Geriatric Psychiatry, 9*(1), 49–57. Available from https://doi.org/10.1097/00019442-200102000-00008.

McDonald, L., & Thomas, C. (2013). Elder abuse through a life course lens. *International Psychogeriatrics, 25*(8), 1235–1243. Available from https://doi.org/10.1017/S104161021300015X.

McGarry, J., & Simpson, C. (2011). Domestic abuse and older women: Exploring the opportunities for service development and care delivery. *The Journal of Adult Protection, 13*(6), 294–301. Available from https://doi.org/10.1108/14668201111194203.

McGarry, J., Simpson, C., & Hinchliff-Smith, K. (2017). Older women, domestic violence and mental health: A consideration of the particular issues for health and healthcare practice. *Journal of Clinical Nursing, 26*(15–16), 2177–2191.

Mezey, N., Post, L., & Maxwell, C. (2002). Redefining intimate partner violence: Women's experience with physical violence and non-physical abuse by age. *International Journal of Sociology and Social Policy, 22*(7/8), 122–154. Available from https://doi.org/10.1108/01443330210790120[34].

Montminy, L. (2005). Older women's experiences of psychological violence in their marital relationships. *Journal of Gerontological Social Work, 46*(2), 3–22.

Nägele, B., Böhm, U., Görgen, T., & Tóth, O. (2010). Intimate partner violence against older women – Summary report. *Daphne project*. Retrieved from: <http://www.ipvow.org/images/ipvow/reports/summary_report_final.pdf>.

National Institute for the Care of the Elderly. (2015). *Into the light: National survey on the mistreatment of older adults*. Retrieved from: <https://cnpea.ca/images/canada-report-june-7-2016-pre-study-lynnmcdonald.pdf>.

O'Connell, H., Chin, A. V., Cunningham, C., & Lawlor, B. (2016). Recent developments: Suicide in older people. *British Medical Journal, 329*(7471), 895–899. Available from https://doi.org/10.1136/bmj.329.7471.895.

O'Neil, B. (2016). *Domestic homicide and homicide-suicide in the older population*. Master's thesis. Graduate Program in Psychology. University of Western Ontario.

Paisner, S. (2018). Five myths about domestic violence. *The Washington Post*. Retrieved from: <https://www.washingtonpost.com/outlook/five-myths/five-myths-about-domestic-violence/2018/02/23/78969748-1819-11e8-b681-2d4d462a1921_story.html?utm_term = .0789e3ec393e>.

Pathak, N., Dhairyawan, R., & Tariq, S. (2019). The experience of domestic violence among older women: A narrative review. *Maturitas, 121*, 63–75. Available from https://doi.org/10.1016/j.maturitas.2018.12.011.

Penhale, B. (2014). *Older women, domestic violence & elder abuse: Recent findings and ongoing challenges*. Retrieved from: <http://www.ncpop.ie/userfiles/file/Seminar%202014/Bridget%20Penhale%20Presentation%2017_9_14.pdf>.

Penhale, B., & Porritt, J. (2010). *Intimate partner violence against older women*. National Report United Kingdom. Retrieved from: <https://www.uea.ac.uk/documents/2397319/2510614/IPVoW + UK + National + Report.pdf/c46ac112-7ec1-4259-9b26-e2cbd575bf4a>.

Roberto, K., & McCann, B. (2018). Violence and abuse in rural older women's lives: A life course perspective. *Journal of Interpersonal Violence*. Available from https://doi.org/10.1177/0886260518755490.

Roberto, K., McCann, B., & Brossoie, N. (2013). Domestic violence in late life: An analysis of national news reports. *Journal of Elder Abuse & Neglect, 25*(3), 230–241. Available from https://doi.org/10.1080/08946566.2012.751825.

Salari, S. (2007). Patterns of intimate partner homicide suicide in later life: Strategies for prevention. *Clinical Interventions in Aging, 2*(3), 441−452.

Spencer, C. (2009). *Law commission of Ontario: Ageism and the law: Emerging concepts and practices in housing and health.* Retrieved from: <https://www.lco-cdo.org/wp-content/uploads/2014/01/older-adults-commissioned-paper-spencer.pdf>.

Stöckl, H., & Penhale, B. (2015). Intimate partner violence and its association with physical and mental health symptoms among older women in Germany. *Journal of Interpersonal Violence,* 30, 3089−3111.

Stone, W. (2018). *Domestic Violence's Overlooked Damage: Concussion and Brain Injury.* Retrieved from: <https://www.washingtonpost.com/national/health-science/domestic-violences-overlooked-damage-concussion-and-brain-injury/2018/06/01/4d86f92a-657c-11e8-81ca-bb14593acaa6_story.html?noredirect = on&utm_term = .b26c588716b5>.

Sutton, D., & Dawson, M. (2017). *Femicide of older women. Learning network brief 31.* London, ON: Learning Network, Centre for Research and Education on Violence Against Women and Children.

United Nations. (2002) *Political declaration and Madrid international plan of action on aging.* Retrieved from: <https://www.un.org/en/events/pastevents/pdfs/Madrid_plan.pdf>.

United Nations DESA. (2013). *Neglect, abuse and violence against older women.* Retrieved from: <https://www.un.org/esa/socdev/documents/ageing/neglect-abuse-violence-older-women.pdf>.

United Nations DESA Population Division. (2015). World population ageing 2015 *(ST/ESA/SER.A/390).* New York: United Nations.

United Nations General Assembly. (2013). Follow-up to the international year of older persons: Second world assembly on ageing: Report of the secretary general *(A/68/167).* New York: United Nations.

United Nations Women. (2017). *Spotlight on sustainable development goal 5: Achieve gender equality and empower all women and girls.* Retrieved from: <http://www.unwomen.org/en/digital-library/multimedia/2017/7/infographic-spotlight-on-sdg-5>.

VEGA Project. (2019). Recognizing and responding safely to family violence. McMaster University. Retrieved from: <https://vegaproject.mcmaster.ca/>.

Violence Against Women and Girls (VAWG). (2016). *Brief on violence against older women.* Retrieved from: <https://www.un.org/esa/socdev/documents/ageing/vawg_brief_on_older_women.pdf>.

Warmling, D., Lindner, S., & Coelho, E. (2017). Intimate partner violence prevalence in the elderly and associated factors: Systematic review. *Ciencia & Saude Coletiva, 22*(9), 3111. Available from https://doi.org/10.1590/1413-81232017229.12312017.

Weaver, D. (2018). *Dementia's hidden darkness: Violence and domestic abuse.* Retrieved from: <https://www.salon.com/2018/11/18/dementias-hidden-darkness-violence-and-domestic-abuse_partner/>.

Williams, L. M. (2003). Understanding child abuse and violence against women: A life course perspective. *Journal of Interpersonal Violence, 18*(4), 441−451. Available from https://doi.org/10.1177/0886260502250842.

World Health Organization, 2008. *A Global Response to Elder Abuse and Neglect: Building Primary Health Care Capacity to Deal with the Problem Worldwide: Main Report.* Retrieved from: <http://www.who.int/ageing/publications/elder_abuse2008/en/>.

World Health Organization. (2012). *Dementia: A public health priority.* Retrieved from: <http://apps.who.int/iris/bitstream/handle/10665/75263/

9789241564458_eng.pdf;jsessionid = 2B0763974B9DA1E90034C8617BD9201E? sequence = 1>.

World Health Organization (2017). *Violence against women. Key facts.* Retrieved from: <https://www.who.int/news-room/fact-sheets/detail/violence-against-women>.

World Health Organization (2019). *Global campaign for violence prevention. Violence Prevention Alliance.* Retrieved from: <https://www.who.int/ violenceprevention/approach/ecology/en/>.

Zink, T., Jacobson, J., Regan, S., & Pabst, S. (2004). Hidden victims: The healthcare needs and experiences of older women in abusive relationships. *Journal of Women's Health (2002)*, *13*(8), 898–908. Available from https://doi.org/10.1089/jwh.2004.13.898.

Zink, T., Regan, S., Jacobson, C. J., & Pabst, S. (2003). Cohort, period, and aging effects: A qualitative study of older women's reasons for remaining in abusive relationships. *Violence Against Women*, *9*(12), 1429–1441.

Case study references

Anonymous. (2016a). Carer who killed wife with dementia had 'fog of fatigue'. *BBC News.* Retrieved from: <https://www.bbc.com/news/av/38242737/carer-who-killed-wife-with-dementia-had-fog-of-fatigue>.

Anonymous. (2016b). Dementia carer 'smothered wife and tried to kill himself.' *BBC News.* Retrieved from: <https://www.bbc.com/news/uk-wales-south-east-wales-38234296>.

Daxer, L. (2016). *Margaret Mayer.* Retrieved from: <https://disability-memorial.org/margaret-mayer>.

Gayle, D. (2016). Family criticises social services over deaths of elderly couple in Wales. *The Guardian.* Retrieved from: <https://www.theguardian.com/uk-news/2016/dec/07/angus-mayer-margaret-alzheimers-coroners-inquest-cardiff>.

Small, P. (2007a). Guilty plea in wife's beating death. *The Star.* Retrieved from: <https://www.thestar.com/news/2007/03/01/guilty_plea_in_wifes_beating_death.html>.

Small, P. (2007b). Man admits killing his wife. *The Star.* Retrieved from: <https://www.thestar.com/news/2007/03/02/man_admits_killing_his_wife.html>.

Wales News Service. (2017). 'He was willing himself to die — it haunts me Dad was being punished' Daughter of man who killed wife says she was 'never angry' with him. *Wales Online.* Retrieved from: <https://www.walesonline.co.uk/news/wales-news/daughter-man-who-killed-dementia-12733307>.

Further reading

Brennan, S. (2012). Victimization of older Canadians, 2009. *Juristat.* Statistics Canada Catalogue no. 85-002-X.

Dawson, M. (2018). *106 women and girls killed by violence: Eight-month report by the Canadian femicide observatory for justice and accountability.* Retrieved from: <https://femicideincanada.ca/sites/default/files/2018-09/CFOJA%20FINAL%20REPORT%20ENG%20V3.pdf>.

Learning Network. (2017). *Issue 19: Femicide of women who are older.* London, ON: Western University.

Domestic homicides in rural communities: challenges in accessing resources

Anna-Lee Straatman[1], Deborah Doherty[2] and Victoria Banman[3]

[1]Centre for Research & Education on Violence against Women & Children, Faculty of Education, Western University, London, ON, Canada [2]Public Legal Education and Information Service New Brunswick, New Brunswick, Canada [3]Banman Counselling, St. Thomas, ON, Canada

Historically, research on domestic violence in rural communities has been very limited (Logan, Walker, & Leukefeld, 2001; Schissel, 1992; Van Hightower, Gorton, & DeMoss, 2000); yet statistics on domestic violence and homicide shows that these problems are at least as prevalent, if not more so, in rural areas as in urban ones (Martz & Saraurer, 2000; Websdale & Johnson, 1997; Websdale, 1998). There are various possible explanations for this lack of exploration of domestic violence in rural communities. It may reflect an urban-centric bias on the part of researchers. Alternatively it may stem from the belief that few differences exist between women's experiences of abuse in urban and rural communities. Research suggests that understanding the social and cultural contexts in which abuse occurs is essential to fully understand the subjective experiences of women living with domestic violence (Doherty & Hornosty, 2001; Logan et al., 2001; Martz & Saraurer, 2000). Such understanding is also essential for the development and design of appropriate and effective programs for helping women. This chapter will feature some of the most recent research to date regarding this context.

Rurality and risk for domestic violence

Definitions of rural vary based on context but are commonly identified with sparsely populated regions with low population

Preventing Domestic Homicides. DOI: https://doi.org/10.1016/B978-0-12-819463-8.00003-4

density (Sandberg, 2013). In Sweden rural areas are defined as areas with at least five inhabitants per square kilometer and cities with population of up to 25,000. In Australia areas are classified according to their population, size, and relative distance to an urban center. The US Census Bureau defines rural as all population, housing, and territory not included within an urbanized area or urban cluster (Holder, Fields, & Lofquist, 2016; Ratcliffe, Burd, Holder, & Fields, 2016). The rural areas of the United States contain 19% of the population. Urban areas and urban clusters which contained the majority of the population, only occupied about 3% of the land area of the country (United States Census Bureau, 2016). Demographics of rural populations in the United States, Canada, and Australia indicate that people living in rural areas tend to be older, experience higher poverty and unemployment rates, and lower education (Baxter, Gray, & Hayes, 2011; Des Meules & Pong, 2006; Holder et al., 2016).

According to the 2011 Census, 19% of Canadians live in rural areas. One definition of rural is areas with fewer than 1000 inhabitants and a population density below 400 people per square kilometer (Statistics Canada, 2012). Although this definition may be useful for some circumstances, such as gathering aggregate national statistics on rural populations, it may not be appropriate when considering the experience of people living in rural areas which have vast geographical expanses that are primarily agricultural or forested. Some communities with populations greater than 1000 are quite isolated but are not necessarily included in official statistics (Zorn, Wuerch, Faller, & Hampton, 2017).

Indigenous people are largely represented in rural, remote, and northern areas of many countries, despite their small representation in the general population. Indigenous people represent less than 5% of the population in Canada, United States, and Australia (Aboriginal Affairs and Northern Development Canada, 2013; Baxter et al., 2011; United States Census Bureau, 2012). More than half of Indigenous people live in the rural and remote regions of Australia (Baxter et al., 2011) and more than half of registered Indians live on reserve. More than half of the reserves in Canada report less than 500 residents (Aboriginal Affairs and Northern Development Canada, 2013).

Rurality is more than just a statistical quantification of geography and location. It also refers to the social, cultural, and economic circumstances which create the context in which women experience intimate partner violence. Often it involves lack of access to services, jobs, and even recreation and leisure activities. A strong patriarchal value system may influence perceptions of domestic violence including blaming and shaming the victim, while normalizing and minimizing abusive behavior (Doherty & Hornosty, 2008).

A critical feature of many rural communities is the prevalence and value placed on hunting, fishing, and outdoor life. This is sometimes referred to as the "hunting culture" or even the "firearm culture" which is often passed down over generations. Unlike the negative connotations associated with the presence of handguns and crime in urban areas, in rural areas hunting is seen to be an activity that supports wildlife conservation activities and wildlife management, and it promotes comradery with other hunters and cohesion within families and across social networks (Arnett & Southwick, 2015). Revenue from hunting activities often contributes to the sustainability of communities. Firearms in rural locations are often used for hunting, and target practice and gun safety tend to be viewed more liberally in these communities as a result of strong community values around these practices (Doherty & Hornosty, 2008). Although there are no official statistics on gun ownership in Canada, the highest rates of police reported firearm-related violent crime in 2016 occurred in northern regions including Nunavut, Northwest Territories, Saskatchewan, and Yukon, all with rates more than double the national average (Cotter, 2018). The rate of violent crime involving a rifle or shotgun was four times higher in rural areas compared to urban areas and five times higher in provincial north regions and the territories.

Constraints and conditions of farming may also contribute to risk for domestic violence victimization of women living in rural communities. Farming can be considered romantically as raising animals on lush, green pastures, or, as a more progressive economic enterprise where animals are raised in large modern facilities. Generally, livestock operations and cash crop farms are part of a business that will have to be divided if a partnership dissolves. Research conducted with farm women in Canada and Australia found that farm women often remained in violent relationships because they valued their property, risked losing their economic investment and their children's inheritance, and often had a personal attachment to the family farm (Wendt & Hornosty, 2010). Women had respect for the values and importance of the family farm and made decisions focused on saving the family farm rather than themselves.

Indeed rurality can be conceived differently depending on one's location, perspective, and experience. One author of this chapter lives on a cash crop farm in southwestern

Ontario—arguably one of the most densely populated regions of Canada—but still considers herself to live in a rural area. Revenue from farming is a major source of income for her household. If she were to leave her farm she would be walking away from her home and business. However, her farm is within close proximity (less than 50 km) to several larger urban centers where she has access to many resources. Yet even in this area (population less than 2000), she does not have access to public transportation, and there are no doctors or police presence in the community. Residents must leave the community and travel minimally 20 km to access any of these services. In other areas, including northern Ontario and the prairie provinces, the distances to travel to access services are much greater. This is particularly challenging when trying to access services in and from fly-in communities (Faller et al., 2018; Moffitt & Fikowski, 2017).

It is important to examine and understand the context of domestic homicides in rural communities. However, it is important to remember that rurality differs in various regions of a country and is impacted by factors such as policy, geography, and economics. While focusing on rural communities contributes to an intersectional analysis of domestic violence, the same focus may contribute to the "othering of rurality—reinforcing images and perceptions of rural locations and rural inhabitants as deviant"—something that may further marginalize rural victims of domestic violence (Sandberg, 2013).

Domestic violence is reported to occur at higher rates in rural than urban communities (Burczycka, Conroy, & Savage, 2018; Mishra et al., 2014; Northcott, 2011; Peek-Asa et al., 2011; Strand & Storey, 2019). In Canada rates of police-reported incidents of domestic violence perpetrated by spouses, former spouses, and family members are much higher in rural than urban areas (Northcott, 2011), and the rate of victimization for both male and female victims in rural areas are significantly higher than in urban areas (Burczycka et al., 2018). Prevalence and incidence studies in other countries show similar patterns (Campo & Tayton, 2015; Strand & Storey, 2019).

Children living in rural populations may also be at greater risk of exposure to domestic violence. A longitudinal study of families who had recently given birth to a child from rural, low-income communities in the United States found that the prevalence of domestic violence in these families ranged from 21% to 41% at any given time during the study reference period (Gustafsson, Cox, & Family Life Project Key Investigators, 2016). More than half of the mothers reported that they or their partner had been physically violent at some point over the course of the 5-year study.

Indigenous people experience domestic violence at higher rates, more likely to experience injury, and more likely to live in rural, remote, and northern communities where access to services is limited (Moffitt & Fikowski, 2017). The intergenerational effects of historical trauma, normalized violence, gossip, community retribution, family and community values, and women's self-preservation have contributed to a culture of remaining silent about domestic violence (Moffitt & Fikowski, 2017). Indigenous women in rural areas report reluctance to seek help based on their experiences with the historical removal and institutionalization of children to residential schools and the child welfare system, and their fear of losing custody of the children (Brassard, Montminy, Bergeron, & Sosa-Sanchez, 2015). Lack of privacy, fear of stigma, and need to protect the family are factors contributing to reluctance to report (Brassard et al., 2015). Chapter 11, Domestic homicide within Indigenous communities: examining violence in the context of historical oppression, provides further insights on intimate partner violence among Indigenous communities.

Domestic homicide in rural populations

Nearly one-quarter (22%) of the domestic homicides in Canada from 2010 to 2015 involved rural populations (Dawson et al., 2018). Of these homicides, almost one-quarter (24%) of the victims were Indigenous. When one considers domestic murder—suicides, the highest rate, outside of the territories, was found in New Brunswick—a largely rural province—followed by Newfoundland and Labrador. Nova Scotia, Manitoba, and Ontario reported among the lowest rates (Dawson et al., 2018). It appears that higher murder—suicide rates tend to be associated with the more rural provinces.

Studies of domestic homicide in the United States have looked at retrospective data to identify those committed in rural areas. The National Violent Death Reporting System examined 17 states between 2005 and 2014 and found that female victim domestic homicide was greater in rural than urban areas. The FBI Supplemental Homicide report from 1980 to 1999 found that the rate of domestic homicide was four times greater in rural areas than in metropolitan areas in the state of North Carolina (Gallup-Black, 2005). Several factors were explored to understand the differences between domestic homicides in rural and suburban areas. While there were some differences such as higher education and employment rates and access to hospitals for those in urban as compared to rural communities, these differences did not appear to be statistically significant. Other contributing factors such as the gender gap in income and proportion of females living in poverty continued to be greater in rural counties, and limited access to shelters and other domestic violence resources and services may also be contributors (Gillespie & Reckdenwald, 2017). Women from rural neighborhoods had a higher risk of being killed by an intimate partner than those in urban and suburban neighborhoods (Beyer, Layde, Hamberger, & Laud, 2015).

Risk factors for domestic homicide in rural communities

Although we must be cautious about extrapolating lethality based only on an understanding of domestic violence risk factors, research has demonstrated that domestic violence and domestic homicide risk factors share a significant degree of overlap (Campbell, 2004; Doherty, 2017). These risk factors are found in both rural and urban environments (Brownridge, 2006; Canadian Centre for Justice Statistics, 2011; DVDRC, 2008), however, the clustering of factors can be quite different for rural women compared to those in urban settings.

Some notable differences were documented in a New Brunswick study (Doherty, 2017) of women killed by their partners. Compared to national statistics on domestic homicide, women victims in this rural province were more likely to be assaulted or killed while living in an intact relationship, whereas in more urban provinces, women were most often killed at or after separation. In addition, there was greater involvement of serious alcohol/drug involvement in the New Brunswick deaths, as well as more depression and threats of suicide in domestic homicide perpetrators. New Brunswick women were more likely than women in Ontario or nationally to be killed with firearms (Canadian Centre for Justice Statistics, 2011; Doherty, 2006). Finally the New Brunswick victims were likely to be older. The average age of the women killed in murder–suicides over the past 5 years in New Brunswick was 55 years, whereas in Ontario, the average age of victims was 33 years (DVDRC, 2015). An aging population is a common feature of rural communities and brings with it some unique challenges of meeting the needs and providing services for older women living with domestic violence. Chapter 2, Older women and domestic homicide, offers a full discussion on the risk factors for domestic homicide of older women.

Separation

Separation is one of the most prevalent factors related to lethality that was found in urban settings. Given that women in rural communities often choose to stay with abusive partners for personal, social, economic, and cultural reasons, the supports and services that could help them to deal with the abuse may need to be different from those available in large urban areas. Several studies have shown that sometimes women who are being abused by their partner cannot, or do not, access services from domestic violence specialists. Sometimes women feel safest using a variety of strategies that are effective for them in the short term (Lindhorst, Nurius, & Macy, 2005; Wendt, Chung, Elder, Hendrick, & Hartwig, 2017) such as visiting family or even learning to endure the abuse. Such strategies may be accompanied by addictions, mental health problems, and various negative coping strategies that can lead to shame and further reduce interaction with domestic violence professionals. It is important that service providers not assume that the most effective intervention for all abused women is leaving the relationship. For example, concerns for pets and livestock or farm animals can inhibit help-seeking behavior. When working with rural women, it is important to recognize the complexity of women's choices in deciding whether to stay or leave (Goodkind, Sullivan, & Bybee, 2004). Understanding the cultural, social, and economic circumstances confronting rural woman experiencing abuse, can help service providers discuss the decision making and options about continuing or ending relationships (Wathen & MacMillan, 2003).

Poverty

Community-level poverty has also been found to predict domestic violence victimization and perpetration for both men and women. The more impoverished the community, the greater the risk for domestic violence (Edwards, Mattingly, Dixon, & Banyard, 2014). Rural counties have higher poverty rates, lower proportion of female-headed households, and females who are unemployed compared with nonrural counties and yet are characterized by a slightly higher proportion of females living in poverty than nonrural counties (Reckdenwald, Yohros, & Szalewski, 2018). The economy of many rural communities is changing, particularly those of farming, logging, mining, and fishing, contributing to further community-level poverty (Rural Think Tank, 2005). As a result, many young people are leaving rural communities to seek employment elsewhere. As population dwindles, the availability of services may also be negatively impacted.

Social and geographical isolation

While small rural communities may be close knit in some ways, this closeness can also lead to a greater sense of isolation for some people experiencing domestic violence for a variety of reasons. Women experience increased social isolation because of domestic violence, not as a lack of contact with other people because of distances (Lanier & Maume, 2009; Wendt, et al, 2017). Local attitudes about family privacy also create barriers to effective intervention and access to services in rural settings (Owen & Carrington, 2015). Women may be protective of the reputation of themselves and their extended family and not be inclined to talk about the abuse they are experiencing, because they are reluctant to become the source of local gossip. Women in rural, regional, and remote locations tend to experience longer periods of domestic violence than women living in rural areas before they seek help. Women may not see distance as a barrier to accessing services, relying on friends and relatives for support (Wendt et al., 2017). Aboriginal women reported stronger family support networks than non-Aboriginal women. In cases where there was no informal support network, some women do not reach out for help at all.

Availability of services

Research has identified lack of access and poor availability to services as a potential barrier to preventing domestic homicides. Fewer health-care services including hospitals, physicians, registered nurses, and dentists were available in rural counties where domestic homicides occurred in the United States (Reckdenwald, Szalewski, & Yohros, 2018). Rural women also reported negative experiences when engaging in formal help seeking from counselors and family physicians. Doctors often either ignored signs of abuse or refused to become involved. Women had limited options when seeking counseling support or medical care (Riddell, Ford-Gilboe, & Leipert, 2009). Counseling services for men are also very limited, restricting interventions to legal responses or leaving men unaccountable for their actions (Wendt et al., 2017).

Service providers experience disheartenment when trying to deal with a web of issues including poverty, unemployment, lack of resources, isolation, Indigenous concerns, and the legal system (Faller et al., 2018; Wuerch, Zorn, Juschka, & Hampton, 2016). Isolation, in terms of distance to services, and distance for police to travel to respond may act as deterrents to victims when requiring or seeking assistance (Faller et al., 2018; Owen & Carrington, 2015). Treatment services for victims and abusers are often located in larger urban centers which require significant travel. These challenges contribute to a sentiment in some areas by service providers of "our hands are tied." Service providers try to provide services, but they may be limited in scope, and at times, the services they are offering are not what is wanted by the victims seeking help (Moffitt & Fikowski, 2017). Other staffing issues, including high-turnover rates, inadequate training, staff shortages, and burnout also contribute to challenges in service provision (Faller et al., 2018; Moffitt & Fikowski, 2017; Wendt et al., 2017; Wuerch et al., 2016).

Location of shelters

When women do leave domestic violence situations, they may find temporary housing with family and friends or seek more formalized accommodation through a shelter or transition house. According to the Canadian Transition Home survey conducted by Statistics Canada, there were 627 shelters for abused women operating in Canada on April 16, 2014, and 32 shelters were located on reserves across Canada (Beattie & Hutchins, 2015). Most reserves are located in rural and remote regions (Waegemakers-Schiff & Turner, 2014). Just over one-third of shelters serve small populations and rural areas (Maki, 2018). Four percent of the shelters served population areas of less than 1000 people (Beattie & Hutchins, 2015; Maki, 2018), and ten shelters were located in fly-in communities (Maki, 2018). Less than half of shelters and transition homes in small and rural communities reported access to public transportation in their community. For the 12 rural shelters, only 4 reported public transportation in their community. Most rural shelters and transition homes reported access to mental health and victim support for children but at a lesser rate than urban and suburban shelters (Maki, 2018).

Firearms

The acceptance of firearms as part of rural culture may be common, but this is reason for concern in the area of domestic violence. Research examining a variety of potential risk factors and the incidence of homicide in the home has concluded that firearm ownership is strongly linked to domestic homicides (Reckdenwald, Szalewski & Yohros, 2018; Doherty, 2006). Firearms account for over half of the female domestic partner homicides in the United States. States with higher firearm restrictions have lower female domestic homicide rates (Gollub & Gardner, 2019; Sivaraman, Ranapurwala, Moracco, & Marshall, 2019). Additionally in the United States, women in rural counties were more likely to be killed with a firearm than those living in nonrural counties (Reckdenwald, Szalewski & Yohros, 2018).

Firearms were also more likely to be used in domestic homicides involving rural, remote, and northern populations in Canada. More than one-third of these homicides involved the use of a firearm, compared to the general population where the most common method of killing was stabbing (Dawson et al., 2018). A study of domestic homicides between 1984 and 2005 in New Brunswick, Canada, found that nearly half (46%) of the women were killed with a firearm, and nearly three-quarters of these homicides (70%) occurred in small towns and rural locations (Doherty, 2006). Moreover knowing that firearms were present in the home often made women living with domestic violence more fearful (Doherty & Hornosty, 2008). Between 2002 and 2010, firearms were present in more than one-quarter of domestic homicides in Ontario (DVDRC, 2014). Domestic homicide perpetrators in Ontario in rural areas were more likely to have access to a firearm and to use that firearm to kill their partner (Banman, 2015).

Case studies

The following two case studies involve a murder−suicide and a triple homicide, all of which occurred in rural areas of Canada in 2014 and 2015.

Unity, Saskatchewan: the case of Shirley Parkinson

Many of the details of this case are available through https://www.cbc.ca/news/canada/saskatchewan/family-of-murder-suicide-victim-shirley-parkinson-issues-warning-1.3221190. For additional references, see references from case studies.

Ms. Shirley Parkinson is remembered as a loving, family-oriented, community-minded mother, daughter, sister, and aunt. She was the oldest of eight children and a primary caregiver for her siblings during childhood and adolescence. Ms. Parkinson and her husband Donald Parkinson, of 27 years, lived on an acreage with their two daughters near the small town of Unity, Saskatchewan, population 2400, located 90 km southeast of North Battleford. Ms. Parkinson continued to be a caregiver in her professional career as a public health nurse and cared for generations of people in her community. She was well known in the community in her capacity as public health nurse. She was a lactation consultant, administered vaccinations in local schools, and taught health courses such as sexual education. She helped to establish a food bank in her community and a community resource center. She was an active member of her church and volunteered as a Brownie leader.

Mr. Parkinson, originally from England, ran a tractor parts business. Ms. Parkinson was killed in a murder—suicide by Mr. Parkinson on September 10, 2014 after he bludgeoned her to death in her sleep. After her death, family members expressed concern regarding Mr. Parkinson's depression, alcoholism, and mental health. Mr. Parkinson became increasingly isolated over time, whereas Ms. Parkinson maintained her professional role and profile in the community. Her siblings believe she was considering separation at the time of her death. It is not known whether Ms. Parkinson chose to reach out to community services for support.

Themes and recommendations

Ms. Parkinson lived in a rural area of Saskatchewan and was well connected and known in her community. She was the public health nurse in the community, a leader, and perhaps considered herself to be a role model. Therefore she may have been reluctant to seek support from other community services as this would have compromised her privacy and that of her husband.

Ms. Parkinson's family was aware of Mr. Parkinson's changing behavior, increased isolation, alcoholism, depression, and emotional abuse but did not recognize these as warning signs for domestic homicide until after the murders occurred. One family member provided Ms. Parkinson with information regarding a support group. There was some indication on behalf of the family that Ms. Parkinson was preparing to leave her husband. Separation is often a very dangerous time that has been identified as a risk factor for domestic homicide. In a letter her family wrote after her death, they highlighted the importance of having a safety plan when separating from a partner and knowing what the resources are as they recognize that this is a very dangerous time in a woman's life (https://assets.documentcloud.org/documents/2388681/break-the-silence.pdf). Ms. Parkinson's family is urging lawmakers, domestic violence workers, and others to be advocates for victims of domestic violence. This advocacy helped facilitate a decision by the Saskatchewan government to begin a domestic violence death review committee to ensure every homicide would receive a thorough independent review and recommendations about how to prevent a death in similar circumstances in the future.

Renfrew County, Ontario: the case of Carol Culleton, Anastasia Kuzyk, and Nathalie Warmerdam

Many of the details outlined in this case can be retrieved from https://www.cbc.ca/news/canada/ottawa/basil-borutski-trial-triple-murder-verdict-1.4407526. For additional references, see the references from case studies.

On September 22, 2015, Mr. Basil Borutski murdered three women that he had intimate relationships with: Carol Culleton, Anastasia Kuzyk, and Nathalie Warmerdam. Mr. Borutski had a history of domestic violence in his marriage, with charges of domestic violence laid three times during his 25-year marriage. His daughters testified on behalf of their mother regarding the abuse she experienced including hair pulling, slapping, attempting to push his wife out of a moving vehicle, and threatening to burn the family home. Charges were dropped each time.

Nathalie Warmerdam

Ms. Warmerdam was 48 years old. She grew up in the Ottawa Valley and lived in Foymount. She was the mother of two children: Adrian, 20 years old, and Valerie, 18 years old. Ms. Warmerdam worked at a hospice in Renfrew. In 2009 she was separating from her husband and met Mr. Borutski who was visiting his father in the hospice. Ms. Warmerdam dated Mr. Borutski and supported him though his own divorce proceedings. Mr. Borutski moved into Ms. Warmerdam's home with her and her two children. Adrian recalls liking Mr. Borutski at first, but Mr. Borutski changed over time. He began drinking heavily. Ms. Warmerdam encouraged him to seek counseling but he refused. In 2011 Ms. Warmerdam posted bail for Mr. Borutski on charges of assault and threatening to kill his exwife. Ms. Warmerdam testified on his behalf to his character in his divorce proceedings but the courts eventually sided with his exwife. One year later, he faced charges of assault against Ms. Warmerdam's son and for threats he made to kill one of their pets. Ms. Warmerdam ended the relationship in 2012. In December 2012 Mr. Borutski was banned from the township where Ms. Warmerdam lived but the order was amended so that he could attend alcohol abuse treatment in the area. In January 2013 Mr. Borutski was released from jail with a 2-year probation order and 10-year weapons ban. Ms. Warmerdam began wearing a mobile tracking device and alarm meant for survivors of domestic violence. Ms. Warmerdam's son Adrian was at home on the morning when his mother was killed.

Anastasia Kuzyk

Ms. Kuzyk was 36 years old. She was a daughter and a sister. She loved dogs and horses and had competed in equestrian events when she was younger. She was a real estate agent and worked at a local bar in Wilno, Ontario, where she met Mr. Borutski. She ignored warnings issued by regulars at the bar or other women who knew him. He would come to her house drunk and demand sex. When she did not comply, he beat her. On one occasion she called police. He was charged with assault, choking, and mischief for setting fire to her belongings. He was found guilty of choking Ms. Kuzyk and sentenced to 17 months in prison and 2 years of probation. He was released in December 2014, after serving 19 months and ordered to a batterer intervention program which he never attended. Ms. Kuzyk was very fearful of him. Ms. Kuzyk's sister Eva was living with her and at home at the time of her death.

Carol Culleton

Ms. Culleton was 66 years old. She grew up in Chalk River, Ontario, the second youngest of five children. She worked in the public service sector for some time but quit to run a business with her husband. The business struggled and closed, at which time she returned to work for the government. She had recently retired after working for about 10 years in the public service sector for the government of Canada. Ms. Culleton's husband died of cancer in May 2012. She lived in North Gower but also owned property in Chalk River and a cottage in Combermere, Ontario, which she was preparing to sell.

Ms. Culleton dated Mr. Borutski in 2013. She met him at the Wilno Tavern, had a casual relationship with him that summer, and then she lost contact with him. About a month before she was killed, Mr. Borutski reappeared in her life. He would show up unannounced and did some landscaping and other work to her cottage that was not solicited. Mr. Borutski exhibited signs of jealousy and anger toward other male friends Ms. Culleton had. On one occasion in a fit of jealousy he tore up her garden. He sent many text messages. He also showed up at her home one time unannounced. On September 21, 2015, Ms. Culleton told Mr. Borutski that she did not want him to come back anymore, that she was seeing someone else. He collected his things but was really upset. Her neighbor told her that Mr. Borutski was stalking her and that she should be careful and call the police. Ms. Culleton promised to lock the door and call 911 if anything happened. On September 22, 2015, Ms. Culleton was found by a real estate agent at the cottage. The agent found a broken front door and Ms. Culleton's body inside the cottage wrapped in a blanket.

On September 22, 2015, Mr. Borutski drove 20 km from his home to Ms. Culleton's cottage in Combermere and strangled her. He then drove Ms. Culleton's car 33 km to Ms. Kuzyk's house in Wilno and shot her. He traveled 32 km to Ms. Warmerdam's house in Foymount and shot her. Three murders were committed that day within a 2-hour time period. Mr. Borutski was subsequently apprehended several hours later about 100 km away in Kinburn near Ottawa, Ontario.

Mr. Borutski was well known to police and engaged with the justice system. His reputation preceded him within the community. Mr. Borutski had a history of domestic violence charges and convictions; uttering threats, stalking, mischief, and broken peace bonds. Throughout his violent history, Mr. Borutski denied responsibility for his actions and behavior, blaming others, seeing himself as the victim and claimed unfair treatment by the police. He also refused to engage in court-ordered counseling. Text messages and notes sent to various people included themes of having been cheated on, judging others, seeking karma, and taking others with him. Mr. Borutski attended his last probation session 1 week before the murders. The probation officer found the meeting unremarkable. In December 2017 he was found guilty of two counts of first-degree murder in the shootings of Ms. Kuzyk and Ms. Warmerdam, and one count of second-degree murder for strangling Ms. Culleton. He was sentenced to life in prison with no chance of parole for 70 years (he was 60 years of age).

Discussion

Risk factors for domestic violence and homicide identified in these two cases include mental health and addictions problems, pending or recent separation, and history of domestic violence. Ms. Culleton had recently told Mr. Borutski that she was seeing someone else and did not want him coming around anymore. Mr. Borutski's history of domestic violence was more well-known than that of Mr. Parkinson. The geographic isolation contributed to delays in awareness of the murders of Ms. Parkinson and Ms. Culleton.

Mr. Borutski and Mr. Parkinson may have benefited from addictions and mental health counseling, anger management, and domestic violence intervention programs. Although many programs were mandated for Mr. Borutski, he was not compliant. Danger was added to this situation when a peace bond was amended so that Mr. Borutski could attend addictions counseling close to where one of his victims lived. Her safety was jeopardized. Stricter enforcement of compliance was required. Ms. Parkinson felt that she could help and/or manage her husband. She may have been reluctant to seek formal help for herself and her husband due to her profile in the community.

Firearms were used as lethal weapons in two of the murders described earlier and the suicide of Mr. Parkinson. As indicated earlier, firearms are more commonly used in domestic homicides of women living in rural and remote areas. Mr. Borutski was banned from owning a gun but gained access to one after finding it in a scrapyard. A heightened awareness about the access to guns as well as a focus on gun violence in rural and remote areas is needed. Women in rural areas are at higher risk of domestic homicide by firearm.

Ms. Kuzyk and Ms. Warmerdam had both sought help from the police and charges were laid. Ms. Warmerdam had supported and encouraged Ms. Kuzyk in pressing charges against Mr. Borutski. Based on media coverage after the murders, it appears that all three women had communicated concerns about Mr. Borutski to family, friends, and neighbors, many of whom were supportive. Ms. Culleton's friends and neighbors encouraged her to call police, concerned about his stalking and harassing behavior. Ms. Warmerdam had engaged in safety planning activities and utilized an alarm which she could press if she was in trouble. Unfortunately she was unable to use it on the day of her murder and it is unlikely that it would have helped, as the murder was committed so quickly. Although Ms. Parkinson's family seemed to be aware of their brother-in-law's mental health and addiction problems, there seems to be limited information that she was reaching out for help.

Themes and recommendations

The cases reviewed highlight critical issues in preventing domestic homicides. Some of the issues are universal for all domestic violence scenarios, and some of the factors raised have special salience for rural communities. These cases had an impact on provincial governments to take action on the issue of domestic violence.

The Saskatchewan media profile of the Parkinson case with the support of her siblings accelerated planning for a domestic violence death review committee and enhanced public awareness. The Renfrew County triple homicide raised the profile of rural domestic violence and increased funding for innovative outreach for violence against women agencies in rural communities across Ontario. The funding was directed to the many barriers in rural communities including isolation, lack of public transportation, challenges in accessing services, and delays in service provision.

Domestic violence touches on all aspects of rurality. Contextualizing risk factors and identifying barriers related to geographical isolation means responding to a lack of affordable housing, lack of public transportation, and child-care options, as well as patriarchal attitudes and beliefs which legitimate male control over women. Formal help seeking is further dampened as the result of familiarity and lack of confidentiality associated with accessing services. This is further complicated when combined with other characteristics of rural communities such as the presence of firearms which have an integral role in rural culture.

The lack of services or the barriers in accessing them fosters a plethora of unmet needs and a poor fit of services which results in a greater risk that rural women will suffer emotional health and mental health consequences and even death (Beattie & Cotter, 2010; Doherty & Berglund, 2008). Research also shows that women suffering poor physical and mental health were less likely to be able to maintain separation when leaving an abusive partner (Afifi et al., 2009). Clearly understanding the realities of women living with violence in rural communities and determining how this impacts their risk for lethality and influences their help-seeking behavior is critical. Availability of services and programs and access to them creates a significant barrier to well-being and safety (Hornosty & Doherty, 2003; Logan et al., 2001).

Promising practices

As noted throughout this chapter, rurality and rural culture may be viewed differently from one community to the next. A one-size-fits-all approach would appear to be unhelpful. A hub and spoke approach to domestic and family violence services in rural and remote areas has been proposed in Australia (Wendt et al., 2017). This approach requires service providers to be visible and able to engage with the community. Services embedded within the local community context are more likely to be successful. Domestic and family violence specialists appear to be best positioned to take up this role but may require an expansion of services to include crisis management, safety planning, short- and long-term counseling, accommodation, children's services, perpetrator programs, advocacy, and community awareness (Wendt et al., 2017).

A promising practice for providing support in rural communities involves home visits. Home visits are conducted for a variety of reasons, with the goal of creating positive change in the home. Service providers indicate that this may be effective in developing relationships, providing ongoing support, and improving mental health of their clients (Wuerch et al., 2016). Another suggestion included providing space attached to a local hospital that can be used as temporary shelter for women in crisis.

Rural communities present unique challenges in addressing domestic violence. The isolation and limited services increase victims' vulnerability. Public awareness is critical. Some rural provinces like New Brunswick have raised the profile of domestic homicides across the province in both rural and urban areas through the Silent Witness Project. Silent Witness is an international initiative which began in Minnesota, United States, and creates exhibits of life-sized red silhouettes representing women who have been victims of domestic homicide to both remember the victim as well as prompt awareness and action for changes to end violence against women (see http://www.silentwitness.ca/home). Honoring these deaths in a very public manner provides a way to raise awareness and hopefully prevent future domestic homicides. Professional training and sector coordination are also critical in rethinking the nature of rural risk assessment, safety planning, and risk management by police, social services, and health services.

Concluding comments

Women experiencing domestic violence in rural communities face many challenges in seeking help, and if necessary, leaving a relationship. Recent research has identified the phenomenon of "putting up, shutting up, and getting on with life" as a coping strategy (Moffitt & Fikowski, 2017). Service providers face many similar challenges—difficulty providing service and gaining trust of the community, particularly in places where historical trauma and oppression have occurred. Solutions must be developed in each community addressing the culture and geography of the community. Innovative strategies will be required to match barriers presented by rural communities. Qualitative studies dealing with domestic violence in rural communities speak to the importance of creating remedies that address the social and cultural experience of violence including location (geography). (DeKeseredy & Schwartz, 2009; Doherty, 2017; Logan et al., 2001). Such an approach is now recognized as essential when examining all vulnerable populations including older women, immigrant women, Indigenous women, and women with disabilities. Place and geography are more than demographic features; they create the social and cultural location in which women experience their lived realities of violence, and in which prevention programs and services must become accessible and respond.

References

Aboriginal Affairs and Northern Development Canada. (2013). *Aboriginal demographics from the 2011 National Household Survey.* Retrieved from <www.aadnc-aandc.gc.ca/eng/1370438978311/1370439050610>.

Afifi, T. O., MacMillan, H., Cox, B. J., Asmundson, G. J. G., Stein, M. B., & Sareen, J. (2009). Mental health correlates of intimate partner violence in marital relationships in a nationally representative sample of males and females. *Journal of Interpersonal Violence, 24*(8), 1398−1417.

Arnett, E. B., & Southwick, R. (2015). Economic and social benefits of hunting in North America. *International Journal of Environmental Studies, 72*(5), 734−745.

Banman, V. L. (2015). *Domestic homicide risk factors: Rural and urban considerations.* Retrieved from Electronic Thesis and Dissertation Repository. (2767).

Baxter, J., Gray, A., & Hayes, M. (2011). *Families in regional, rural and remote Australia.* Melbourne: Australian Institute of Family Studies. Retrieved from <https://aifs.gov.au/sites/default/files/publication-documents/fs201103.pdf>.

Beattie, S., & Cotter, A. (2010). *Homicide in Canada 2009* (catalogue number 85-002-X). Retrieved from Statistics Canada <http://www.statcan.gc.ca/pub/85-002-x/2010003/article/11352-eng.htm>.

Beattie, S. & Hutchins, H. (2015). *Shelters for abused women in Canada, 2014* (catalogue number 85-002-X). Retrieved from Statistics Canada <https://www150.statcan.gc.ca/n1/pub/85-002-x/2015001/article/14207-eng.htm>.

Beyer, K. M., Layde, P. M., Hamberger, K. L., & Laud, P. W. (2015). Does neighborhood environment differentiate intimate partner femicides from other femicides? *Violence Against Women, 21*(1), 49−64. Available from https://doi.org/10.1177/1077801214564075.

Brassard, R., Montminy, L., Bergeron, A. S., & Sosa-Sanchez, I. A. (2015). Application of intersectional analysis to data on domestic violence against

Aboriginal women living in remote communities in the province of Quebec. *Aboriginal Policy Studies, 4*(1), 3–23.

Brownridge, D. (2006). Violence against women post-separation. *Aggression and Violent Behaviour, 11*(5), 514–530.

Burczycka, M., Conroy, S., & Savage, L. (2018) *Family violence in Canada: A statistical profile 2017* (catalogue number 85-002-X). Retrieved from Statistics Canada <https://www150.statcan.gc.ca/n1/pub/85-002-x/2018001/article/54978-eng.htm>.

Campbell, J. C. (2004). Helping women understand their risk in situations of intimate partner violence. *Journal of Interpersonal Violence, 19*(12), 1464–1477. Available from https://doi.org/10.1177/0886260504269698.

Campo, M., & Tayton, S. (2015). *Domestic and family violence in regional, rural and remote communities.* Australian Institute of Family Studies.

Canadian Centre for Justice Statistics. (2011). *Family violence in Canada: A statistical profile 2011* (catalogue number 85-002-X). Retrieved from Statistics Canada <http://www.statcan.gc.ca/pub/85-002-x/2013001/article/11805-eng.pdf>.

Cotter, A. (2018). *Firearms and violent crime in Canada, 2016* (catalogue number 85-005-X). Retrieved from Statistics Canada: <https://www150.statcan.gc.ca/n1/pub/85-005-x/2018001/article/54980-eng.htm>.

Dawson, M., Sutton, D., Jaffe, P., Straatman, A. L., Poon, J., Gosse, M., & Sandhu, G. (2018). *One is too many: Trends and patterns in domestic homicide in Canada 2010-2015.* Canadian domestic homicide prevention initiative with vulnerable populations. Retrieved from <http://cdhpi.ca/sites/cdhpi.ca/files/CDHPI-REPORTDEC2_DEC_FINAL.pdf>.

DeKeseredy, W. S., & Schwartz, M. D. (2009). *Dangerous exits: Escaping abusive relationships in rural America.* New Brunswick, NJ: Rutgers University Press.

Des Meules, M., & Pong, R. (2006). How healthy are rural Canadians? An assessment of their health status and health determinants. *Canadian Institute for Health Information*, ISBN 10: 1-55392-881-4.

Doherty, D. (2006). Domestic homicide in New Brunswick: An overview of some contributing factors. *Atlantis, 30*(3), 1–20.

Doherty, D. & Berglund, D. (2008). *Psychological abuse: A discussion paper.* Public Health Agency of Canada. Retrieved from <http://www.phac-aspc.gc.ca/sfv-avf/sources/fv/fv-psych-abus/index-eng.php>.

Doherty, D. & Hornosty, J. (2001). *Responding to wife abuse in farm and rural communities searching for solutions that work.* Saskatchewan Institute of Public Policy. Retrieved from <http://citeseerx.ist.psu.edu/viewdoc/download?doi = 10.1.1.582.1977&rep = rep1&type = pdf>.

Doherty, D. & Hornosty, J. (2008). *Exploring the links: Firearms, family violence and animal abuse in rural communities.* Canada Firearms Centre, Royal Canadian Mounted Police and Public Safety Canada. Retrieved from <http://www.legal-info-legale.nb.ca/en/uploads/file/pdfs/Family_Violence_Firearms_Animal_Abuse.pdf>.

Doherty, D. (2017). Rethinking safety planning: A self-directed tool for rural women. In T. Augusta-Scott, K. Scott, & L. M. Tutty (Eds.), *Innovations in interventions to address intimate partner violence: Research and practice* (pp. 18–32). Routledge Press.

Domestic Violence Death Review Committee (DVDRC). (2008). *Annual report to the Chief Coroner.* Toronto, ON: Office of the Chief Coroner.

Domestic Violence Death Review Committee (DVDRC). (2014). *Annual report to the Chief Coroner.* Toronto, ON: Office of the Chief Coroner.

Domestic Violence Death Review Committee (DVDRC). (2015). *Annual report to the Chief Coroner*. Toronto, ON: Office of the Chief Coroner.

Edwards, K. M., Mattingly, M. J., Dixon, K. J., & Banyard, V. L. (2014). Community matters: Intimate partner violence among rural young adults. *American Journal of Community Psychology, 53*(1−2), 198−207.

Faller, N. Y., Wuerch, M. A., Hampton, M. R., Barton, S., Fraehlich, C., Juschka, D., & Zederayko, A. (2018). A web of disheartenment with hope on the horizon: Intimate Partner violence in rural and northern communities. *Journal of Interpersonal Violence*. Available from https://doi.org/10.1177/0886260518789141.

Gallup-Black, A. (2005). Twenty years of rural and urban trends in family and intimate partner homicide. Does place matter? *Homicide Studies, 9*(2), 149−173.

Gillespie, L. K., & Reckdenwald, A. (2017). Gender equality, place, and female-victim intimate partner homicide: A county-level analysis in North Carolina. *Feminist Criminology, 12*(2), 171−191.

Gollub, E. L., & Gardner, M. (2019). Firearm legislation and firearm use n female intimate partner homicide using National Violent Death Reporting System data. *Preventive Medicine* (118), 216−219. Available from https://doi.org/10.1016/j-ypmed.2018.11.007.

Goodkind, J. R., Sullivan, C. M., & Bybee, D. I. (2004). A contextual analysis of battered women's safety planning. *Violence Against Women, 10*(5), 514−533. Available from https://doi.org/10.1177/1077801204264368.

Gustafsson, H. C., Cox, M. J., & Family Life Project Key Investigators. (2016). Intimate partner violence in rural low-income families: Correlates and change in prevalence over the first 5 years of a child's life. *Journal of Family Violence, 31*(1), 49−60. Available from https://doi.org/10.1007/s10896-015-9760-4.

Holder, K., Fields, A., & Lofquist, D. (2016). *Rurality matters*. US Census Blog. United States Census Bureau. Retrieved from <https://www.census.gov/newsroom/blogs/random-samplings/2016/12/rurality_matters.html>.

Hornosty, J., & Doherty, D. (2003). Responding to wife abuse in farm and rural communities: Searching for solutions that work. In R. Blake, & A. Nurse (Eds.), *The trajectories of rural life: New perspectives on rural Canada* (pp. 37−53). Regina, SK: Canadian Plains Research Centre.

Lanier, C., & Maume, M. O. (2009). Intimate partner violence and social isolation across the rural/urban divide. *Violence Against Women, 15*(11), 1311−1330. Available from https://doi.org/10.1177/1077801209346711.

Lindhorst, T., Nurius, P., & Macy, R. J. (2005). Contextualized assessment with battered women: Strategic safety planning to cope with multiple harms. *Journal of Social Work Education, 41*(2), 331−352.

Logan, T., Walker, R., & Leukefeld, C. (2001). Rural, urban influenced, and urban differences among domestic violence arrestees. *Journal of Interpersonal Violence, 16*, 266−283. Available from https://doi.org/10.1177/088626001016003006.

Maki, K. (2018). *Mapping VAW shelters and transition houses: Initial finding of a national survey*. Women's Shelters Canada. Retrieved from <https://endvaw.ca/wp-content/uploads/2018/10/Mapping-VAW-Shelters-2018.pdf>.

Martz, D. & Sarurer, D. (2000). *Domestic violence and the experiences of rural women in east central Saskatchewan*. Centre for Rural Studies and Enrichment. Retrieved from <http://www.pwhce.ca/pdf/domestic-viol.pdf>.

Mishra, A., Patne, S., Tiwari, R., Srivastava, D. K., Gour, N., & Bansal, M. (2014). A cross-sectional study to find out the prevalence of different types of domestic violence in Gwalior City and to identify the various risk and protective factors for domestic violence. *Indian Journal of Community Medicine, 39*(1), 21−25. Available from https://doi.org/10.4103/0970-0218.126348.

Moffitt, P., & Fikowski, H. (2017). *Northwest Territories research project for territorial stakeholders. Rural and northern community response to intimate partner violence.* Retrieved from <http://www2.uregina.ca/ipv/>.

Northcott, M. (2011). Domestic violence in rural Canada. *Victims of Crime Research Digest, 4*(4), 9–14.

Owen, S., & Carrington, K. (2015). Domestic violence (DV) service provision and the architecture of rural life: An Australian case study. *Journal of Rural Studies, 39*, 229–238. Available from https://doi.org/10.1016/j.jrurstud.2014.11.004.

Peek-Asa, C., Wallis, A., Harland, K., Beyer, K., Dickey, P., & Saftlas, A. (2011). Rural disparity in domestic violence prevalence and access to resources. *Journal of Women's Health, 20*(11), 1743–1749.

Ratcliffe, M., Burd, C., Holder, K., & Fields, A. (2016). *Defining rural at the U.S. Census Bureau. American community survey and geography brief.* United States Census Bureau. Retrieved from <https://www.census.gov/content/dam/Census/library/publications/2016/acs/acsgeo-1.pdf>.

Reckdenwald, A., Szalewski, A., & Yohros, A. (2018). Place, injury patterns, and female-victim intimate partner homicide. *Violence Against Women, 25*(6), 654–676. Available from https://doi.org/10.1177/1077801218797467.

Reckdenwald, A., Yohros, A., & Szalewski, A. (2018). Health care professionals, rurality, and intimate femicide. *Homicide Studies, 22*(2), 161–187. Available from https://doi.org/10.1177/1088767917744592.

Riddell, T., Ford-Gilboe, M., & Leipert, B. (2009). Strategies used by rural women to stop, avoid, or escape from intimate partner violence. *Health Care for Women International, 30*(1-2), 134–159.

Rural Think Tank (2005). *Understanding issues families face living in rural and remote communities.* Catholic Family Counselling Centre. Retrieved from <https://www.canada.ca/content/dam/phac-aspc/migration/phac-aspc/hp-ps/dca-dea/publications/rtt-grr-2005/pdf/rtt-grr-2005_e.pdf>.

Sandberg, L. (2013). Backward, dumb and violent hillbillies? Rural geographies and intersectional studies on intimate partner violence. *Affilia, 28*(4), 350–365.

Schissel, B. (1992). Rural crime, policing and related issues. In D. Hay, & G. Basran (Eds.), *Rural sociology in Canada.* Toronto, ON: Oxford University Press.

Sivaraman, J. J., Ranapurwala, S. I., Moracco, K. E., & Marshall, S. W. (2019). Association of state firearm legislation with female intimate partner homicide. *American Journal of Preventive Medicine, 56*(1), 125–133. Available from https://doi.org/10.1016/j.amepre.2018.09.007.

Statistics Canada. (2012). *Canada's rural population since 1851. Census in brief* (catalogue number 98-310-X2011003). Retrieved from Statistics Canada <https://www12.statcan.gc.ca/census-recensement/2011/as-sa/98-310-x/98-310-x2011003_2-eng.pdf>.

Strand, S. J., & Storey, J. E. (2019). Intimate partner violence in urban, rural, and remote areas: An investigation of offense severity and risk factors. *Violence Against Women, 25*(2), 188–207. Available from https://doi.org/10.1177/1077801218766611.

United States Census Bureau. (2012). *The American Indian and Alaska native population: 2010.* Retrieved from <www.census.gov/prod/cen2010/briefs/c2010br-10.pdf>.

United States Census Bureau. (2016). *American community survey 2015.* United States Census Bureau. Retrieved from <https://www.census.gov/newsroom/press-releases/2016/cb16-210.html>.

Van Hightower, N., Gorton, J., & DeMoss, C. (2000). Predictive models of domestic violence and fear of intimate partners among migrant and seasonal farm worker women. *Journal of Family Violence, 15*(2), 137–153.

Waegemakers-Schiff, J. & Turner, A. (2014). *Housing first in rural Canada: Rural homelessness & housing first across 22 Canadian communities.* Canadian Observatory on Homelessness. Retrieved from <https://www.homelesshub.ca/sites/default/files/attachments/Rural_Homelessness_in_Canada_2014.pdf>.

Wathen, C. N., & MacMillan, H. L. (2003). Interventions for violence against women: Scientific review. *The Journal of the American Medical Association, 289*(5), 589–600.

Websdale, N. (1998). *Rural women battering and the justice system: An ethnography* (Vol. 6). Sage.

Websdale, N., & Johnson, B. (1997). The policing of domestic violence in rural and urban areas: The voices of battered women in Kentucky. *Policing and Society: An International Journal, 6*(4), 297–317.

Wendt, S., Chung, D., Elder, A., Hendrick, A., & Hartwig, A. (2017). *Seeking help for domestic and family violence: Exploring regional, rural, and remote women's coping experiences: Key findings and future directions.* Australia's National Research Organisation for Women's Safety Limited. Retrieved from <https://www.anrows.org.au/publication/seeking-help-for-domestic-and-family-violence-exploring-regional-rural-and-remote-womens-coping-experiences-key-findings/>.

Wendt, S., & Hornosty, J. (2010). Understanding contexts of family violence in rural, farming communities: Implications for rural women's health. *Rural Society, 20*(1), 51–63.

Wuerch, M. A., Zorn, K. G., Juschka, D., & Hampton, M. R. (2016). Responding to intimate partner violence: Challenges faced among service providers in northern communities. *Journal of Interpersonal Violence, 34*(4), 691–711.

Zorn, K., Wuerch, M. A., Faller, N., & Hampton, M. R. (2017). Perspectives on regional differences and intimate partner violence in Canada: A qualitative examination. *Journal of Family Violence, 32*, 633–644.

References from case studies

Allen, B. (September 10, 2015). *Family of murder-suicide victim Shirley Parkinson issues warning. CBC News.* Retrieved from <https://www.cbc.ca/news>.

Boesveld, S. (January 23, 2018). *The Renfrew County murders are not an anomaly. Chatelaine.* Retrieved from <https://www.chatelaine.com/living>.

Helmer, A. (November 24, 2017). *Timeline: From 1982 to 2015, a history of Basil Borutski. Ottawa Citizen.* Retrieved from <https://ottawacitizen.com>.

Nease, K. (November 24, 2017a). *Basil Borutski guilty of murdering 3 women in shocking killing rampage. CBC News.* Retrieved from <https://www.cbc.ca/news>.

Nease, K. (December 4, 2017b). *Basil Borutski's history of violence. CBC News.* Retrieved from <https://www.cbc.ca/news>.

Nease, K. (December 6, 2017c). *Basil Borutski will die in prison for "vicious, cold-blooded murder of 3 women". CBC News.* Retrieved from <https://www.cbc.ca/news>.

Further reading

Australian Domestic and Family Violence Death Review Network. (2018). *Data report 2018*. Syndey, AU: Domestic Violence Death Review Team.

Brennan, S. (2011). *Violent victimization of Aboriginal women in the Canadian provinces, 2009*. Juristat (catalogue number 85-002-X).

Dudgeon, A., & Evanson, T. (2014). Intimate partner violence in rural U.S. areas: What every nurse should know. *American Journal of Nursing, 114*(5), 26−35. Available from https://doi.org/10.1097/01.NAJ.0000446771.02202.35.

Domestic homicides within LGBTQ2S+ communities: barriers in disclosing relationships and violence

Katherine Rossiter[1], Katherine Reif[2] and Olivia Fischer[3]
[1]*FREDA Centre for Research on Violence Against Women and Children, School of Criminology, Simon Fraser University, and Ending Violence Association of British Columbia, Canada* [2]*Centre for Research & Education on Violence Against Women & Children, Faculty of Education, Western University, London, ON, Canada* [3]*Counselling Psychology, University of British Columbia, and Ending Violence Association of British Columbia, Canada*

Despite decades of research on domestic violence within the cisgender heterosexual population, our understanding of domestic violence within lesbian, gay, bisexual, transgender, queer, and Two-Spirit (LGBTQ2S+) communities is still in its infancy (see, e.g., Girshick, 2002; Island & Letellier, 1991; Kaschak, 2001; Leventhal & Lundy, 1999; Lobel, 1986; McClennen & Gunther, 1999; Renzetti & Miley, 1996; Renzetti, 1992; Ristock, 2002). While research in this area has been growing since the late 1980s (Ristock, 2011, p. 4; Rollè, Giardina, Caldarera, Gerino, & Brustia, 2018), between the years 2000 and 2015, only 3% of 14,200 research articles published on domestic violence focused on the experiences of lesbian, gay, and bisexual people (Edwards, Sylaska, & Neal, 2015). Research on domestic violence in the lives of transgender and nonbinary people and LGBTQ2S+ people of color is even more limited (Decker, Littleton, & Edwards, 2018; Ristock, 2011; Taylor & Ristock, 2011; Walker, 2015). In 2017 approximately 5% of the adult population in the United States identified as LGBT, reflecting a steady increase in this population since 2012 (Newport, 2018), and while only 2%–5% of all domestic homicides are categorized as involving LGBTQ2S+ partners (Burczycka, Conroy, & Savage, 2018; Fox, 2004; Gannoni & Cussen, 2014; Ibrahim, 2019; Office for National Statistics, 2018), the needs and experiences of LGBTQ2S+ communities must be better understood.

Preventing Domestic Homicides. DOI: https://doi.org/10.1016/B978-0-12-819463-8.00004-6

This chapter summarizes the literature on domestic violence and homicide within LGBTQ2S+ communities, beginning with key terminology. We then discuss the incidence of domestic violence and homicide within this population and the nature, dynamics, causes, and contexts within which this violence occurs. We review three domestic homicide cases involving LGBTQ2S+ individuals, identify major themes and recommendations from each case, and discuss lessons learned to inform domestic homicide prevention strategies. We conclude the chapter with recommendations for future research, legislation, policy, and practice.

What do we mean by LGBTQ2S+ communities and domestic violence?

Terminology relevant to LGBTQ2S+ communities is constantly evolving, and identity labels are fluid and hold different meanings for the people who use them (Canadian Centre for Gender and Sexual Diversity, 2018; QMUNITY, 2018). Our use of the term "LGBTQ2S+ communities" is meant to be inclusive of a wide range of sexual orientations, gender identities, and gender expressions. While the nuances of language and terminology used within the LGBTQ2S+ community are beyond the scope of this chapter, we highlight some of the key terms used.

Gender identity is an individual's internal sense of their gender (e.g., cisgender man or woman, transgender, nonbinary, gender nonconfirming, genderqueer, gender-fluid, gender creative, agender), while *sexual orientation* refers to a person's sexual and/or romantic attraction to others (e.g., heterosexual, lesbian, gay, bisexual, pansexual). *Queer* is an umbrella term that has been reclaimed by LGBTQ2S+ communities and is used to describe sexual and/or gender identities that fall outside of societal norms. Although LGBTQ2S+ communities are gaining visibility and acceptance in society, heterosexism, and cissexism (i.e., the privileging of heterosexual and cisgender identities); homophobia, biphobia, and transphobia (i.e., negative attitudes and discrimination toward LGBTQ2S+ people); and transmisogyny (hatred of trans women, see Serano, 2007) are prevalent within heteronormative and cisnormative social contexts, creating vulnerabilities to violence for LGBTQ2S+ people in society and within intimate relationships (Simpson, 2018). The term *Two-Spirit* is used by many Indigenous people "to identify a range of roles and identities which may span, and even complicate, distinctions between gender, sex, and sexuality" (Hunt, 2016, p. 5); however, not all Indigenous LGBTQ people identify as Two-Spirit.

While this book focuses on "domestic" violence and homicides, Ristock (2005) notes that the term "domestic violence" does not fit well for many LGBTQ2S+ individuals. The term is strongly associated with heterosexual relationships and is rooted in assumptions of gendered roles, including male perpetrator and female victim, which can erase the violence that occurs within LGBTQ2S+ intimate relationships (Ristock, 2005). This term may also imply that partners are cohabitating or that the violence is occurring in the home; however, some LGBTQ2S+ people may be unable to live with their partners due to safety concerns, including fear of hate violence or discrimination from landlords (Messinger, 2017). Conversely LGBTQ2S+ youth who have been kicked out of their family homes due to homophobia, biphobia, or transphobia may be vulnerable to housing insecurity, unemployment, poverty, and homelessness and feel they have little choice but to live with an abusive partner, putting them at increased risk of violence and homicide (Abramovich, 2013; DeFilippis, 2016; Messinger, 2017).

In publications on domestic violence within LGBTQ2S+ communities, the terms "same-sex" or "same-gender" are often used; however, these terms are not inclusive of diverse LGBTQ2S+ identities and relationships. For the purposes of this chapter, we use the language of domestic violence and homicide within LGBTQ2S+ communities to refer to domestic violence involving current or former intimate partners (including dating partners) where at least one of the individuals identifies as LGBTQ2S+ .

Domestic violence within LGBTQ2S+ communities

Despite population growth, and ongoing activism and community organizing to increase visibility, access, and inclusion, and human rights protections, LGBTQ2S+ people continue to face stigma, discrimination, and violence. Research with LGBTQ2S+ communities suggests that the rate of domestic violence is equal or greater than in heterosexual relationships (Decker et al., 2018; Ristock, 2005). LGBTQ2S+ people experience the same forms of domestic violence and abuse as heterosexual and cisgender people (e.g., physical, sexual, verbal, emotional, financial, spiritual) (Edwards et al., 2015; Ristock, 2005); however, the dynamics of domestic violence and the tactics used by perpetrators to exert power and control may differ slightly within LGBTQ2S+ communities (Roe & Jagodinsky, n.d.).

For example, violence and abuse may involve threatening to disclose a partner's sexual and/or gender identity to others without their consent ("outing" them), potentially threatening employment, housing, child custody, immigration status, and family relationships (Ristock, 2005). Conversely abusive partners who are not "out" themselves may "closet" their partner by forcing them to hide their sexual orientation or gender identity to avoid stigma and discrimination (Canadian Centre for Gender and Sexual Diversity, 2017). An abuser may intentionally use incorrect gender pronouns for their partner ("misgendering") or refer to them by a name they no longer use ("deadnaming"), which can contribute to "trans erasure" (Dunne, Raynor, Cottrell, & Pinnock, 2017; Thieme & Saunders, 2018). Abusers may isolate their partners from queer spaces, queer communities, and "chosen family" (Weston, 1991); reinforce internalized homophobia, biphobia, and/or transphobia; and/or minimize or normalize violence and abuse within LGBTQ2S+ relationships (Roe & Jagodinsky, n.d.). They may also use privilege to increase their partner's financial dependence on them and/or control their partner's access to gender-affirming medication or surgery (Canadian Centre for Gender and Sexual Diversity, 2017; Wirtz, Poteat, Malik, & Glass, 2018).

Domestic violence occurs in LGBTQ2S+ communities for many of the same reasons as domestic violence within heterosexual and cisgender populations. However, there are unique factors underlying relationship violence and abuse within LGBTQ2S+ communities, such as internalized homophobia, biphobia, and transphobia, and the impacts of colonization (see Chapter 11: Domestic homicide within Indigenous communities: examining violence in the context of historical oppression) and "minority stress" (Mendoza, 2011; Messinger, 2017; Taylor & Ristock, 2011). Power imbalances based on degree of "outness," ability to "pass," access to resources, and HIV status can also increase vulnerabilities to domestic violence among LGBTQ2S+ communities (Messinger, 2017).

While LGBTQ2S+ people may report both perpetrating and experiencing domestic violence in their lives, there is little research on the directionality of domestic violence within this community, and research findings appear to be inconclusive (Edwards et al., 2015; Messinger, 2017). Yet stereotypes and myths about LGBTQ2S+ people and their relationships may lead to assumptions that violence is not serious or that it is bidirectional. Framing domestic violence in LGBTQ2S+ relationships as "mutual abuse" can minimize this violence (Messinger, 2017; Rainbow, 2016; Ristock, 2005) and lead to inadequate police responses, such as mutual arrests or no arrests in cases where police are unable to determine who is the primary aggressor.

Barriers to support

LGBTQ2S+ communities face significant barriers to support and protect from domestic violence, health, and justice services. To access domestic violence services, they must disclose that they have experienced domestic violence; yet they may not have the language to name their experience as such. To access inclusive services, they must disclose their sexual orientation and/or gender identity, which many LGBTQ2S+ individuals may choose not to for fear of stigma and discrimination, or for fear of drawing negative attention to the LGBTQ2S+ community, thereby fueling discrimination. Individuals who disclose neither their queer identity nor their victim status may be described as "double closeted" (Canadian Centre for Gender and Sexual Diversity, 2017), which can contribute to risk of ongoing domestic violence and abuse (Messinger, 2017).

Victims of domestic violence may avoid accessing health care for physical or psychological injuries due to discrimination in health-care settings. Accessing the justice system may be dangerous for some LGBTQ2S+ survivors, particularly transgender survivors, nonstatus survivors, and LGBTQ2S+ survivors who do sex work. Unfortunately domestic violence services, including women's shelters and support groups, may be unsafe for survivors whose same-sex abusers can access the same service and/or inaccessible for gender diverse survivors (Lyons et al., 2016).

Only 3% of domestic violence incidents reported to police in Canada involved same-sex partners, and those incidents reported to police are more likely to involve serious assaults or weapons; yet charges are less likely to be laid than in heterosexual domestic violence cases (Ibrahim, 2019). Domestic violence survivors may have legitimate concerns about confidentiality and personal safety within LGBTQ2S+ communities, which are relatively small, especially in rural communities where there may be fewer resources and options for survivors, and less immediate access to safety and police protection (Ibrahim, 2019) (see Chapter 3: Domestic homicides in rural communities: challenges in accessing resources).

Domestic homicide within LGBTQ2S+ communities

There are several unique methodological challenges in researching domestic homicide within LGBTQ2S+ communities. Official data sources may fail to identify the sexual orientation and/or gender identity of victims and perpetrators or may inaccurately report on the nature of their relationship, such that the incident is never "counted" as a case of LGBTQ2S+ domestic homicide (Gannoni & Cussen, 2014; National Coalition of Anti-Violence Programs, 2016). Domestic violence and homicide may also be obscured if cases are prosecuted as hate crimes in an effort to secure a more severe punishment, or if they occur as part of a series of homicides, as in the case of Canadian serial killer, Mr. McArthur, who targeted and killed eight men between 2010 and 2017, most of whom had ties to Toronto's "Gay Village" and some of whom he reportedly had a romantic and/or sexual relationship with, though the exact nature of these relationships remains unclear. LGBTQ2S+ domestic homicides are especially likely to be missed in jurisdictions where same-sex marriage is illegal (Messinger, 2017). Finally intersecting identities are often overlooked in official statistics such that very little is known about domestic violence and homicide in racialized LGBTQ2S+ communities.

Research findings and national survey data suggest that between 2% and 5% of domestic homicides in Canada, the United States, the United Kingdom, and Australia occur within LGBTQ2S+ communities, a small proportion compared with the heterosexual population (Burczycka et al., 2018; Fox, 2004; Gannoni & Cussen, 2014; Ibrahim, 2019; Office for National Statistics, 2018). Between 2009 and 2017, of the 760 domestic homicides committed in Canada, 36 (5%) involved same-sex intimate partners (Ibrahim, 2019). Of the documented same-sex homicides in Canada over the past 20 years, 86% involved men who killed a male intimate partner. Same-sex domestic homicides were more likely than heterosexual domestic homicides to involve current boyfriends or girlfriends (38% vs 11%), and less likely to involve current or former spouses, or former boyfriends or girlfriends (Ibrahim, 2019). Same-sex domestic homicides were more likely than heterosexual domestic homicides to be motivated by an argument or quarrel (40% vs 37%) and less likely to be motivated by frustration, anger, despair, or jealousy (Ibrahim, 2019).

According to the US Supplementary Homicide Reports, 15 (2%) of the 928 homicides in 2016 were coded as occurring within a "homosexual relationship." Of the total 51,007 cases of domestic homicide between 1976 and 2001, 2% were coded as occurring within a "homosexual" relationship; the majority (2%) of victims were gay men, and a minority (less than 1%) were lesbian women (Fox, 2004; Mize & Shackelford, 2008). In the United Kingdom, in the year ending March 2018, seven (3%) male-perpetrated domestic homicides were committee against a male partner or expartner and only one (3%) female-perpetrated domestic homicide was committed against a female partner or expartner (Office for National Statistics, 2018). In Australia data from the National Homicide Monitoring Program show that 2% of the 1536 domestic homicides that occurred between 1989–1990 and 2009–2010 involved same-sex partners (Gannoni & Cussen, 2014). As in the United States, the most common motive was a domestic (25%) or other (13%) argument; in 22% of cases, there was no apparent motive, or the motive was unknown, and jealousy was the apparent motive in 9% of homicides (Gannoni & Cussen, 2014).

National statistics compiled by government agencies, based on police, coroners, and/or medical examiners' reports, are limited in explaining domestic homicide within LGBTQ2S+ communities. They rarely capture diverse sexual and gender identities (e.g., if a victim was not "out" to others or their legal identification was not changed before their death) or capture detailed information that would highlight the intersecting identities of victims (e.g., bisexual men of color, older lesbian women, transgender refugees).

Due to the limitations of official records, some community organizations and initiatives have maintained their own records of LGBT+ homicides. For example, the National Coalition of Anti-Violence Programs has released annual reports on LGBTQ and HIV-affected domestic violence since the late 1990s. Its most recent report indicates that, of the fifteen LGBTQ domestic violence-related homicides in 2016, nine of the victims (60%) were cisgender men, three of the victims (20%) were cisgender women, two of the victims (13%) were transgender women, one victim (less than 1%) was gender nonconforming, and nine of the victims (60%) were people of color (all of the transgender women and gender nonconforming victims). Ten victims (67%) were killed by a current romantic or sexual partner, four victims (27%) were killed by a former partner, and one victim (less than 1%) was killed by police in the context of a domestic violence incident (National Coalition of Anti-Violence Programs, 2017). This information helps us to better understand the particular vulnerabilities of people within LGBTQ2S+ communities to domestic homicide. In Case studies, we review three such cases, selected to illustrate diverse LGBTQ2S+ communities, based on available public documentation.

Case studies

In this section, we examine the individual circumstances, intersecting identities, and systemic issues in three LGBTQ2S+

domestic homicide cases from various countries. Details about the homicides were publicly available through coroners' reports and/or media reports; however, it is important to note that domestic homicides involving LGBTQ2S+ communities may be sensationalized in the media. Each case highlights important lessons that can be learned and shared with the public, professionals, and systems involved in responding to domestic violence within LGBTQ2S+ communities. It is hoped that the overlapping themes emerging from our analysis of the cases will contribute to the prevention of domestic homicides within LGBTQ2S+ communities.

Massachusetts, United States: The case of Ms. Cochrane Rintala

Many of the details highlighted in this case can be accessed from: https://www.bostonmagazine.com/news/2013/05/28/cara-rintala-murder-trial/Additional and resources are available in References from case studies.

This case describes a homicide perpetrated by Ms. Rintala (aged 43) against her same-sex spouse, Ms. Cochrane Rintala (aged 37). The 2010 homicide represented the first case in the State of Massachusetts' history where a woman was charged for killing her wife, 6 years after Massachusetts became the first State in the United States to legalize same-sex marriage (Wolf, 2015).

The couple, who began their relationship in 2002, was described as an improbable match, despite the fact that both worked as paramedics. In 2005 Ms. Cochrane Rintala moved into Ms. Rintala's residence in Granby, Hampshire County, Massachusetts. Two years later, they adopted a newborn child, Brianna, and were married.

The women's relationship was marked by turbulence from the onset, with reports of physical abuse, involvement of police, and restraining orders made against one another. Ms. Cochrane Rintala's coworkers indicated they saw bruises on her throughout the years; however, she often attributed her injuries to causes other than domestic violence. In 2008 Ms. Cochrane Rintala sought a restraining order against Ms. Rintala for physical abuse, which led to Ms. Rintala's arrest and subsequent charges of assault and battery. At Ms. Cochrane Rintala's request, this charge was later dismissed. In May 2009 Ms. Rintala was distressed and told a judge that Ms. Cochrane Rintala had threatened to take away her home, livelihood, and daughter, and that she was scared. The judge was unmoved by her pleading and frustrated by their ongoing arguments. He expressed that he was close to filing criminal charges against both women and threatened to involve the Department of Children and Families if they did not resolve their disputes.

In June 2009 Ms. Cochrane Rintala began a relationship with another woman and moved in with her. However, after accumulating debt by using her new partner's credit cards, she left the relationship and returned to living with Ms. Rintala. The couple separately filed for divorce in 2009 but did not follow through. Despite significant debt, the couple embarked on a cruise that winter. They were described by their church Reverend as "aglow" upon their return; the Reverend also indicated that they were looking for meaning in their lives and balance in their relationship.

On the evening of March 28, 2010, Ms. Cochrane Rintala was working an overnight shift. Ms. Rintala had a male friend over to visit their residence. Ms. Cochrane Rintala found out that this acquaintance was visiting and became furious at the thought of him and Ms. Rintala spending time together. She and Ms. Rintala engaged in a heated text conversation. The same night, Ms. Cochrane Rintala made future plans for a male coworker to come over a few nights later when Ms. Rintala was scheduled to work. On March 29, 2010, Ms. Rintala was found crying and sitting on the floor in the basement, which was stained with ceiling paint and blood after a call by a neighbor that was prompted by Ms. Rintala. Ms. Cochrane Rintala's body, covered in paint, lay on Ms. Rintala's lap. She had three wounds to her scalp and blood marks on her face.

According to the prosecutor at the trial, Ms. Rintala engaged in an elaborate cover-up of the crime, including the creation of an alibi by running multiple errands with her daughter, making several calls to Ms. Cochrane Rintala, and contaminating the crime scene with paint. Ms. Rintala was indicted on a first-degree murder charge on October 11, 2013; however, this trial and a second trial in 2014 resulted in a deadlocked jury. She was found guilty of first-degree murder on October 7, 2016, and was given a mandatory life sentence with no possibility of parole.

Themes and recommendations

This case draws attention to domestic violence among women in same-sex relationships, a problem that has historically been trivialized due to the myth that it is less serious than violence within heterosexual relationships (Messinger, 2017). Misperceptions of women as nonviolent and/or incapable of causing significant injury, and assumptions about the bidirectional nature of violence in same-sex relationships may have contributed to the deadlocked jury in this case (Ristock, 2003).

This case illustrates the need for increased awareness of domestic violence within LGBTQ2S+ communities, particularly among police and justice system personnel. Likewise there is a need for appropriate referrals to domestic violence services that are inclusive, affirming, and responsive to the needs of LGBTQ2S+ victims/survivors. Services are also needed for LGBTQ2S+ domestic violence perpetrators, recognizing that they may both have perpetrated and been a victim of domestic violence, and that perpetrators may have experienced minority stress, including violence and discrimination, which may have contributed to their violent behavior. The extent to which other agencies (e.g., child protective services) were involved in this case is unknown; however, it is evident that there were risk factors present (e.g., history of violence, threats, previous separation). The couple's child was also at risk as a result of being exposed to domestic violence, as a lack of service provision to couples experiencing domestic violence may increase the risk to children in cases of domestic violence (Lawson, 2019) (see Chapter 8: Child homicides in the context of domestic violence: when the plight of children is overlooked).

Queensland, Australia: The case of Ms. Prasetyo

Many of the details highlighted in this case can be accessed from: https://www.courts.qld.gov.au/__data/assets/pdf_file/0008/583883/osc-ar-2016-2017.pdf. Additional resources are available in References from case studies.

This case involves a homicide—suicide that occurred between October 3 and 4, 2014, in Queensland, Australia, in which Ms. Prasetyo was killed by Mr. Volke who then died during police intervention. Ms. Prasetyo, a transgender woman of color, was stabbed and dismembered by her cisgender male spouse, Mr. Volke. Both parties were 27-years-old at the time of their deaths and resided together in a Brisbane apartment.

The couple met in Melbourne in 2013 while Mr. Volke was working in adult clubs; he and Ms. Prasetyo traveled together before settling in Queensland. They were married in August 2013. Their marriage was described as one of convenience; she had helped him obtain employment to pay off a significant amount of debt, and he had helped her obtain a visa to stay in Australia. Both Mr. Volke and Ms. Prasetyo worked as independent sex workers.

The relationship between Ms. Prasetyo and Mr. Volke was described as volatile and worsened to the point that arguments could be overheard by neighbors. According to friends, Mr. Volke did not believe that Ms. Prasetyo was faithful and had threatened to harm her. Her former employer reported that Mr. Volke had previously assaulted her. In email communications to a former partner, Mr. Volke indicated that Ms. Prasetyo monitored his usage of social media and email and had threatened to tell his family about their arrangement if he left her. However, there were no reports of Mr. Volke being violent in previous relationships and neither partner had prior police involvement.

There is little information available on Ms. Prasetyo. It was reported that she felt isolated and was unsatisfied with residing in Brisbane and missed her family back home in Indonesia. She reportedly worked to support her family. Her intersecting identities as a transgender woman of color and sex worker may have increased her risk of violence while also making her violent death less visible in the media.

A friend described Mr. Volke as in "poor mental health" and "paranoid." He had a history of anxiety and depression and, according to his parents and former partner, had attempted suicide in 2006. He was referred for psychiatric treatment in 2007 and was determined to be suffering from moderate depression and sleep disturbance. It is unknown if he received treatment when traveling overseas. According to his former partner, Mr. Volke was concerned about his circumstances relative to living with Ms. Prasetyo and was experiencing suicidal ideation. It was reported that Mr. Volke was worried that his occupation and relationship would cause embarrassment to his family.

The couple was heard arguing on October 2, 2014, and, shortly after the murder (which was believed to have occurred a day later), neighbors reported a foul smell emanating from their apartment. These concerns came to the attention of the building managers who, after finding blood stains on the carpet, called police to conduct a welfare check. On October 4, 2014, when police arrived at his apartment, Mr. Volke indicated that he and Ms. Prasetyo had fought but that she had left, and he was unaware of her whereabouts. Mr. Volke was asked to secure his dogs before letting police in, but instead he locked the door and fled the apartment through another exit. He was later located with self-inflicted cuts to his wrists and neck and was pronounced dead. Upon entering the couple's apartment, the responding officers discovered Ms. Prasetyo's dismembered body in the unit. An inquest was undertaken in May 2017 as a result of Mr. Volke's death occurring during police intervention.

Themes and recommendations

The deaths in this case appeared to have been domestic violence-related; however, missed opportunities for intervention could not be identified, as the couple had little interaction with support networks. The case, however, draws attention to the hidden nature of domestic violence against members of the transgender community, particularly transgender people of color whose work is highly stigmatized. Transgender people experience exceptionally high rates of domestic violence (Stotzer, 2009), and there is an urgent need for greater awareness and more inclusive system responses. The Special Taskforce on Domestic and Family Violence in Queensland has recommended that the government enhance their domestic violence public awareness campaigns to include LGBTQ-specific elements to increase awareness of domestic violence within these communities, remove barriers to seeking support, and educate LGBTQ2S+ communities on where to seek support. The Taskforce highlighted a lack of adequate responses by service providers to the unique needs and concerns of the LGBTQ community, which contributes to barriers to help-seeking (Special Taskforce on Domestic and Family Violence in Queensland, 2015). Research on domestic violence service providers in New South Wales has shown that a majority feels incompetent in providing services to transgender clients (Constable, De Castro, Knapman, & Baulch, 2011), indicating an evident gap in service delivery.

This case also highlights the intersecting forms of oppression experienced by transgender women of color involved in sex work. Transgender women, particularly those who are racialized, often experience discrimination in their lives, including in the workplace, which can lead them to seek alternative employment such as sex work (Nadal, Vargas, Meterko, Hamit, & McLean, 2012). The case also draws attention to the risk to victims of abusive partners who are dealing with untreated mental illness and suicidal ideation (see Chapter 7: Perpetrator mental health: depression and suicidality as risk factors for domestic homicide).

Ontario, Canada: The case of Mr. Heddington

Many of the details highlighted in this case can be accessed from: https://www.dailyrecord.co.uk/news/crime/fatal-vows-wife-who-killed-1738026. Additional resources are available in References from case studies.

This case involves a homicide perpetrated in self-defense by Ms. Rudavsky (aged 27) against her abusive partner, Mr. Heddington (aged 30), on September 21, 2002. Mr. Heddington and Ms. Rudavsky met in 2002 on a farm in Glencoe, Ontario. Ms. Rudavsky left her partner at the time to move in with Mr. Heddington. They dated for 4 months before reportedly getting married. The couple was together for 7 months prior to the homicide. Reportedly Ms. Rudavsky identified as a cisgender heterosexual woman and Mr. Heddington as a transgender man. According to Mr. Heddington's family, he began to identify as male at the age of 14. He strove to embody stereotypically masculine traits through his physical appearance, mannerisms, and aggression and was described as a violent person.

Ms. Rudavsky experienced escalating domestic violence shortly after the start of the relationship, with reports of Mr. Heddington hitting her, torturing her, threatening her with a gun, and threatening to kill her family. Family and friends noticed that Ms. Rudavsky had sustained injuries from violence but when she was admitted to hospital with life-threatening injuries, she denied the abuse.

The couple moved to Chatham, Ontario, approximately 1 hour from family and friends. Friends began to worry about Mr. Heddington's possessive behavior, Ms. Rudavsky's isolation from friends, and her notable weight loss. According to family and friends, Mr. Heddington controlled Ms. Rudavsky's food intake and was critical of her for not acting more "ladylike." Police and medical reports indicate a history of abusive behavior by Mr. Heddington in at least three prior relationships.

The night of the incident, Ms. Rudavsky stabbed Mr. Heddington with a knife after breaking away from his grip when he was choking her. When responding police officers found her tending to Mr. Heddington, she stated that a burglar caused his injuries. However, Mr. Heddington was conscious at the time and indicated that it was Ms. Rudavsky who stabbed him. Paramedics responding to the incident discovered, en route to the hospital, that Mr. Heddington had a prosthetic penis. Ms. Rudavsky indicated that she was unaware that Mr. Heddington was transgender.

Ms. Rudavsky was arrested and, after Mr. Heddington's death, she was charged with murder. The second-degree murder charge was dropped when it was determined that she had Stockholm syndrome and had acted in self-defense.

Themes and recommendations

This case draws attention to the reality that domestic homicides are not always committed by domestic violence perpetrators; rather they can be perpetrated by victims in response to the violence they have experienced within a context of coercive control. As friends and family appear to have been aware of violence within this relationship, they may have benefitted from the availability of educational resources and information on how to provide support to victims and talk to perpetrators. In addition, a major theme in this case is the fact that the perpetrator did not disclose his transgender identity to his spouse. Transgender individuals do not always feel comfortable or safe sharing their transgender identity with others, even intimate partners, due to the potential for transphobia and transprejudice. This is reflected in media reports on this case that sensationalized Mr. Heddington's transgender identity and demonstrated an overall lack of sensitivity to transgender individuals. The media reported Mr. Heddington "actually being a woman," disregarding his gender identity in the article headline, "Woman Killed Husband Then Found Out 'He' Was a 'She'." Societal disregard and discrimination toward transgender individuals can impede help-seeking, which may include batterer intervention programs for perpetrators and safety planning for victims.

Toxic masculinity also seems to be at work in this case. Trans men sometimes look to hegemonic constructions of masculinity when embodying their gender identity (Abelson, 2014). This mirroring may lead to increased violence, aggression, and reinforcing stereotypical gender roles, as a result of toxic masculinity, a manifestation of hegemonic masculinity that can enforce the adoption of strict gender roles through expressions of aggression and dominance over others (Parent, Gobble, & Rochlen, 2018).

Discussion

Despite relatively low rates of domestic homicide, LGBTQ2S+ communities experience equal or greater rates of domestic violence than heterosexual and cisgender populations (Decker et al., 2018; Edwards et al., 2015). LGBTQ2S+ domestic violence survivors face numerous barriers to support and safety, including a lack of LGBTQ-specific domestic violence programs, lack of knowledge among mainstream domestic violence service providers, and discrimination when accessing domestic violence, health, and justice services. Limited research on domestic violence and homicide within LGBTQ2S+ communities, and the failure of governments to prioritize and allocate resources to programs for LGBTQ2S+ survivors and perpetrators, mean we still have little knowledge about the true incidence of the problem, effective and inclusive prevention and intervention programs to address this issue, and legislation and policy to address vulnerabilities to domestic violence and homicide for LGBTQ2S+ communities.

The research and cases discussed in this chapter illustrate the unique issues and barriers to safety for LGBTQ2S+ communities at risk of domestic violence and homicide, and the ways in which marginalization and discrimination of LGBTQ2S+ communities contributes to vulnerabilities to violence. In the following, we summarize the lessons that can be learned from research and cases of domestic homicide within LGBTQ2S+ communities and make recommendations for research, legislation, policy, and practice that will contribute to the prevention of domestic homicides within LGBTQ2S+ communities.

The case of Ms. Prasetyo points to the particular vulnerabilities of LGBTQ2S+ people who are marginalized and isolated because of their sexual orientation and gender identity, as well as their employment and/or immigration status. Both Ms. Prasetyo's and Ms. Cochrane Rintala's case pointed to the vulnerabilities created by financial dependency on an abusive partner. The case of Ms. Cochrane Rintala also highlights the significant lack of knowledge about LGBTQ2S+ domestic violence among health and justice responders, and missed opportunities for prevention and intervention, particularly in light of the presence of risk factors for escalating and lethal violence. The case of Mr. Heddington reminds us that fear of transphobia and transprejudice can exist not only in society but also within intimate relationships and that some domestic homicides are perpetrated in self-defense after years of abuse within a context of coercive control.

Recommendations for future research

Research on the subject of domestic violence and homicide in LGBTQ2S+ communities will be strengthened by common definitions of these communities that reflect a wide range of identities and relationship types, including one-time sexual encounters, short-term dating relationships, long-term monogamous partnerships, and polyamorous relationships, regardless of cohabitation or marital status. Researchers must also apply an intersectional framework when seeking to better understand the unique vulnerabilities of LGBTQ2S+ survivors and barriers to accessing support and protection.

Research is desperately needed to better understand the experiences and needs of transgender and nonbinary people. According to Decker et al. (2018), "work focused on the experiences of transgender individuals remains almost entirely overshadowed by research focused on [domestic violence] among cisgender sexual minorities" (p. 270). We must also learn more about the particular experiences and needs of LGBTQ2S+ people of color, including newcomers and Indigenous and Two-Spirit people, to improve access to inclusive and culturally relevant domestic violence services.

Further research is needed to understand domestic violence and homicide perpetration within LGBTQ2S+ communities and to advance theories that explain these forms of violence, beyond discrimination, and minority stress. Research is also needed to identify protective factors in the lives of LGBTQ2S+ perpetrators and survivors and to evaluate the efficacy of LGBTQ-specific domestic violence prevention and intervention programs so that effective programs can be replicated (Decker et al., 2018).

Recommendations for legislation and policy

Human rights legislation must include protections against discrimination on the grounds of sexual orientation and gender identity to fully protect members of LGBTQ2S+ communities. Protections against discrimination in housing, employment, health care, and social services, will increase the likelihood that LGBTQ2S+ people will be able to live their lives free of discrimination, which may prevent some of the conditions that increase risk of domestic violence and/or limit individuals from options and choices that could enhance their safety.

Same-sex marriages and civil unions are performed or fully/partially recognized in many countries around the world. Recognizing same-sex marriages may mean that LGBTQ2S+ domestic partnerships are more accepted in society, more visible in the community, and more likely to be recorded in domestic homicide files involving partners who may otherwise be "missed" based on assumptions or active attempts to misrepresent the people involved (e.g., as friends, roommates, or acquaintances).

Government and/or organizational policies that address domestic violence and homicide must be inclusive of LGBTQ2S+ survivors. These policies should use gender-inclusive language, where possible, to acknowledge that people of all gender identities may be survivors of domestic violence and homicide, while emphasizing the gendered nature of domestic violence and homicide, crimes that disproportionately affect sexual and gender minorities (e.g., cisgender women, transgender women, and bisexual people).

Recommendations for practice

The violence against women sector has, for decades, focused on raising awareness of men's violence against women and developing programs and services to increase safety and support for heterosexual cisgender women experiencing domestic violence (Tabibi, Kubow, & Baker, 2017). However, despite advances in protecting women from male violence, the needs of LGBTQ2S+ domestic violence survivors have not been adequately addressed. LGBTQ-specific and inclusive domestic violence programs continue to be developed, but there is a need for more antiviolence programs in LGBTQ-specific agencies and more LGBTQ-specific programs in domestic violence agencies, along with greater cross-sector collaboration to develop and deliver innovative programs.

Training for service providers in the domestic violence, health, justice, child protection, and social services sectors is needed. All service providers should be offered mandatory agency-wide anti-oppression/antidiscrimination training as well as training on the unique and varied circumstances, contexts, and needs of LGBTQ2S+ domestic violence survivors (Messinger, 2017; Ristock, 2011). Education on LGBTQ2S+ domestic violence should be delivered by trainers with subject matter expertise and/or relevant lived experience and should include information about the prevalence, nature, causes, and impacts of domestic violence in LGBTQ2S+ people's relationships, as well as barriers to help-seeking (Messinger, 2017). Training should also address risk assessment and safety planning in LGBTQ2S+ communities, so that service providers do not have to rely on mainstream risk assessment and safety planning tools, thereby missing important risk factors, safety considerations, and information about the social contexts within which domestic violence is perpetrated in LGBTQ2S+ communities (Rollè et al., 2018).

Training on domestic violence and homicide within LGBTQ2S+ communities should also be integrated into postsecondary education for future health professionals (e.g., counselors, nurses, physicians, and psychiatrists), justice system personnel (e.g., police, probation officers, lawyers, and judges), and social workers so that front-line responders are more knowledgeable and better equipped to identify and respond to domestic violence within LGBTQ2S+ communities. To increase visibility of the LGBTQ2S+ community from an early age and validate and normalize LGBTQ2S+ relationships, public education and awareness must also be integrated into the grade-school education system. Healthy relationships and sex education curricula must be inclusive so that LGBTQ2S+ people see themselves and their experiences reflected in the curricula.

Finally all sectors with a responsibility to respond to domestic violence should assess how well their promotional materials, intake forms and assessment instruments, programming, and facilities are meeting the needs of LGBTQ2S+ survivors (Ristock, 2005) and make a concerted effort to recruit and hire LGBTQ2S+ staff (Renarde, 2016).

Conclusion

LGBTQ2S+ survivors of domestic violence continue to face enormous barriers to services and safety due to a lack of LGBTQ-specific and/or inclusive domestic violence services and/or discriminatory attitudes and behaviors among front-line responders, which may lead them not to access services, thereby increasing their risk of ongoing or escalating violence and homicide.

Domestic homicide victims may not be identified as LGBTQ2S+ because they are not "out" to many people in their lives or because first responders or the media fail to identify any romantic or sexual relationship with the perpetrator. There is a dearth of domestic homicide research focused on LGBTQ2S+ communities, in all their diversity, and we must fill gaps in our knowledge to inform legislation, policy, programs, and best practices to improve protections for sexual and gender minorities, and increase access to inclusive services where they can receive relevant and inclusive supports, including risk assessment and safety planning, to reduce the risk of domestic homicide.

References

Abelson, M. J. (2014). Dangerous privilege: Trans men, masculinities, and changing perceptions of safety. *Sociological Forum, 29*(3), 549–570. Available from https://doi:10.1111/socf.12103.

Abramovich, A. I. (2013). No fixed address: Young, queer, and restless. Toronto: Canadian Observatory on Homelessness. Retrieved from <https://www.homelesshub.ca/resource/23-no-fixed-address-young-queer-and-restless>.

Burczycka, M, Conroy, S, & Savage, L. (2018). *Family violence in Canada: A statistical profile, 2017.* (Report No. 85-002-X). Retrieved from <https://www150.statcan.gc.ca/n1/pub/85-002-x/2018001/article/54978/tbl/tbl2.10-eng.htm>.

Canadian Centre for Gender and Sexual Diversity. (2017). *Creating services that are here to help: A guidebook for LGBTQ2S+ and intimate partner violence service providers in Canada.* Retrieved from <http://ccgsd-ccdgs.org/wp-content/uploads/2017/08/IPV-Guidebook-10_10_17.pdf>.

Canadian Centre for Gender and Sexual Diversity. (2018). *CCGSD queer vocabulary.* Retrieved from <http://ccgsd-ccdgs.org/wp-content/uploads/2018/08/CCGSD-Vocabulary.pdf>.

Decker, M., Littleton, H. L., & Edwards, K. M. (2018). An updated review of the literature on LGBTQ+ intimate partner violence. *Current Sexual Health Reports, 10,* 265−272. Available from https://doi.org/10.1007/s11930-018-0173-2.

DeFilippis, J. N. (2016). "What about the rest of us?" An overview of LGBT poverty issues and a call to action. *Journal of Progressive Human Services, 27*(3), 143. Available from https://doi.org/10.1080/10428232.2016.1198673.

Dunne, M. J., Raynor, L. A., Cottrell, E. K., & Pinnock, W. J. A. (2017). Interviews with patients and providers on transgender and gender nonconforming health data collection in the electronic health record. *Transgender Health, 2*(1), 1−7. Available from https://doi.org/10.1089/trgh.2016.0041.

Edwards, K., Sylaska, K. M., & Neal, A. M. (2015). Intimate partner violence among sexual minority populations: A critical review of the literature and agenda for future research. *Psychology of Violence, 5*(2), 112−121. Available from https://doi.org/10.1037/a0038656.

Fox, J. A. (2004). *Uniform crime reports: Supplemental homicide reports, 1976−2001. Compiled by Northeastern University, College of Criminal Justice. ICSPR version.* Ann Arbor, MI: Inter-university Consortium for Political and Social Research [Producer and Distributor]. Available from https://doi.org/10.3886/ICPSR20100.v1.

Gannoni, A., & Cussen, T. (2014). *Same-sex intimate partner homicide in Australia.* Canberra, Australia: Australian Institute of Criminology, Australian Government. Retrieved from <www.aic.gov.au/media_library/publications/tandi_pdf/tandi469.pdf>.

Girshick, L. B. (2002). *Woman-to-woman sexual violence: Does she call it rape?* Lebanon, England: University Press of New England.

Hunt, S. (2016). *An introduction to the health of two-spirit people: Historical, contemporary and emergent issues.* National Collaborating Centre for Aboriginal Health (NCCAH). Retrieved from <https://www.ccnsa-nccah.ca/docs/emerging/RPT-HealthTwoSpirit-Hunt-EN.pdf>.

Ibrahim, D. (2019). *Police-reported violence among same-sex intimate partners in Canada, 2009 to 2017.* (Report No. 85-002-X). Retrieved from https://www150.statcan.gc.ca/n1/en/pub/85-002-x/2019001/article/00005-eng.pdf?st = 0cDzvqd-.

Island, D., & Letellier, P. (1991). *Men who beat the men who love them: Battered gay men and domestic violence.* Binghamton, NY: Haworth Press.

Kaschak, E. (2001). *Intimate betrayal: Domestic violence in lesbian relationships.* New York: Haworth Press.

Leventhal, B., & Lundy, S. (1999). *Same-sex domestic violence: Strategies for change.* Thousand Oaks, CA: Sage Publications.

Lobel, K. (1986). *Naming the violence: Speaking out about lesbian battering (Report of the national coalition against domestic violence lesbian task force).* Seattle, WA: Seal Press.

Lyons, T., Krüsi, A., Pierre, L., Smith, A., Small, W., & Shannon, K. (2016). Experiences of trans women and two-spirit persons accessing women-specific health and housing services in a downtown neighbourhood of Vancouver, Canada. *LGBT Health, 3*(5), 373–378.

McClennen, J. C., & Gunther, J. J. (1999). *A professional's guide to understanding gay and lesbian domestic violence: Understanding practice interventions.* Lewiston, NY: Edwin Mellen Press.

Mendoza, J. (2011). The impact of minority stress on gay male partner abuse. In J. L. Ristock (Ed.), *Intimate partner violence in LGBTQ lives* (pp. 169–181). NY: Routledge.

Messinger, A. M. (2017). *LGBTQ intimate partner violence: Lessons for policy, practice, and research.* Oakland, CA: University of California Press. Available from https://doi.org/10.1525/j.ctt1j2n8sf.

Mize, K. D., & Shackelford, T. K. (2008). Intimate partner homicide methods in heterosexual, gay, and lesbian relationships. *Violence and Victims, 23*(1), 98. Available from https://doi.org/10.1891/0886-6708.23.1.98.

National Coalition of Anti-Violence Programs (NCAVP). (2016). *Lesbian, gay, bisexual, transgender, queer, and HIV-affected intimate partner violence in 2015: A report from the National Coalition of Anti-Violence Programs.* New York: Emily Waters. Retrieved from <https://avp.org/wp-content/uploads/2017/04/2015_ncavp_lgbtqipvreport.pdf>.

National Coalition of Anti-Violence Programs (NCAVP). (2017). *Lesbian, gay, bisexual, transgender, queer, and HIV-affected intimate partner violence in 2016: A report from the National Coalition of Anti-Violence Programs.* New York: Emily Waters. Retrieved from <http://avp.org/wp-content/uploads/2017/11/NCAVP-IPV-Report-2016.pdf>.

Newport, F. (May 22, 2018). *In U.S., estimate of LGBT population rises to 4.5%.* Retrieved from <https://news.gallup.com/poll/234863/estimate-lgbt-population-rises.aspx>.

Office for National Statistics. (2018). *Domestic abuse in England and Wales: Year ending March 2018.* Retrieved from <https://www.ons.gov.uk/peoplepopulationandcommunity/crimeandjustice/bulletins/domesticabuseinenglandandwales/yearendingmarch2018>.

QMUNITY. (2018). *Queer terminology from A to Q.* Retrieved from <https://qmunity.ca/wp-content/uploads/2019/06/Queer-Glossary_2019_02.pdf>.

Rainbow, P. L. (2016). Through a queer lens: Challenging our heteronormative response to women's intimate partner violence. In J. Patterson (Ed.), *Queering sexual violence: Radical voices from within the anti-violence movement* (pp. 195–200). Riverdale, NY: Riverdale Ave Books.

Renarde, G. (2016). Notes from the domestic violence casebook: Oppression of queer clients by queer service providers. In J. Patterson (Ed.), *Queering sexual violence: Radical voices from within the anti-violence movement* (pp. 243–246). Riverdale, NY: Riverdale Ave Books.

Renzetti, C. M. (1992). *Violent betrayal: Partner abuse in lesbian relationships.* Newbury Park, CA: Sage Publications.

Renzetti, C. M., & Miley, C. H. (1996). *Violence in gay and lesbian domestic partnerships.* New York: Haworth Press.

Ristock, J. L. (2002). *No more secrets: Violence in lesbian relationships*. New York: Routledge Press.

Ristock, J. (2005). *Relationship violence in lesbian/gay/bisexual/transgender/queer [LGBTQ] communities: Moving beyond a gender-based framework*. *Violence against Women Online Resources*. Retrieved from <https://www.njep-ipsacourse.org/PDFs/Ristock-RelationshipViolenceinLGBTQCommunities.pdf>.

Ristock, J. L. (2011). Introduction: Intimate partner violence in LGBTQ lives. In J. L. Ristock (Ed.), *Intimate partner violence in LGBTQ lives* (pp. 1–9). New York: Routledge.

Roe & Jagodinsky. (n.d.). *Gay, lesbian, bisexual and trans power and control wheel*. Retrieved from <http://www.ncdsv.org/images/TCFV_glbt_wheel.pdf>.

Rollè, L., Giardina, G., Caldarera, A. M., Gerino, E., & Brustia, P. (2018). When intimate partner violence meets same sex couples: A review of same sex intimate partner violence. *Frontiers in Psychology, 9*, 1506. Available from https://doi.org/10.3389/fpsyg.2018.01506.

Serano, J. (2007). *Whipping girl: A transsexual woman on sexism and the scapegoating of femininity*. Emeryville, CA: Seal Press.

Simpson, L. (2018). *Violent victimization of lesbians, gays and bisexuals in Canada, 2014, Canadian Centre for Justice Statistics*. Retrieved from https://www150.statcan.gc.ca/n1/en/pub/85-002-x/2018001/article/54923-eng.pdf?st = XYTGjRgX.

Tabibi, J., Kubow, M., & Baker, L. (2017). *Gender diversity in the VAW sector: Identifying barriers and recommendations for consideration – A discussion paper informed by the learning network knowledge exchange, November 2016*. London, Canada: Centre for Research & Education on Violence Against Women & Children.

Taylor, C. G., & Ristock, J. L. (2011). "We are all Treaty people": An anti-oppressive research ethics of solidarity with Indigenous LGBTQ people living with partner violence. In J. L. Ristock (Ed.), *Intimate partner violence in LGBTQ lives* (pp. 301–319). New York: Routledge.

Thieme, K., & Saunders, M. A. S. (2018). How do you wish to be cited? Citation practices and a scholarly community of care in trans studies research articles. *Journal of English for Academic Purposes, 32*, 80–90.

Walker, J. K. (2015). Investigating trans people's vulnerabilities to intimate partner violence/abuse. *Partner Abuse, 6*(1), 107–125.

Weston, K. (1991). *Families we choose: Lesbians, gays, kinship*. New York: Columbia University Press.

Wirtz, A. L., Poteat, T. C., Malik, M., & Glass, N. (2018). Gender-based violence against transgender people in the United States: A call for research and programming. *Trauma, Violence & Abuse*. Available from https://doi.org/10.1177/1524838018757749.

References from case studies

Aldridge, M. L., & Browne, K. D. (2003). Perpetrators of spousal homicide: A review. *Trauma, Violence & Abuse, 4*(3), 265–276. Available from https://doi.org/10.1177/1524838003004003005.

Barry, S. (2016a). *Day 1 of 3rd Cara Rintala murder trial: Defense says Annamarie Cochrane Rintala knew her killer, but it wasn't defendant*. Retrieved from <https://www.masslive.com/news/2016/09/day_1_of_third_cara_rintala_mu.html>.

Barry, S. (2016a). *Witness in Cara Rintala murder trial: 2-year-old said, 'Mommy's in the basement'*. Retrieved from <https://www.masslive.com/news/2016/09/witness_in_cara_rintala_murder.htm>.

Constable, A., De Castro, N., Knapman, R., & Baulch, M. (2011). *One size does not fit all: Gap analysis of NSW domestic violence support services in relation to gay, lesbian, bisexual, transgender and intersex communities' needs.* Executive Summary and Recommendations, ACON, Sydney. Retrieved from <https://nla.gov.au/nla.obj-489138563/view>.

Coroners Court of Queensland. (2017). *Inquest into the deaths of Marcus Peter Volke and Mayang Prasetyo.* Retrieved from <https://www.courts.qld.gov.au/__data/assets/pdf_file/0006/521277/cif-volke-mp-prasetyo-m-20170519.pdf>.

Daily Mail Reporter. (2012). Wife kills abusive husband in self-defence only to discover 'he' was actually a woman wearing prosthetic penis. *Daily Mail.* Retrieved from <https://www.dailymail.co.uk/femail/article-2242991/Wife-kills-abusive-husband-self-defense-discover-actually-woman-wearing-prosthetic-penis.html>.

Elisha, E., Idisis, Y., Timor, U., & Addad, M. (2010). Typology of intimate partner homicide: Personal, interpersonal, and environmental characteristics of men who murdered their female intimate partner. *International Journal of Offender Therapy and Comparative Criminology, 54*(4), 494–516. Available from https://doi.org/10.1177/0306624X09338379.

English, B. (2012). *Gay spouse murder case puts focus on long-hidden problem. Boston Globe.* Retrieved from <https://www.bostonglobe.com/metro/2012/02/24/gay-spouse-murder-case-granby-puts-focus-same-sex-violence/vBgnFcgNaGoWZQZWe2683K/story.html>.

Green, J. (2005). Part of the package: Ideas of masculinity among male-identified transpeople. *Men and Masculinities, 7*(3), 291–299.

Haak, A. M. (2014). *The embodiment of masculinity among trans identified men* (Unpublished doctoral dissertation). Minnesota State University, Mankato, Minnesota.

Khalik, J. (2017). Marcus Volke murder-suicide 'reminder of violence in LGBTI community'. *The Australian.* Retrieved from <https://www.theaustralian.com.au/news/marcus-volke-murdersuicide-reminder-of-violence-in-lgbti-community/news-story/baa587c3409917eadf8243feb4478b33>.

Kyriacou, K. (2014). Dark story behind the murder – Suicide of Mayang Prasetyo and Marcus Volke in Teneriffe. *The Courier Mail.* Retrieved from <https://www.couriermail.com.au/news/queensland/dark-story-behind-the-murdersuicide-of-mayang-prasetyo-and-marcus-volke-in-teneriffe/news-story/324fc63892a5771cf7010e04dbbdd7cf>.

Lawson, J. (2019). Domestic violence as child maltreatment: Differential risks and outcomes among cases referred to child welfare agencies for domestic violence exposure. *Children and Youth Services Review, 98*, 32–41.

Majchrowicz, M. (2016). Cara Rintala sentenced to life in prison without parole. *Daily Hampshire Gazette.* Retrieved from <https://www.gazettenet.com/Cara-Rintala-sentenced-to-life-in-prison-5346835>.

McGinniss, J. (2013). Reasonable doubt: The Cara Rintala murder trial. *Boston Magazine.* Retrieved from <https://www.bostonmagazine.com/news/2013/05/28/cara-rintala-murder-trial/>.

Nadal, K. L., Vargas, V., Meterko, V., Hamit, S., & McLean, K. (2012). Transgender female sex workers: Personal perspectives, gender identity development, and psychological processes. In M. A. Paludi (Ed.), *Managing diversity in today's workplace: Strategies for employees and employers: Vol. 1. Gender, race, sexual orientation, ethnicity, and power* (pp. 123–153). Santa Barbara, CA: Praeger.

Parent, M. C., Gobble, T. D., & Rochlen, A. (2018). Social media behavior, toxic masculinity, and depression. *Psychology of Men & Masculinity*. Available from https://doi.org/10.1037/men0000156.

Ristock, J. L. (2003). Exploring dynamics of abusive lesbian relationships: Preliminary analysis of a multisite, qualitative study. *American Journal of Community Psychology, 31*(3), 329–341. Available from https://doi.org/10.1023/A:1023971006882.

Shortland, G. (2017). *'Passionate' paramedic strangled, thrown downstairs and covered in paint by her wife*. Retrieved from <https://www.mirror.co.uk/news/real-life-stories/passionate-paramedic-strangled-thrown-downstairs-9739146>.

Special Taskforce on Domestic and Family Violence in Queensland. (2015). Not now, not ever: Putting an end to domestic and family violence in Queensland. Department of Communities, Child Safety and Disability Services.

Stotzer, R. L. (2009). Violence against transgender people: A review of United States data. *Aggression and Violent Behavior, 14*(3), 170–179. Available from https://doi.org/10.1016/j.avb.2009.01.006.

The Mirror. (2013). *Fatal vows: The woman who killed her husband in self-defence, then found he was a she - The Rudavsky case*. Retrieved from <https://www.mirror.co.uk/features/fatal-vows-woman-who-killed-1736278>.

Wolf, R. (2015). From Massachusetts, lessons on gay marriage – And divorce. *USA Today*. Retrieved from <https://www.usatoday.com/story/news/nation/2015/05/17/same-sex-marriage-massachusetts-supreme-court/27368009/>.

Domestic homicides in teens and young adult dating relationships: ignoring the dangers of dangerous relationships

Jordan Fairbairn[1], Peter Jaffe[2] and Corinne Qureshi[3]

[1]Department of Sociology, King's University College at Western University, ON, Canada [2]Centre for Research & Education on Violence Against Women & Children, Faculty of Education, Western University, London, ON, Canada [3]Faculty of Education, Western University, ON, Canada

Introduction

Adolescents and young adults experience some of the highest rates of domestic homicide (Sinha, 2013a, 2013b), yet have received relatively little attention in this area of prevention research. There is, however, a growing body of work on dating violence and its associated harms. Domestic violence in youth dating relationships is increasingly recognized as a public health problem causing serious psychological and physical harms to victims (Martin, Houston, Mmari, & Decker, 2012). The risks for harm and even lethal violence underscore the importance of making connections between dating violence and domestic homicide.

We begin this chapter by briefly defining and discussing youth dating violence and highlighting current research on the relationship between dating violence and homicide. We then present three case studies of domestic homicides involving young victims and discuss how these cases fit with our knowledge of risk factors for domestic homicide, and how we might use this knowledge to prevent future deaths. Preventing domestic homicides among teens and young adults involves understanding the unique circumstances of this age group as well as the links to dating violence and domestic homicide more

Preventing Domestic Homicides. DOI: https://doi.org/10.1016/B978-0-12-819463-8.00005-8

broadly. To explore these issues, we draw from the social—ecological model of violence (Bronfenbrenner, 1979; Heise, 1998) to underscore the importance of considering community and social capacity to recognize high-risk cases and act to support victims in a timely manner. As these cases demonstrate, victims experience significant barriers to receiving adequate and timely support addressing stalking, harassment, and generally abusive behaviors, and accessing effective interventions to prevent this violence from turning lethal.

Youth, dating violence, and domestic homicide

Defining youth

In this chapter, we are focusing on adolescents (teenagers) as well as emerging adults. Adolescence generally refers to the developmental period when individuals are approximately between the ages of 12 and 17 years old (Arnett, 2000). The Mental Health Commission of Canada (MHCC, 2015) uses the term "emerging adults" to describe individuals aged 16—25 years old to underscore that youth is a dynamic process of growth and change, and not a fixed span of time categorized by age (Arnett, 2000; Carver et al., 2015). The term emerging adults acknowledges that young adults are in a transitional stage to adulthood characterized by an increase in responsibilities and independence. During the emerging adulthood phase, developmental competencies that started forming in adolescence continue as individuals explore various roles and life paths, whereas they may also remain partially or fully financially dependent on others (Arnett, 2000; Carver et al., 2015). This transitional stage is also a time where many individuals have their first more serious romantic relationship(s).

Dating violence

"Dating violence" can be understood as a subcategory of "domestic violence" and "intimate partner violence." This violence specifically involves dating partners (as opposed to spouses or common-law partners) and, like domestic violence and intimate partner violence more broadly, can involve a range of abusive behaviors including psychological, verbal, and emotional abuses, sexual violence, and physical assaults (Sinha, 2013a, 2013b). More recently acts that constitute dating violence have expanded to include stalking and digital or cyber dating abuse (Borrajo, Gámez-Guadix, & Calvete, 2015; Zweig, Dank, Yahner, & Lachman, 2013). Young women between the ages of

15 and 24 years are the highest risk age group for experiencing dating violence in their relationships (Beaupré, 2014; Brown, 2013; Johnson & Colpitts, n.d.). Prevalence rates of physical violence are estimated to be between 10% and 20%, with emotional abuse and controlling behaviors significantly higher, ∼30%−50% (Helm, Baker, Berlin, & Kimura, 2017). This abuse has been linked to numerous chronic and lasting physical and mental health effects, including increased rates of depression, anxiety, substance use, suicide ideations, eating disorders, early pregnancy, risky sexual behaviors, serious injuries, and revictimization in college and adult relationships (Barter, McCarry, Berridge, & Evans, 2009; Exner-Cortens, Eckenrode, & Rothman, 2013; Lutwak, Dill, & Saliba, 2013; Vagi, Rothman, Latzman, Tharp, & Hall, 2013). It is important to pay attention to youth dating relationships that may be at risk of violence. Youth learn relationship dynamics and patterns from early romantic relationships that may likely carry into later stages of life (Wincentak, Connolly, & Card, 2016), and violence perpetrated and experienced earlier in life has the potential to escalate as youth mature into adulthood (Williams, Connolly, Pepler, Craig, & Laporte, 2008). In rare cases, this abuse turns lethal.

Domestic homicide

Domestic homicide is the killing of a current or former intimate partner, including a spouse, common-law, or dating partner (Carcach & James, 1998; Dawson et al., 2018). Women are approximately four out of five victims of domestic homicide (Burczycka, Conroy, & Savage, 2018). In Canada there were 960 domestic homicides from 2003 to 13. Young women of ages 15−24 are at high risk for domestic homicide (Sinha, 2013a, 2013b), and there is growing awareness of this elevated risk and associated risk factors among domestic violence researchers and prevention experts (DVDRC, 2015; Jouriles, Grych, Rosenfield, McDonald, & Dodson, 2011; Niolon, et al., 2015; Smith & Donnelly, 2001). According to the Canadian Domestic Homicide Prevention Initiative, 10% of domestic homicide cases from 2010 to 15 involved youth couples (Dawson et al., 2018).

Existing research on homicides in the context of dating relationships has been furthered by the emergence of domestic violence death review committees (DVDRCs, also often called "fatality review committees") in the United States, Canada, New Zealand, Australia, and the United Kingdom (see Dawson, 2017; Websdale, 2003). These committees play an important role in identifying risk factors for domestic homicide and making recommendations to prevent future homicides. Furthermore these reviews provide valuable insights into the prevention of these tragedies through professional and public awareness as well as enhanced risk assessment, safety planning, and risk management (Jaffe, Fairbairn, & Sapardanis, 2018). When assessing potentially dangerous dating relationships, research and review committees have noted that several important factors to consider include significant age differences, controlling behavior, and rejection and/or relationship termination.

Age differences

A significant age difference between the perpetrator and victim has been identified as a factor associated with domestic homicide cases. This risk factor is gendered, in that age difference is a risk factor for women whose male partners are significantly older. The Ontario Domestic Violence Death Review Committee (2015) notes that this disparity is generally nine or more years. The Washington State fatality review team observed that youth victims were often in relationships with older partners: on average 5.8 years older than their female partners (WSDVFR, 2012). This finding echoes the results from other research that has suggested that age disparity between youth in intimate relationships is a significant risk factor for domestic homicide (Coyne-Beasley, Moracco, & Casteel, 2003; Glass, Laughon, Rutto, Bevacqua, & Campbell, 2008).

Controlling behavior

Research suggests a relationship between controlling behaviors and adolescent dating abuse (Giordano, Soto, Manning, & Longmore, 2010; Taylor, Joseph, & Mumford, 2017). Glass et al. (2008) sought to identify risk factors for youth femicide by comparing cases of femicide to cases of abused female youth and found that the younger victims of homicide were more likely to have experienced controlling behavior from their partner (e.g., extreme jealousy) than older victims. Although controlling behavior such as extreme jealously and possessiveness may be a risk factor at all ages, Glass et al.'s (2008) work suggests that a male partner's jealous and controlling behaviors approximately doubled the risk of femicide for female youth when compared to older adult women. There is also a danger that controlling behaviors may be normalized among youth as demonstrating the level of love and commitment (Glass et al., 2008). Others have cautioned that we must take these behaviors seriously, explaining that controlling behaviors should not be minimized simply because they may not be criminal (Taylor et al, 2017).

Rejection

Current or pending separation is one of the most significant risk factors in domestic homicide broadly (DVDRC, 2015). For youth this separation may involve ending a relationship, or rejecting an individual's advances in the first place. The Washington State fatality review team assessed cases of 38 victims who were under the age of 21 when they were killed by their husbands or boyfriends and observed that 45% had ended their relationship or were attempting to end their relationship (WSDVFR, 2012). Coyne-Beasley et al. (2003) examined femicide cases for older adolescents (ages 15–18) occurring in North Carolina between 1990 and 95 and found that rejection was the most commonly cited reason for the homicide. The rejection occurred when the young woman had separated from the male perpetrator, or when the victim would not participate in a desired relationship. Dating relationships are often shorter in duration than spousal or common-law relationships, and this shorter timeframe may limit the ability of people around the victim to understand the potential for violence, including lethal violence.

Prevention and intervention

A growing body of work focuses on interventions to reduce dating violence among adolescents and young adults in recent years (Crooks, Jaffe, Caely, Kerry, & Deinera, 2019; Crooks, Scott, Wolfe, Chiodo, & Killip, 2007; Jaffe et al., 2018). However, significant knowledge gaps surrounding effective prevention among marginalized groups remain. Specifically Crooks et al. (2019) noted that "there is a lack of evidence-based strategies for preventing IPV among Indigenous youth; lesbian, gay, bisexual, transgender, questioning+ [LGBTQ+] youth; and young women with disabilities, even though these groups are at elevated risk for experiencing violence" (p. 29). Researchers have also noted gaps in addressing intimate partner violence among rural young adults (Edwards, Mattingly, Dixon, & Banyard, 2014).

Relationship violence prevention for young adults should be multilevel and focused on communities and collective efficacy rather than simply individual- and relationship-based solutions (Edwards et al., 2014). In understanding this violence, we need to explore how communities and institutions are functioning to support youth experiencing dating violence. The social—ecological model, originally developed by Bronfenbrenner (1979) and adapted by others (e.g., Dahlberg & Krug 2002; Heise, 1998), combines various levels of influence (ecologies) to understand complex phenomena such as violence (Heise, 1998). This model recognizes the intersections of individual-, relationship-, community-, and societal-level factors that are related to various forms of violence such as domestic homicides. Much work to prevent violence against women and girls has historically focused on the individual and relationship levels (Johnson & Dawson, 2011). In exploring the following case studies, we emphasize the need to strengthen community- and societal-based responses to dating violence.

Case studies

Statistics collected on dating violence and homicide do not detail the individual realities of these deaths and the suffering of surviving family members and friends. This section is dedicated to discussing three cases that highlight the unique vulnerabilities of dating violence. These homicides have all received public review through media accounts, trials, and/or published death reviews. Although the following three cases come from different countries, there are important overlapping themes. Each case highlights barriers that victims encountered in seeking safety and points to valuable lessons that professionals from various legal, social service, health and education systems can take away in terms of how to prevent similar deaths in the future.

Salt Lake City, UT: the case of Lauren McCluskey and Melvin Rowland

Many of the details outlined in this case can be retrieved from: https://thinkprogress.org/mccluskey-university-of-utah-warned-police-about-ex-boyfriend-6-times-bc08aed0fad5/. For additional references, see References from case studies.

On October 22, 2018, Lauren McCluskey, a 21-year-old student at the University of Utah, was killed by her former boyfriend, 37-year-old Melvin Rowland, who later committed suicide. McCluskey and Rowland's relationship reportedly ended on October 10, 2018, after McCluskey discovered that her partner had been lying about his age and his criminal background as a registered sex offender. Following the breakup, McCluskey's parents contacted campus police to ask that McCluskey receive protection during a meeting with Rowland for him to return her car. Although these requests were met, McCluskey's subsequent attempts to receive help were not. McCluskey's killing followed her many attempts to seek help from various officials in the weeks and days leading up to her murder, including university housing officials, campus police, and 911 dispatch. For example, McCluskey contacted police officers six times in the 10 days leading up to her death, reporting threatening text messages received from her expartner, pointing to details of his criminal record and demonstrating a persistent and unwavering sense of fear for her life. In her contacts with campus police, 911 dispatch, and the university detective assigned to her case, McCluskey was consistently rerouted without receiving adequate attention from any of these protective services.

Information from authorities suggests that McCluskey's case was not viewed as requiring urgent attention for several reasons, including the threatening text messages reportedly did not reach the level of harassment; more time was needed to assess the threat level Rowland posed and the extortion proof McCluskey had brought forward; Salt Lake City Police insisted that McCluskey's case remain within the jurisdiction of campus police. There are also questions about the way her information was handled. In a disturbing call to 911 dispatch (Weaver & Tumulty, 2018), McCluskey can be heard telling police of her concerns that someone from the campus police was feeding information to her perpetrator, as Rowland had been reporting details of her police involvement back to her as it unfolded. McCluskey was redirected, once again, to campus police. Ultimately McCluskey's parents were the last people to contact campus police, and called 911 after hearing their daughter being attacked while they were on the phone with her. By the time police responded, Rowland had shot and killed McCluskey.

Themes and recommendations

Lauren McCluskey's death occurred despite the presence of several risk factors, repeated contact with authorities, and a circle of security that included supportive friends and family. There are various individual- and relationship-level risk factors present in this case, including an age gap between the McCluskey and Rowland, Rowland's criminal record and his history of disobeying legal authorities, their recent separation, and the fact that McCluskey was involved in a new dating relationship. What is striking, however, is the lack of effective community and societal-level supports available to McCluskey. There were inadequate crisis responses and supports offered by of the college campus, begging questions such as would support have looked different if McCluskey had been older or a nonstudent? Why were more inquiries into the details of McCluskey's concerns not made? Where were McCluskey's protective supports in the interim while police conducted investigations? The lack of urgency of police response does not align with the risks shown by the couple's recent separation, McCluskey's fear of her expartner, and the physical evidence of threatening text messages. Furthermore it speaks to the lack of training and understanding of domestic violence by these frontline responders. McCluskey's case calls for faster police response in terms of investigation and protection, especially for cases demonstrating these significant risk factors.

The slow police response appears to have been driven in part by shifting responsibility and a lack of information sharing among authorities. McCluskey was redirected several times by campus police and 911 operators. It is unclear what, if any, risk assessments, safety planning, and risk management strategies were implemented. Given that McCluskey was repeatedly redirected to campus police who are less likely to have received formal, in-depth domestic violence intervention training and resources, it seems unlikely that adequate domestic violence risk and safety tools were being used. This case underscores the need for proper training for officers such as campus police, who were reportedly not familiar with conducting criminal background searches and parole standards. Training standards are critical components of care of at-risk individuals, and those working in the front lines such as high school and postsecondary student services have firsthand access to student populations that largely consists of young people, many of whom are in dating relationships. Thus it is recommended that police officers, both on and off campus, receive more in-depth training and coursework on domestic violence that considers a feminist perspective, risk factors of domestic homicide, communication strategies for dealing with victims of domestic violence, and information on the prevalence and severity of dating violence.

Gateshead, England: the case of Alice Ruggles and Trimaan Dhillon

Many of the details outlined in this case can be retrieved from: https://www.telegraph.co.uk/news/2018/09/12/police-face-disciplinary-action-blunders-stalker-murder/; https://www.theguardian.com/uk-news/2018/sep/12/two-police-officers-disciplined-alice-ruggles-murder-case; https://www.telegraph.co.uk/news/2017/04/26/soldier-gets-life-stalking-murdering-former-girlfriend/; https://www.gateshead.gov.uk/article/11258/Domestic-homicide-review-into-death-of-Alice-Ruggles.

On October 12, 2016, 26-year-old Trimaan Dhillon killed his exgirlfriend, 24-year-old Alice Ruggles, by cutting her throat. The couple had reportedly met online earlier in 2016 and dated until Ruggles ended the relationship later that year, after which Dhillon began harassing her via phone messages, hacking into her social media accounts, and showing up outside her residence late at night. Dhillon refused to accept the fact that the relationship was over and became jealous when he discovered Ruggles was in a new relationship. He engaged in a campaign of stalking involving unwanted late-night visits to her home, leaving chocolates and flowers, threatening to publish sexually explicit images of Ruggles, and eventually threatening to create a fake dating profile to harm her reputation. Unbeknownst to her, a prior girlfriend had to get a restraining order to protect herself from Dhillon.

Ruggles had reported Dhillon's stalking behavior to the police just 11 days before her death. Police initially told Ruggles they would issue Dhillon a warning that he would be arrested if he continued to contact her. However, they instead redirected her concerns to Dhillon's military supervisors, who spoke to Dhillon about his behavior but ultimately shifted responsibility back onto the police to issue official warnings. Five days before the murder, the police had given the victim the choice to press charges and she declined out of sympathy for the perpetrator. This process was inconsistent with police policies at that time. In the words of the prosecutor at trial: "Sadly the dilemma this young girl was left in is obvious. She was scared and worried by his behavior but she had cared for and even loved him at one time," he added. "Generously she decided not to have him arrested and she paid for that decision with her life five days later." Dhillon was convicted of the murder and sentence to life in prison in April 2017.

Later investigation into the police officers in charge of handling Ruggles' case revealed that one had been accused of misconduct and the other of unsatisfactory performance prior to Ruggles' reports. Reports also indicate that one officer dealing with Ruggles' case felt that the 120 miles of distance between Ruggles and Dhillon was a sufficient barrier to prevent future threats or actual violence. However, just days later, Dhillon drove that 120 miles and killed Alice Ruggles. An internal police investigation by the Independent Office for Police Conduct found police misconduct and disciplined two of the officers involved for not recognizing the perpetrator's behavior as stalking rather than harassment, as well as leaving the decision to charge with the victim. One of the officers was found to have offered poor supervision in this case. Both officers were required to take additional training. A subsequent death review report highlighted the many missed opportunities by the police and military to intervene earlier in the case to prevent the homicide. The committee published a thorough 20-point action plan with timelines and responsibilities of key government agencies (see https://www.gateshead.gov.uk/article/11258/Domestic-homicide-review-into-death-of-Alice-Ruggles).

The Ruggles family has started a foundation to recognize the critical risk represented by stalking (see https://www.alicerugglestrust.org/). The foundation "exists to raise awareness of coercive control and stalking, to ensure that relevant legislation is effective and adhered to, and to bring about lasting improvements in the management of perpetrators and the protection of victims". In her mother's words; "We believe there are important lessons to be learned from what happened to Alice. We didn't think that she was the sort of girl that something like this could happen to. We welcomed him into our family, and he came across as a normal person. Unfortunately, he was a cruel manipulative bully who made Alice miserable and took her away from us. With hindsight, there were many signs of stalking and coercive behavior that we did not recognize. Everybody should know about these signs."

Themes and recommendations

Like Lauren McCluskey, responsibility for Alice Ruggles's case was passed back and forth between the larger community police agency and the workplace-specific authorities (Dhillon's military supervisors). In addition, Ruggles' case demonstrates a lack of understanding by the authorities of the potential for lethal violence that existed. Officers viewed Dhillon's behavior as harassment rather than stalking, and this appeared to limit the attention and protection extended to Ruggles prior to her death. Stalking behaviors are a known risk factor for domestic homicide (Kivisto, 2015; McFarlane, Campbell, & Watson, 2002). Therefore both police officers and military staff (i.e., Dhillon's employers) demonstrated a lack of understanding of the risk that Ruggles faced. Reports suggest that the fact that Dhillon had no prior history of physical violence against Ruggles may have caused authorities to take his behavior less seriously. There was evidence at the trial that a former girlfriend was frightened enough to obtain a restraining order, although it is not clear if the police had access to this information. Although a history of physical violence is an important risk factor for domestic homicide, the absence of this history does not mean a victim is safe—particularly when there are other red flags related to stalking behavior.

Further it is both notable and concerning that military authorities felt that this case "was a civil matter" and that "simply because he is a soldier doesn't mean we as his employer have any role to play" (Evans, 2018, para 7). The lack of a comprehensive understanding of domestic violence and the role of the employer in preventing domestic violence (see Wathen, MacGregor, & MacQuarrie, 2015) is apparent. In both McCluskey and Ruggles' cases, the community and societal supports were inadequate to address the individual- and relationship-level risk factors. In fact the college and military settings harmed McCluskey and Ruggles through institutional inaction at a time where rapidly evolving situations required urgent responses. It is not just that comprehensive and rapid community and societal responses could have helped save lives; it is that the inadequate awareness of risk factors, trivializing attitudes, and bureaucratic indifference are themselves risk factors for domestic homicide.

Dayton, OH: the case of LaShonda Childs and Trendell Goodwin

Many of the details outlined in this case can be retrieved from: https://rollingout.com/2018/10/04/how-a-girl-17-put-out-a-warning-before-being-killed-by-her-ex-boyfriend-28/. For additional references, see References from Case Studies.

LaShonda Childs was 17 years old when she was shot and killed by her 28-year-old expartner Trendell Goodwin on October 2, 2018. Childs and Goodwin met in September 2017, when Goodwin lied about his age, telling Childs he was 20 years old. Prior to his relationship with Childs, Goodwin had a criminal record, a history of violating court orders, and a history of threatening behavior in his previous relationships. This was in addition to the known extensive history of abuse in their year-long relationship. News reports detail Childs' complaints to Dayton police from January to March of 2018 that document her concerns about Goodwin. Goodwin harassed Childs, calling her up to 70 times per day and stealing and breaking her phones. Childs had also shared these concerns publicly via Facebook 2 weeks before she was killed, reporting that Goodwin broke windows, stalked her, held her hostage in her home, bit her several times, burned her, and shot up her house. Childs was seemingly aware of the danger she was in and attempted to make others aware of her situation, noting, "If you see the signs don't ignore it y'all. Domestic violence is real not just in movies" (Shaw, 2018, para 5).

Childs went to police with signs of physical abuse in early 2018. Her initial concerns received attention, as Goodwin was arrested in February 2018. However, after the relationship ended and the abusive behavior escalated, Childs requested a protection order. On September 10, 2018, a municipal court judge ordered an additional year of probation for Goodwin, and continued a preexisting protection order that instructed Goodwin to stay 500 feet away from Childs and prohibited him from contacting her by phone (Gokavi, 2018). Goodwin repeatedly violated this order, however, culminating on October 2 when Childs called 911 to report that Goodwin was holding a gun to her new boyfriends' head. By the time the police responded to the call, Childs had been shot and died later that day.

Goodwin's known history of criminal offending included being arrested approximately 15 times starting in 2011 (Gokavi, 2018). Most of these cases were not prosecuted. In addition to arrests for assaults against Childs, there were arrests and accounts related to assaults against numerous other women, including violation of protective orders. Court reports also indicate that Goodwin had served minimal time for his previous sentences: for example, serving 19 days of a 180-day sentence for misdemeanor assault and spending 1 year of an initial 2016 sentence of 5 years on probation for carrying a concealed weapon.

Themes and recommendations

This case highlights the inadequacy of criminal justice response to domestic violence and its limited capacity to keep victims safe in the face of escalating violence. Despite a long history of general offending and violence against women, Goodwin was extended leniency in risk management regarding his previous offences. Police were aware of Goodwin's abusive and threatening behavior toward Childs yet the community protections extended to Childs were evidently inadequate. Childs' case should have been flagged as high risk due to factors such as a history of previous and ongoing violence in the relationship; her ongoing and escalating fear for her safety; separation; stalking; a new partner in Childs' life; him disobeying authority; a significant age difference between the Childs and Goodwin; access to a weapon; and a history of violence in previous relationships. Childs' case is representative of the lack of coherence in risk assessment, risk management, and safety planning. It does not appear that there were any risk assessments conducted or safety plans in place for Childs, and that existing risk management strategies directed at Goodwin were unsuccessful or not enforced (e.g., protection order, orders for home detention, and counseling following earlier misdemeanor assaults). While Goodwin was demonstrably a repeat offender and dangerous person, Childs' could perhaps have been kept safe with increased efficiency and effectiveness of criminal justice response and improved risk management strategies, whereby offenders are surveyed more closely and violations of court orders are taken seriously with legal consequences.

However, this case also demonstrates that additional, domestic violence-specific expertise is needed to coordinate high-risk cases. Childs, although seemingly aware of the danger she was in and attempting to publicize this through social media, was lacking in community and societal supports, perhaps in part due to Childs' youth. In addition, as a young Black woman, Childs was facing unique societal challenges related to historical discrimination and institutional racism. While more in-depth analysis would be needed to determine how these factors played out in Childs' case specifically, it is evident that severe and ongoing abuse was not taken as seriously as it needed to be in the weeks leading to her death and that Childs was not able to access to the social supports necessary for adequate safety planning. Her brother Jaylon saw his sister's death as a lesson to other teens in abusive relationships, saying "I just want to tell all the young girls, all the females, families, friends, if you see the signs, don't ignore them ...do what you got to do. Use the resources. There's too many out here not to" (from https:// www.whio.com/news/local/dayton-shooting-victim-death-deva stating-for-family/ovXqfSIyxXkPsd1rScOnyH/).

Discussion

Youth dating violence literature and the cases discussed here highlight important themes regarding prevention, community responses, and management of high-risk cases. While much of this discussion is also applicable to preventing domestic homicides more broadly, these ideas are particularly salient and/or take on unique forms when viewed in the context of youth dating violence and with the aim of improving community and justice response to this violence.

Understanding youth dating relationships as high-risk cases

Youth risk for domestic homicide increases when the community and institutions surrounding the potential victim and perpetrator communities do not recognize high-risk cases. Each of these case studies represents high-risk cases involving relatively short-term relationships. Because of the brief nature of the relationships, there was either no known history or a short-lived history of abuse prior to the relationship ending. The abuse began and/or escalated after the relationship ended, and, based on media accounts, it does not appear that anyone outside of the victim and their immediate circle (family, friends) grasped the volatility of the situation and danger they were in.

Youth dating relationships and breakups may not be well understood and are frequently trivialized by older adults in positions or authority. In addition to previous violence, separation and stalking are important risk factors for domestic homicide (Kivisto, 2015; McFarlane et al., 2002; Office of the Chief Coroner, 2016). Digital harassment and stalking also need to be better understood. Not only are they a mechanism to repeatedly harass and threaten victims from a distance, but also abusers can use digital tracking features (GPS, location information) to have more access to their expartner's whereabouts, particularly if they have stolen passwords, phones, etc. Young men's abusive behaviors such as stalking and digital harassment are often normalized postbreakup as "just trying to get her back." These are cases where accessing supports and gathering information such as conducting risk assessments needs to happen quickly. There are many risk assessment tools that could be utilized (see Campbell, Hilton, Kropp, Dawson, & Jaffe, 2016; Messing & Thaller, 2013), but this requires young women to be able to connect with the correct supports in a timely way. Furthermore these assessments are not an end in themselves, but must lead to safety planning for the victim and risk management strategies for the perpetrator (Campbell et al., 2016). The case studies discussed here demonstrate that dating violence situations can be rapidly evolving, particularly in transitional periods such as recent separation and/or the presence of a new partner, as the abusive partner grows increasingly desperate in his attempts to regain control. In these cases, the timelines of translating risk assessment findings into management and planning actions is crucial.

Youth-specific prevention

In addition to interventions for high-risk cases, dating violence prevention is a long-term pursuit. In this regard, research suggests that assessment and prevention need to be youth specific. For example, prevention programs need to consider the different stages of teen relationships (Helm et al., 2017; for a discussion of youth-specific prevention programming in schools, see Jaffe et al., 2018). These initiatives should recognize that youth may describe their dating violence experiences differently than older adults. For example, Martin et al. (2012) observed that youth participants used dating violence language not typically heard among adults (e.g., "drama," "disrespect"). There have been adolescent-specific tools developed to document and predict teen dating violence (see Aizpitarte et al., 2017; Cohen, Shorey, Menon, & Temple, 2018; Wolfe et al., 2001). Principles underlying such tools are that risk assessment tools for adolescent dating violence should consider unique characteristics of dating romantic relationships (i.e., age-development period specificity) and that they should be culturally appropriate (Aizpitarte et al., 2017). Aizpitarte et al. (2017) developed the Violence in Adolescents' Dating Relationships Inventory based on interviews with adolescents, focus groups, and experts' judgments. They tested it with 466 adolescents from Guatemala, Mexico, and Spain. Among other features, this instrument is important for youth dating violence in that it includes items specific to new relational ways for perpetrating abuse, capturing "not only overtly violent acts but also more subtle acts that more often occur in dating relationships, including those taking place with the aid of new technologies" (p. 2642).

Community readiness to help

In each of the cases discussed in this chapter, there is a gap between the help that the victim sought and the help they received. When victims seek help, supports need to be there. This requires preparing those around them to take abuse reports seriously and to know how to help. Thus potential help-givers need preparation if they are to provide effective support (Hedge, Sianko, & McDonell, 2017). In these case studies, whether it was campus authorities (housing, campus police), police, military supervisors, or a social media network, victims made their concerns known and were met with little in terms of concrete protections. Lack of awareness of high-risk cases, insufficient training, and knowledge of how to support the victim and manage the perpetrator, and/or a feeling that it was not their role to do so may have all been contributing factors. Violence prevention programming frequently emphasizes the role of the individual bystander in preventing acts of violence (Banyard, Moynihan, & Plante, 2007; Storer, Casey, & Herrenkohl, 2016); community organizations and institutions need the same focus. Campus police, military supervisors, and other institutions charged with the supervision and protection of youth must understand their roles and responsibilities regarding preventing violence. Furthermore as these cases demonstrate, effective collaboration needs to be viewed as a violence prevention strategy. Individuals experiencing dating violence likely do not have the knowledge or resources to coordinate various officials and levels of bureaucracy (nor should they have to).

In general there are many frontline stakeholders who may have the opportunity to intervene in youth domestic violence situations, but face challenges related to preparedness to support (see Jaffe et al., 2018). Educators may lack the training, time, or perceived mandate to address healthy relationship and dating violence prevention (Chiodo, 2017). Family and emergency doctors, as well as mental health and social services, may be able to identify youth at risk based on injuries and/or emotional distress, and provide support and referral. In dating violence prevention research, youth describe preferred resource centers as those that are confidential and safe, with empathetic, nonjudgmental staff (Martin et al., 2012). It is therefore important that any skills and knowledge training implemented at a community and structural level build these principles into the foundation of service provision.

Universal prevention

Youth who have previously perpetrated dating violence are more likely to offend again (Cohen et al., 2018). While risk assessment, risk management, and safety planning are all key elements of intervention to prevent lethal violence, the big picture of dating violence prevention requires stopping violence before it starts. Prevention efforts need to focus on the development and maintenance of healthy relationships (Johnson, Giordano, Manning, & Longmore, 2015), and to begin early, with late childhood and early adolescence being ideal times for messaging and intervention (Latzman, Vivolo-Kantor, Niolon, & Ghazarian, 2015; Orpinas, Nahapetyan, & Truszczynski, 2017). Prevention responses also should address culturally relevant risk factors and actively engage youth from the community and cultural contexts in which these risk factors exist (Hautala, Sittner Hartshorn, Armenta, & Whitbeck, 2017). This includes developing dating violence prevention programs that specifically address the needs and vulnerabilities of LGBT youth (Dank, Lachman, Zweig, & Yahner, 2014).

There are several evidence-based approaches to preventing youth dating violence, including programs such as Safe Dates (Foshee et al., 2004), Shifting Boundaries (Taylor, Stein, Mumford, & Woods, 2013), and the Fourth R (Wolfe et al., 2009; for an in-depth discussion of these programs, see Jaffe et al., 2018 and Crooks et al., 2019, 2007). These universal programs aim to promote nonviolent and respectful relationships, and acknowledge the need to do more than target victims and perpetrators. Additional aspects include how the broader peer group can recognize dating violence, intervene, and/or support those who are seeking help.

Future research

Preventing deaths in youth dating relationships requires evidence informed practices. More research is needed on the risk factors associated with severe dating violence among emerging adult populations and to bridge this knowledge with findings from domestic violence death review committees' recommendations surrounding youth domestic homicides. One example of an interdisciplinary Canadian initiative is the work of "Breaking the Uncomfortable Silence," developed in response to the 2006 murder of Natalie Novak by her abusive exboyfriend. Natalie's parents, Dawn and Ed Novak, have been vocal advocates and educators about the predictable and preventable nature of their daughter's killing, and the need for education about domestic violence signs and risk factors for lethality so that friends and family know how to help (more information about their work can be found online at natalienovakfund.com).

Beyond risk factors, collaborative work might explore how community organizations and large institutions such as college campuses and military bases can ensure they are equipped to support those currently experiencing and/or perpetrating domestic violence, including those who are going through volatile situations such as high-stress separations from a partner and are worried about their well-being. This work might include documenting available social, financial, and criminal justice supports and evaluating their effectiveness.

Finally the unique aspects of dating violence and barriers faced by youth as a broad population must be explored with a recognition of the heterogeneous nature of youth. Research should continue to build a knowledge base among dating violence experiences of LGBT youth (see Dank et al., 2014), racialized individuals, and those living with disabilities, with a specific focus on their experiences accessing supports and an assessment of how their domestic homicide risk may be elevated based on discriminatory attitudes and practices at a variety of levels (relationship, community, and structural).

Concluding comments

The three case studies discussed in this chapter highlight the need to strengthen community- and societal-based responses to dating violence, particularly as it pertains to high-risk cases. In each case, the available protections were not timely enough or sufficiently strong to keep these young women safe. The unfortunate reality is that, in high-risk dating violence cases, there is not the time to monitor the situation and passively observe escalating violence. Individuals, community leaders, and institutional representatives adjacent to the situation need training and resources to be able to recognize and respond to high-risk cases quickly, collaboratively, and effectively. We cannot gamble that the abuser will "get over it" or "move on". Young lives depend on it.

References

Aizpitarte, A., Alonso-Arbiol, I., Van de Vijver, F. J., Perdomo, M. C., Galvez-Sobral, J. A., & Garcia-Lopez, E. (2017). Development of a dating violence assessment tool for late adolescence across three countries: The Violence in

Adolescents' Dating Relationships Inventory (VADRI). *Journal of Interpersonal Violence, 32*(17), 2626–2646.

Arnett, J. J. (2000). Emerging adulthood: A theory of development from the late teens through the twenties. *American Psychologist, 55*(5), 469–480.

Banyard, V. L., Moynihan, M. M., & Plante, E. G. (2007). Sexual violence prevention through bystander education: An experimental evaluation. *Journal of Community Psychology, 35*(4), 463–481.

Barter, C., McCarry, M., Berridge, D., & Evans, K. (2009). *Partner exploitation and violence in teenage intimate relationships: Executive summary.* London, UK: NSPCC.

Beaupré, P. (2014). Section 2: Intimate partner violence. *Juristat, Statistics Canada* (Catalogue Number 85-002-x).

Borrajo, E., Gámez-Guadix, M., & Calvete, E. (2015). Cyber dating abuse: Prevalence, context, and relationship with offline dating aggression. *Psychological Reports, 116*(2), 565–585.

Bronfenbrenner, U. (1979). *The ecology of human development: Experiments by nature and design.* Cambridge, MA: Harvard University Press.

Brown, V. (2013). Gang member perpetrated domestic violence: A new conversation. *University of Maryland Law Journal of Race, Religion, Gender and Class, 2*(7), 1–21.

Burczycka, M., Conroy, S., & Savage, L. (2018). Family violence in Canada: A statistical profile, 2017 (Catalogue Number 85-002-X). Retrieved from <https://www150.statcan.gc.ca/n1/pub/85-002-x/2018001/article/54978-eng.pdf>.

Campbell, M., Hilton, N. Z., Kropp, P. R., Dawson, M., & Jaffe, P. (2016). *Domestic violence risk assessment: Informing safety planning & risk management.* London, ON: Canadian Domestic Homicide Prevention Initiative. Available from <http://cdhpi.ca/domestic-violence-risk-assessment-informing-safety-planning-risk-management-brief>.

Carcach, C., & James, M. (1998). *Homicide between intimate partners in Australia. Trends & Issues in Crime and Criminal Justice* (p. 90) Canberra: Australian Institute of Criminology.

Carver, J., Cappelli, M., Davidson, S., Caldwell, W., Bélair, M., & Vloe, M. (2015). *Taking the next step forward: Building a responsive mental health and addictions system for emerging adults.* Mental Health Commission of Canada.

Chiodo, D. G. (2017). *A qualitative study of the fidelity of implementation of an evidence-based healthy relationships program* (Doctoral dissertation). The University of Western Ontario.

Cohen, J. R., Shorey, R. C., Menon, S. V., & Temple, J. R. (2018). Predicting teen dating violence perpetration. *Pediatrics, 141*(4), e20172790.

Coyne-Beasley, T., Moracco, K. E., & Casteel, M. J. (2003). Adolescent femicide: A population-based study. *Archives of Pediatrics & Adolescent Medicine, 157*(4), 355–360.

Crooks, C. V., Scott, K. L., Wolfe, D. A., Chiodo, D., & Killip, S. (2007). Understanding the link between childhood maltreatment and violent delinquency: What do schools have to add? *Child Maltreatment, 12*(3), 269–280.

Crooks, C. V., Jaffe, P., Caely, D., Kerry, A., & Deinera, E.-C. (2019). Preventing gender-based violence among adolescents and young adults: Lessons from 25 years of program development and evaluation. *Violence Against Women, 25* (1), 29–55. (01).

Dahlberg, L. L., & Krug, E. G. (2002). Violence - A global public health problem. In E. Krug, L. Dahlberg, J. Mercy, A. Zwi, & R. Lozano (Eds.), *World report on violence and health* (pp. 1–56)). Geneva, Switzerland: World Health Organization.

Dank, M., Lachman, P., Zweig, J. M., & Yahner, J. (2014). Dating violence experiences of lesbian, gay, bisexual, and transgender youth. *Journal of Youth and Adolescence, 43*(5), 846–857.

Dawson, M. (Ed.), (2017). *Domestic homicides and death reviews: An international perspective.* London: Palgrave Macmillan.

Dawson, M., Sutton, D., Jaffe, P., Straatman, A., Poon, J., Gosse, M., ... & Sandhu, G. (2018). One is too many: Trends and Patterns in Domestic Homicides in Canada 2010-2015. *Canadian domestic homicide prevention initiative with vulnerable populations.* Available from <www.cdhpi.ca>.

Domestic Violence Death Review Committee. (2015). *2013-14 Annual report to the chief coroner.* Toronto, Canada.

Edwards, K. M., Mattingly, M. J., Dixon, K. J., & Banyard, V. L. (2014). Community matters: Intimate partner violence among rural young adults. *American Journal of Community Psychology, 53*(1-2), 198–207.

Exner-Cortens, D., Eckenrode, J., & Rothman, E. (2013). Longitudinal associations between teen dating violence victimization and adverse health outcomes. *Pediatrics, 131*(1), 71–78.

Foshee, V. A., Bauman, K. E., Ennett, S. T., Linder, G. F., Benefield, T., & Suchindran, C. (2004). Assessing the long-term effects of the Safe Dates program and a booster in preventing and reducing adolescent dating violence victimization and perpetration. *American Journal of Public Health, 94*(4), 619–624.

Glass, N., Laughon, K., Rutto, C., Bevacqua, J., & Campbell, J. (2008). Young adult intimate partner femicide: An exploratory study. *Homicide Studies: An Interdisciplinary and International Journal, 12*(2), 177–187.

Giordano, P. C., Soto, D. A., Manning, W. D., & Longmore, M. A. (2010). The characteristics of romantic relationships associated with teen dating violence. *Social Science Research, 39*(6), 863–874.

Hautala, D. S., Sittner Hartshorn, K. J., Armenta, B., & Whitbeck, L. (2017). Prevalence and correlates of physical dating violence among North American Indigenous adolescents. *Youth & Society, 49*(3), 295–317.

Hedge, J. M., Sianko, N., & McDonell, J. R. (2017). Professional help-seeking for adolescent dating violence in the rural south: The role of social support and informal help-seeking. *Violence Against Women, 23*(12), 1442–1461.

Heise, L. (1998). Violence against women: An integrated, ecological framework. *Violence Against Women, 4*(3), 262–290.

Helm, S., Baker, C. K., Berlin, J., & Kimura, S. (2017). Getting in, being in, staying in, and getting out: Adolescents' descriptions of dating and dating violence. *Youth & Society, 49*(3), 318–340.

Jaffe, P., Fairbairn, J., & Sapardanis, K. (2018). Youth dating violence and homicide. In D. A. Wolfe, & J. R. Temple (Eds.), *Adolescent dating violence: Theory, research, and prevention.* Elsevier Academic Press.

Johnson, H., & Colpitts, E. (n.d). *Fact sheet: Violence against women in Canada.* Ottawa, ON. Retrieved from <http://www.cwhn.ca/sites/default/files/CRIAW %20-FACTSHEET%20Violence%20against%20women%20-%20long% 20version.pdf>.

Johnson, H., & Dawson, M. (2011). *Violence against women in Canada: Research and policy perspectives.* Don Mills, ON: Oxford University Press Canada.

Johnson, W. L., Giordano, P. C., Manning, W. D., & Longmore, M. A. (2015). The age–IPV curve: Changes in the perpetration of intimate partner violence during adolescence and young adulthood. *Journal of Youth and Adolescence, 44*(3), 708–726.

Jouriles, E. N., Grych, J. H., Rosenfield, D., McDonald, R., & Dodson, M. C. (2011). Automatic cognitions and teen dating violence. *Psychology of Violence, 1*(4), 302–314.

Kivisto, A. J. (2015). Male perpetrators of intimate partner homicide: A review and proposed typology. *Journal of the American Academy of Psychiatry and The Law, 43*(3), 300–312.

Latzman, N. E., Vivolo-Kantor, A. M., Niolon, P. H., & Ghazarian, S. R. (2015). Predicting adolescent dating violence perpetration: Role of exposure to intimate partner violence and parenting practices. *American Journal of Preventive Medicine, 49*(3), 476–482.

Lutwak, N., Dill, C., & Saliba, A. (2013). Dating violence must be addressed in the public health forum. *Journal of Women's Health, 22*(4), 393–394.

Martin, C. E., Houston, A. M., Mmari, K. N., & Decker, M. R. (2012). Urban teens and young adults describe drama, disrespect, dating violence and help-seeking preferences. *Maternal and Child Health Journal, 16*(5), 957–966.

McFarlane, J., Campbell, J. C., & Watson, K. (2002). Intimate partner stalking and femicide: Urgent implications for women's safety. *Behavioral Sciences & The Law, 20*(1–2), 51–68.

The Mental Health Commission of Canada (MHCC). (2015). <https://www.mentalhealthcommission.ca/English/mental-health-emerging-adults>.

Messing, J. T., & Thaller, J. (2013). The average predictive validity of intimate partner violence risk assessment instruments. *Journal of Interpersonal Violence, 28*(7), 1537–1558.

Niolon, P. H., Vivolo-Kantor, A., Latzman, N. E., Valle, L. A., Kuoh, H., Burton, T., ... Tharp, A. T. (2015). Prevalence of teen dating violence and co-occurring risk factors among middle school youth in high-risk urban communities. *Journal of Adolescent Health, 56*(2), S5–S13.

Orpinas, P., Nahapetyan, L., & Truszczynski, N. (2017). Low and increasing trajectories of perpetration of physical dating violence: 7-Year associations with suicidal ideation, weapons, and substance use. *Journal of Youth and Adolescence, 46*(5), 970–981.

Sinha, M. (2013a). Family violence in Canada: A statistical profile, 2011. *Juristat* (Catalogue no. 85-002-X).

Sinha, M. (2013b). *Measuring violence against women: Statistical trends.* (Catalogue number 85-002-X).

Smith, D. M., & Donnelly, J. (2001). Adolescent dating violence: A multi-systemic approach of enhancing awareness in educators, parents, and society. *Journal of Prevention & Intervention in the Community, 21*(1), 53–56.

Storer, H. L., Casey, E., & Herrenkohl, T. (2016). Efficacy of bystander programs to prevent dating abuse among youth and young adults: A review of the literature. *Trauma, Violence & Abuse, 17*(3), 256–269.

Taylor, B., Joseph, H., & Mumford, E. (2017). Romantic relationship characteristics and adolescent relationship abuse in a probability-based sample of youth. *Journal of Interpersonal Violence*, 0886260517730566.

Taylor, B. G., Stein, N. D., Mumford, E. A., & Woods, D. (2013). Shifting boundaries: An experimental evaluation of a dating violence prevention program in middle schools. *Prevention Science, 14*(1), 64–76.

Vagi, K. J., Rothman, E. F., Latzman, N. E., Tharp, A. T., & Hall, D. M. (2013). Beyond correlates: A review of risk and protective factors for adolescent dating violence perpetration. *Journal of Youth and Adolescence, 42*(4), 633–649.

Washington State Domestic Violence Fatality Review (2012). *Teen victims of domestic violence homicide in Washington State.* Washington State Coalition against Domestic Violence.

Wathen, C. N., MacGregor, J. C., & MacQuarrie, B. J. (2015). The impact of domestic violence in the workplace: Results from a pan-Canadian survey. *Journal of Occupational and Environmental Medicine, 57*(7), e65.

Websdale, N. (2003). Reviewing domestic violence deaths. *National Institute of Justice Journal, 250*, 26−31.

Williams, T. S., Connolly, J., Pepler, D., Craig, W., & Laporte, L. (2008). Risk models of dating aggression across different adolescent relationships: A developmental psychopathology approach. *Journal of Consulting and Clinical Psychology, 76*, 622−632.

Wincentak, K., Connolly, J., & Card, N. (2016). Teen dating violence: A meta-analytic review of prevalence rates. *Psychology of Violence*. Available from https://doi.org/10.1037/a0040194.

Wolfe, D. A., Crooks, C., Jaffe, P., Chiodo, D., Hughes, R., Ellis, W., ... Donner, A. (2009). A school-based program to prevent adolescent dating violence: A cluster randomized trial. *Archives of Pediatrics & Adolescent Medicine, 163*(8), 692−699.

Wolfe, D. A., Scott, K., Reitzel-Jaffe, D., Wekerle, C., Grasley, C., & Straatman, A. L. (2001). Development and validation of the conflict in adolescent dating relationships inventory. *Psychological Assessment, 13*, 277−293.

Zweig, J. M., Dank, M., Yahner, J., & Lachman, P. (2013). The rate of cyber dating abuse among teens and how it relates to other forms of teen dating violence. *Journal of Youth and Adolescence, 42*(7), 1063−1077.

References from case studies

Evans, M. (2018). *Woman was murdered by stalker ex-boyfriend after police blunders, report finds.* Retrieved from <https://www.telegraph.co.uk/news/2018/09/12/police-face-disciplinary-action-blunders-stalker-murder/>.

Gibbs, L. (2018). *College track star warned police about her ex-boyfriend 6 times in the 10 days before he killed her.* Retrieved from <https://thinkprogress.org/mccluskey-university-of-utah-warned-police-about-ex-boyfriend-6-times-bc08aed0fad5/>.

Gokavi, M. (2018). *Court records: Man had history of violence against teen who was shot to death.* Retrieved from <https://www.whio.com/news/local/shooting-victim-reportedly-shows-grandview-hospital/o1U3RnUJM6McIGKiDn4e7K/>.

Office of the Chief Coroner of Ontario. (2016). *Domestic violence death review committee 2016 annual report.* Toronto, Canada.

Shaw, A.R. (2018). *Girl, 17, gave this warning before being killed by her 28-year-old ex-boyfriend.* Retrieved from <https://rollingout.com/2018/10/04/how-a-girl-17-put-out-a-warning-before-being-killed-by-her-ex-boyfriend-28/>.

Weaver, J. & Tumulty, B. (2018). *911 calls from Lauren McCluskey released for the first time.* Retrieved from <https://kutv.com/news/local/911-calls-from-lauren-mccluskey-released-for-the-first-time>.

Further reading

Breaking the Uncomfortable Silence: Natalie's Story. Western University. <http://extraordinary.westernu.ca/endviolence/natalie-novak.html>.

Campbell, J. C., Webster, D. W., & Glass, N. (2009). The danger assessment validation of a lethality risk assessment instrument for intimate partner femicide. *Journal of Interpersonal Violence, 24*(4), 653−674.

Coroners Service Death Review Panel. (2016). *Report to the Chief Coroner of British Columbia, 2010-2015.* British Columbia, Canada.

Fairbairn, J., Jaffe, P., & Dawson, M. (2017). Challenges in defining domestic homicide: Considerations for research and practice. In M. Dawson (Ed.), *Domestic homicides and death reviews* (pp. 201–228). London, UK: Palgrave Macmillan.

Natalie Novak Fund: Education & Prevention of Relationship Violence. <https://www.natalienovakfund.com/#home>.

Vagi, K. J., Olsen, E., Basile, K. C., & Vivolo-Kantor, A. M. (2015). Teen dating violence (physical and sexual) among U.S high school students: Findings from the 2013 National Youth Risk Behavior Survey. *JAMA Pediatrics, 169*(5), 474–482.

Domestic homicide in immigrant communities: lessons learned

Sepali Guruge[1], Abir Al Jamal[2], Sarah Yercich[3], Misha Dhillon[4], Katherine Rossiter[3,4], Randal David[5] and Meineka Kulasinghe[6]

[1]Ryerson University, Daphne Cockwell School of Nursing, Victoria, Toronto, ON, Canada [2]Muslim Resource Centre for Social Support and Integration, London, ON, Canada [3]FREDA Centre for Research on Violence Against Women and Children, School of Criminology, Simon Fraser University, Vancouver, BC, Canada [4]Ending Violence Association of British Columbia, Vancouver, BC, Canada [5]Centre for Research & Education on Violence against Women & Children, Faculty of Education, Western University, London, ON, Canada [6]King's University College, Western University, London, ON, Canada

Introduction

Domestic violence (DV) is recognized as a significant social issue worldwide that affects people of all ages, races, and backgrounds (World Health Organization, 2012). Canadian statistics indicate that the rate of DV is comparable among immigrants and nonimmigrants (Ibrahim, 2018). However, some researchers suggest that immigrants are at greater risk for DV due to a range of migration histories and a diversity of cultural values and norms (Pan et al., 2006). Systematic reviews of the literature indicate that domestic homicide (DH) committed by immigrants is not a major contributor to the overall prevalence of DH, but researchers suggest that further research on DH in immigrant populations is warranted (Vatnar, Friestad, & Bjørkly, 2017). This chapter provides a contextual understanding of DH in immigrant communities using three case studies: two within the Canadian context and one in Australia. We present a brief summary of the literature and identify two theoretical frameworks that can be used to understand the micro-, meso-, and macrolevel factors related to DH: the ecosystemic/ecological and intersectional frameworks. The case studies discussed reveal missed opportunities, lessons learned, and implications for practice and future research on DH in immigrant communities.

Preventing Domestic Homicides. DOI: https://doi.org/10.1016/B978-0-12-819463-8.00006-X

Definitions and statistics

Immigration is the process by which people move to a new country for settlement purposes (International Organization for Migration, 2017). The category of "immigrant" is not limited to any particular legal status, reason for migration, and length of stay in a new country (Han, 2009; Menjívar & Salcido, 2002; United Nations Educational, Scientific, & Cultural Organization, 2017). More than half of all immigrants live in only 10 countries, including the United States, the United Kingdom, Canada, and Australia (United Nations, 2017). A considerable portion of the population of these countries is foreign-born: about 15% in the United States (United Nations, 2017); 15% in the United Kingdom (United Nations, 2017); 22% in Canada (Statistics Canada, 2017); and 28% in Australia (Phillips & Simon-Davies, 2017). The term "refugee" refers to immigrants who migrate involuntarily or by force, for reasons that may include war, political or religious persecution, or natural disasters (United Nations Educational, Scientific, & Cultural Organization, 2017). As of 2017, there were 26 million refugees and asylum seekers worldwide (United Nations, 2017). In 2017, 102,800 refugees were resettled across the globe, including: 33,400 in the United States; 26,600 in Canada; 15,100 in Australia; and 6200 in the United Kingdom (United Nations High Commissioner for Refugees, 2018).

Literature review

Immigrants have diverse lived experiences, migration journeys, and sociocultural and economic backgrounds. Understanding DH in immigrant communities requires a framework that captures this heterogeneity. The risk factors for DH among immigrants are multifaceted, interconnected, and situated within the contexts of the country of origin and the country of settlement. Limited research attention has been paid to DH in immigrant communities, and within the existing research, the risks and vulnerabilities of immigrants tend to be examined using a primarily "culture-blaming" lens. A common assumption is that immigrants' (homogeneous) cultural and religious backgrounds create barriers to help-seeking, thereby elevating risk of and vulnerability to DH (Burnman, Smailes, & Chantier, 2004; Raj & Silverman, 2002). These problematic assumptions are often reflected in policy making and service provision and thus compromise the safety of immigrants by failing to appropriately address their unique, multifaceted concerns, needs, and experiences in policy and practice.

The experiences of as well as the risks for DV and complexity of victims' vulnerabilities must be understood within individual, community, cultural, societal, and structural contexts, both pre- and postmigration (Guruge, 2012; Guruge, Khanlou, & Gastaldo, 2010). Risk factors are related to intersecting social identities (e.g., gender identity, race, social class, age, ability, religion, sexual orientation, and history) (Guruge et al., 2010) as well as structural barriers faced by immigrants, such as: (1) precarious immigration status and sponsorship expectations (Guruge, 2012; Hassan et al., 2011; Hyman & Forte, 2006); (2) unfamiliarity with and/or inaccessibility of systems (Jackson, Yercich, Godard, & Lee, 2018; Keller & Brennan, 2007; Rothman, Gupta, Pavlos, Dang, & Coutinho, 2007; Vaughan et al., 2015); (3) a lack of culturally and linguistically relevant information, services, and support (Guruge & Humphreys, 2009); (4) experiences of discrimination and racism (Edelstein, 2013; Guruge & Humphreys, 2009; Trijbetz, 2011); (5) patriarchal ideologies emphasizing male dominance, control, and entitlement (in both pre- and postmigration contexts) (Muhammad, 2010; West, 2015); (6) a lack of recognition of credentials and skills that result in un/underemployment, poverty, housing instability, and financial dependence (Guruge, Collins, & Bender, 2010; Guruge et al., 2010; Jackson et al., 2018; Kim & Sung, 2016; Muhammad, 2010; West, 2015); (7) geographic, community, cultural, and social isolation (Trijbetz, 2011); and (8) a lack of culturally integrated approaches for dealing with perpetrators. Therefore when focusing on DH within immigrant communities, it is vital to consider diversity in terms of social identities, and premigration journeys and experiences of various forms of violence and traumas, as well as the postmigration factors and contexts described earlier.

Theoretical frameworks

We combine an ecosystemic (ecological) framework (Gitterman & Germain, 1976) with an intersectional lens (Cho, Crenshaw, & McCall, 2013; Guruge, 2012; Guruge & Khanlou, 2004) to explore the contexts within which DH occurs within immigrant communities. Utilizing this integrated approach, we explore how individuals and families are situated within the intersection of a range of micro-, meso-, and macrolevel factors that come together to create power imbalances, inequalities, and vulnerabilities (Cho et al., 2013; Guruge & Khanlou, 2004). For example, community norms and values dictate expected modes of interaction and practices of help-seeking that may be shaped by the collective self (Triandis,

1989; Triandis, 1999). The power dynamics within these ecosystems evolve and intersect to force individuals to conform to family, community, and societal values and beliefs (even though the influences are not always unidirectional). Overall the intersections of gender identity, race, ethnicity, class, nationality, religion, immigration status, sexual orientation, education, language, culture, and ability, among other factors in the context of postmigration structural barriers, may create situations of high risk of DV (Ahmad, Riaz, Barata, & Stewart, 2004; Chokshi, 2007) and DH for immigrants.

Case studies

This section summarizes three DH cases within immigrant populations and explores important overlapping themes. The majority of the risk factors identified in these cases are adopted from the Office of the Chief Coroner (2018) but are highlighted within immigrant contexts.

London, Canada: the case of Ms. El-Birani

Many of the details outlined in this case can be retrieved from: http://neighboursfriendsandfamilies.ca/blog/voices-survivors-part-1-mahas-story. For additional references, see the References for case studies.

On April 11, 2012, Ms. El-Birani, aged 50, was killed by her husband, Mr. El-Birani, aged 53, in their family home. In 1982 Ms. El-Birani had married Mr. El-Birani in Lebanon. Mr. El-Birani had witnessed his mother being killed during armed conflict. The couple migrated to Canada in 1989 with their three daughters, hoping for a better life. The family moved to London, Ontario, to be close to Mr. El-Birani's extended family. Ms. El-Birani earned an Early Childhood Education diploma. She was employed and was the primary provider for her family. Their daughters were pursuing education and also worked and contributed to the family income. Mr. El-Birani was unemployed and stayed at home. He used to socialize with his siblings and a few friends.

One of their daughters described Ms. El-Birani as a religious person, and, in comparison, described Mr. El-Birani as not religious, very controlling, tyrannical, and someone who would cause arguments in public. Mr. El-Birani reportedly blamed his aggressive and controlling behavior on his wife and their daughters. He had been diagnosed with clinical depression and paranoia. His health-care providers reportedly connected his abusive behaviors to his mental health problems, and as a result, Ms. El-Birani and her daughters tolerated the abuse. Their extended family was aware of the abuse but reportedly did not intervene.

In 2005 Mr. El-Birani's abusive behavior escalated overtime to the point when he physically abused their daughters, stopped them from attending school, locked them inside the house, and threw his eldest daughter and her child out of the home. The daughters phoned Ms. El-Birani who came home and pleaded with Mr. El-Birani to let their daughters leave safely. Instead he forcibly removed Ms. El-Birani's hijab and physically pushed her out of the home. The police were called and Mr. El-Birani was formally charged and a protection order was put in place. He was also mandated to attend an anger management program. Due to the protection order, Mr. El-Birani went to live with his siblings, but after a short time they negotiated with Ms. El-Birani to allow him to live in the house and promised they would find him alternate accommodation to live alone, which never happened. Ms. El-Birani and her children were shamed and blamed by their extended family and the wider community for calling the police and reporting the abuse. One year before Ms. El-Birani's murder, their family doctor had reportedly stated that it was good that Ms. El-Birani did not leave Mr. El-Birani.

Upon Mr. El-Birani's completion of the mandated anger management program, Ms. El-Birani received a letter from the organization stating that he showed no signs of repentance or accountability for his abusive acts. Later when Mr. El-Birani tried to strangle his wife during another abusive incident, the daughters reached out to their extended family who had advised them not to call the police and that they no longer wanted to be involved. Following this, the cycle of violence continued and escalated without any formal or informal support. At the time of Ms. El-Birani's murder, she was living in a basement suite within their home, while Mr. El-Birani lived in the rest of the home. In April 2012, Ms. El-Birani contacted his therapist who advised Ms. El-Birani to call 911 if he became violent. A week later, Mr. El-Birani stabbed Ms. El-Birani 25 times in her upper body. She died at the door of their house, apparently trying to escape. Mr. El-Birani was sentenced to life in prison with no possibility of parole for 10 years. Following the trial, their three daughters feared for their own lives and left Canada; they now live in Lebanon.

Themes

This tragedy reveals how the pre- and postmigration context can affect an immigrant family at risk of DV or DH. It demonstrates many missed opportunities by extended family, friends, community members, and service providers to stop the violence and prevent Ms. El-Birani from being killed.

Employment

Mr. El-Birani experienced chronic unemployment; the underlying factors that caused unemployment within the postmigration context were not revealed. This information would have provided an in-depth understanding of the impact of being unemployed on his mental health and family, taking into consideration Mr. El-Birani's premigration education and employment. On the other hand, Ms. El-Birani upgraded her education, became gainfully employed, and took on the role of the primary breadwinner, and their daughters also contributed to the household expenses. The reversal of traditional gender roles was a key risk factor for this family. Within the postmigration context, men may experience a decline and/or loss of status and employment. This change can significantly impact the man's identity as a provider, a fundamental aspect of their collective self.

Isolation

The El-Birani family moved to London to be closer to family, yet they experienced isolation from their extended family and community as a result of the abuse, and even more so after reporting the abuse. Following police involvement, Mr. El-Birani became isolated even from his siblings and stayed home without any support.

Separation

Ms. El-Birani and their daughters continued to live in the same location as the perpetrator after separation, with no indication that the protection order was lifted.

Feelings of shame, stigma, and helplessness

Ms. El-Birani and their daughters were subjected to abuse, experienced shame, and felt trapped. The family was stigmatized for reporting abuse, and Ms. El-Birani did not want their daughters being further judged by the community. Eventually the family became discouraged from seeking formal help and sequestered themselves.

Mental health

Mr. El-Birani suffered mental health problems and reportedly had tried to commit suicide. He witnessed the death of his mother during combat, and there is no evidence of the exploration of this trauma. This case highlights the importance of addressing unresolved premigration trauma. Trauma must be explored within cultural context as it plays a key role in interpreting mental health, DV, and its impact on the individual and their family, and the strategies to address DV. Similarly it is important to explore stressors such as the loss of familiar social support, and adjusting to a new country where families need to navigate new systems, language, and cultural differences, which can exert tension within the family, and in many instances, interplay as risk of DV (Baobaid, Ashbourne, Tam, Badahdah, & Al Jamal, 2018).

Coercive control, intimidation, and abuse

Mr. El-Birani was controlling and abusive. This behavior might incorrectly be attributed to culture, a problematic assumption which impedes immigrant victims of DV from seeking help. However, acknowledging that the behavior is embedded within patriarchal attitudes that are prevalent across cultures and communities would contribute to creating a safe space for women to seek help.

History of abuse

Ms. El-Birani had experienced abuse throughout her marriage, and Mr. El-Birani also abused their daughters. The violence had escalated in frequency and severity following incidents such as contact with police, family involvement, separation, most noticeably before the homicide.

Informal social support

Mr. El-Birani's extended family added to the risk and vulnerability of Ms. El-Birani and their daughters. While Ms. El-Birani's extended family resided in their country of origin, one of their daughters reported that they were supportive. Separation from extended family affects their well-being. Within collectivist cultures, family support is often expected when conflict arises. Existing informal supports, such as friends, were reportedly unaware of the severity of the risk to Ms. El-Birani. This indicates the need to explore and assess the availability and effectiveness of informal support as a risk or protective factor.

Formal support

The family had resided in Canada for over 20 years yet they were unfamiliar with specialized services, with the exception of their knowledge of DV shelters. This raises questions about the extent of information available to immigrant families and communities to seek help for DV. When the police were involved, Mr. El-Birani was charged and a protection order was put in place. Although their eldest daughter had her child with her during the incident, there was no mention of child protection involvement. Mr. El-Birani had a therapist but was not engaged. The healthcare professionals appear to have undermined risk, which raises a question about the importance of sharing risk assessments or levels of risk with all professionals involved. In this case, there was no indication that a risk assessment was conducted, coordination among service providers, referral to other services, or follow-up with the family regarding risk management and safety planning. After the tragedy, it was found that a risk assessment completed by one daughter had indicated that Ms. El-Birani was at a high risk for DH.

Lessons learned from this tragedy highlight the importance of understanding the intersecting and contextual risk factors facing immigrants. These risk factors affect the family, and more specifically victims, by increasing their vulnerabilities and creating unique barriers that impede them from seeking help. Service providers need to assess and analyze risk factors within a cultural context to have a holistic understanding of the underlying factors that will inform effective risk management and safety planning. Coordinated and culturally integrative interventions where service providers work with victims and perpetrators are key to mitigate DH risk and enhance DV victims' safety.

Geraldton, Australia: the case of Dr. Liyanage

Many of the details outlined in this case can be retrieved from: https://thenewdaily.com.au/news/state/wa/2017/03/06/doctor-killed-abusive-husband-speaks/. For additional references, see References for case studies.

On June 24, 2014, 34-year-old Dr. Liyanage killed her husband Dr. Athukorala, aged 51, as he slept in their bedroom. Dr. Liyanage met Dr. Athukorala during their Pathology fellowship in Sri Lanka in 2009 and fell in love with him. Despite her friends' concerns about his manipulative behavior and advice that she should leave him, she accepted his marriage proposal. Dr. Liyanage believed that her options to marry were limited because she was sexually active with Dr. Athukorala before marriage (and he was her first sexual partner), and, as the eldest daughter, she did not want to burden her family.

The couple migrated to Australia in 2011 and settled in Geraldton. Shortly thereafter Dr. Athukorala began abusing Dr. Liyanage physically, sexually, psychologically, emotionally, and financially. He reportedly forced her to perform sexual acts, which he streamed online to strangers so he could in turn access child pornography. Dr. Athukorala took intimate photos with girls during the couple's vacation in Sri Lanka. Dr. Athukorala also coerced Dr. Liyanage into inviting a young girl to their house and was planning to have sex with her; Dr. Liyanage told the girl to leave if she wanted to.

In 2013 both Dr. Liyanage and Dr. Athukorala worked at Geraldton Regional Hospital. Dr. Liyanage was accepted and loved by her colleagues, whereas Dr. Athukorala reportedly felt superior to his colleagues and became irate when he was unable to control them. Over time, Dr. Athukorala's abuse intensified and, on many occasions, Dr. Liyanage was unable to go to work because of the abuse; Dr. Athukorala would call in sick on her behalf. Dr. Liyanage tried to leave Dr. Athukorala at least six times but he was able to coerce her to come back by threatening to share her private information. He monitored her every move inside and outside the home.

Dr. Liyanage reached out to her friends in Sri Lanka who encouraged her to return to Sri Lanka. Her mother-in-law accused her of being a disobedient wife and ordered her to stay with Dr. Athukorala. Dr. Liyanage felt extreme shame and helplessness, and often considered suicide, but the thought of her family's sorrow if she acted on her suicidal ideation stopped her. She was fearful that the legal systems would not be able to help her in Australia nor protect her family in Sri Lanka.

Dr. Liyanage was sentenced to four years in prison for manslaughter and released after two and a half years. Dr. Liyanage was at risk of deportation, but Australia's Immigration Minister reinstated her visa so she could stay in the country upon her release. Dr. Liyanage disclosed that the first time she felt free was when she was in prison.

Themes

This case illustrates the intersectionality of a range of factors at the micro-, meso-, and macrolevels of a person's country of origin and their new country that created unique and heightened risk of, and vulnerability to, DH.

Cultural beliefs

The idea that premarital sex reduces a woman's prospects of finding a suitable partner is rooted in the patriarchal belief that virginity is associated with sexual premarital purity and family honor. Where such beliefs are prevalent, premarital sex, even with the prospective husband, will bring disgrace to the whole family (Hunjan & Towson, 2007).

Age

There was a major age difference between the couple ($\sim$20 years). Dr. Liyanage was 29 years old when she met Dr. Athukorala (average age at first marriage in Sri Lanka was 23 years) (United Nations, Department of Economic, & Social Affairs, Population Division, 2013). Dr. Liyanage reportedly felt obligated to marry him to save face for the family, avoid scandal, and not become a burden.

Feelings of extreme shame and helplessness

Dr. Liyanage was unable to seek help for various reasons noted earlier including the severity, frequency, and types of abuse she experienced, which created extreme shame and helplessness. Her mother-in-law also contributed to this sense of shame by accusing Dr. Liyanage of being a disobedient wife. Even though Dr. Liyanage was highly educated and spoke English fluently, she faced significant barriers to seeking help.

Isolation

As a new immigrant in a small city, Dr. Liyanage experienced geographic and social isolation especially in the context of Dr. Athukorala's monitoring of her activities in and outside the home. Reportedly Dr. Athukorala had forced Dr. Liyanage to sever her ties with her parents and family in Sri Lanka prior to migration.

Coercive control, intimidation, and abuse

Dr. Athukorala intimidated Dr. Liyanage in various ways, and when she tried to leave him, he coerced her to return using threats against her and her family, including reportedly threatening to share sexual videos. Dr. Athukorala also controlled her finances.

History of abuse

Dr. Athukorala began abusing Dr. Liyanage when they were still in Sri Lanka, and the severity and frequency of this abuse increased over time.

Workplace dynamics

Dr. Athukorala was not happy with his colleagues, whereas Dr. Liyanage felt accepted and loved at work. There was evidence that the abuse had direct impact on her work and workplace. Reportedly the hospital staff did not see any signs of DV, even when her husband called her workplace on her behalf to report absence from work.

Informal social support

Dr. Liyanage's informal support was both a risk factor and a protective factor. She was separated from her family and her supportive friends who lived in Sri Lanka. Her mother-in-law attributed her son's abusive behavior to Dr. Liyanage being a disobedient wife. It is not clear what informal support she had in Australia. (See Chapter 10: Domestic violence and homicide in the workplace, for more information on DV and the workplace).

Formal support

Dr. Liyanage was not connected to any DV services and there were no known disclosures of abuse to anyone in Australia.

Impediments to help-seeking

Dr. Liyanage felt unable to seek help from formal support due to her distrust in the legal system's ability to protect her in Australia and her family in Sri Lanka. This is a common factor for immigrant women who fear for the safety of their families, especially when/where police in the pre- and/or postmigration contexts cannot be trusted and/or women victims of DV are not given adequate protection.

This case highlights how applying an intersectionality lens informs the exploration of aforementioned risks. Lack of awareness of the signs of DV or attributing signs of DV to cultural practices creates a huge missed opportunity in the workplace; for some women their workplace may be the only place where they may be able to obtain support to deal with DV.

Victoria, Canada: the case of Ms. Park

Many of the details outlined in this case can be retrieved from: https://rcybc.ca/sites/default/files/documents/pdf/reports_publications/honouring_christian_lee.pdf. For additional references, see References for case studies.

On September 4, 2007, Ms. Park was killed by her estranged husband, Mr. Lee. After killing Ms. Park, Mr. Lee also killed their

6-year-old son, Christian, his mother-in-law, Ms. Chun, and father-in-law, Mr. Park. Mr. Lee then killed himself.

Mr. Lee had immigrated to Canada as a young child and was described as having assimilated well into Canadian culture. Ms. Park immigrated from Korea to Canada in her early twenties. She met Mr. Lee approximately a year after arriving in Canada and married him in 2004. Mr. Lee was previously married to another (Korean) woman, and he blamed his lack of fluency in Korean culture as a reason for the breakdown of that marriage. Ms. Park and Mr. Lee owned a Korean restaurant together. Ms. Park's parents moved in with the couple. Ms. Park was not fluent in English, so she was reliant on Mr. Lee's ability to navigate Canadian systems. Mr. Lee had been part of the Canadian Armed Forces for 12 years, but he also had a lengthy history of criminal behavior that included involvement with law enforcement and the criminal justice system. He had allegedly set a restaurant on fire, assaulted colleagues on numerous occasions, and in July 2006 was charged with threatening and holding a man hostage. Mr. Lee was also being sued by a former employee of the restaurant as a result of two alleged incidents: a knife wound requiring stitches and another physical assault that included choking, hitting, and throwing the employee against a wall.

Based on the accounts of many people, Ms. Park and Mr. Lee seemed to live a relatively stable life. However, Ms. Park had experienced many years of abuse from Mr. Lee. In 2003 she called the Victoria Police Department to report the abuse, but Mr. Lee was not charged. On the advice of a family friend who was aware of the DV, Mr. Lee and Ms. Park started marriage counseling in the summer of 2007, where she disclosed a lengthy history of abuse from Mr. Lee and her multiple attempts to leave him. Ms. Park called the police again in July 2007, but by the time police arrived Mr. Lee had calmed down. Mr. Lee and Ms. Park were in a car accident in August 2007. Ms. Park later told police that Mr. Lee was trying to kill her in the accident because she had told him that she was planning on divorcing him. She had also disclosed a longstanding history of physical, emotional, psychological, and sexual abuse, intimidation tactics, and fear for her own life and those of her son and family. Police issued a protection order, blocking Mr. Lee's access to Ms. Park, the home, and restaurant, and also barred him from possessing knives or other weapons, but Mr. Lee continued to have access to their son Christian. Police recommended that Mr. Lee be held in custody until a hearing because he stated that he would not follow orders, but a judge released Mr. Lee on bail citing lack of evidence, and his belief that there were inconsistencies in Ms. Park's reporting history. Mr. Lee had informed the marriage counselor of his suicidal ideation.

By mid-August 2007, Ms. Park had taken many precautions for her and her family's safety, including multiple disclosures to service providers of abuse and of Mr. Lee's breaches of the protection and bail orders. Victoria police contacted Mr. Lee to confirm that he understood the conditions of the orders. The court reviewed the evidence of Mr. Lee breaching his bail, but the court date was stayed to September 4, 2007. At 3 a.m. on the day of court, Mr. Lee entered Ms. Park's home through an unsecured window, and repeatedly stabbed to death Ms. Park, Ms. Park's parents, Christian. Mr. Lee phoned 911 and subsequently stabbed himself to death. This case resulted in a review by the Representative for Children and Youth, a Coroner's Inquest, and a wave of legislative and policy reform to improve the response to DV in BC (Representative for Children and Youth, 2009).

Themes

This tragedy demonstrates many missed opportunities at the meso- and macrolevels to prevent DH.

Employment

Mr. Lee was unemployed prior to the homicide. There appear to have been many conflicts at work including litigation with former employees. He experienced financial hardships due to unemployment as a result of postprotection order.

Involvement with the criminal justice system

Mr. Lee had a history of aggression involving his colleagues and staff. While police issues a protection order there was no condition against him seeing Christian. (See Chapter 8: Child homicides in the context of domestic violence: when the plight of children is overlooked, for more information about children at risk of DH.) Even after Mr. Lee told the police upon his release that he would not abide by the protection order (which he subsequently breached several times), he was released on bail.

Language barrier

Ms. Park was not fluent in English thus relied on Mr. Lee for translation and system navigation. There were no readily accessible linguistically appropriate information and/or support.

Separation

Ms. Park attempted to leave Mr. Lee several times and had informed him of her intention to divorce him on the day of the car accident.

Prior threats to kill

Mr. Lee had threatened to kill Ms. Park and him if she were to leave him.

History of abuse

Ms. Park had experienced a lengthy history of abuse by Mr. Lee, which began prior to their marriage. (See Chapter 5: Domestic homicides in teens and young adult dating relationships: ignoring the dangers of dangerous relationships, for information on violence in young adult dating.)

Stalking

Mr. Lee began to stalk Ms. Park and their son after receiving the protection order.

Suicidality

A month before the murder, Mr. Lee had reported that he was experiencing suicidal ideation.

Access to weapons

Mr. Lee had military training and access to knives, and had a history of using them against others.

Informal support

Ms. Park had support from her parents who lived with her, and a family friend who knew about the abuse and advised the couple to seek help.

Formal support

Ms. Park had sought formal support after a few extreme incidents. She had shared with police her nervousness when talking to authority figures. Multiple service providers became involved with the family after the car accident and Mr. Lee's threats to kill Ms. Park.

The system lacked effective risk assessment, risk management, and coordination among the various services involved with the family. It is notable that in the months preceding the homicide, a marriage counselor, police, and courts were aware of the history and severity of DV, but none of these contacts resulted in an in-depth assessment and information sharing about level of risk and coordinated interventions.

Discussion and implications for practice and future research

The women involved in the three cases presented had endured lengthy histories of violence, experienced several types of abuse, and faced multiple intersecting risks for DV and systemic barriers that increased their risk of DH. The consideration of risk factors is crucial for interventions in and prevention of DV, as is the acknowledgment and understanding that some risk factors can escalate DV into DH (Dawson, Jaffe, Campbell, Lucas, & Kerr, 2017). However, few studies have examined how these key risk factors intersect to create conditions that may lead to DH (Dawson & Piscitelli, 2017), specifically within immigrant contexts.

Immigrant women often face multiple intersecting barriers that impede help-seeking in postmigration and (re)settlement contexts. For example, they often do not receive accurate information about existing services for women experiencing DV (Erez, Adelman, & Gregory, 2009; Guruge & Humphreys, 2009) and face barriers to navigating the legal and justice system, which can be discriminatory, racist, and/or culturalist. Further many of the available services are not culturally safe and responsive, which acts as an additional barrier to safety for immigrant women (Guruge & Humphreys, 2009; Guruge et al., 2010). Immigrant women are also often fearful of their or their families' immigration status being revoked (Dawson et al., 2017). At the community level, women may be concerned about losing the limited social network and support they have in the new country because of stigma, shame, and blame that may result from calling the police (Guruge & Humphreys, 2009; Guruge et al., 2010). Additionally abusers' threats to harm the women's families are a legitimate concern (Erez et al., 2009). Concerns about justice and DV services seemed to play a key role in all of the cases reviewed. For Ms. El-Birani and Dr. Liyanage, extended family members' non-supportive response to their victimization added to risk.

Immigrant women may share some commonalities in their lived experiences and postmigration realities, but immigrants are also heterogeneous with unique experiences and circumstances (VAWnet, 2012a). Practitioners must pay careful attention to the complex and diverse intersecting factors faced by immigrant women and their families to effectively address DV

(Campbell et al., 2003; Guruge, 2012; Uehling, Bouroncle, Roeber, Tashima, & Crain, 2011) and prevent DH. The intersecting factors at the micro- and mesolevels can shape women's 'collective self,' and in turn, their lived experiences and whether/how they define and/or disclose abuse (Pan et al., 2006). Practitioners must also recognize cultural similarities, differences, and complexities when developing effective interventions and responses to DV (Ely, 2004; James, 2010). Attribution of patriarchal values to certain cultures or religions is unacceptable and erroneous (Patil, 2013), and can create impediments for abused immigrant women to report abuse and seek help. Effective responses to the unique needs of immigrant women must be culturally informed.

There is also a need for culturally informed public educational programs to raise awareness of DV and its effects on individuals, families, and communities (Du Mont et al., 2012; Guruge, Tiwari, & Lucea, 2010). Similarly, programs are needed to provide information to service providers working with newcomer women and children about risk factors to facilitate effective responses to DV (Du Mont et al., 2012; VAWnet, 2012a). Such programs need to acknowledge the complexities of dealing with family violence in collectivist cultures and in the communities where dissolution of a marital relationship is highly discouraged and potentially viewed as shameful.

Culturally informed risk assessments are recommended to assess the diverse intersecting risk factors, severity, and lethality among immigrant populations (Du Mont et al., 2012). However, few culturally informed risk assessment tools are available (Rossiter et al., 2018; Yercich & Rossiter, 2018). Practitioners are encouraged to use "structured professional judgement" in identifying risk factors and recognizing the intersecting nature of these complex risk factors; this technique has demonstrated its effectiveness in identifying risk of DV in some settings (Newman, 2010; Northcott, 2012 as cited in Backhouse & Toivonen, 2018). Special consideration should be given toward assessing and analyzing risk effectively across cultures and understand the contextual risk factors unique to immigrant populations. Traditional risk assessment tools are geared toward nonimmigrant populations, so professionals working with immigrant women experiencing abuse must address the risk factors that may be specific to these populations that capture premigration trauma, postmigration stressors, and shifts in gender roles and previous family dynamics.

The complexity of DV necessitates an acknowledgment of the need to engage men and boys in preventing and responding to DV

(United Nations Human Rights Council, 2017). Taking into consideration immigrant contexts, culturally integrative and responsive risk management programs for perpetrators are recommended to address contextual and intersectional risk factors and help abusers recognize patriarchal attitudes that promote abuse (Dabby & Poore, 2007). There is a need for research that can contextualize DV within immigrants' pre- and postmigration experiences (Guruge et al., 2010). Research on risk factors for DV across cultures is limited, and without contextualizing any program or service within immigrant experiences, assessing the risk of a perpetrator for lethality may be misinterpreted. Risks should be interpreted with strong consideration given to the perpetrator's mental health and the impact on the victim, as ignoring these aspects has high risk of lethality for women. The lack of culturally informed programs and services for perpetrators increases the risk of violence and lethality against women. Collaborative services and cross-sector initiatives to manage risk and maximize the safety of victims are also recommended (Polaschek, 2016 as cited in Backhouse & Toivonen, 2018; VAWnet, 2012b).

When developing safety plans with immigrant women experiencing DV, practitioners need to be aware of potentially unique needs including stresses around immigration status. Moreover practitioners should consider how women perceive safety (Midlarsky, Venkataramani-Kothari, & Plante, 2006; Yercich & Rossiter, 2018). Practitioners should build on the protective factors within each specific cultural belief system and help provide social support to meet the unique needs of women experiencing DV to ensure their safety, improve their well-being, and facilitate their empowerment and agency. There is an uniqueness to how individuals interpret and give meaning to their journey and how they perceive and conceptualize significant social issues.

Culturally informed integrative and collaborative services to assess and manage risk and enhance safety are important in addressing DV, interrupting abuse, and mitigating risk. Collaboration among and across diverse organizations promotes collective responses to immigrant women experiencing DV, prevents service duplication, and allows women to access a range of services. Collaboration also allows service providers to assess risk, share information, undertake safety planning, and tailor interventions that meet the needs of and secure safety and support for immigrant women as well as services for abusers and other family members (Baobaid & Ashbourne, 2016; Whitaker et al., 2007). More opportunities are needed for service providers to be trained in such integrative models of service to enhance their capacity to conduct and analyze risk assessments and recognize unique risk factors, as well as to create risk management strategies and safety plans within immigrant contexts.

Finally service providers working with immigrant women, men, children, and families need to meaningfully apply cultural humility within their practice. Cultural humility can improve their awareness of DV and the diverse and intersecting factors that affect the lived experiences and evolving notion of the self for victims of DV. The relationships between practitioners and immigrant women, men, children, and families should be based on respect through acknowledgment that cultures are fluid, recognition of the inherent power imbalance in client—professional relationships, ongoing critical reflection of self, continuous learning, and working in conjunction with immigrant families and communities (Fisher-Borne, Cain, & Martin, 2015; Foronda, Baptiste, Reinholdt, & Ousman, 2016).

Implications for policy

Culturally safe, responsive, and proactive approaches to policy and programs that support victims and survivors of DV are needed because immigrant women may lack the cultural and legal literacy of their destination countries. Some immigrant women may feel most comfortable with receiving support from their close ethnic networks rather than formal supports (Shirwadkar, 2004) therefore educational programs should strive to promote knowledge transfer organically through programming that is aimed at language and/or cultural communities (Shirwadkar, 2004) in general. Service providers should collaborate with informal support networks to ensure that DV, when disclosed or discovered, can be effectively addressed and safety of women and children can be promoted.

Legislative protections should address the unique risk factors that make disclosing abuse and accessing supports challenging for immigrant women (Guruge, 2007). For example, some countries have immigration policies that have provisions in place to protect abused women who do not have permanent residence or citizenship from deportation (Ghafournia, 2011). However, barriers continue to exist within such policies, such as placing the burden of proof on the victims, including the need to obtain statutory declarations from medical or allied health professionals, which is challenging for immigrant women who may be isolated and/or accompanied to health appointments by their abusers (Ghafournia, 2011). Recent shifts in Canadian spousal sponsorship policy reflect an understanding of the uneven power dynamics and potential abuses that can occur within sponsorship relationships by abolishing the two-year rule which previously required sponsored spouses/partners to reside with their sponsor for 2 years to retain their immigration status (Jackson et al., 2018). Ultimately protective legislative systems need to take a holistic approach to supporting victims of DV and be more understanding of the various risk factors that often exacerbate the vulnerability of immigrant women.

Future research

As previously noted, gaps exist in the literature with respect to identifying risk factors unique to DV and DH within immigrant communities. These gaps are further evidenced by the reviews of the case studies in this chapter, which indicate a need for future research given the complexity and heterogeneity of risk factors for escalating and potentially lethal violence for immigrants who experience DV. Future research is needed to assess the variations in DV conceptualization among immigrant populations, especially with a specific focus on the contexts within which DH is more likely to occur. Similarly research is needed to examine the impact of integration stressors on immigrant families in Canada to address DV among immigrant communities. Research on the effectiveness of existing risk assessment tools used with immigrant populations is recommended as is work on the suitability of existing risk management and safety planning strategies with immigrant populations. Finally research is needed to examine and assess the effectiveness of collaborations among service providers working with immigrant populations and addressing DV as well as evaluation of existing collaborative and culturally integrative responses.

References

Ahmad, F., Riaz, S., Barata, P., & Stewart, D. E. (2004). Patriarchal beliefs and perceptions of abuse among South Asian immigrant women. *Violence Against Women, 10*(3), 262–282. Available from https://doi.org/10.1177/1077801203256000.
Backhouse, C., & Toivonen, C. (2018). *National Risk Assessment Principles for domestic and family violence: Companion resource. A summary of the evidence-base supporting the development and implementation of the National Risk Assessment Principles for domestic and family violence (ANROWS Insights 09/2018)*. Sydney, NSW: ANROWS.
Baobaid, M., & Ashbourne, L. M. (2016). *Enhancing culturally integrative family safety response in Muslim communities*. England, UK: Taylor & Francis.
Baobaid, M., Ashbourne, L., Tam, D., Badahdah, A., & Al Jamal, A. (2018). *Pre- and Post-Migration stressors and marital relations among Arab refugee families in Canada*. Doha, Qatar: Doha International Family Institute.
Burnman, E., Smailes, S. L., & Chantier, K. (2004). 'Culture' as a barrier to service provision and delivery: Domestic violence services for minoritized women.

Critical Social Policy, 24(3), 332–357. Available from https://doi.org/10.1177/026101830044363.

Campbell, J. C., Webster, D., Koziol-McLain, J., Block, C., Campbell, D., Curry, M. A., . . . Laughon, K. (2003). Risk factors for femicide in abusive relationships: Results from a multisite case control study. *American Journal of Public Health, 93*(7), 1089–1097.

Cho, S., Crenshaw, K. W., & McCall, L. (2013). Toward a field of intersectionality studies: Theory, applications, and praxis. *Signs: Journal of Women in Culture and Society, 38*(4), 785–810. Available from https://doi.org/10.1086/669608.

Chokshi, R. (2007). *South Asian immigrant women & abuse: Identifying intersecting issues and culturally appropriate solutions* (Unpublished Master's thesis). Toronto, ON: Ryerson University.

Dabby, C., & Poore, G. (2007). *Engendering change: Transforming gender roles in Asian and Pacific Islander communities.* San Francisco, CA: Asian and Pacific Islander Institute on Domestic Violence.

Dawson, M., Jaffe, P., Campbell, M., Lucas, W., & Kerr, K. (2017). Canada. In M. Dawson (Ed.), *Domestic homicides and death reviews: An international perspective* (pp. 59–90). New York: Springer.

Dawson, M., & Piscitelli, A. (2017). Risk factors in domestic homicides: Identifying common clusters in the Canadian context. *Journal of Interpersonal Violence,* 1–12. Available from https://doi.org/10.1177/0886260517729404.

Du Mont, J., Hyman, I., O'Brien, K., White, M. E., Odette, F., & Tyyska, V. (2012). Factors associated with intimate partner violence by a former partner by immigration status and length of residence in Canada. *Annals of Epidemiology, 22*(11), 772–777. Available from https://doi.org/10.1016/j.annepidem.2012.09.001.

Edelstein, A. A. (2013). Culture transition, acculturation and intimate partner homicide. *SpringerPlus, 2*(1), 338. Available from https://doi.org/10.1186/2193-1801-2-338.

Ely, G. E. (2004). Domestic violence and immigrant communities in the United States: A review of women's unique needs and recommendations for social work practice and research. *Stress, Trauma and Crisis: An International Journal, 7*(4), 223–241. Available from https://doi.org/10.1080/15434610490888027.

Erez, E., Adelman, M., & Gregory, C. (2009). Intersections of immigration and domestic violence: Voices of battered immigrant women. *Feminist Criminology, 4*(1), 32–56. Available from https://doi.org/10.1177/1557085108325413.

Fisher-Borne, M., Cain, J. M., & Martin, S. L. (2015). From mastery to accountability: Cultural humility as an alternative to cultural competence. *Social Work Education, 34*(2), 165–181. Available from https://doi.org/10.1080/02615479.2014.977244.

Foronda, C., Baptiste, D. L., Reinholdt, M. M., & Ousman, K. (2016). Cultural humility: A concept analysis. *Journal of Transcultural Nursing, 27*(3), 210–217. Available from https://doi.org/10.1177/1043659615592677.

Ghafournia, N. (2011). Battered at home, played down in policy: Migrant women and domestic violence in Australia. *Aggression and Violent Behavior, 16*(3), 207–213. Available from https://doi.org/10.1016/j.avb.2011.02.009.

Gitterman, A., & Germain, C. B. (1976). Social work practice: A life model. *Social Service Review, 50*(4), 601–610. Available from https://doi.org/10.1086/643430.

Guruge, S. (2007). *The influence of gender, racial, social, and economic inequalities on the production of and responses to intimate partner violence in the post-migration context.* Toronto, ON: University of Toronto, Unpublished dissertation.

Guruge, S. (2012). Intimate partner violence: A global health perspective. *Canadian Journal of Nursing (Special Issue on Global Health)*, *44*(4), 36–64.

Guruge, S., Collins, E., & Bender, A. (2010). Working with immigrant women: Guidelines for mental health. *Canadian Issues* (Summer 2010), 114–118.

Guruge, S., & Humphreys, J. (2009). Barriers that affect abused immigrant women's access to and use of formal social supports. *Canadian Journal of Nursing Research*, *41*(3), 64–84.

Guruge, S., & Khanlou, N. (2004). Intersectionalities of influence: Researching the health of immigrant and refugee women. *Canadian Journal of Nursing Research*, *36*(3), 32–47.

Guruge, S., Khanlou, N., & Gastaldo, D. (2010). Intimate male partner violence in the migration process: Intersections of gender, race, and class. *Journal of Advanced Nursing*, *66*(1), 103–113. Available from https://doi.org/10.1111/j.1365-2648.2009.05184.x.

Guruge, S., Shirpak, R., Zanchetta, M., Gastaldo, D., Hyman, I., & Sidani, S. (2010). A meta-synthesis of post-migration changes in marital relationships in Canada. *Canadian Journal of Public Health*, *101*(4), 327–331. Available from https://doi.org/10.1007/BF03405296.

Guruge, S., Tiwari, A., & Lucea, M. B. (2010). *International perspectives on family violence*. New York: Springer.

Han, J. H. J. (2009). *Safety for immigrant, refugee and non-status women: A literature review.* Retrieved from <http://endingviolence.org/files/uploads/IWP_Lit_Review_for_website_May_2010.pdf>.

Hassan, G., Thombs, B., Rousseau, C., Kirmayer, L. J., Feightner, J., Ueffing, E., & Pottie, K. (2011). Appendix 13: Intimate partner violence: Evidence review for newly arriving immigrants. *Canadian Medical Association Journal*, *7*, 1–13.

Hunjan, S., & Towson, S. (2007). "Virginity is everything": Sexuality in the context of intimate partner violence in the South Asian community. In S. Das Dasgupta (Ed.), *Body evidence: Intimate violence against South Asian women in America* (pp. 53–67). Piscataway, NJ: Rutgers University Press.

Hyman, I., & Forte, T. (2006). The association between length of stay in Canada and intimate partner violence among immigrant women. *American Journal of Public Health*, *96*(4), 654.

Ibrahim, D. (2018). *Family violence in Canada: A statistical profile, 2014. Juristat, Statistics Canada, Catalogue no. 85-002-X.* Retrieved from <https://www150.statcan.gc.ca/n1/en/pub/85-002-x/2016001/article/14303-eng.pdf?st = cZhBqFKw>.

International Organization for Migration. (2017). *Key migration terms.* Retrieved from <https://www.iom.int/key-migration-terms>.

Jackson, M., Yercich, S., Godard, L., & Lee, H. (2018). *Building Supports Phase III, the policy component: Immigration, refugee, and settlement; housing; and health.* Retrieved from <http://www.fredacentre.com/wp-content/uploads/2010/09/Building-Supports-Phase-3-report-final3pdfMay2018.pdf>.

James, K. (2010). Domestic violence within refugee families: Intersecting patriarchal culture and the refugee experience. *Australian and New Zealand Journal of Family Therapy*, *31*(3), 275–284. Available from https://doi.org/10.1375/anft.31.3.275.

Keller, E. M., & Brennan, P. K. (2007). Cultural considerations and challenges to service delivery for Sudanese victims of domestic violence: Insights from service providers and actors in the criminal justice system. *International Review of Victimology*, *14*(1), 115–141. Available from https://doi.org/10.1177/026975800701400107.

Kim, C., & Sung, H.-G. (2016). Characteristics and risk factors of Chinese immigrant intimate partner violence victims in New York City and the role of supportive networks. *The Family Journal, 24*(1), 60. Available from https://doi.org/10.1177/1066480715615632.

Menjívar, C., & Salcido, O. (2002). Immigrant women and domestic violence: Common experiences in different countries. *Gender & Society, 16*(6), 898–920. Available from https://doi.org/10.1177/089124302237894.

Midlarsky, E., Venkataramani-Kothari, A., & Plante, M. (2006). Domestic violence in the Chinese and South Asian immigrant communities. *Annals of the New York Academy of Sciences, 1087*, 279–300.

Muhammad, A. A. (2010). Preliminary Examination of so-called "honour killings" in Canada *(CAT. No. J4-23/2013E-PDF)*. Ottawa, ON: Government of Canada. Retrieved from http://www.justice.gc.ca/eng/rp-pr/cj-jp/fv-vf/hk-ch/hk_eng.pdf.

Newman, C. (2010). *Expert domestic violence risk assessments in the family courts.* Retrieved from http://bds-research.com/Assessments/DVI/Research/domestic_violence_risk_assessment_in_family_court.pdf.

Office of the Chief Coroner. (2018). *Domestic Violence Death Review Committee 2017 annual report.* Toronto, ON: Queen's Printer for Ontario. Retrieved from https://www.mcscs.jus.gov.on.ca/english/deathinvestigations/OfficeChiefCoroner/Publicationsandreports/DVDRC2017.html.

Pan, A., Daley, S., Rivera, L. M., Williams, K., Lingle, D., & Reznik, V. (2006). Understanding the role of culture in domestic violence: The Ahimsa Project for safe families. *Journal of Immigrant and Minority Health, 8*(1), 35–43. Available from https://doi.org/10.1007/s10903-006-6340-y.

Patil, V. (2013). From patriarchy to intersectionality: A transnational feminist assessment of how far we've really come. *Signs: Journal of Women in Culture and Society, 38*(4), 847–867. Available from https://doi.org/10.1086/669560.

Phillips, J., & Simon-Davies, J. (2017). *Migration to Australia: A quick guide to the statistics.* Retrieved from <https://www.aph.gov.au/About_Parliament/Parliamentary_Departments/Parliamentary_Library/pubs/rp/rp1617/Quick_Guides/MigrationStatistics>.

Raj, A., & Silverman, J. (2002). Violence against immigrant women: The roles of culture, context, and legal immigrant status on intimate partner violence. *Violence Against Women, 8*(3), 367–398. Available from https://doi.org/10.1177/10778010222183107.

Rossiter, K. R., Yercich, S., Baobaid, M., Al Jamal, A., David, R., Fairbairn, J., ... Jaffe, P. (2018). *Domestic violence in immigrant and refugee populations: Culturally-informed risk and safety strategies (4).* London, ON: Canadian Domestic Homicide Prevention Initiative, ISBN: 978-1-988412-13-9.

Rothman, E. F., Gupta, J., Pavlos, C., Dang, Q., & Coutinho, P. (2007). Batterer intervention program enrollment and completion among immigrant men in Massachusetts. *Violence Against Women, 13*(5), 527–543. Available from https://doi.org/10.1177/1077801207300720.

Shirwadkar, S. (2004). Canadian domestic violence policy and Indian immigrant women. *Violence Against Women, 10*(8), 860–879. Available from https://doi.org/10.1177/1077801204266310.

Statistics Canada. (2017). *Immigration and ethnocultural diversity: Key results from the 2016 Census.* Retrieved from <https://www150.statcan.gc.ca/n1/daily-quotidien/171025/dq171025b-eng.htm>.

Triandis, H. C. (1989). The self and social behavior in differing cultural contexts. *Psychological Review, 96*(3), 506.

Triandis, H. C. (1999). Cross-cultural psychology. *Asian Journal of Social Psychology, 2*(1), 127–143.

Trijbetz, T. (2011). *Domestic and family violence and people from immigrant and refugee backgrounds.* Retrieved from <http://www.mhima.org.au/pdfs/Domestic%20and%20family%20violence_fact%20sheet%2011.pdf>.

Uehling, G., Bouroncle, A., Roeber, C., Tashima, N., & Crain, C. (2011). Preventing partner violence in refugee and immigrant communities. *Forced Migration Review, 38,* 50–51.

United Nations. (2017). *International Migration Report 2017.* Retrieved from <http://www.un.org/en/development/desa/population/migration/publications/migrationreport/docs/MigrationReport2017.pdf>.

United Nations, Department of Economic and Social Affairs, Population Division. (2013). *World Fertility Report 2012.* United Nations Publication.

United Nations Educational, Scientific, and Cultural Organization. (2017). *Social and human sciences, International migration.* Retrieved from <http://www.unesco.org/new/en/social-and-human-sciences/themes/international-migration/glossary/migrant/>.

United Nations High Commissioner for Refugees. (2018). *Global trends: Forced displacement in 2017.* Retrieved from <https://www.unhcr.org/5b27be547.pdf>.

United Nations Human Rights Council. (2017). *Accelerating efforts to eliminate violence against women* (Publication No. A/HRC/35/L.15). Retrieved from <https://documents-dds-ny.un.org/doc/UNDOC/LTD/G17/165/68/PDF/G1716568.pdf?OpenElement>.

Vatnar, S. K. B., Friestad, C., & Bjørkly, S. (2017). Intimate partner homicide, immigration and citizenship: Evidence from Norway 1990–2012. *Journal of Scandinavian Studies in Criminology and Crime Prevention, 18*(2), 103–122. Available from https://doi.org/10.1080/14043858.2017.1394629.

Vaughan, C., Murdolo, A., Murray, L., Davis, E., Chen, J., Block, K., . . . Warr, D. (2015). ASPIRE: A multi-site community-based participatory research project to increase understanding of the dynamics of violence against immigrant and refugee women in Australia. *BMC Public Health, 15,* 1–9. Available from https://doi.org/10.1186/s12889-015-2634-0.

VAWnet. (2012a). *Addressing domestic violence in immigrant communities: Critical issues for culturally competent services.* Harrisburg, PA: Rana, S.

VAWnet. (2012b). *Practical considerations for parenting interventions for men who batter.* Harrisburg, PA: Scott, K.

West, C. M. (2015). African immigrant women and intimate partner violence: A systematic review. *Journal of Aggression, Maltreatment & Trauma,* 1–14. Available from https://doi.org/10.1080/10926771.2016.1116479.

Whitaker, D. J., Baker, C. K., Pratt, C., Reed, E., Suri, S., Pavlos, C., . . . Silverman, J. (2007). A network model for providing culturally competent services for intimate partner violence and sexual violence. *Violence Against Women, 13*(2), 190–209. Available from https://doi.org/10.1177/1077801206296984.

World Health Organization. (2012). *Understanding and addressing violence against women.* Retrieved from <http://apps.who.int/iris/bitstream/10665/77432/1/WHO_RHR_12.36_eng.pdf>.

Yercich, S., & Rossiter, K. R. (2018). Immigrant and refugee populations. In N. Jeffrey, J. Fairbairn, M. Campbell, M. Dawson, P. Jaffe, & A.-L. Straatman (Eds.), *Canadian Domestic Homicide Prevention Initiative with Vulnerable Populations (CDHPIVP) literature review on risk assessment, risk management and safety planning.* London, ON: Canadian Domestic Homicide Prevention Initiative, ISBN: 978-1-988412-27-6.

References for case studies

Chamari Liyanage

Budge, D. (2016). *Allow Chamari Liyanage to remain in Australia.* Available from Change.org. Retrieved from <https://www.change.org/p/peter-dutton-mp-allow-dr-chamari-liyanage-to-remain-in-australia>.

Christian, B. (2016, February 6). *Geraldton doctor murder trial: Chamari Liyanage tried to drown herself after abuse, court hears. ABC News.* Retrieved from <https://www.abc.net.au/news/2016-02-09/geraldton-doctor-murder-trial-chamari-liyanage-suicidal-trapped/7152626>.

Christian, B. (2016, February 9). *Murder-accused doctor 'forced to watch' husband's sexual encounter with teen. ABC News.* Retrieved from <https://www.abc.net.au/news/2016-02-10/murdered-doctor-forced-wife-to-watch-teen-sexual-encounter/7157424>.

Day, L. (2016, November 22). *Doctor Chamari Liyanage, who killed abusive husband with mallet, appeals to Peter Dutton to stay in Australia. ABC News.* Retrieved from <https://www.abc.net.au/news/2016-11-22/doctor-who-killed-abusive-husband-appeals-to-stay-in-australia/8047094>.

Day, L. (2017, March 6). *'I thought he would change': Doctor who killed abusive husband speaks out. The New Daily.* Retrieved from <https://thenewdaily.com.au/news/state/wa/2017/03/06/doctor-killed-abusive-husband-speaks/>.

Laurie, V. (2016, February 26). *Notes tell of a violent spiral into death and jail. The Australian.* Retrieved from <https://www.theaustralian.com.au/news/nation/notes-tell-of-a-violent-spiral-into-death-and-jail/news-story/b87d3dfbe3c515fc5c7e70c514815f55>.

Solmundson, J. (2016, February 15). *Murder accused 'beaten until she could not breathe.' The West Australian.* Retrieved from <https://thewest.com.au/news/oceania/murder-accused-beaten-until-she-could-not-breathe-ng-ya-330866>.

Solmundson, J. (2016, February 17). *Doctor planned teen sex, court told. Geraldton Guardian.* Retrieved from <http://pressreader.com/australia/geraldton-guardian/20160217/281573764753383>.

The Sunday Times. (2018, July 1). *Why she finally broke.* Retrieved from <https://www.pressreader.com/australia/the-sunday-times/20180701/284588833480441>.

The Sunday Times. (2018, July 1). *What happened in Geraldton.* Retrieved from <https://www.pressreader.com/australia/the-sunday-times/20180701/284584538513145>.

Tallier, S. (2016, February 15). *Husband urged murder-accused doctor to have affairs, Geraldton court told. ABC News.* Retrieved from <https://abc.net.au/7.30/doctor-who-killed-her-abusive-husband-speaks-out/8329820>.

Sonia El-Birani

Carruthers, D. (2017, October 18). *Domestic killing activist urges positive outrage. The London Free Press.* Retrieved from <https://lfpress.com/2017/10/18/domestic-killing-activist-urges-positive-outrage/wcm/cb811f56-033e-0d89-fcc7-4803a90219d1>.

El-Birani, A. (2017, April 19). *Voices of survivors: Part 2 Alham's story. Neighbours, Friends, and Families.* Retrieved from <http://neighboursfriendsandfamilies.ca/blog/voices-survivors-part-2-ahlams-story>.

El-Birani, H. (2017, April 27). *Voices of survivors: Part 3 Houda's story. Neighbours, Friends, and Families.* Retrieved from <http://neighboursfriendsandfamilies.ca/blog/voices-survivors-part-3-houdas-story>.

El-Birani, M. (2017, April 17). *Voices of survivors: Part 1 Maha's story. Neighbours, Friends, and Families*. Retrieved from <http://neighboursfriendsandfamilies. ca/blog/voices-survivors-part-1-mahas-story>.

Neighbours, Friends & Families. (2018, November 1). *Fatal Silence* [Video file]. *Neighbours, Friends, and Families*. Retrieved from <https://www.youtube. com/watch?v = J_zUJI4Xpzs>.

Paparella, N. (2014, April 22). *Guilty plea, life sentence in 2012 south London murder. CTV London*. Retrieved from <https://london.ctvnews.ca/guilty-plea-life-sentence-in-2012-south-london-murder-1.1786828>.

Sims, J. (2014, April 22). *Chawki El-Birani's sentenced to life in killing of wife. The London Free Press*. Retrieved from <https://lfpress.com/2014/04/22/chawki-el-biranis-sentenced-to-life-in-killing-of-wife/wcm/baf00375-a3e3-8be1-4dc2-7be7daf5dad4>.

Yong Sun Park

CBC News. (2008, May 1). *Sunny Park feared being killed, newly released video shows. CBC News*. Retrieved from <https://www.cbc.ca/news/canada/british-columbia/sunny-park-feared-being-killed-newly-released-video-shows-1.704187>.

CTV News. (2007, September 5). *Oak Bay husband was facing criminal charges. CTV News*. Retrieved from <https://www.ctvnews.ca/oak-bay-husband-was-facing-criminal-charges-1.255022>.

Hunter, J. (2007, September 4). *Killings stun wealthy B.C. neighbourhood. The Globe and Mail*. Retrieved from <https://www.theglobeandmail.com/news/national/killings-stun-wealthy-bc-neighbourhood/article1081510>.

Hunter, J. (2008, May 9). *How an inquest highlighted the cracks in Peter Lee's peaceful, kind facade. The Globe and Mail*. Retrieved from <https://www.theglobeandmail.com/news/national/how-an-inquest-highlighted-the-cracks-in-peter-lees-peaceful-kind-facade/article1202748/>.

Meissner, D. (2007, September 6). *Dad in B.C. mass killing had violent past. The Star*. Retrieved from <https://www.thestar.com/news/canada/2007/09/06/dad_in_bc_mass_killing_had_violent_past.htm>.

Ministry of Public Safety and Solicitor General. (2009). *Verdict at the Coroner's Inquest into the deaths of Kum Lea Chun, Moon Kyu Park, Christian Thomas Lee, Yong Sun Park, Hyun Joon Lee (File Nos.:2007:0168:0139/40/41/42/43)*. Victoria, BC: Province of British Columbia. Retrieved from https://www2.gov. bc.ca/assets/gov/birth-adoption-death-marriage-and-divorce/deaths/coronors-service/inquest/2009/verdict-park-lee-chun-18-dec-2009.pdf.

Representative for Children and Youth. (2009). *Honouring Christian Lee – No private matter: Protecting children living with domestic violence*. Victoria, BC: Turpel-Lafond, M.E. Retrieved from https://rcybc.ca/sites/default/files/documents/pdf/reports_publications/honouring_christian_lee.pdf.

The Canadian Press. (2009, December 14). *4-Murder inquest hears justice official's warning. CBC News*. Retrieved from <https://www.cbc.ca/news/canada/british-columbia/4-murder-inquest-hears-justice-official-s-warning-1.809702>.

Perpetrator mental health: depression and suicidality as risk factors for domestic homicide

Katreena Scott[1], Casey L. Oliver[2] and Polly Cheng[2]
[1]Department of Applied Psychology and Human Development, University of Toronto, Toronto, ON, Canada [2]Centre for Research & Education on Violence Against Women & Children, Western University, London, ON, Canada

Introduction

> *But if I wasn't ever going to be happy again, then I would make sure that they wouldn't be alive to enjoy their happiness.*
> —**Hikaru, Revenge Road**

The notion that a man is so in love with his partner that to lose her would be a fate "worse than death" is common enough to be a trope in books, songs, movies, anime, comics, TV, and video games. Romantic heroes vow that "without you, life is not worth living" and "if I can't have you, no one will." Given the prevalence of these ideas, there is surprisingly little scholarship exploring the relationship between domestic violence (DV) perpetration, depression, and suicidality (Sesar, Šimic, & Dodaj, 2015). In fact it is only fairly recently that depression has been considered as a risk factor for perpetration of lethal DV. Depression and suicidality are not included in many DV risk assessment instruments (Hilton, Harris, Rice, Houghton, & Eke, 2008), and there is uneven appreciation in the DV, justice, and mental health fields of the importance of these factors as they relate to DV. This chapter will shed light on this important area of research, outlining the nature of depression and suicidality as risk factors for domestic homicide by male perpetrators. Considerations relevant to the mental health of female perpetrators of DV homicide are outlined in Chapter 12, Future directions on promoting domestic homicide prevention in diverse populations.

Preventing Domestic Homicides. DOI: https://doi.org/10.1016/B978-0-12-819463-8.00007-1

Depression and suicidality in perpetrators of domestic homicide

Perpetrator depression and suicidality emerged as concerns in the early 1990s from DV death/fatality review processes (Johnson, Lutz, & Websdale, 1999). This was, in part, due to the recognition that homicide—suicide, although a rare crime, is relatively common in the context of domestic homicides (Flynn et al., 2009; Zeppegno et al., 2019). For example, considering homicides in Sweden between 1990 and 1999, Belfrage and Rying (2004) found that rates of suicide were four times higher following domestic homicides as compared to homicides not committed in the context of DV. Examining data from the supplemental homicide survey in Canada, Brennan and Boyce (2013) reported that between 2001 and 2011, there were 344 murder—suicides in Canada, resulting in the deaths of 419 victims and 344 accused. Ninety-five percent of those accused were male and, in 77% of these incidents, at least one of the victims was related to the accused, most often a current or former spouse. Analyzing data from the National Violent Death Reporting System in the United States, Velopulos, Carmichael, Zakrison, and Crandall (2019) reported that between the years 2003 and 2015, of the 6131 domestic homicides involving opposite sex partners, homicide—suicides occurred in 47% of the cases involving a female victim and a male suspect (which made up the majority of cases) and 12% of cases involving a female perpetrator and a male victim. Finally using data compiled from detailed media, court and statistical documents in Canada between 2010 and 2015, of the 442 accused domestic homicide perpetrators, 21% died by suicide and another 7% attempted suicide following the homicide (Dawson et al., 2018).

Domestic violence death review committee (DVDRC) work has also highlighted that both suicidal ideation and depression are fairly commonly identified in retrospect in perpetrators of domestic homicide, even when such cases do not involve suicide or attempted suicide (Aldridge & Browne, 2003; Dawson & Piscitelli, 2017). For example, based on a review of 188 cases of domestic homicide recorded in England and Wales between April 2011 and March 2013, Bridger, Strang, Parkinson, and Sherman (2017) reported high rates of depression, with 40% of the male offenders known by someone, though not often by police, as suffering from suicidal ideation, self-harm, or as attempting suicide.

Complexities in examining the role of depression in perpetrators of domestic violence

Given the relatively high prevalence of homicide–suicide in DV-related killings and the recognition of depression and suicidality in DVDRCs, why have these factors not figured more prominently in past discussions of the characteristics, predictors, risk assessment, and risk management of DV perpetrators? There are three broader contextual reasons for the lack of attention to depression and suicidality in DV perpetrators, all of which are worth exploring due to their intersections with recommendations for change.

Mental health and homicide in police and criminal data

A first reason that the association between depression, suicidality, and domestic homicide has been underexamined has to do with how mental health is considered within police data and in criminal justice models of offending and homicide. In beginning this discussion, it is important to acknowledge that the intersection between policing/justice and mental health is complex and surfaces many ethical dilemmas and concerns including those around responsibility for crimes (i.e., at what point should a mentally ill offender be deemed not guilty for reasons of insanity), privacy of information (i.e., how much personal medical information should be shared with and recorded by police), discrimination against mentally ill people by police and within the justice system, along with many other issues (e.g., see special issue edited by Lurigio & Watson, 2010). Despite the attention to mental illness in these debates, offender mental health is generally absent from theories and models of crime and criminal recidivism (Link, Ward, & Stansfield, 2019). Internalizing/affective mental health problems (including depression, post-traumatic stress disorder, anxiety, phobias) are broadly discounted as criminogenic needs and dynamic risk factors, at least for male offenders, in most major theories of criminal behavior (Basto-Pereira, Comecanha, Ribeiro, & Maia, 2015). For example, the Risk, Needs, Responsivity model, which has been the predominant model of offender rehabilitation for many years, deems internalizing mental health problems to be unimportant to understanding risk for recidivism and inappropriate targets for intervention aimed at reducing reoffending (Bonta & Andrews, 2007; Campbell, French, & Gendreau, 2009; Polaschek, 2012). In theories of the development of delinquency, when internalizing problems are considered, they are often conceptualized as protective against offending, at least among males (Loeber, Stouthamer-Loeber, & White, 1999; Wibbelink, Hoeve, Stams, & Oort, 2017). A significant body of prospective research supports these theories showing either null or negative associations between depression (and other mood disorders) and offending/reoffending (i.e., the presence of depression predicts less criminal behavior; Bonta, Blais, & Wilson, 2014; Grann, Danesh, & Fazel, 2008; Hein et al., 2017; Ritakallio et al., 2008).

Mental illness has figured more prominently as a potential risk factor in studies of homicide. Studies in high-income countries exploring the possible connections between mental health and homicide (not specific to DV) generally find that between 8% and 23% of all homicide perpetrators are mentally ill at the time of the offense, suggesting that although the overall number of homicides perpetrated by those with serious mental illnesses is low, there is an association between serious mental illness and homicide (Bridger et al., 2017; Dawson & Piscitelli, 2017; Liem & Koenraadt, 2008; Minero, Barker, & Bedford, 2017; Rosenbaum & Bennett, 1986; Statistics Canada, 2015; Taylor & Gunn, 1999). Mental illnesses most consistently associated with homicide are schizophrenia and other psychotic disorders, with studies estimating a 7- to 20-fold increase in risk of homicide perpetration among persons with schizophrenia over the general population (Fazel, Gulati, Linsell, Geddes, & Grann, 2009; Wallace et al., 1998). Although mental illnesses featuring psychosis show the strongest association to homicide overall, there is some evidence that, within perpetrators of domestic homicide, affective disorders are more common. In one of the strongest studies in this area, Oram, Flynn, Shaw, Appleby, and Howard (2013) linked data across the UK Home Office Police National Computer and the National Confidential Inquiry into Suicide and Homicide by People with Mental Illness on 1180 convicted perpetrators of domestic homicide (i.e., homicide—suicide cases were not included). These researchers found depression to be present in 13% of perpetrators at the time of the offense, symptoms of psychosis to be present in 7% of cases, and any mental illness (excluding those related to substance use) to be present in 20% of offenders. Thus, although mental illnesses that include features of psychosis may be more strongly associated to homicide in general, there appear to be higher rates of affective disorders in the specific subset of homicides against intimate partners and family members.

Recognition of domestic violence within mental health services

Within the study of mental health, depression, and suicide are the focus of innumerable studies exploring predictors, impacts, risk assessment tools and strategies, prevention and intervention initiatives, stigma, etc. Very few of these studies explore suicidality or depression as a potential risk to others. To some extent, this makes sense—instances of homicide–suicide are relatively rare when considered against the rate of suicide overall (McPhedran et al., 2018). However, the degree of neglect of DV within the study of depression and suicidality goes beyond what might be expected from the data alone, reflecting broader bifurcation of the fields of mental health and DV (Mason, Wolf, O'Rinn, & Ene, 2017; Oram, Khalifeh, & Howard, 2017). It is still the case that many of the core services for DV survivors, DV perpetrators, and for children who have been exposed to DV are found outside of traditional mental health services. Better connections need to be made between these fields in general and in the study of depression and suicidality in particular.

This being said, there are a handful of researchers crossing fields to explore similarities and differences between homicides that do and do not involve suicide (e.g., Banks, Crandall, Sklar, & Bauer, 2008; Bourget, Gagne, & Whitehurst, 2010; Dobash, Dobash, Cavanagh, & Lewis, 2004; Liem, Barber, Markwalder, Killias, & Nieuwbeerta, 2010). On the basis of a systematic review and metaanalysis of 27 studies, Panczak et al. (2013) found that perpetrators of domestic homicide–suicide were more likely to be male, older, and married or formerly married than perpetrators of homicide or those who died from suicide. Perpetrators of homicide–suicide were less likely than simple homicide perpetrators to be under the influence of alcohol, to be unemployed, and to have a known history of DV perpetration and less likely than those who committed suicide to have a previous suicide attempt. On the basis of these results, Panczak suggested that homicide–suicide may need to be understood as distinct from both simple homicides and suicides in characteristics and risk factors. Other studies, and particularly those that have limited their comparisons to homicide and homicide–suicide in the context of DV, have generally confirmed these differences. Vatnar, Friestad, and Bjørkly (2019), for example, reviewed 177 domestic homicides in Norway between 1990 and 2012. They concluded that perpetrators of domestic homicide—suicide were less socially marginalized (i.e., older, more often employed, married or common-law, less likely to have a criminal history) than domestic homicide perpetrators but did not differ in terms of DV history and often had similar motives. In one of the only studies to examine depression, as opposed to suicidality, Oliver and Jaffe (2018) compared 30 domestic homicide cases in which there was no history of depression and/or substance use in the perpetrator, 28 in which there was evidence that the perpetrator was depressed, 15 with only substance abuse, and 13 perpetrators with comorbid depression and substance abuse. Results found that perpetrators with comorbid mental health and substance use problems tended to have a greater number of risk factors and were involved with more service providers than men without such problems; however, beyond this, few substantive differences were noted for the depressed only group compared to the other three beyond what might be expected (i.e., perpetrators with depression were more likely to have threatened suicide in the past). Finally Salari and Sillito (2016) examined the intention behind the murders in cases of domestic homicide and domestic homicide—suicide, particularly whether the primary intent behind homicide—suicides was suicide or homicide. They found that among younger and middle-aged perpetrators, the majority (74%—80%) had primary homicidal intentions, whereas perpetrators in the elder group (60 years and up) had primary suicidal intentions (63%). Perpetrators whose primary intention was homicide typically had a history of DV, threatened the victim, isolated the victim, exerted power and control, stalked and/or kidnaped the victim, had a protective order or the victim feared for their safety, committed crimes against the victim, inflicted severe wounds during the homicide, and killed others in addition to their (former) partner. Perpetrators with a primary suicidal intention typically exhibited depressive symptomatology that included sad or depressed mood, previous suicide attempts, and/or ideation. They also experienced financial trouble, turmoil, confusion, as well as tended to have victims who were unaware of impending danger. Salari and Sillito (2016) also noted that risk of harm tended to be less obvious in cases where suicide was the primary intention, emphasizing the need for professionals to be better trained to question both homicidal and suicidal intentions directly.

In summary in the handful of studies that have compared domestic homicide—suicide to domestic homicide, it has been found that homicide–suicide perpetrators tend to be older, less socially disadvantaged, and less likely to have involvement with the criminal justice system, emphasizing the importance of the mental health system in recognizing and managing domestic homicide risk.

Association of mental health with domestic violence offending

A final deterrence to recognizing the association between depression, suicidality, and DV lethality risk comes from the study of the characteristics of men who abuse and assault their partners and is, to a fairly large extent, a legacy of early work in the field. In the 1970s when research began in earnest on DV and its impacts, there was a need to wrestle the understanding of abuse perpetration away from solely individually based, psychopathological explanations to theories rooted in patriarchal power structures and social acceptance of violence against women. Intervention programs for abusers had a significant resocialization component, and a strong focus on personal accountability, emphasizing that the men who perpetrate violence in their intimate relationships do so because they choose to and because they can get away with it (Austin & Dankwort, 1999; Gondolf, 2015). In this early work there was a strong reaction against explanations of DV perpetration that were seen as potentially mitigating personal responsibility for abuse, including those that highlighted mental health and substance use difficulties (e.g., Bennett & Piet, 1999). Around the same time, women's advocates, abuse survivors, and leaders in intervention for abusive men were working to raise awareness of patterns of psychological abuse and the fact that men sometimes used threats of suicide as a control tactic and a means of keeping their partners from leaving the relationship (Healey, Smith, & O'Sullivan, 1999; Shepard & Campbell, 1992). Such work was not meant to discard the potential risk of suicidality; rather, it was viewed as necessary to raise awareness that the presentation of domestically violent men (mostly as victims needing professionals to help their "bad" partners) seldom matched the reality of the abuse they were perpetrating (Logan, 2017; Myhill & Hohl, 2016).

As understanding of DV grew, more complex and multifaceted theories and models of DV perpetration emerged that recognized the interplay of societal, family of origin, individual, and situational risk factors for abuse perpetration including substance use, personality disorders, and psychological distress (Capaldi, Knoble, Shortt, & Kim, 2012; Smith Slep, Foran, & Heyman, 2014). However, even within these models, research has confirmed that, although rates of mental health problems are higher than population averages, a majority of men who perpetrate DV do not have diagnosable mental health illnesses (Gondolf, 1999; Shorey, Febres, Brasfield, & Stuart, 2012). Moreover, with the exception of substance abuse, mental health variables do not consistently predict or moderate intervention outcome (i.e., depressed or suicidal perpetrators do not do consistently worse in intervention than men who are not depressed or suicidal) (Grann & Wedin, 2002; Huss & Ralston, 2008). This being said, there is consistent evidence for a weak to moderate effect for depression as a risk factor for men's perpetration of DV (Fleming et al., 2015; Pan, Neidig, & O'Leary, 1994 and a metaanalytic review by Spencer, Cafferky, & Stith, 2016). Additionally the relationship between depression and abuse seems to be stronger when more severe DV perpetration is considered. Birkley and Eckhardt (2015), for example, found support for a moderate effect of depression and other internalizing negative emotions on DV perpetration and a moderator effect for DV severity such that men (and women) who perpetrated moderate to severe DV reported higher levels of negative emotion than those who reported low to moderate DV. Similarly in Schumacher, Feldbau-Kohn, Slep, and Heyman's (2001) metaanalytic review, male perpetrators of severe DV were more likely to exhibit depressive symptomatology than perpetrators of less severe abuse. Research such as this has prompted what are now robust conversations about how to best address both DV perpetration and the mental health needs of men who abuse their partners (Gilchrist, Radcliffe, McMurran, & Gilchrist, 2015; Gondolf, 2009).

Recommendations for addressing depression and suicidality as risk factors for domestic violence homicide

Summarizing from the earlier discussion, DVDRCs have played a critical role in highlighting the association between depression, suicidality, and lethal DV. Criminologist, mental health professionals, and intervention services for DV are now working to integrate knowledge of this association into research, policy, and practice. Recommendations have been made for improvements in practice across fields. Within the criminal justice system, it has been recommended that standardized DV risk assessments include items tapping depression and suicidality in perpetrators of DV. DVDRC's have also recommended that when risk for lethality is high (for any reason including suicidality), police and other actors within the criminal justice system increase vigilance and contribute to multiagency efforts to manage risk. Ongoing education for all police service personnel on DV, suicide, and mental health issues has been emphasized. It has also been recommended that specialist DV services, including those associated with the criminal justice system, include questions on their crisis line, intake, and safety planning forms to ensure that advocates routinely ask about abusers' suicidal attempts or threats and safety plan accordingly.

An extensive set of recommendations have also been advanced for health services providers. Family doctors and/or other general health practitioners (e.g., naturopathic doctors, nurses) are frequently in contact with domestic homicide perpetrators around mental health issues in the months prior to the homicide (Coben & Friedman, 2002). Flynn, Gask, Appleby, and Shaw (2016), for example, found that 77% of domestic homicide–suicide perpetrators were in contact with a general practitioner within the year of the murder, 42% of whom mentioned psychological problems. Recognizing these contacts as a potential opportunity to prevent homicides, DVDRCs have recommended that professional colleges and accreditation bodies for these groups (e.g., College of Physicians, Nurses, Naturopathic Doctors) develop and promote educational programs for new and practicing professionals that highlight the warning signs and dynamics of DV and the potential for lethality, especially in patients who have a history of depression, substance abuse, report problems, or conflict in their relationship and/or whose relationships are dissolving. It has been further recommended that training include the importance of follow-up with victims of DV to ensure that they received the proper information and guidance.

Mental health and allied health professionals working directly with patients presenting with mental health concerns including practitioners in medicine, nursing, social work, psychology, psychiatry, addictions, and others are the focus of additional recommendations. These professionals are also fairly often in contact with the perpetrators of domestic homicide in the months prior to the offense (Campbell, Glass, Sharps, Laughon, & Bloom, 2007). Oram et al. (2013), for example, found that, in a population-based study, 25% of domestic homicide perpetrators had previous contact with mental health services within their lifetime and 15% had contact in the year leading up to the homicide. It has been recommended that training for all mental health professionals includes information on the link between depression, suicidal ideation, and domestic homicide and that routine screening for DV be implemented in depressed and suicidal clients in general mental health settings. Such a change would also require that mental health professionals become skilled in safety planning with potential victims, risk management with potential perpetrators, and have the capacity to recognize how abusers might use suicidal threats as a tactic of control. DVDRCs have recommended greater collaboration between DV specialist and mental health service providers in general, and have specifically called for joint work to establish clear guidelines regarding when the combination of DV and suicidal threats signals clear danger to others and triggers providers' duty to warn potential victims.

Finally DVDRCs have recommended general public education campaigns for family members, friends, and workplaces around the importance of DV risk factors, including the potentially lethal combination of DV history, separation, depression, and suicidal or homicidal thoughts or threats. General education should also have the aim of overcoming cultural barriers and the feelings of shame and stigma related to mental health issues.

In the following, two cases of DV homicide are presented in which perpetrator mental health was a known concern. In the first case, health and mental health practitioners were among the only professionals in a position to recognize DV homicide risk. In the second case, the complexities of working across criminal justice and mental health services are illustrated.

Edmonton, Alberta, Canada: the case of Jeanne Cathleen Heard

Many of the details outlined in this case can be retrieved from: https://open.alberta.ca/dataset/94fb907b-beb2-4320-aecf-cb99227e0df2/resource/38d4f695-8bce-4856-a13c-fd5bdfcb51c5/download/2015-fatality-report-lagolindo.pdf.

Ms. Jeanne Cathleen Heard was 47 years old when she was murdered by Mr. Dwayne Richard Poirier (46 years old). Ms. Heard and Mr. Poirier started a relationship in 2006 and moved in together in 2007. Problems started shortly afterward. Over the course of their relationship, both Ms. Heard and Mr. Poirier had taken out various emergency protection orders against one another. They were also both involved with mental health services. In June 2010 Ms. Heard died as a result of strangulation. It is speculated that after strangling Ms. Heard, Mr. Poirier removed the gas cap from the natural gas line in their home. Gas then leaked into the home and some electrical or fire source ignited the house into a bomb. The resulting house explosion was ruled a homicide–suicide. Mr. Poirier was killed along with two neighbors. The explosion also caused over 3.5 million dollars in damage to the neighborhood.

Ms. Heard had a significant history of contact with mental health professionals. Over the course of their relationship, she had been seen by mental health professionals due to childhood trauma and was involved in individual and group therapy terminating about 2 years prior to her death. She was diagnosed with depression and was given medication to help alleviate the symptoms. Ms. Heard was also referred to a mental health professional to assist her in leaving the violent relationship with Mr. Poirier. However, neither her family physician nor the mental health professional documented that Ms. Heard's safety was compromised in the relationship. In the last appointment with her family physician during the month of her murder she told them that "he's gotten counselling, I've gotten counselling—it's okay."

Mr. Poirier had both mental and physical health concerns and had been connected with his family physician, mental health professionals, and with a mental health clinic. He battled anxiety, depression, and suicidal ideation. His family physician and the mental health professionals working with him knew about his volatile relationship with Ms. Heard. The last appointment with his physician was in the month before the homicide–suicide occurred. The physician noted that Mr. Poirier's mental health difficulties were being managed. Mr. Poirier was also connected with a psychiatrist who carried out safety and security planning with him to keep him safe from suicide but did not, as far as is recorded, consider or address the possibility of homicide.

A suicide note was written by Mr. Poirier and was emailed to a social worker who he had been connected with a year prior. The note was written moments before his death and described his remorse at having killed Ms. Heard. He stated that her killing occurred after a fight between the couple erupted over deciding to separate and divide their property.

Themes and recommendations

Mental health is a primary theme within this case, as both the victim and perpetrator were struggling with mental health concerns. As exemplified, medical and mental health professionals failed to recognize risk associated with DV and did not engage in either safety planning with Ms. Heard or risk management with Mr. Poirier around such risks. Neither the psychiatrist who carried out safety and security planning with Mr. Poirier nor the mental health professionals working with him connected his suicidality with risk to Ms. Heard. Similarly the mental and medical health professionals working with Ms. Heard around the time she was separating from Mr. Poirier failed to recognize risk and initiate safety planning. With better recognition of the association of domestic homicide to separation, depression, and suicidality, professionals involved may have been able to more accurately assess and manage Mr. Poirier's risk and work with Ms. Heard to ensure that she had a strong protection plan in place while she was separating from Mr. Poirier. Collaborative health teams that include medical and mental health professionals and professionals with expertise in DV, with the ability to openly share information, may be helpful in closing these gaps and preventing future domestic homicides.

There are a number of initiatives currently being pursued to improve the way in which medical and mental health professionals recognize and respond to DV. One example is an initiative through the Oklahoma Domestic Violence Fatality Review Board that has resulted in a specialized Mental Health and Domestic Violence committee that has brought awareness to the relationship between mental health, suicidality, and DV (Oklahoma Domestic Violence Fatality Review Board, 2014). This initiative has also established DV liaison positions within mental health and substance abuse agencies across the state. The development of committees such as this one could assist in the unification of professionals from across sectors and prompt collaborative case management in situations like Ms. Heard and Mr. Poirier's.

In the case of Ms. Heard, police were also involved as there had been numerous emergency protective orders executed between Mr. Poirier and Ms. Heard. Despite the multiple occasions when police would have been aware of the violence in their relationship, only one standardized DV risk assessment had ever been completed in this case. Thus a main recommendation from the public fatality inquiry into this case was the mandatory completion of such tools in every DV incident so that officers can discern cases that are at a high level of risk for future violence and put into place integrated risk management.

Finally this case is yet another example of the fact that separation can be a time when violence increases and risk for lethal victimization escalates. Professionals, including physicians and police officers, should inform victims that they may be at more risk when attempting to leave their violent partner. This important risk does not seem to have been factored in, or addressed, by mental health professionals working with either Ms. Heard or Mr. Poirier. Risks and stresses associated with separation, had they been considered, may have assisted in the implementation of strategies to keep Ms. Heard safe and prevent Mr. Poirier's death.

Southend-on-Sea, Essex, England: the case of Jeannette Goodwin

Many of the details outlined in this case can be retrieved from: https://www.safeguardingsouthend.co.uk/pdfs/domestic%20homicide/DHR_Full_Report_of_AB_and_YZ_Feb_2014.pdf.

Ms. Jeannette Goodwin was a 47-year-old woman from Southend who was murdered by her expartner, Mr. Martin Bunch, 44 years old, on July 24, 2011. Ms. Goodwin was a wife and a mother to three children, one of whom lived with her part-time. Mr. Bunch had previously been married for 22 years and was a father to three children. Ms. Goodwin and Mr. Bunch had known each other for eight years and an affair commenced between them in mid-2010. They did not live together, and Mr. Bunch's permanent address was unclear at the time of the murder. Ms. Goodwin called off the affair in early 2011 which initiated a string of DV incidents. Specifically Ms. Goodwin had contacted police a total of seven times following a variety of stalking and violent behaviors which included abusive texts, phone calls, and physical abuse. The police arrested Mr. Bunch several times on charges of harassment and battery and eventually installed panic alarms in Ms. Goodwin's home for safety. Ms. Goodwin was fearful about making a statement to police due to potential retaliation from Mr. Bunch; however, she ultimately submitted a witness statement. Ms. Goodwin initiated further security features on her home through what is known as a sanctuary scheme, and this was completed in the month before her death. Ms. Goodwin had been connected with agencies in her community, including DV victim support.

Mr. Bunch also had considerable contact with service providers prior to the murder of Ms. Goodwin. Between 1986 and 2011, Mr. Bunch had acquired a total of 79 convictions, including multiple offenses against persons and offenses against court, police, and prison staff. He had a long history of struggling with anger, anxiety, suicidality, depression, and alcohol abuse. As early as 2008, he had received a community order that included alcohol treatment and fines. He also received referrals to services to address substance on his own accord through his general practitioner. Although Mr. Bunch did not successfully complete court-ordered intervention for drinking, he did access and complete community-based substance abuse services to which he was referred by his general practitioner. Most of these services focused solely on his abuse of alcohol and were of short duration. There was no evidence of screening, discussion, or concern about DV from community drug and alcohol services.

Mr. Bunch had also been in contact with services due to concerns about suicidality. In March of 2011, Mr. Bunch presented at emergency having taken an overdose of alcohol and tablets. He was assessed by a psychiatric nurse, but no disorders or concerns about DV or ongoing risk of self-harm were noted. In early June 2011 police received a report that Mr. Bunch was threatening to harm himself and others. He was found having injected tablets and attempts were made to have him assessed by a criminal justice psychiatrist mental health specialist. In mid-June he was seen by a consultant at a local hospital where he was judged to be dysphoric, angry, and anxious with mild-to-moderate depression. No suicidal thoughts were noted, no DV assessment was undertaken, and Mr. Bunch was discharged to the care of his general practitioner. In the weeks before the murder, Mr. Bunch's family had also connected him with mental health services to provide him with assistance for both his depression and alcohol abuse. On the day of her murder, Ms. Goodwin had contacted police stating that she was scared for her safety after Mr. Bunch was found on her property in breach of his bail conditions. Police did not immediately dispatch a unit to respond to this call. Later that day, Ms. Goodwin activated her panic alarm system, which resulted in police attending her home and finding her dead from multiple stab wounds. Mr. Bunch has since received a life sentence.

Themes and recommendations

In reviewing this case, there are a variety of themes and recommendations that arise. Some considerations are relevant to the role of the criminal justice system and apply across cases, regardless of possible intersections with mental health. These include the need for consistent standardized risk assessment measures, timely response to high-risk situations, appropriate consideration of past breaches in sentencing, and the importance of sharing information. In retrospective review, it was noted that Mr. Bunch had not paid any of his previous fines or completed unpaid work orders associated with his sentences. He did not show up for all of his court dates that prevented the initiation of a full risk assessment by Essex Probation. Mr. Bunch breached bail conditions numerous times for numerous offences, including contacting Ms. Goodwin, staying out past curfew, and removing a monitoring tag. However, bail was continuously granted on subsequent offences, and there was a lack of integrated follow-up for these various offenses. There is a need for courts and probation to take into account past failures to comply with authority when deciding on the result of subsequent hearings and risk management plans for domestic offenders. Although this recommendation applies to all cases, such complications (i.e., missed appointments, multiple bail violations) may be particularly likely to arise in the context of cases where perpetrators are also suffering from addiction and/or mental health problems and are poorly functioning overall.

Ms. Goodwin's death also illustrates the many gaps in risk management between the criminal justice and mental health systems. Within the mental health system, Mr. Bunch's depression, drinking, and suicidal tendencies were seen in isolation and not connected to his criminal history and risk to Ms. Goodwin. Mr. Bunch's general practitioner was the main health provider dealing with his condition, which given the nature and severity of risk, is problematic. A major missed opportunity was the provision of mental health services by a coordinating mental health practitioner trained in DV. This type of professional could have assisted in the mitigation of risk by accurately assessing the improvement or worsening of Mr. Bunch's condition and communicating this information to Ms. Goodwin and other professionals involved. The Essex mental health trust oversaw the mental health and substance abuse agencies in this case. They have since implemented a DV policy and mandatory DV training for their staff members.

Finally it is worth reflecting on Mr. Bunch's possible experiences accessing help. It has been well-established help-seeking in general is more of a problem for men than women, especially those who endorse strongly masculine norms (Seidler, Dawes, Rice, Oliffe, & Dhillon, 2016; Yousaf, Grunfeld, & Hunter, 2015).

Defying these patterns, Mr. Bunch had, on numerous occasions, sought out help for his difficulties, but with seemingly limited success. He was discharged from alcohol treatment and was often only able to access treatment on a short-term basis. Unfortunately this is not atypical of the response of the mental health system to men who struggle with DV alongside mental health and substance use problems. Studies of domestically violent men who try to reach out for services often find that they are treated with a lack of empathy by service providers who are sometimes afraid to engage and may treat them with high levels of negative judgment (Lipsky, Caetano, & Roy-Byrne, 2011; Rose et al., 2011). Thus even when men's mental health needs are recognized and/or they have reached out for help, having a history of perpetrating DV may act as an additional barrier to accessing intervention.

General discussion and implications

DV homicide risk associated with perpetrator depression and suicidality need to be more broadly recognized within criminal justice, health, mental health, and DV services. In the cases reviewed in this chapter, the perpetrators had contact with medical and mental health providers or programs in their communities who did not recognize DV-related risks. General and specialized mental health professionals should be able to recognize and address risks associated with DV and mental health and/or relationship concerns. Professional training on this topic is needed for practicing service providers, and education curricula for new professionals needs to be updated to include provisions for assessment and management risk for domestic homicide. Women who present with a history of DV and concern about the mental health of their partners/expartners need to be taken seriously. Men who present with relationship concerns, obsessive thoughts, depression, and suicidality need to be properly assessed for DV risks. General mental health service providers need to make their services more accessible and responsive to those who have been victims and perpetrators of DV. Greater collaboration is also needed across mental health, justice, and DV specialist services so that those cases presenting as highly concerning can be collaboratively managed. The intersections between mental health and domestic homicide also need to be more deeply examined in research. Most existing research on depression, suicidality, and DV perpetration is retrospective or correlational: these variables need to be examined prospectively as predictors of subsequent domestic violent offending. It is also important to examine whether reductions in depression create corresponding reductions in risk for perpetrating DV and on the conditions under which suicidality and homicidality are most likely to be related.

Finally it is important to acknowledge that there are many questions about the intersection of mental health and DV that have not been covered in this chapter. Herein the focus was on depression and suicidality in male perpetrators of domestic homicide. For nonlethal DV perpetration, another area of mental health plays an important role—substance abuse. The many and varied intersection of substance abuse and DV perpetration were not covered in this chapter (however see Van Dorn, Volavka, & Johnson, 2012). We also did not explore the potentially additive concerns that might exist for individuals with DV risk factors and severe mental illnesses such as disorders that include delusional symptoms. There has been very little work done in this area, though from the extant literature, it may be hypothesized that serious mental illness would add to the risk of serious and potentially lethal DV perpetration (Lipsky et al., 2011). Finally this chapter did not discuss female perpetrators of homicide, which is a population in which affective disorders, including depression, are also known to be more prevalent and whose victims are most likely to be children or other family members (Golenkov, Large, Nielssen, & Tsymbalova, 2016; Masle, Goreta, & Jukić, 2000; Schanda et al., 2004).

In summary, this chapter underscores the importance of mental health to DV lethality risk. It emphasizes the necessity of collaboration among service providers to address both violence-specific and mental health-specific concerns in perpetrators of DV so that perpetrator mental health concerns are effectively managed and victims are better protected.

References

Aldridge, M. L., & Browne, K. D. (2003). Perpetrators of spousal homicide: A review. *Trauma, Violence & Abuse, 4,* 265–276.

Austin, J. B., & Dankwort, J. (1999). Standards for batterer programs: A review and analysis. *Journal of Interpersonal Violence, 14,* 152–168.

Banks, L., Crandall, C., Sklar, D., & Bauer, M. (2008). A comparison of intimate partner homicide to intimate partner homicide-suicide: One hundred and twenty-four New Mexico cases. *Violence Against Women, 14,* 1065–1078.

Basto-Pereira, M., Comecanha, R., Ribeiro, S., & Maia, A. (2015). Long-term predictors of crime desistance in juvenile delinquents: A systematic review of longitudinal studies. *Aggression and Violent Behavior, 25,* 332–342.

Belfrage, H., & Rying, M. (2004). Characteristics of spousal homicide perpetrators: A study of all cases of spousal homicide in Sweden 1990-1999. *Criminal Behaviour and Mental Health, 14,* 121–133.

Bennett, L., & Piet, M. (1999). Standards for batterer intervention programs: In whose interest? *Violence Against Women, 5,* 6–24.

Birkley, E. L., & Eckhardt, C. I. (2015). Anger, hostility, internalizing negative emotions, and intimate partner violence perpetration: A meta-analytic review. *Clinical Psychology Review, 37,* 40–56.

Bonta, J., & Andrews, D. A. (2007). Risk-need-responsivity model for offender assessment and rehabilitation. *Rehabilitation, 6,* 1–22.

Bonta, J., Blais, J., & Wilson, H. A. (2014). A theoretically informed meta-analysis of the risk for general and violent recidivism for mentally disordered offenders. *Aggression and Violent Behavior, 19,* 278–287.

Bourget, D., Gagne, P., & Whitehurst, L. (2010). Domestic homicide and homicide-suicide: The older offender. *The Journal of the American Academy of Psychiatry and the Law, 38,* 305–311.

Brennan, S. & Boyce, J. (2013). Section 2: Family-related murder-suicides. *Juristat.* Retrieved from <https://www150.statcan.gc.ca/n1/pub/85-002-x/2013001/article/11805/11805-2-eng.htm>.

Bridger, E., Strang, H., Parkinson, J., & Sherman, L. W. (2017). Intimate partner homicide in England and Wales 2011-2013: Pathways to prediction from multi-agency domestic homicide reviews. *Cambridge Journal of Evidence-Based Policing, 1,* 93–104.

Campbell, J. C., Glass, N., Sharps, P. W., Laughon, K., & Bloom, T. (2007). Intimate partner homicide: Review and implications of research and policy. *Trauma, Violence & Abuse, 8,* 246–269.

Campbell, M. A., French, S., & Gendreau, P. (2009). The prediction of violence in adult offenders: A meta-analytic comparison of instruments and methods of assessment. *Criminal Justice and Behavior, 36,* 567–590.

Capaldi, D. M., Knoble, N. B., Shortt, J. W., & Kim, H. K. (2012). A systematic review of risk factors for intimate partner violence. *Partner Abuse, 3,* 231–280.

Coben, J. H., & Friedman, D. I. (2002). Health care use by perpetrators of domestic violence. *The Journal of Emergency Medicine, 22,* 313–317.

Dawson, M., & Piscitelli, A. (2017). Risk factors in domestic homicides: Identifying common clusters in the Canadian context. *Journal of Interpersonal Violence.* Available from https://doi.org/10.1177/0886260517729404.

Dawson, M., Sutton, D., Jaffe, P., Straatman, A., Poon, J., Gosse, M., Peters, O. & Sandhu, G. (2018). *One is too many: Trends and patterns in domestic homicides in Canada 2010-2015. Canadian Domestic Homicide Prevention Initiative with Vulnerable Populations.* Retrieved July 2, 2019 from <http://cdhpi.ca/sites/cdhpi.ca/files/CDHPI-REPORTRV.pdf>.

Dobash, R. E., Dobash, R. P., Cavanagh, K., & Lewis, R. (2004). Not an ordinary killer - Just an ordinary guy: When men murder an intimate woman partner. *Violence Against Women, 10,* 577–605.

Fazel, S., Gulati, G., Linsell, L., Geddes, J. R., & Grann, M. (2009). Schizophrenia and violence: Systematic review and meta-analysis. *PLoS Medicine, 6*(8), e1000120.

Fleming, P. J., McCleary-Sills, J., Morton, M., Levtov, R., Heilman, B., & Barker, G. (2015). Risk factors for men's lifetime perpetration of physical violence against intimate partners: Results from the international men and gender equality survey (IMAGES) in eight countries. *PLoS One, 10*(3), e0118639.

Flynn, S., Gask, L., Appleby, L., & Shaw, J. (2016). Homicide—suicide and the role of mental disorder: A national consecutive case series. *Social Psychiatry and Psychiatric Epidemiology, 51*, 877–884.

Flynn, S., Swinson, N., While, D., Hunt, I. M., Roscoe, A., Rodway, C., ... Shaw, J. (2009). Homicide followed by suicide: A cross-sectional study. *The Journal of Forensic Psychiatry & Psychology, 20*, 306–321.

Gilchrist, G., Radcliffe, P., McMurran, M., & Gilchrist, L. (2015). The need for evidence-based responses to address intimate partner violence perpetration among male substance misusers. *Criminal Behaviour & Mental Health, 25*, 233–238.

Golenkov, A., Large, M., Nielssen, O., & Tsymbalova, A. (2016). Homicide and mental disorder in a region with a high homicide rate. *Asian Journal of Psychiatry, 23*, 87–92.

Gondolf, E. W. (1999). MCMI results for batterer program participants in four cities: Less "pathological" than expected. *Journal of Family Violence, 14*, 1–17.

Gondolf, E. W. (2009). Implementing mental health treatment for batterer program participants: Interagency breakdowns and underlying issues. *Violence Against Women, 15*, 638–655.

Gondolf, E. W. (2015). *Gender-based perspectives on batterer programs: Program leaders on history, approach, research, and development.* Lexington Books.

Grann, M., Danesh, J., & Fazel, S. (2008). The association between psychiatric diagnosis and violent re-offending in adult offenders in the community. *BMC Psychiatry, 8*, 92.

Grann, M., & Wedin, I. (2002). Risk factors for recidivism among spousal assault and spousal homicide offenders. *Psychology, Crime and Law, 8*, 5–23.

Healey, K., Smith, C., & O'Sullivan, C. (1999). *Batterer intervention: Program approaches and criminal justice strategies.* DIANE Publishing.

Hein, S., Barbot, B., Square, A., Chapman, J., Geib, C. F., & Grigorenko, E. L. (2017). Violent offending among juveniles: A 7-year longitudinal study of recidivism, desistance, and associations with mental health. *Law and Human Behavior, 41*, 273.

Hilton, N. Z., Harris, G. T., Rice, M. E., Houghton, R. E., & Eke, A. W. (2008). An in depth actuarial assessment for wife assault recidivism: The domestic violence risk appraisal guide. *Law and Human Behavior, 32*, 150–163.

Huss, M. T., & Ralston, A. (2008). Do batterer subtypes actually matter? Treatment completion, treatment response, and recidivism across a batterer typology. *Criminal Justice and Behavior, 35*, 710–724.

Johnson, J. A., Lutz, V. L., & Websdale, N. (1999). Death by intimacy: Risk factors for domestic violence. *Pace Law Review, 20*, 263.

Liem, M., Barber, C., Markwalder, N., Killias, M., & Nieuwbeerta, P. (2010). Homicide-suicide and other violent deaths: An international comparison. *Forensic Science International, 207*, 70–76.

Liem, M., & Koenraadt, F. (2008). Familicide: A comparison with spousal and child homicide by mentally disordered perpetrators. *Criminal Behaviour and Mental Health, 18*, 306–318.

Link, N. W., Ward, J. T., & Stansfield, R. (2019). Consequences of mental and physical health for reentry and recidivism: Toward a health-based model of desistance. *Criminology*, 1–30.

Lipsky, S., Caetano, R., & Roy-Byrne, P. (2011). Triple jeopardy: Impact of partner violence perpetration, mental health and substance use on perceived unmet need for mental health care among men. *Social Psychiatry and Psychiatric Epidemiology, 46*, 843–852.

Loeber, R., Stouthamer-Loeber, M., & White, H. R. (1999). Developmental aspects of delinquency and internalizing problems and their association with persistent juvenile substance use between ages 7 and 18. *Journal of Clinical Child Psychology, 28*, 322–332.

Logan, T. K. (2017). "If I can't have you nobody will": Explicit threats in the context of coercive control. *Violence and Victims, 32*, 126–140.

Lurigio, A. J., & Watson, A. C. (2010). The police and people with mental illness: New approaches to a longstanding problem. *Journal of Police Crisis Negotiations, 10*, 3–14.

Masle, L. M., Goreta, M., & Jukić, V. (2000). The comparison of forensic-psychiatric traits between female and male perpetrators of murder or attempted murder. *Collegium Antropologicum, 24*, 91–99.

Mason, R., Wolf, M., O'Rinn, S., & Ene, G. (2017). Making connections across silos: Intimate partner violence, mental health, and substance use. *BMC Women's Health, 17*, 29.

McPhedran, S., Eriksson, L., Mazerolle, P., De Leo, D., Johnson, H., & Wortley, R. (2018). Characteristics of homicide-suicide in Australia: A comparison with homicide-only and suicide-only cases. *Journal of Interpersonal Violence, 33*, 1805–1829.

Minero, V. A., Barker, E., & Bedford, R. (2017). Method of homicide and severe mental illness: A systematic review. *Aggression and Violent Behavior, 37*, 52–62.

Myhill, A., & Hohl, K. (2016). The "golden thread" coercive control and risk assessment for domestic violence. *Journal of Interpersonal Violence*. Available from https://doi.org/10.1177/0886260516675464.

Oklahoma Domestic Violence Fatality Review Board. (2014). Domestic violence homicide in Oklahoma: A report of the Oklahoma Domestic Violence Fatality Review Board 2014. Oklahoma City, OK.

Oliver, C. L., & Jaffe, P. G. (2018). Comorbid depression and substance abuse in domestic homicide: Missed opportunities in the assessment and management of mental illness in perpetrators. *Journal of Interpersonal Violence*. Available from https://doi.org/10.1177/0886260518815140.

Oram, S., Flynn, S. M., Shaw, J., Appleby, L., & Howard, L. M. (2013). Mental illness and domestic homicide: A population-based descriptive study. *Psychiatric Services, 64*(10), 1006–1011.

Oram, S., Khalifeh, H., & Howard, L. M. (2017). Violence against women and mental health. *The Lancet Psychiatry, 4*(2), 159–170.

Pan, H. S., Neidig, P. H., & O'Leary, K. D. (1994). Predicting mild and severe husband-to-wife physical aggression. *Journal of Consulting and Clinical Psychology, 62*(5), 975–981.

Panczak, R., Geissbuhler, M., Zwahlen, M., Killias, M., Tal, K., & Egger, M. (2013). Homicide-suicides compared to homicides and suicides: Systematic review and meta-analysis. *Forensic Science International, 233*, 28–36.

Polaschek, D. L. (2012). An appraisal of the risk-need-responsivity (RNR) model of offender rehabilitation and its application in correctional treatment. *Legal and Criminological Psychology, 17*, 1–17.

Ritakallio, M., Koivisto, A. M., von der Pahlen, B., Pelkonen, M., Marttunen, M., & Kaltiala-Heino, R. (2008). Continuity, comorbidity and longitudinal associations between depression and antisocial behavior in middle adolescence: A 2-year prospective follow-up study. *Journal of Adolescence, 31*, 355–370.

Rose, D., Trevillion, K., Woodall, A., Morgan, C., Feder, G., & Howard, L. (2011). Barriers and facilitators of disclosures of domestic violence by mental health service users: Qualitative study. *The British Journal of Psychiatry, 198*, 189–194.

Rosenbaum, M., & Bennett, B. (1986). Homicide and depression. *The American Journal of Psychiatry, 143,* 367–370.

Salari, S., & Sillito, C. L. F. (2016). Intimate partner homicide-suicide: Perpetrator primary intent across young, middle, and elder adult age categories. *Aggression and Violent Behavior, 26,* 26–34.

Schanda, H., Knecht, G., Schreinze, D., Stompe, T., Ortwein-Swoboda, G., & Waldhoer, T. (2004). Homicide and major mental disorders: A 25-year study. *Acta Psychiatrica Scandinavica, 110,* 98–107.

Schumacher, J. A., Feldbau-Kohn, S., Slep, A. M. S., & Heyman, R. E. (2001). Risk factors for male-to-female partner physical abuse. *Aggression and Violent Behavior, 6,* 281–352.

Seidler, Z. E., Dawes, A. J., Rice, S. M., Oliffe, J. L., & Dhillon, H. M. (2016). The role of masculinity in men's help-seeking for depression: A systematic review. *Clinical Psychology Review, 49,* 106–118.

Sesar, K., Šimic, N., & Dodaj, A. (2015). Differences in symptoms of depression, anxiety and stress between victims and perpetrators of intimate partner violence. *Journal of Sociology and Social Work, 3,* 63–72.

Shepard, M. F., & Campbell, J. A. (1992). The abusive behavior Inventory: A measure of psychological and physical abuse. *Journal of Interpersonal Violence, 7,* 291–305.

Shorey, R. C., Febres, J., Brasfield, H., & Stuart, G. L. (2012). The prevalence of mental health problems in men arrested for domestic violence. *Journal of Family Violence, 27,* 741–748.

Smith Slep, A. M., Foran, H. M., & Heyman, R. E. (2014). An ecological model of intimate partner violence perpetration at different levels of severity. *Journal of Family Psychology, 28,* 470.

Spencer, C., Cafferky, B., & Stith, S. M. (2016). Gender differences in risk markers for perpetration of physical partner violence: Results from a meta-analytic review. *Journal of Family Violence, 31,* 981–984.

Statistics Canada. (2015). Homicide in Canada, 2014. *Juristat, Statistics Canada.* Retrieved July 2, 2019 from <https://www150.statcan.gc.ca/n1/en/pub/85-002-x/2015001/article/14244-eng.pdf?st = cQvqkgGF>.

Taylor, P. J., & Gunn, J. (1999). Homicides by people with mental illness: Myth and reality. *British Journal of Psychiatry, 17,* 9–14.

Van Dorn, R., Volavka, J., & Johnson, N. (2012). Mental disorder and violence: Is there a relationship beyond substance use? *Social Psychiatry and Psychiatric Epidemiology, 47,* 487–503.

Vatnar, S. K., Friestad, C., & Bjørkly, S. (2019). A comparison of intimate partner homicide with intimate partner homicide-suicide: Evidence from a Norwegian national 22-year cohort. *Journal of Interpersonal Violence.* Available from https://doi.org/10.1177/0886260519849656.

Velopulos, C. G., Carmichael, H., Zakrison, T. L., & Crandall, M. (2019). Comparison of male and female victims of intimate partner homicide and bidirectionality - An analysis of the National Violence Death Reporting System. *The Journal of Trauma and Acute Care Surgery.* Available from https://doi.org/10.1097/TA.0000000000002276.

Wallace, C., Mullen, P., Burgess, P., Palmer, S., Ruschena, D., & Browne, C. (1998). Serious criminal offending and mental disorder case linkage study. *British Journal of Psychiatry, 172,* 477–484.

Wibbelink, C. J., Hoeve, M., Stams, G. J. J., & Oort, F. J. (2017). A meta-analysis of the association between mental disorders and juvenile recidivism. *Aggression and Violent Behavior, 33,* 78–90.

Yousaf, O., Grunfeld, E. A., & Hunter, M. S. (2015). A systematic review of the factors associated with delays in medical and psychological help-seeking among men. *Health Psychology Review, 9,* 264–276.

Zeppegno, P., Gramaglia, C., di Marco, S., Guerriero, C., Consol, C., Loreti, L., ... Sarchiapone, M. (2019). Intimate partner homicide suicide: A mini-review of the literature (2012–2018). *Current Psychiatry Reports, 21,* 13.

Additional references

First case

Cawley, L., & Melley, J. (September 11, 2012). Murderer Martin Bunch 'said he was a danger', family claims. *The British Broadcasting Corporation.* Retrieved from <https://www.bbc.com/news/uk-england-essex-19555119>.

Taylor, D. (October 30, 2012). Police criticised over murder of Jeanette Goodwin. *The Guardian.* Retrieved from <https://www.theguardian.com/society/2012/oct/30/essex-police-criticised-domestic-murder>.

Second case

Court documents paint a picture of domestic violence. (June 25, 2010). *CTV News Edmonton.* Retrieved from <https://edmonton.ctvnews.ca/court-documents-paint-a-picture-of-domestic-violence-1.526343>.

Kleiss, K. (June 25, 2010). Couple who died in Edmonton house explosion had violent, volatile relationship. *The Edmonton Journal.* Retrieved from <http://www.edmontonjournal.com/news/couple + died + edmonton + house + explosion + violent + volatile + relationship/3200980/story.html>.

Perkel, C. (February 19, 2015). Fatal Edmonton house blast report says better family violence programs needed. *The Huffington Post.* Retrieved from <https://www.huffingtonpost.ca/2015/02/19/fatal-edmonton-house-blas_n_6714954.html>.

Child homicides in the context of domestic violence: when the plight of children is overlooked

Katreena Scott[1], Laura Olszowy[2], Michael Saxton[2] and Katherine Reif[2]

[1]*Department of Applied Psychology and Human Development, University of Toronto, Toronto, ON, Canada* [2]*Centre for Research and Education on Violence Against Women and Children, Faculty of Education, Western University, London, ON, Canada*

Introduction

I never want anyone to be sitting where I'm sitting and to have lost their son, because I can never get him [Luke] back. Rosie Batty, outspoken advocate and domestic violence (DV) survivor, spoken October 20, 2014, at the inquest into the death of her 11-year-old son Luke who was killed by her abusive expartner Greg Anderson after years of DV.

Children in families where there is a domestic homicide always pay a heavy price (Alisic, Krishna, Groot, & Frederick, 2015; Jaffe, Campbell, Hamilton, & Juodis, 2012; Lewandowski, McFarlane, Campbell, Gary, & Barenski, 2004). Children lose parents and are vulnerable to a cascade of impacts and adversities associated with that loss. They are directly and indirectly traumatized by the murder itself, sometimes being direct witnesses or being the first ones on the scene and other times experiencing trauma associated with indirect knowledge of events. Too often, children carry crushing guilt associated with a misperception that, if they had only behaved differently, reached out sooner or been "better" in some way, then they could have prevented the homicide from occurring. Children also sometimes pay the ultimate price as victims of homicide, killed as an act of DV-related revenge against their mother.

Remarkably children have very seldom been the focus of research on DV homicide and their deaths are only sometimes included in DV death review committee (DVDRC) work (Jaffe,

Preventing Domestic Homicides. DOI: https://doi.org/10.1016/B978-0-12-819463-8.00008-3

Campbell, Reif, Fairbairn, & David, 2017). The few studies that have been conducted in this area find that many of the major risk factors for DV homicide apply equally to understanding risk to children. For example, in a recent Canadian study, Hamilton, Jaffe, and Campbell (2013) compared DV homicides without children (44 cases), those with children present in the home but not killed (27 cases) and those which included children as homicide victims (13 cases). Findings suggested no difference in the risk factors across these cases—the top 10 risk factors associated with DV homicide (e.g., separation, previous DV, stalking, depression of perpetrator, escalation of violence) were equally prevalent in each group of cases. What differentiated the groups was the number of professionals and agencies involved. In cases involving child death, there were significantly more agencies involved (9.3) as compared to those where children were present (6.3) and those with no children in the home (4.1). It is especially tragic that, even with this greater number of professionals involved, no one had been able to act to prevent these deaths. This chapter is devoted to lessons learned from DV homicide cases that also involve the killing of children.

Child homicide in context

Recognizing that one death is too many, how common is child homicide in the context of DV? On the basis of results from DVDRCs across North America, Jaffe et al. (2012) estimate that approximately 7% of DV homicide victims are children. In an additional 22% of cases, children are direct witnesses, and in a further 30%, they are present at the scene. Other research suggests that 20% of DV homicides involve third-party victims (including children) apart from intimate partners (Smith, Fowler, & Niolon, 2014). Clearly cases involving children are not an anomaly.

It is also useful to ask: Of all child homicide cases, what proportion are DV related? Globally an estimated 95,000 children are murdered each year (UNICEF, 2014). Parents are the single most common perpetrators, making up a slight majority in lower-income countries (56%) and almost two-thirds (64%) of perpetrators in higher-income countries (Stöckl, Dekel, Morris-Gehring, Watts, & Abrahams, 2017). Characteristics of child homicide cases vary predictably along a number of lines, including age and perpetrator motive. In adolescence, acquaintances make up the highest proportion of homicide perpetrators, though parents make up a distressingly close second highest proportion. Very young infants, and particularly nonaticides (i.e., killing a child within 24 hours of birth), are perpetrated most often by (young) mothers in the context of a pregnancy that was unwanted and, in many cases, hidden from friends, family, and/or work colleagues. Fathers are most often implicated in homicides of older children and stepchildren in the context of extreme discipline or as an act of revenge against a spouse (Benítez-Borrego, Guàrdia-Olmos, & Aliaga-Moore, 2013; Eriksson, Mazerolle, Wortley, & Johnson, 2016; Liem & Koenraadt, 2008). The latter killings, which make up the second most common form of father-perpetrated filicide, have been described as intentional, perpetrated in response to a mother's attempts or threats to leave the relationship and most often by men who had a history of perpetrating DV (Dawson, 2015; Dixon, Krienert, & Walsh, 2013; Eriksson et al., 2016).

In summary a substantial minority of DV homicides also involve the murder of a child, and a significant subsample of all children killed are killed by their fathers in the context of DV. This chapter is organized on the basis of agencies typically involved in DV risk assessment and management in families with children and uses case studies to illustrate ways in which these agencies might have acted to prevent DV homicide. We begin with police, as police are often a pivotal entry point to a network of social and legal institutions that can provide greater safety as well as support for families (Berkman & Esserman, 2004). We then consider child protection services (CPS) and family court services, both of which are socially mandated to act in the best interests of the safety and well-being of the child. Finally we consider the role of shelters and other women's advocacy services.

Role of police services

Recognizing the critical role of police as first responders and as an agency likely have ongoing involvement in complex DV cases, many recommendations for DV homicide prevention focus on risk assessment, monitoring, and management by police. Viewed through the lens of potential risk to children, three recommendations stand out. The first is for better information sharing and collaboration across police services and CPS to coordinate efforts, share information about the level and nature of risk, and to collaborate to monitor, manage, and reduce risk of harm. Such sharing of information is important because police and CPS often have different, but equally important, information relevant to assessing and managing risk. Moreover perpetrators of completed and attempted domestic homicides are frequently known to both police and the child protection system, with one study reporting that these fathers were three times more likely to have previously been reported for child abuse than men who perpetrated DV but not attempted homicide (Campbell, 2004). Unfortunately research is fairly consistent in finding that, in cases of DV, communication between police and CPS services is incomplete and inconsistent (Øverlien & Aas, 2016; Saltiel, 2015; Stanley, Miller, Richardson Foster, & Thomson, 2010).

A second major area of recommendation is for ongoing monitoring of high-risk DV perpetrators, particularly in the context of separation and disputed custody and access. The Ontario DVDRC, for example, recommends that police receive ongoing training on appropriate responses to DV cases that involve custody and access in light of potential danger to the victim and/or the children involved. It has been further recommended that a proactive approach be used (e.g., doing check-ins on offenders to ensure bail conditions compliance; assess and respond proactively to changes in dynamic risk for reoffense), rather than one solely based on responding to calls to police, and that such approaches be coordinated with other service providers (and in particular, with CPS). This recommendation calls for police to become part of an active risk-management plan in situations of high risk for lethality. Such actions may be particularly important for perpetrators awaiting trial, judgement, or sentencing, when no other justice personal (e.g., probation officers) are involved.

Finally a number of commentators have recommended that police attend more to children on the scene of arrest and immediately afterward (Richardson-Foster, Stanley, Miller, & Thomson, 2012). Available research suggests that police have rather limited interactions with children, may view children as observers on the sidelines rather than primary or secondary victims of DV, and often report having limited training and competency in addressing the impact of exposure to DV on children (Richardson-Foster et al., 2012). There are, however, substantial benefits to police speaking with children who are living in a home where DV is occurring (Berkman & Esserman, 2004; Richardson-Foster et al., 2012). Police involvement with children has been shown to improve victim satisfaction and increase the likelihood of contacting the police in the future (Richardson-Foster et al., 2012). Additionally police–child interactions seem to improve information gathering, thereby aiding in the assessment of risk as well as potentially strengthening the evidence available to the prosecution of DV perpetrators (Richardson-Foster et al., 2012). The above point is of particular importance given the evidence that suggests children living in a home with DV are aware of coercive control taking place in the family, are affected by these controlling dynamics, and continually attempt to make sense of these experiences (Callaghan, Alexander, Sixsmith, & Fellin, 2018). Moreover prior research has shown that children have a desire for police officers to involve them in the process of DV investigations and for their perspectives and needs to be better seen, heard, and believed by the police (Holt, Buckley, & Whelan, 2008). The following case study highlights problems and concerns with sharing information, coordinating risk-management responses, and talking with police, as well as with the absence of proactive monitoring of the potential perpetrator.

Case study: Mary Shipstone, United Kingdom

Many of the details outlined in this case can be retrieved from: http://www.eastsussexlscb.org.uk/wp-content/uploads/SCR-Child-P-Overview-Report-Published-March-.16.pdf.

On September 11, 2014, seven-year-old Mary Shipstone was killed by her father. Her father, Mr. Yasser Alromisse, 46, killed himself on scene. At the time of the homicide, there was a family court order preventing contact between Mr. Alromisse and his daughter and police were aware of heightened concerns resulting from the fact that the family's address had been inadvertently shared with Mr. Alromisse a few months earlier. The family was known to numerous agencies and police services as a result of concerns about DV and child abuse.

Ms. Lyndsey Shipstone and Mr. Alromisse married in 2005 and had Mary in 2006. Ms. Shipstone also had a son with special needs from a previous relationship. In 2008 there were two contacts with police and social services due to violence that Mr. Alromisse perpetrated in the family, once against Ms. Shipstone and once against her son. In both cases there was a brief investigation and warnings, but no other actions. In early 2009 Ms. Shipstone left the relationship with Mr. Alromisse and family court proceedings began. Mr. Alromisse applied for custody of Mary and, in his submission to the court, accused Ms. Shipstone of abuse and neglect of her children, including sexual abuse allegations. Conversely Ms. Shipstone informed the court that she was a victim of DV and alleged Mr. Alromisse was physically abusive toward her children. The court granted custody of Mary to Ms. Shipstone and ordered Mr. Alromisse have supervised access.

In 2010 Mr. Alromisse and Ms. Shipstone renewed their relationship and Mr. Alromisse became a frequent visitor to the home, despite a court order to stay away from the family home and to have his access to Mary supervised. Police were notified of Mr. Alromisse's violation of his court order on two different occasions, once by the maternal grandmother (June 2010) and another time by social services responsible for children (September 2010). Child protection wanted Mr. Alromisse to undergo an assessment and/or utilize supervised contact to ensure child safety; Mr. Alromisse was refusing. Police attended the home in response to both calls, noted information in both cases, but indicated that there was no current role for them.

There was an escalation of concerns in May of 2011 involving involvement of CPS and police when Ms. Shipstone ended the relationship again. At this point, there was a cross-system recognition of heightened risk of DV and a coordinated, multiagency effort was undertaken to assess and manage risk. There were a number of complicating factors including Ms. Shipstone's distrust of the process and a short move out of the country, which were managed by the team. Over the next three years, the situation was one of semiregular court involvement around custody and access, ongoing child protection involvement, and some supervised visitation between Mr. Alromisse and Mary. Mr. Alromisse made a series of applications through the family courts to gain greater access to Mary. On several occasions the court ordered to arrange supervised or indirect access to Mary, often with recommendation that Mr. Alromisse receive therapeutic intervention. For example, in 2011 a court-ordered assessment by a psychologist recommended that due to impact of DV on the family and difficulties that arose from Mr. Alromisse's personality and temperament, indirect contact be maintained until further therapeutic interventions were undertaken by Mr. Alromisse. About a year later (November 2012) and despite the fact that Mr. Alromisse had not completed any intervention, the family court ordered further supervised contact. In January of that same year, it was decided by social services that there was no longer a need for a child protection plan; this decision coincided with the family moving locations and the transfer of their child protection file to the local authority. At around the same time, funding from child protection for supervised access ended and access was made indirect until payment was arranged by Mr. Alromisse. In August 2013 the family court noted that there had not been any further direct or indirect contact. A next supervised contact session took place in October 2013, which was Mr. Alromisse's first contact with Mary in approximately 10 months. Ms. Shipstone indicated that Mary reacted badly to the contact and a hold was placed on further supervised access sessions.

In April 2014 Ms. Shipstone reported to the police that her legal counsel had inadvertently revealed her new address to Mr. Alromisse in legal documents. She voiced concern that he would try to remove Mary and was worried for the safety of her children. The police recorded this information and sought to pass it on to her neighborhood police division for further action; it was passed in error to the wrong division where it was closed without further action. In August 2014 Mr. Alromisse sought action from social services to arrange supervised contact; this was at odds with the order made by the family court. In September 2014 the case was allocated to a Children and Family Court Advisory and Support Service worker who began to make arrangements to gather information and see Mary before the next hearing. Before this meeting could occur, Mr. Alromisse came to the house, shot Mary twice and then turned the gun on himself.

There are multiple lessons to be learned from the murder of Mary Shipstone and the suicide of Mr. Alromisse. Some of these are relevant to cultural differences and perpetrator mental health, which are issues highlighted in Chapter 6, Domestic homicide in immigrant communities: lessons learned, and Chapter 7, Perpetrator mental health: depression and suicidality as risk factors for domestic homicide. Others concern ubiquitous issues with coordination of multiple services and challenges of having multiple jurisdictions involved. In this chapter, we highlight lessons that are specific to understanding police services and risk to children. First events that occurred early in this case are illustrative of concerns around the ways in which police and child protection collaborate to share information and manage risk associated with DV. In this case, as in many others, there was a disconnect between the evaluation and risk-management steps put in place by child protection and police. Specifically despite a court order, a plan for assessment and supervised access, and a call directly from CPS, police deemed the "on the scene" situation to be low risk and nonproblematic. There is also no evidence from the case that police interviewed Ms. Shipstone and Mr. Alromisse's children at this time, so their perspectives on this situation were likely not considered. Thus early opportunities to coordinate across services to assess the risk that Mr. Alromisse posed to his family, engage him in intervention to manage and change this risk, partner with

Ms. Shipstone in the development of safety strategies, and meet the needs of the children in the family were missed.

A second lesson highlights the potential role for police in proactive monitoring of risk. Once the higher-risk nature of the case had been recognized, strong, coordinated protective plans were put in place by the professionals; however, these plans were almost exclusively focused on "hardening the target," that is, protecting Ms. Shipstone and the children to make it more difficult for Mr. Alromisse to harm them. The residence of Ms. Shipstone and the children was changed and hidden, her compliance with maintaining no-contact was monitored, and orders were put in place to limit and supervise Mr. Alromisse's contact with his child. However, no proactive steps were taken to engage in ongoing monitoring and management of Mr. Alromisse's level of risk. In this case, as a result of Mr. Alromisse's ongoing reluctance to engage with professionals, police might have been the only professionals who could have reached out to him to for proactive risk management. A key time for this would have been when the family was transferred to a new jurisdiction, at which point a proactive policing plan might have had an officer meet with Mr. Alromisse, assess his current risk level, and begin risk management, potentially in collaboration with child protection. Instead because Ms. Shipstone was maintaining no-contact with Mr. Alromisse and there was ongoing denial of unsupervised access, police and CPS were comfortable with a less intense risk-management plan; a comfort that might have changed had the lens included ongoing assessment of Mr. Alromisse's risk for offending alongside that of Ms. Shipstone's capacity to act in protectively.

Role of child protection and family court

Two other agencies often involved in DV homicides involving children are children protection (CPS) and courts adjudicating on the basis of family law (herein called family court). Child protection and family courts share a principle commitment to prioritizing children in decision making. Within both of these systems, substantial attention has been placed on better recognizing the impact of DV on children. Over the past two decades, CPS jurisdictions have increasingly recognized that living with DV is, in and of itself, a potential form of emotional harm and thus a child protection concern that should be investigated via mandatory reporting. Once jurisdictions recognize exposure to DV as a form of child maltreatment it typically becomes one of the leading reasons for reporting to child protection. This is now the case across Australia, Canada, and the United Kingdom (Child Family Community Australia, 2017; Department for Education, 2018; Public Health Agency of Canada, 2010). Child protection has thus become a critical partner in assessing, managing, and changing DV-related risk to children.

Within family courts, there has been a similar shift over the past few decades from seeing DV as an adult issue not relevant to custody and access decisions to understanding that both historic and ongoing DV is critical to consideration of the best interests of the child (e.g., Bala et al., 1998; Symons, 2010). Such recognition has been based on evidence of the deleterious effects of child exposure to DV, the persistence of DV postseparation, the overlap of concerns about parenting, and the potential risk of lethality to children and their mothers. These findings, along with efforts of DV and child advocates, have led to significant legislative changes across a number of countries including the United States, Australia, New Zealand, and most recently, Canada, to directly require consideration of DV in postseparation parenting plans.

Despite the significant changes made by both the child protection and family court systems, DV death reviews continue to emphasize significant improvements needed in both settings. A first major recommendation is for better recognition and assessment of DV and risk for DV lethality. In CPS, extensive research on practice with families where there is DV speaks to the challenges that child protection workers have accurately identifying the presence of DV and the associated levels of risk to children and their caregivers (Bourassa, Lavergne, Damant, Lessard, & Turcotte, 2006; Jenney, Mishna, Alaggia, & Scott, 2014; Lapierre & Côté, 2011; Postmus & Merritt, 2010; Radford, Blacklock, & Iwi, 2006; Shlonsky & Friend, 2007). For example, a small Canadian study focusing on child protection workers' practices with DV cases highlighted that the presence or absence or DV had relatively little influence on decision making relative to consideration of referral source and frequency and severity of violence (Hughes & Chau, 2012). Another Canadian study with child protection workers found that only about 60% of workers conduct a systematic evaluation for the presence of DV in their cases (Bourassa et al., 2006). Obstacles to effectively detecting DV included parents' denial of the DV, lack of physical evidence, heavy workloads of caseworkers, lack of awareness of violence in small communities, lack of cooperation by the parents, short duration of interventions, and fear of endangering the victim. Broader, more frequent, and high-level training of all

CPS staff and supervisors in DV is frequently recommended (Bourassa et al., 2006; Button & Payne, 2009; Fusco, 2013).

Adequate recognition of DV is also a problem within the family court system. There have been persistent concerns expressed by specialist women's services that DV perpetration is underrecognized and, even when acknowledged, is not given sufficient weight in decisions around contact and parenting plans (Harrison, 2008; Hunt & Macleod, 2008; Rivera, Zeoli, & Sullivan, 2012; Trinder, Firth, & Jenks, 2009). Commentators in Australia, Canada, United Kingdom, United States, and elsewhere have pointed out that DV allegations made by women in the context of parental separation are often met with skepticism and suspicion that the allegation is being utilized to limit the involvement of the other parent, especially if there has not been previous involvement of police or other authorities (Jaffe, Crooks, & Bala, 2009). Reviews of practice continue to find that the rights of fathers and potential benefits of father–child contact outweigh the potential harms and dangers of ongoing DV in judges' decision making (Godbout, Parent, & Saint-Jacques, 2015; Harrison, 2008; Rivera et al., 2012). For example, in a recent UK study, MacDonald (2016) reviewed reports by a specialized advisory service on 70 families, finding that women and children's accounts of fathers' violence tended to be seen as irrelevant and were disregarded in report recommendations, especially when there was no external evidence (i.e., police charges) to corroborate allegations.

A second significant problem identified within both child protection and family courts is a predominant focus on mothers and their role in protecting children from DV exposure as opposed to fathers' behavior and evidence of change in abusive behaviors. Within child protection, this manifests as pressure for women to be appropriately "protective" of their children's potential DV exposure and in case decisions that are based on this protectiveness (Alaggia, Gadalla, Shlonsky, Jenney, & Daciuk, 2015; Humphreys & Absler, 2011). Accordingly it is not unusual for CPS DV cases to be open or closed on the basis of mothers' appreciation of the impact of DV on her children and willingness to engage in protective actions (i.e., separation, use of no-contact orders) without there ever having been contact or risk-reducing intervention with the perpetrator of DV and without a plan in place to monitor and manage his ongoing risk. Such practices persist for a number of reasons, including a narrow interpretation of CPS mandate to protect children, workers' difficulty engaging fathers, and a lack of training, skills, and resources to manage the risk of DV perpetrators behaviors in frontline staff (Jenney et al., 2014; Lapierre & Côté, 2011; Stanley, Miller, Richardson Foster, & Thomson, 2011). A lack of collaboration across organizations in providing services to manage and change risk is another contributing factor (Edelson, Gassman-Pines, & Hill, 2006; Lessard et al., 2010). While CPS agencies are continuing to work to improve practice with fathers in general, and DV perpetrating men in particular, child protection workers need continued training, supervision, and support to better support (rather than blame) DV victims and to increase their skills and confidence in working with perpetrators of DV (Stanley & Humphreys, 2014).

Women survivors of DV face similarly high-stakes scrutiny in family court where allegations of historic and potentially ongoing DV, if considered by the judge to be unfounded and potentially malicious, can result in her being perceived as an "unfriendly" parent unwilling to work together with the father of their children and/or as engaging in willful alienation of the children against their father (Jaffe, Ashbourne, & Mamo, 2010). Parental alienation, although not accepted as a clinical syndrome or diagnosis, is still used in arguments in court and is a real concern for those raising allegations of abuse. The courts put such an emphasis on resolving custody disputes with some form of a shared parenting or joint custody plan that it is difficult to even raise allegations of violence without compelling evidence. The courts want friendly coparenting parents and the allegations of abuse are counteracted by allegations of alienation and the argument that the parent (usually mother) raising these concerns is intentionally undermining the father–child relationship. Many victims retreat from this system and come to an unsafe parenting arrangement because of the emotional and financial burden of ongoing family court disputes (Meier & Dickson, 2017; Meier, 2009).

Finally problems have been noted in the fact that both the child protection and family court system seldom apply a lens of DV lethality risk to understanding children's situations (Alaggia et al., 2015; Jenney et al., 2014). It has been argued that the field of child protection has been slow to realize that helping establish safety for the mother is synonymous with ensuring safety for the children (Hughes, Chau, & Poff, 2011; Shlonsky & Friend, 2007). Ironically while many child protection investigations involving DV result in the requirement that the mother to separate from the abuser—an action known to increase risk in the short term—this "protective" action often leads child protection to reduce monitoring and involvement (Hughes et al., 2011). Other research suggests that the child protection system may be reluctant to become involved in cases where parents with an alleged history of DV are separated and in dispute over custody or access (factors that can contribute to risk for lethality) for fear of being drawn into the dispute (Lessard et al., 2010). Similarly there have been many calls for better assessment of the potential for lethal DV risk as part of family court proceedings. Jaffe and colleagues, for example, have called for the use of differential intervention strategies to be implemented to address cases of DV as soon as possible after the beginning of a family's involvement in the family court system (Jaffe et al., 2009). In this model, concerns about DV would lead immediately to a different stream of processing (i.e., an "off ramp" from the traffic of more typical cases) with access to specialized assessors able to assess level of risk, supervised visitation services and intervention opportunities for all members of the family to manage risk, and court monitoring of progress.

The following case is one in which both child protection and family court had longstanding roles. There were multiple missed opportunities to intervene.

Case study—Jared Osidacz

Many of the details outlined in this case can be retrieved from: http://www.springtideresources.org/sites/all/files/Osidacz_Inquest_Recommendations.pdf.

Jared Osidacz, age 8, was killed by his father, Mr. Andrew Osidacz, on March 18, 2006, in Brantford, Ontario, during a court-ordered unsupervised access visit. His parents had separated four years prior following a serious domestic assault by Mr. Osidacz. Immediately precipitating the homicide was an altercation between Mr. Osidacz and his recently estranged girlfriend, Ms. Ferrell. Mr. Osidacz went to her home with Jared and was allowed in because Jared and her same-age daughter were friends. Mr. Osidacz stabbed Ms. Ferrell and her daughter Sarah multiple times. Jared intervened and was fatally stabbed by Mr. Osidacz. Immediately following these events, Mr. Osidacz drove to the home of his exwife (and Jared's mother) Ms. Julie Craven. He forcibly entered the home of Ms. Craven and in a distraught state told her he had killed Jared. He had a large knife to her throat for 45 minutes during which time he contacted his mother by phone, told her Jared was dead, and told her to come to Ms. Craven's house. The police arrived at the home a short time later. Upon seeing

Mr. Osidacz with the knife to Ms. Craven's neck, the police officer shot him. He died at the scene.

Ms. Craven and Mr. Osidacz met in March 1996 in Brantford, Ontario. Their courtship was brief. Ms. Craven became pregnant and the couple was quickly engaged and married. During Ms. Craven's pregnancy, Mr. Osidacz began to exhibit controlling tactics and signs of emotional abuse. Following Jared's birth, Ms. Craven described Mr. Osidacz's controlling behaviors as escalating, including restricting her parents' access to Jared, providing her with minimal financial resources, and spending increasingly longer periods of time in his basement office. A particularly contentious issue between them was the baby videos of Jared that Mr. Osidacz had hidden from her. This was the catalyst for the fight in April 2002 that resulted in Ms. Craven trying to break the lock to his office and Mr. Osidacz responding by banging her head into the door several times. Following this assault, the police were contacted and Mr. Osidacz was arrested. The couple did not reunite after this incident. During the police investigation, a taping machine was discovered in Mr. Osidacz's office and he was also charged with illegally recording Ms. Craven's phone calls. The police notified the child protection authorities and an investigation ensued. All the parties were interviewed, including Jared. According to the record, Jared stated he knew about the assault and he was aware of the ongoing conflict between his parents. The child protection worker determined that the mother was protective and closed the file. Both parents were admonished for exposing Jared to ongoing conflict. Family court also became involved. An interim family court order was issued granting Ms. Craven custody and Mr. Osidacz liberal access.

Over the following four years, Jared's family was involved with multiple agencies. In retrospect, there were also multiple additional indicators of Mr. Osidacz's escalating level of risk for perpetrating violence. Mr. Osidacz pleaded guilty in criminal court to assaulting Ms. Craven in 2002 and was placed on probation with terms that prohibited him from direct contact with Ms. Craven. Due to inappropriate behavior, he was discharged and then readmitted to court-ordered DV intervention program. Despite his guilty plea, Mr. Osidacz remained adamant that he was not guilty of assaulting Ms. Craven. Eventually he was allowed to complete his treatment through an online anger management course, which he reported he completed by listening to tapes in his car. In September 2003 Mr. Osidacz was charged with a breach for approaching Ms. Craven and Jared in a parking lot as he tried to get Jared to go with him. Around the same time, Ms. Craven notified the police that she found hundreds of rounds of ammunition in her laundry room that she believed were recently placed there. She believed Mr. Osidacz was responsible and told the police she was worried that she and Jared were still in danger. By this point, Mr. Osidacz was in a new relationship with a woman, Ms. Ferrell, who had a daughter the same age as Jared. The police had Ms. Craven bring the ammunition into the station and they notified CPS. During CPS investigation, Ms. Craven shared her worries about Mr. Osidacz's family and her fear for Jared's safety. She also tried to get the CPS investigator to look at the violent pornography she found that belonged to Mr. Osidacz. Mr. Osidacz's account differed from Ms. Craven's and CPS characterized the case as one of conflict, rather than ongoing DV. The file was closed, and the parents were again advised that their exposing Jared to adult conflict could be a reason to find him in need of protection. There was ongoing family court involvement. Eventually a custody and access assessment was recommended. In March 2004, the custody and access assessor recommended to family court that Ms. Craven be awarded sole custody with Mr. Osidacz having unsupervised access every other weekend.

In December 2004 Mr. Osidacz appeared in criminal court for a breach of probation; the charges were dropped. Here Ms. Craven obtained a one-year-peace bond against Mr. Osidacz, expiring in December 2005. Mr. Osidacz's attacks against Ms. Ferrell, her daughter, Ms. Craven and his killing of Jared occurred three months later. With respect to this case, there were several opportunities missed by child protection and the family court system. CPS opened an investigation on two occasions. On the first occasion, shortly after Mr. Osidacz's initial assault, an investigation was opened and closed quickly on the basis of the protective actions that Ms. Craven was taking. CPS was involved again in 2003 following Mr. Osidacz's breach of probation and as a result of concerns reported by police that Mr. Osidacz may be inappropriately using Jared as a lever in ongoing conflict. CPS ended up doing a fairly intensive investigation, including interviews with many members of the family. What appeared to be weighed most heavily in investigation were the multiple conflicting allegations of Ms. Craven and Mr. Osidacz, the lack of concerns expressed by Ms. Ferrell, and the seemingly good relationship between Mr. Osidacz and Jared. Not heavily weighed were DV risk factors including the history of coercive control tactics reported by Ms. Craven, the seriousness of Mr. Osidacz's initial assault, problems with Mr. Osidacz's engagement with intervention, and clear evidence for lack of change (i.e., ongoing denial), Mr. Osidacz's failure to comply with court orders, evidence of ongoing custody and access disputes, recent evidence of fear in Ms. Craven, and obsessiveness in Mr. Osidacz. As a result, instead of implementing a plan for monitoring, managing, and changing Mr. Osidacz's level of risk, both parents were admonished for discussing adult conflict with Jared and warned against any further allegations of emotional harm regarding Jared. This case thus provides an excellent example of the "double-edged sword" that women who have been victims of DV are required to walk as a result of a general lack of appreciation of DV-related risk. Ms. Craven's disclosures and concerns about DV-related risk were not interpreted as credible and valid and, as a result, she (along with Mr. Osidacz) was warned that further reports to the Society about allegations of emotional harm regarding Jared would result in more intrusive child protection action.

Jared's case also illuminates the failings of the legal system and how the lack of information sharing and coordination between criminal court, family court, police, and child protection impacted assessment and management of risk. Key in this case was an apparent lack of appreciation in family court of DV-related risk factors. Soon after Mr. Osidacz assaulted Ms. Craven and they separated, and before the criminal case was heard, Mr. Osidacz was given liberal, unsupervised access. Following this decision, and despite the accumulation of DV-related risks including Mr. Osidacz's criminal charge, his ongoing denial of the assault, his removal from an intervention program as a result of poor accountability, his breech of a no-contact order and Ms. Craven's expressed fears and concerns, there was no substantial change to this initial order. In retrospect, no one in the family court system applied a DV lens to understanding the ongoing and escalating pattern of Mr. Osidacz's risk for perpetrating lethal assault.

Role of shelter services

Shelter services are a third service essential to preventing child homicide in the context of DV. Shelter work is often crisis based and focused on immediate needs for housing, clothing, and food, though shelters also provide longer-term services including transitional and permanent housing (Baker, Billhardt, Warren, Rollins, & Glass, 2010). Although these basic adult-focused needs are often predominant in the day-to-day work of shelters, violence against women services have long recognized the impacts on children of living with DV (Hester, 2011). Grounding this work is an understanding that children's safety and well-being needs are usually best met by increasing the strengths and competencies of their mothers and recognizing that mothers' decisions about leaving or remaining in an abusive relationship, seeking or not seeking help, are most often guided by her concerns about her children (Petrucci & Mills, 2002).

Recognizing the needs of children exposed to DV, shelters increasingly incorporate programs and activities that provide mothers with trauma and violence-informed parenting skills to support them in strengthening their relationship with their children. Shelters are also working directly to meet the array of psychosocial needs of children in these situations (Chanmugam, Kemter, & Goodwin, 2015). They are, for example, increasingly incorporating practices that recognize the impact of trauma on children (Ezell, McDonald, & Jouriles, 2000; Stephens, McDonald, & Jouriles, 2000) and working on partnering with more generalist service providers to become a conduit to child-specific supports such as case management, counseling, school integration, and child mental health services (Groves & Gewirtz, 2006). Shelters have also began to directly involve children and youth in safety planning, especially during the period of heightened risk after separation (Chanmugam & Hall, 2012). Although there have been few empirically strong evaluations of shelter programs for children, increasing safety is often the primary goal of most children's programs (Poole, Beran, & Thurston, 2008). For children who have unsupervised visitation with perpetrators of DV, safety planning goals can focus on empowerment, management of fear and anxiety, and critical thinking skills acquisition that decrease violence potential (Chanmugam & Hall, 2012; Hardesty & Campbell, 2004).

When considering the role of shelters in promoting the safety of children, DVDRCs often focus recommendations on their essential role in coordinated, cross-agency, system-wide response to high-risk DV cases, including collaboration between shelter advocates and the child protection system. This is a recognized area of tension in the field. Part of this tension comes from the aforementioned tendency of CPS to inappropriately blame mothers when they are unable to protect their children against exposure to DV of which she herself is a victim, CPS's reliance on separation as an (misdirected) indicator of increased child safety, and an often degendered view of DV as a reflection of general dysfunction in the family (Hester, 2011).

Tension also arises from the differential focus on women's empowerment and child safety which, although often aligned, can be in conflict. For example, a women at shelter maybe struggling with addiction and mental health issues (potentially as a result of DV victimization) and, as a result, be emotionally or physically abusive and neglectful to her children. For these complex cases, cross-sector agreement and guidelines on how to proceed are important, but only sometimes in place (Hester, 2011). Other challenges are those of time within each sector for communication and collaboration (Langenderfer-Magruder, Alven, Wilke, & Spinelli, 2019). Notwithstanding these challenges, there are ongoing efforts across both of these systems for better collaboration, particularly in working with cases deemed at high risk for lethality, to maximize the ways shelters can work collaboratively with other services to provide a seamless and supportive response to the woman and her children. The following case emphasizes the potential for shelters to work alongside CPS and other services to address risk to children.

Toronto, Ontario: the case of Ms. Zahra Abdille, Faris Abdille, and Zain Abdille

Many of the details outlined in this case can be retrieved from: https://www.thestar.com/news/crime/2014/12/04/triple_homicide_slaying_victim_told_friend_she_was_afraid_of_her_husband.html.

Ms. Zahra Abdille, aged 43, and her two sons, Faris (aged 13) and Zain (aged 8), were killed by her partner and their father, Mr. Yusuf Osman Abdille, aged 50, on Saturday November 29, 2014. The homicides were followed by the perpetrator's suicide. The victims were killed in their apartment and Mr. Abdille subsequently jumped onto a highway where he was struck by a car and died.

Ms. Abdille was born in Somalia and grew up in Kenya before moving to Canada in the late 1990s. She met Mr. Abdille in 1997, and they were married a year later in Toronto. She began working as a public health nurse in 2007 and completed a master's degree and nurse practitioner's certificate at Ryerson University in 2012. Ms. Abdille was described as focused on bettering herself and providing a better life for her children.

Ms. Abdille came to a DV shelter in Toronto with her children on July 10, 2013, and stayed there for ~2−3 weeks. Staff were aware that she was escaping a long-term abusive relation-ship and that she wanted to end her marriage. Reportedly she did not wish to report the violence to police, as she did not want her husband arrested. While at the shelter, she took time off work to care for and support her children. According to the shelter's Executive Director, Mr. Abdille called her numerous times, as many as 50 calls in a single day. Friends were aware of Ms. Abdille's fears about her husband, as well as her concerns for her children. Notwithstanding these fears, people from her community encouraged her to go back home and work things out with Mr. Abdille.

While at the shelter, Ms. Abdille attempted to obtain an emergency court order to get interim custody of her children, which would have also granted her a restraining order against her husband. She was turned away, however, as a result of being unable to produce certain pertinent documents (e.g., income tax returns, receipts for daycare). As Ms. Abdille did not qualify for legal aid to challenge custody issues and could not afford a lawyer, as she faced the prospect of paying rent on her own. On July 23, Ms. Abdille left the shelter and told the staff that she was moving with her children into a rental property. However, she reportedly moved back into the apartment that she shared with Mr. Abdille. A friend stated that she had offered for her to stay at her house, but Ms. Abdille declined due to her belief that Mr. Abdille would find her there. A shelter worker felt that Ms. Abdille may have been unable to afford rent in the city, and as a result, was forced to return to the perpetrator, which was commonplace for many other women in the shelter. According to her friend, she was afraid of the perpetrator, but did not believe that he would hurt her children, and this is likely the reason that she chose to return to their home, coupled with the fear of stigma associated with being a victim of DV. A short time after she returned home with her children, Mr. Abdille killed everyone in the family, including himself.

This case highlights a variety of challenges that were faced by Ms. Abdille as she attempted to flee her abusive partner. It was described, in retrospect, by the Chair of the DVDRC as "a homicide waiting to happen" (Carville, 2015). As described by the Executive Director of the shelter she visited, she attempted to access help for herself and her children but "fell through the cracks" in that she was unable to qualify for the support that was needed, rendering her helpless and "forced" to return to the perpetrator. The challenges she faced were further com-pounded by Ms. Abdille, a woman of color, facing stigmatiza-tion by her community for being a victim of DV. Overall, this case highlights the lack of funding and support (e.g., affordable housing, income support, legal services) for victims in similar circumstances, issues that are frequently noted in DVDRC reports. DVDRCs have also recommended that shelters provide support to victims to navigate multiple services and systems. Recommendations from the DVDRC specific to this case, for example, focused on having social services adopt a more "hands-on" approach with victims to assist them with navigating the system and administering standardized risk assessment tools in order to identify cases that are high risk. The availability of such services may have helped ensure that Ms. Abdille and her children had access to safe housing and greater support within their cultural community. There may also have been a role for greater collaboration and communication between the shelter and family court.

A more complicated, controversial issue in this case is the potential role of shelters in enlisting CPS to help monitor and manage risk. Despite evidence of ongoing risk of child exposure to DV, CPS were not involved. If viewed through the lens of whether or not Ms. Abdille was acting protectively and of empowering women in their choices, these actions make sense—Ms. Abdille was fleeing an abusive relationship and attempting to put protections in place for herself and her children. However, when viewed through the lens of risk to children, this is a situation where there are multiple indications of risk and no involvement of any system (at least on public record) that was attempting to intervene and manage the risk at its source: Mr. Abdille. Given Ms. Abdille's concern about involving the police, child protection was an obvious partner with the potential capacity to engage, assess, monitor, and manage Mr. Abdille's risk of DV.

Discussion

DV-related homicides involving children appear predictable and preventable with hindsight. A distressingly high proportion of child homicides are DV related with multiple warning signs prior to the tragedy. In this chapter, we highlighted recommendations made by DVDRC's for police services, CPS, family courts, and shelters services to better prevent DV-related homicides against children and provided case examples of where such recommendations might have applied. It is clear that there is still much that needs to be done. For one, better data on victim–perpetrator relationships need to be collected for homicides (Stöckl et al., 2017), and DV-related child deaths need to be consistently included in DVDRC reports. Standardized lethality risk assessment tools that are appropriate to child-focused agencies may also be needed. Although it is useful to know that risk to children is captured in typically used DV lethality assessment instruments, continued research is this area is useful to determine if there are additional factors specific to children that might improve the understanding of risk. To our knowledge, there is currently only one tool available that attempts to do this: The Bernardo's Domestic Violence Risk Identification Matrix (Healy & Bell, 2005) assesses for DV risk/vulnerability and protective measures needed to support children and families. This tool is more of a structured guide that has a great deal of face validity but has not been tested empirically in the decade since its development (Jaffe et al., 2017). More research on tools such as this, along with greater consideration of how existing tools might best be used in child-focused settings, is warranted.

In addition to putting greater focus on children in review and research, a number of practice developments are needed. Those in key protective roles including police, child protection, and shelters need to continue to improve their capacity to work collaboratively to manage these often complicated and high-risk cases. Police need to continue to develop and consistently implement child-focused "best law enforcement practices" that include assessing whether child exposed to DV needs service (Hamby, Finkelhor, & Turner, 2015). Within child protection, frontline workers need practice frameworks and opportunities to develop greater skills for working with families where DV is a concern. Shelters need to be partners in safety planning with children and in continuing to work in coordination with multiple services to articulate and manage risk. Finally continued advocacy is needed within family courts to ensure that DV is adequately recognized and that DV-related risks and harms are better balanced against the rights of fathers and potential benefits of father—child contact.

Fortunately there are ongoing initiatives to improve response to DV. More and more communities are implementing multi-agency risk assessment and management teams that bring together various agencies to collaborate in DV cases at high risk for lethality (e.g., Robinson, 2006; Stanley & Humphreys, 2014). Models are being explored in practice including some that bring together partner agencies in regular high-risk case conferences and others that collaborate through colocation of services for victims, and ongoing research explores how these teams are able to work most effectively (Robinson & Payton, 2016; Robinson & Tregidga, 2007). Greater and better collaboration between specialist DV services and child protection is also a significant ongoing focus of work. On the basis of a scoping review of collaborative CPS and DV specialist practice (Macvean, Humphreys, & Healey, 2018) and a two-year action research project, the Pathways in Research In Collaborative Inter-Agency project team in Australia identified enablers of collaboration and put forward a collaborative framework for child protection and specialist domestic and family violence services (Healey, Connolly, & Humphreys, 2018). This work integrates Mandel's work on the Safe and Together model of practice (Mandel, 2010) and explores the potential for father-focused interventions such as Caring Dads (McConnell, Barnard, & Taylor, 2017; Scott & Lishak, 2012) to contribute to managing and changing perpetrator risk to children and mothers. Within family court, a number of authors have put forward frameworks to help court officials better deal with DV cases. Jaffe and colleagues have provided a model for differential processing of DV cases to facilitate better assessment and safer decision making (Jaffe et al., 2008), and the Battered Women's Justice project has developed and disseminated practice models to aid in the assessment of level, nature, and impact of DV (Davis, 2015). There has been ongoing work to support better training of custody evaluators and family court judges (Saunders, 2015) and to develop court-linked services to support safety for separating families where there is DV (Pulido, Forrester, & Lacina, 2011; Stern & Oehme, 2010).

Finally to close this chapter, it is useful to look outward once again to the lives of children. Although our focus herein has been on specialist services with a specific mandate to address DV, there are many other social institutions for children and families that were not included in our review. These include schools, childcare centers, child mental health services, recreational sporting organizations, community centers, faith-based communities, and others. These agencies provide important supports to children and families. As recommended by DVDRCs, it is critical that public education be extended to these locations so that public awareness and recognition of DV are improved. Such messaging also needs to include education that DV is not just an "adult issue," but one with central importance to the health and well-being of children. Such care by all of our social institutions will help to these tragedies from occurring to our communities' most vulnerable.

References

Alaggia, R., Gadalla, T. M., Shlonsky, A., Jenney, A., & Daciuk, J. (2015). Does differential response make a difference: Examining domestic violence cases in child protection services. *Child & Family Social Work, 20,* 83–95.

Alisic, E., Krishna, R. N., Groot, A., & Frederick, J. W. (2015). Children's mental health and well-being after parental intimate partner homicide: A systematic review. *Clinical Child and Family Psychology Review, 18,* 328–345.

Baker, C. K., Billhardt, K. A., Warren, J., Rollins, C., & Glass, N. E. (2010). Domestic violence, housing instability, and homelessness: A review of housing policies and program practices for meeting the needs of survivors. *Aggression and Violent Behavior, 15,* 430–439.

Bala, N., Bertrand, L., Paetsch, J., Knoppers, B. M., Hornick, J. P., Noel, J., . . .& Miklas, S. W. (1998). *Spousal violence in custody and access disputes: Recommendation for reform.* Report for the status of women Canada. Retrieved January 2019 from <http://citeseerx.ist.psu.edu/viewdoc/download;jsessionid = 29FC8F18E787A51E435339EF6C3BC83A?doi = 10.1.1.494.4574&rep = rep1&type = pdf>.

Benítez-Borrego, S., Guàrdia-Olmos, J., & Aliaga-Moore, A. (2013). Child homicide by parents in Chile: A gender-based study and analysis of post-filicide attempted suicide. *International Journal of Law and Psychiatry, 36,* 55–64.

Berkman, M., & Esserman, D. (2004). *Police in the lives of young children exposed to domestic violence. Paper #4 in the University of Iowa Schechter, Susan. Early childhood, domestic violence, and poverty: Helping young children and their families series.* Iowa City, IA: School of Social Work, University of Iowa.

Bourassa, C., Lavergne, C., Damant, D., Lessard, G., & Turcotte, P. (2006). Awareness and detection of the co-occurrence of interparental violence and child abuse: Child welfare worker's perspective. *Children and Youth Services Review, 28,* 1312–1328.

Button, D. M., & Payne, B. K. (2009). Training child protective services workers about domestic violence: Needs, strategies, and barriers. *Children and Youth Services Review, 31,* 364–369.

Callaghan, J. E., Alexander, J. H., Sixsmith, J., & Fellin, L. C. (2018). Beyond "witnessing": Children's experiences of coercive control in domestic violence and abuse. *Journal of Interpersonal Violence, 33,* 1551–1581.

Campbell, J. C. (2004). Helping women understand their risk in situations of intimate partner violence. *Journal of Interpersonal Violence, 19,* 1464–1477.

Carville, O. (January 29, 2015). Abdille triple homicide prompts renewed calls for change in Ontario domestic-violence system. *The Star.* Retrieved from <https://www.thestar.com/news/gta/2015/01/29/abdille-triple-homicide-prompts-renewed-calls-for-change-in-ontario-domestic-violence-system.html>.

Chanmugam, A., & Hall, K. (2012). Safety planning with children and adolescents in domestic violence shelters. *Violence and Victims, 27,* 831–848.

Chanmugam, A., Kemter, A. J., & Goodwin, K. H. (2015). Educational services for children in domestic violence shelters: Perspectives of shelter personnel. *Child and Adolescent Social Work Journal, 32,* 405–415.

Child Family Community Australia. (2017). *The prevalence of child abuse and neglect.* Melbourne, Australia: Australian Institute of Family Studies. Retrieved from <www.aifs.gov.au/cfca/publications/prevalence-child-abuse-and-neglect>.

Dawson, M. (2015). Canadian trends in filicide by gender of the accused, 1961−2011. *Child Abuse & Neglect, 47,* 162−174.

Davis, G. (2015). A systematic approach to domestic abuse-informed child custody decision making in family law cases. *Family Court Review, 53,* 565−577.

Department for Education. (2018). *Characteristics of children in need: 2017 to 2018. Government of United Kingdom.* Retrieved from <https://assets. publishing.service.gov.uk/government/uploads/system/uploads/ attachment_data/file/762527/Characteristics_of_children_in_need_2017-18. pdf>.

Dixon, S., Krienert, J. L., & Walsh, J. (2013). Filicide: A gendered profile of offender, victim, and event characteristics in a national sample of reported incidents, 1995−2009. *Journal of Crime and Justice, 37,* 339−355.

Edelson, J., Gassman-Pines, J., & Hill, M. (2006). Defining child exposure to domestic violence as neglect: Minnesota's difficult experience. *Social Work, 51,* 167−174.

Eriksson, L., Mazerolle, P., Wortley, R., & Johnson, H. (2016). Maternal and paternal filicide: Case studies from the Australian Homicide Project. *Child Abuse Review, 25,* 17−30.

Ezell, E., McDonald, R., & Jouriles, E. (2000). Helping children of battered women: A review of research, sampling of programs, and presentation of Project SUPPORT. In J. Vincent, & E. Jouriles (Eds.), *Domestic violence: Guidelines for research-informed practice* (pp. 144−170). London: Jessica Kingsley.

Fusco, R. A. (2013). "It's hard enough to deal with all the abuse issues": Child welfare workers' experiences with intimate partner violence on their caseloads. *Children and Youth Services Review, 35,* 1946.

Groves, B. M., & Gewirtz, A. (2006). Interventions and promising approaches for children exposed to domestic violence. *Children Exposed to Violence,* 107−133.

Godbout, E., Parent, C., & Saint-Jacques, M. C. (2015). Positions taken by judges and custody experts on issues relating to the best interests of children in custody disputes in Quebec. *International Journal of Law, Policy and the Family, 29,* 272−300.

Hamby, S., Finkelhor, D., & Turner, H. (2015). Intervention following family violence: Best practices and helpseeking obstacles in a nationally representative sample of families with children. *Psychology of Violence, 5,* 325.

Hamilton, L. H. A., Jaffe, P. G., & Campbell, M. (2013). Assessing children's risk for homicide in the context of domestic violence. *Journal of Family Violence, 28,* 179−189.

Hardesty, J. L., & Campbell, J. C. (2004). Safety planning for abused women and their children. In P. G. Jaffe, L. L. Baker, & A. J. Cunningham (Eds.), *Protecting children from domestic violence: Strategies for community intervention* (pp. 89−100). New York: Guilford Press.

Harrison, C. (2008). Implacably hostile or appropriately protective? Women managing child contact in the context of domestic violence. *Violence Against Women, 14,* 381−405.

Healey, L., Connolly, M., & Humphreys, C. (2018). A collaborative practice framework for child protection and specialist domestic and family violence services: Bridging the research and practice divide. *Australian Social Work, 71,* 228−237.

Healy, J., & Bell, M. (2005). *Assessing the risks to children from domestic violence. Policy and Practice Briefing* (p. 7) .

Hester, M. (2011). The three planet model: Towards an understanding of contradictions in approaches to women and children's safety in contexts of domestic violence. *British Journal of Social Work, 41,* 837–853.

Holt, S., Buckley, H., & Whelan, S. (2008). The impact of exposure to domestic violence on children and young people: A review of the literature. *Child Abuse & Neglect, 32,* 797–810.

Hughes, J., & Chau, S. (2012). Children's best interest and intimate partner violence in the Canadian family law and child protection systems. *Critical Social Policy, 32,* 677–695.

Hughes, J., Chau, S., & Poff, D. C. (2011). "They're not my favourite people": What mothers who have experienced intimate partner violence say about involvement in the child protection system. *Children and Youth Services Review, 33,* 1084–1089.

Humphreys, C., & Absler, D. (2011). History repeating: Child protection responses to domestic violence. *Child & Family Social Work, 16,* 464–473.

Hunt, J., & Macleod, A. (2008). *Outcomes of applications to court for contact orders after parental separation or divorce.* Oxford Centre for Family Law and Policy Department of Social Policy and Social Work University of Oxford. Retrieved June 2, 2019 from <https://dera.ioe.ac.uk/9145/1/outcomes-applications-contact-orders.pdf>.

Jaffe, P. G., Ashbourne, D., & Mamo, A. A. (2010). Early identification and prevention of parent–child alienation: A framework for balancing risks and benefits of intervention. *Family Court Review, 48,* 136–152.

Jaffe, P. G., Campbell, M., Hamilton, L. H., & Juodis, M. (2012). Child in danger of domestic homicide. *Child Abuse and Neglect the International Journal, 36,* 71.

Jaffe, P. G., Crooks, C. V., & Bala, N. (2009). A framework for addressing allegations of domestic violence in child custody disputes. *Journal of Child Custody, 6,* 169–188.

Jaffe, P., Campbell, M., Reif, K., Fairbairn, J., & David, R. (2017). *Children killed in the context of domestic violence: International perspectives from death review committees. Domestic homicides and death reviews* (pp. 317–343). London: Palgrave Macmillan.

Jenney, A., Mishna, F., Alaggia, R., & Scott, K. (2014). Doing the right thing? (Re) Considering risk assessment and safety planning in child protection work with domestic violence cases. *Children and Youth Services Review, 47,* 92–101.

Langenderfer-Magruder, L., Alven, L., Wilke, D. J., & Spinelli, C. (2019). "Getting Everyone on the Same Page": Child welfare workers' collaboration challenges on cases involving intimate partner violence. *Journal of Family Violence, 34,* 21–31.

Lapierre, S., & Côté, I. (2011). "I made her realise that I could be there for her, that I could support her": Child protection practices with women in domestic violence cases. *Child Care in Practice, 17,* 311–325.

Lessard, G., Flynn, C., Turcotte, P., Damant, D., Vézina, J. F., Godin, M. F., ... Rock, L. (2010). Child custody issues and co-occurrence of intimate partner violence and child maltreatment: Controversies and points of agreement amongst practitioners. *Child & Family Social Work, 15,* 492–500.

Lewandowski, L. A., McFarlane, J., Campbell, J. C., Gary, F., & Barenski, C. (2004). "He Killed My Mommy!" Murder or attempted murder of a child's mother. *Journal of Family Violence, 19,* 211–220.

Liem, M., & Koenraadt, F. (2008). Filicide: A comparative study of maternal versus paternal child homicide. *Criminal Behaviour and Mental Health, 18,* 166–176.

Macvean, M. L., Humphreys, C., & Healey, L. (2018). Facilitating the collaborative interface between child protection and specialist domestic violence services: A scoping review. *Australian Social Work, 71*, 148–161.

Macdonald, G. S. (2016). Domestic violence and private family court proceedings: Promoting child welfare or promoting contact? *Violence Against Women, 22*, 832–852.

Mandel, D. (2010). Child welfare and domestic violence: Tackling the themes and thorny questions that stand in the way of collaboration and improvement of child welfare practice. *Violence Against Women, 16*, 530–536.

McConnell, N., Barnard, M., & Taylor, J. (2017). Caring Dads Safer Children: Families' perspectives on an intervention for maltreating fathers. *Psychology of Violence, 7*(3), 406.

Meier, J. S. (2009). A historical perspective on parental alienation syndrome and parental alienation. *Journal of Child Custody, 6*(3-4), 232–257.

Meier, J. S., & Dickson, S. (2017). Mapping gender: Shedding empirical light on family courts' treatment of cases involving abuse and alienation. *Law & Inequality, 35*, 311.

Øverlien, C., & Aas, G. (2016). The police patrols and children experiencing domestic violence. *Police Practice and Research, 17*, 434–447.

Petrucci, C. J., & Mills, L. G. (2002). Domestic violence assessment: Current practices and new models for improved child welfare interventions. *Brief Treatment and Crisis Intervention, 2*, 153.

Poole, A., Beran, T., & Thurston, W. E. (2008). Direct and indirect services for children in domestic violence shelters. *Journal of Family Violence, 23*, 679–686.

Postmus, J. L., & Merritt, D. H. (2010). When child abuse overlaps with domestic violence: The factors that influence child protection workers' beliefs. *Children and Youth Services Review, 32*, 309–317.

Public Health Agency of Canada. (2010). *Canadian incidence study of reported child abuse and neglect - 2008: Major findings*. Ottawa, ON: Public Health Agency of Canada. Retrieved from <https://cwrp.ca/sites/default/files/publications/en/CIS-2008-rprt-eng.pdf>.

Pulido, M. L., Forrester, S. P., & Lacina, J. M. (2011). Raising the bar: Why supervised visitation providers should be required to meet standards for service provision. *Family Court Review, 49*, 379–387.

Radford, L., Blacklock, N., & Iwi, K. (2006). Domestic violence risk assessment and safety planning in child protection – Assessing perpetrators. In C. Humphreys, & N. Stanley (Eds.), *Domestic violence and child protection: Directions for good practice* (pp. 171–189). London: Jessica Kingsley Publishers.

Richardson-Foster, H., Stanley, N., Miller, P., & Thomson, G. (2012). Police intervention in domestic violence incidents where children are present: Police and children's perspectives. *Policing and Society, 22*, 220–234.

Rivera, E. A., Zeoli, A. M., & Sullivan, C. M. (2012). Abused mothers' safety concerns and court mediators' custody recommendations. *Journal of family violence, 27*, 321–332.

Robinson, A. L. (2006). Reducing repeat victimization among high-risk victims of domestic violence: The benefits of a coordinated community response in Cardiff, Wales. *Violence Against Women, 12*, 761–788.

Robinson, A., & Payton, J. (2016). *Independent advocacy and multi-agency responses to domestic violence. Domestic violence* (pp. 249–271). London: Palgrave Macmillan.

Robinson, A. L., & Tregidga, J. (2007). The perceptions of high-risk victims of domestic violence to a coordinated community response in Cardiff, Wales. *Violence Against Women, 13*, 1130−1148.

Saltiel, D. (2015). *Observing front line decision making in child protection,* . *British Journal of Social Work* (46, pp. 2104−2119).

Saunders, D. G. (2015). Research based recommendations for child custody evaluation practices and policies in cases of intimate partner violence. *Journal of Child Custody, 12*, 71−92. Available from https://doi.org/10.1080/15379418.2015.1037052.

Scott, K. L., & Lishak, V. (2012). Intervention for maltreating fathers: Statistically and clinically significant change. *Child Abuse & Neglect, 36*, 680−684.

Shlonsky, A., & Friend, C. (2007). Double jeopardy: Risk assessment in the context of child maltreatment and domestic violence. *Brief Treatment and Crisis Intervention, 7*(4), 253.

Smith, S. G., Fowler, K. A., & Niolon, P. H. (2014). Intimate partner homicide and corollary victims in 16 states: National Violent Death Reporting System, 2003−2009. *American Journal of Public Health, 104*, 461−466.

Stanley, N., & Humphreys, C. (2014). Multi-agency risk assessment and management for children and families experiencing domestic violence. *Children and Youth Services Review, 47*, 78−85.

Stanley, N., Miller, P., Richardson Foster, H., & Thomson, G. (2010). *Children and families experiencing domestic violence: Police and children's social services responses.* London: NSPCC. Available at <www.nspcc.org.uk/Inform/research/Findings/children_experiencing_domestic_violence_wda68549.html>Accessed 30.04.19.

Stanley, N., Miller, P., Richardson Foster, H., & Thomson, G. (2011). A stop−start response: Social services' interventions with children and families notified following domestic violence incidents. *The British Journal of Social Work, 41*, 296−313.

Stephens, N., McDonald, R., & Jouriles, E. N. (2000). Helping children who reside at shelters for battered women: Lessons learned. *Journal of Aggression, Maltreatment & Trauma, 3*, 147−160.

Stern, N., & Oehme, K. (2010). A comprehensive blueprint for a crucial service: Florida's new supervised visitation strategy. *Journal of Law & Family Studies, 12*, 199.

Stöckl, H., Dekel, B., Morris-Gehring, A., Watts, C., & Abrahams, N. (2017). Child homicide perpetrators worldwide: A systematic review. *BMJ Paediatrics Open, 1*(1).

Symons, D. K. (2010). A review of the practice and science of child custody and access assessment in the United States and Canada. *Professional Psychology: Research and Practice, 41*, 267.

Trinder, L., Firth, A., & Jenks, C. (2009). 'So presumably things have moved on since then?' The management of risk allegations in child contact dispute resolution. *International Journal of Law, Policy and the Family, 24*, 29−53.

UNICEF. (2014). *Hidden in plain sight: A statistical analysis of violence against children.* New York: UNICEF, United Nations Children's Fund.

Additional media sources

<https://www.ola.org/en/legislative-business/committees/regulations-private-bills/parliament-38/transcripts/committee-transcript-2006-aug-29#P243_51477>.

<https://www.thestar.com/news/gta/2015/02/01/failure-of-criminal-family-courts-to-share-information-puts-lives-at-risk.html>.
<https://www.thestar.com/news/gta/2015/01/29/abdille-triple-homicide-prompts-renewed-calls-for-change-in-ontario-domestic-violence-system.html>.
<https://www.thestar.com/news/crime/2014/12/04/triple_homicide_slaying_victim_told_friend_she_was_afraid_of_her_husband.html>.
<https://www.theglobeandmail.com/news/toronto/mourners-at-slain-toronto-familys-funeral-shoulder-blame/article21981276/>.
<https://torontosun.com/2014/12/03/man-who-died-on-dvp-idd-as-husband-father-of-murder-victims/wcm/50a6eeb3-c7f4-4972-9a66-fc0b04453040>.

Domestic homicides with police and military: understanding the risks enhanced by trauma and workplace culture

Barbara MacQuarrie[1], Michael Saxton[1], Laura Olszowy[1], Peter Jaffe[1] and Verona Singer[2]

[1]Centre for Research & Education on Violence Against Women & Children, Faculty of Education, Western University, London, ON, Canada [2]Department of Criminology, Saint Mary's University, Halifax, Nova Scotia, Canada

Introduction

This chapter explores two high-risk professions in which the work itself exposes members to risk factors for domestic homicide: police officers and military personnel. Before exploring these phenomena, it is essential to recognize that the overwhelming majority of military personnel and police officers deal with stressful jobs but do not assault their partners. However, limited research (Blumenstein, Fridell, & Jones, 2012; Garvey, 2015; Gershon, 1999; MacManus & Wessely, 2012; Roslin, 2016; Stinson & Liederbach, 2013) and media coverage of these tragedies reinforce an association with a higher incidence of domestic violence (DV) in these groups compared to the general population (MacManus & Wessely, 2012). Overall the research into these careers and DV has lagged behind public perception and is reviewed in this chapter, together with homicide case studies that illustrate some consistent themes and recommendations to address the problem.

Police and military are covered together in this chapter due to shared features of risk for domestic homicide. Traditionally they are male-dominated professions infused with strong patriarchal values. In both occupations, controlled aggression may be required to deal with life-threatening events that also become a source of trauma. Given this, it is unsurprising that both careers are also associated with the development of mental

Preventing Domestic Homicides. DOI: https://doi.org/10.1016/B978-0-12-819463-8.00009-5

health disorders like posttraumatic stress disorder (PTSD). The strength and courage of police and soldiers are highly valued, but acknowledging vulnerability and seeking help are widely perceived as incongruent with those qualities. There are questions about whether the cultures of these organizations reinforce violence against women. This chapter begins with a review of what we know about military and police DV and homicide. We examine the association of particular risk factors arising from involvement in these professions with DV. To supplement the emerging literature, we examine high-profile trage-dies for lessons learned. We conclude with recommendations for practice and future research.

Domestic violence and homicide in the military

Higher rates of sexual violence against women have been docu-mented within all male-dominated institutions (Bostock & Daley, 2007), including the military (Statistics Canada, 2018). The 1993 federal government report by the Canadian Panel on Violence Against Women concluded that there was an irony in "the mili-tary's mandate to defend the country and insure nationwide peace; yet, women within its ambit – citizens of the very population the Canadian military is supposed to protect – are mistreated and abused" (Marshall, Vaillancourt, & Canadian Panel on Violence Against Women, 1993, p. 253). Indeed conclusions from an exter-nal review of violence against women in the military by retired Supreme Court Justice Deschamps show that little has changed:

> *One of the key findings of the External Review Authority (the ERA) is that there is an underlying sexualized culture in the CAF [Canadian Armed Forces] that is hostile to women and LGTBQ members, and conducive to more serious incidents of sexual harassment and assault. Cultural change is therefore key. It is not enough to simply revise policies or to repeat the mantra of 'zero tolerance.' Leaders must acknowledge that sexual misconduct is a real and serious problem for the organization, one that requires their own direct and sustained attention*

Deschamps (2015, p. i)

The author goes on to suggest that the problem cannot be attributed to badly behaved individuals, but rather implicates a military culture where "unwelcome sexual conduct... contributes to a hostile organizational culture – includ[ing] sexual comments or jokes that are not necessarily addressed to a particular person, but which create a negative sexualized environment."

(Deschamps, 2015, p. 5). These dynamics are associated with all forms of violence against women, including DV.

The inherent risks for violence against women who are members of the military extend to military partners and spouses as well. Although it is challenging to research DV in the military, because of the implications of reporting this behavior (Sparrow, Kwan, Howard, Fear, & MacManus, 2017), some estimates of prevalence put rates as high as threefold more common among active soldiers and veterans than the general population (MacManus & Wessely, 2012). US studies demonstrate that reported rates of sexual assault in the military are higher than those reported in the general population. A systematic review of studies suggests that between 1 in 3 and 1 and 10 women report experiencing an attempted or completed rape while serving in the US military (Turchik & Wilson, 2010). Some have also suggested that DV perpetrated by military members is more severe than that perpetrated by the general civilian population (Trevillion et al., 2015). There are many theories for the severity and the frequency of military DV that include stress, repeated separations through deployments, mental illness, substance abuse, and a lack of access to treatment (Gierisch et al., 2013; Shaller, 2012; Sparrow et al., 2017).

There are several risk factors for DV associated with the military. For instance, the military includes many young and nonmarried individuals, the highest risk age group for experiencing DV. Mental health disorders from combat exposure have been linked to DV (Marshall, Panuzio, & Taft, 2005) with PTSD receiving the most attention. Some studies have found that hyperarousal symptoms are heightened in combat veterans. That increases their appraisal of threat, which could be associated with DV (Semiatin, Torres, LaMotte, Portnoy, & Murphy, 2017). Desensitization to violence is another risk factor. Desensitization may lead to increased interpersonal violence in general, and violence toward women specifically (Haddock, 2006). The military environment also promotes hypermasculinity, an extreme form of masculinity based on beliefs endorsing polarized, and stereotypical gender roles. This environment emphasizes control, power, competition, and tolerating pain, rather than disclosure of assaults (Rosen, Knudson, & Fancher, 2003).

In later years, family stresses like adjustments to nonmilitary life, ongoing financial dependency, and ongoing mental health problems may compound the risk for DV (Patton, McNally, & Fremouw, 2015; Trevillion et al., 2015). Adding to the complexity of these problems is the stigma related to experiencing mental health concerns and military veterans' reluctance to self-identify and seek assistance (Shaller, 2012). Both active duty service members and veterans have difficulty seeking mental health care. Although this stigma is beginning to ease, those who wish to get help continue to fear not being taken seriously, job loss, or being looked down upon by their leaders and fellow service members Although soldiers frequently report alcohol concerns, very few are referred for treatment (Milliken, Auchterlonie, & Hoge, 2007). Insufficient treatment facilities on military bases can compound the problem (Shaller, 2012).

At the same time, military spouses and partners are reluctant to disclose the violence. They fear job loss when they are dependent on their spouse for housing and economic security. Partners and spouses also often experience isolation resulting from frequent moves and are unable to learn about and establish trusting relationships with potential sources of support. These issues are further complicated by a lack of trust in how complaints are dealt with by supervisors (Harrison & Laliberte, 1994; McQueen Fergusson Centre & RESOLVE, 2000).

Domestic violence and homicide in policing

Law enforcement is a unique job with specific training and a work culture that may increase the risk of violence at home. Like the military, the prevalence of DV is difficult to establish within police families, though estimates of officer-perpetrated DV have ranged from 10% to 40% (Blumenstein et al., 2012; Garvey, 2015; Gershon, 1999; Stinson & Liederbach, 2013). Although there continue to be significant gaps in research on the extent and the impact of police-perpetrated DV, available research has recognized that the nature of policing work can increase the risk for DV perpetration. Some point to the "spillover" of police training and culture as influences that can contribute to violence occurring at home. For instance, Johnson, Todd, and Subramanian (2005) highlighted that many risk factors associated with the perpetration of DV in the general population show up in police culture and police work. These can be broken down into three clusters: (1) attitudes and behaviors instilled as part of police training, (2) the masculine and authoritarian nature of traditional police culture, and (3) officers' work stress and resulting mental health problems and burnout (Johnson et al., 2005; Oehme, Prost, & Saunders, 2016).

Similar to the military, police officers face an exceptional level of work-related stress and are likely to experience exposure to violent and traumatic situations. Without proper support, this stress can have a multitude of effects, including a negative impact on intimate relationships. Previous research has documented higher rates of job stress, PTSD, and substance use for police officers exposed to violence and traumatic situations while on the job (Gershon, 2000; Neidig, Russell, & Seng, 1992; Saunders, Prost, & Oehme, 2016; Stinson & Liederbach, 2013). Like the military, police culture also embraces values of hypermasculinity, and officers may have difficulty "turning off" their work role while at home. These have been identified as potential correlates of police-perpetrated DV (Johnson, 2010; Oehme et al., 2016). Authoritarianism, cynicism, and burnout are other elements of traditional police culture connected to a higher risk of DV (Blumenstein et al., 2012).

Perhaps one of the most complex associations between DV and the role of a police officer is related to their regular use of coercive force and control over people. Police are trained in interrogation techniques and the appropriate use of power and coercive force. They are sometimes required to use physical force to maintain compliance (Stinson & Liederbach, 2013). If misused, the skills, culture, and training that are characteristic of policing can create a formidable, highly trained perpetrator of DV (Garvey, 2015; Johnson et al., 2005).

For many victims, reporting DV by a police officer is tremendously difficult. Partners of police officers must report the abusive spouse to his or her workplace, making confidentiality for the survivor and the abusive partner difficult. Solidarity with coworkers is vital for police officers who rely heavily on the support of colleagues for safety and support in their role as law enforcement (Garvey, 2015). As a result, survivors may not be believed, or complaints may be minimized (Mazzola, 2013). A "code of silence" that emphasizes secrecy and discourages reporting of colleagues' misconduct (Roslin, 2016) also serves as a barrier to disclosing or reporting DV (Oehme et al., 2016).

The consequences of reporting a police officer for DV can also deter victims. In the United States, the introduction of the Lautenberg Amendment prohibits police officers from owning or using a gun if they convicted of a misdemeanor crime of DV. This places victims in a difficult situation. While they want the violence to end, they may not want their partners' career to end. Also police officers have a unique understanding of how police investigate crimes. The National Center on Women and Policing (2013) highlights that police perpetrators of DV are readily able to manipulate the criminal justice system and shift blame to victims. These factors all contribute to victims' silence and reluctance to report (Lonsway, 2006; Russell & Pappas,

2018). Consequently, too often, police officers are not held accountable for their actions (Roslin, 2016).

Those trying to escape a violent relationship face additional barriers when leaving a police officer (Ammons, 2004). Escaping a violent relationship can involve many vital supports, including women's shelters and community services. However, police officers have knowledge of local shelter locations and other community resources available to victims of DV. Coupled with police professional training, skills, equipment, and job mobility make it relatively easy for officers who are abusive to their partners to find and monitor victims. Separation is generally a time of increased risk for homicide. Victims leaving a police officer, particularly when the relationship has been severely violent, face extreme vulnerability due to the officer's awareness of community resources, the means to locate the victim, and training and skills in the use of coercion and force (Ammons, 2004).

Potential risk factors associated with domestic homicide in the military and policing

The earlier discussion highlights several risk factors identified by DVDRCs that are particularly relevant to the military and police. Both professions have ready *access to firearms* as well as the training and skills to utilize them. Careers in policing and in the military involve high levels of stress and ongoing exposure to violence at work. These are prototypical environments for the development of PTSD and related *mental health concerns*, including *depression* and *substance use*, both of which are well-established risk factors for domestic homicide.

DV and domestic homicide are also associated with *misogynistic attitudes, which* are more likely to be found within patriarchal workplaces. There is considerable evidence about how military and police institutions support these cultural norms. *The routine use of power and control to gain compliance* is another risk factor. There is evidence to show that police training, as well as professional life, can contribute to a perpetrator's arsenal of techniques and tactics of abuse (Wetendorf, 2000). Among members of the military, combat exposure correlates with intimate partner violence perpetration (Marshall et al., 2005), but interestingly, Orcutt, King, and King (2003) found a negative direct association between combat exposure and partner aggression when controlling for PTSD symptoms.

Added to these career-related risk factors are a number of other more general risk factors that may play a significant role within police and military populations. Some research suggests that individuals who join the military are more likely to come from troubled families with a *history of abuse* (Blosnich, Dichter, Cerulli, Batten, & Bossarte, 2014; Langhinrichsen-Rohling, Neidig, & Thorn, 1995). Military personnel and families tend to be younger than other career-oriented workplaces (Clever & Segal, 2013), triggering DV risks associated with *younger age groups*. While these risk factors are not specific to police and military personnel, they are part of the fabric of these professions, leading to workplace cultures that may inadvertently support DV.

There are also several *victim vulnerability* factors that impede help seeking in victims of DV. There may be a heightened concern that reporting will result in criminal proceedings and employment loss in policing and the military. Victims are concerned about not being believed, and these issues are compounded if both the victim and perpetrator are employed within the same institution. The ability of police to monitor efforts to seek help interferes with a victim's ability to find support. Together these factors can deter a victim from coming forward.

The following case studies provide insight on how these risk factors can play out within domestic homicide tragedies.

Case study military

Desmond murder—suicide

On January 3, 2017, close to supper time, 33-year-old Lionel Desmond shot and killed his wife Shanna Desmond, 31 years old, his daughter Aaliyah, 10 years old, and his mother Brenda Desmond, 52 years old, before turning the gun on himself in their home in the rural African Nova Scotian community of Upper Big Tracadie. Mr. Desmond was a former corporal in the Canadian Armed Forces who had served two tours in Afghanistan. One of the guns used to kill the family was a semiautomatic Soviet military-style weapon which Mr. Desmond purchased a few days before the murder—suicide from a local outdoor store.

Lionel Desmond met Shanna Borden when they were in high school in Guysborough County. He joined the military shortly after graduation, and their daughter Aaliyah was born just before he was deployed to Afghanistan in 2007. Ms. Desmond had recently graduated from a university nursing program and had taken a position at a hospital in a neighboring town. Brenda Desmond, Mr. Desmond's mother, was visiting the family for the Christmas holidays at the time of the murder.

Relatives say Desmond did not get the help or support he needed upon his return home to Nova Scotia nor from St. Martha's Hospital in Antigonish where he tried to access mental health services 3 days before the murder–suicide. Family members state Desmond's lack of treatment for the posttraumatic stress contributed to this tragedy and that he fell through the cracks of the federal and provincial government systems. However, in a Facebook posting in early December 2016, Mr. Desmond stated he was diagnosed with postconcussion and PTSD and was treated at a joint forces' personnel facility in New Brunswick that supports ill and injured members for one year before his medical discharge. Mr. Desmond then went to Montreal for 3 months to receive further treatment for his PTSD. After his medical discharge in 2015, Mr. and Ms. Desmond accessed marital counseling and went to many medical appointments.

Sisters of Mr. Desmond stated their brother was a radically changed person when he returned home in 2015. His sense of humor had diminished, and he seemed withdrawn. He experienced waking up in cold sweats and was constantly in a defensive posture backing into corners with his back against the wall. Family members of Mr. Desmond early on called for a public inquiry. They wanted to know why St. Martha's Hospital and Veteran's Affairs failed to provide adequate care to Mr. Desmond for his PTSD. The premier of the province stated the health authority would review what services were offered to Desmond and whether protocols were followed.

It is important to recognize the context of the community in which the Desmond's lived. Upper Big Tracadie is a rural community and is mostly African Nova Scotian. There are historical experiences of discrimination and racism that continue to the present day. This context likely prevents many African Nova Scotian women from reporting abuse for fear of a racist response from the police and justice system. Many women may also worry that reporting abuse will keep alive stereotypes that African Canadian men are violent. Additionally there are fewer supports in rural communities, and women experiencing violence face additional barriers to access services, including having to leave the community as well as difficulty in staying anonymous.

There were mixed public reactions and tensions in the small community regarding whether this murder–suicide was caused by DV or PTSD. One commentator, Dr. Ardath Whynacht, a professor of sociology at Mount Allison University in New Brunswick, stated that in her opinion, DV was a significant factor in the murder–suicide. There were reports of prior domestic abuse that seemed to be acknowledged on social media by Mr. Desmond (Renzetti, 2017). In a Facebook post on December 2016, Mr. Desmond stated he was sorry for being jealous and overcontrolling to his wife and his vulgar outbursts to family. He attributed his violent behaviors to the postconcussion disorder. Dr. Whynacht opined that a diagnosis of PTSD does not necessarily lead to violence, so to view this murder−suicide from only one lens may provide an incomplete picture (MacDonald, 2017). Rev. Elaine Walcott, a relative of the Desmond's and a spiritual adviser, from a neighboring village, took an opposing view. She said shifting the blame to DV would only succeed in "perpetuating stereotypical images and pitting members of the black community against each other" (The Canadian Press, 2017).

On May 24, 2017, the Nova Scotia Minister of Justice announced an inquiry under the Fatality's Investigative Act would be held to examine the Desmonds' deaths. The inquiry will investigate multiple issues surrounding the circumstances under which the deaths occurred, including whether Mr. Desmond had access to appropriate mental health services and treatment for occupational stress injuries and whether his family had access to appropriate DV intervention services.

In this case, the history of DV was a risk factor for homicide. By the perpetrator's admission, he was jealous and controlling and these were also known risk factors. The perpetrator's training in the use of weapons and his easy access to a gun also constitute risk factors. Mental health problems and specifically PTSD was a significant risk factor. The question of whether or not it was the primary cause of the murder−suicide is a question being explored in the inquiry. Importantly the African Nova Scotian identities of both the perpetrator and the victim, as well as their rural location, are intersectional factors that potentially contributed to victim vulnerability. The victim would have had limited options for support in her rural community, and she may have hesitated to reach out to the supports that did exist for fear of experiencing racism herself and out of fear of reinforcing stereotypes about violent black men.

Case studies policing

Ontario domestic violence death review committee police-involved cases

The following section contains three domestic homicide cases perpetrated by police officers in Canada, which were reviewed by the Ontario DVDRC. The Ontario DVDRC has published at least three annual reports (2005, 2010, and 2012) containing reviews of domestic homicide cases perpetrated by a police officer.

The first case was a homicide—suicide perpetrated by a 22-year police veteran in 2003. The couple was in the process of a divorce. The victim described the perpetrator as self-centered and controlling and felt they were no longer compatible. The perpetrator reportedly felt betrayed, hurt, and vulnerable as a result of the divorce proceedings. The perpetrator had been involved in an on duty altercation several years earlier. Shortly before the homicide, the victim mentioned the divorce in front of the couple's daughter, which was a triggering event. The perpetrator retrieved his service firearm while off duty and returned to the home where he killed the victim before he killed himself.

The second case took place in 2007 and involved a female perpetrator and male victim who were ending their relationship. Both the perpetrator and victim were respected senior police officers in their community. The couple, long-time colleagues and friends outside the workplace, were both separated from their spouses and began their relationship while they were both still married. It was reported that the perpetrator struggled with mental health issues exacerbated by relationship losses and grief. In the days leading up to the homicide, it is believed that the victim told the perpetrator he intended to reunite with his wife. The perpetrator was reportedly exceedingly distressed by the breakup and was not eating or sleeping well for 2 days before the homicide. Close friends were concerned about her. On the night of the homicide, the perpetrator asked the victim to reconsider ending it and promised to follow any conditions he might impose on their reunification. The couple saw one another at the victim's residence before he drove the perpetrator home. She retrieved her service firearm from the station while off duty and the victim waited in the car. Once they arrived at her residence, she shot and killed him and then herself.

The third case was a homicide perpetrated by a retired police officer in 2008. The victim expressed concern about her husband's health problems and increasingly severe drinking. The victim shared concerns with a friend about her husband's alcohol-fueled anger. He would occasionally get mad at the victim for working too much. On the morning of the homicide, a friend of the perpetrator came to pick him up for a hunting trip. The perpetrator appeared drunk and was stumbling when he told his friend he had shot his wife.

These cases highlight several risk factors that are commonly identified in cases of domestic homicides, but that also have a unique policing angle to them. Prior DV was identified in some of the cases, which highlights the importance of addressing officer-involved domestic violence (OIDV) as a potential precedent for police-perpetrated domestic homicides.

Separation is widely known to be a dangerous time when there has been DV in a relationship. In two of these situations, separation was pending. That risk was compounded by access to firearms, which increases risk of lethality, not only in the context of separation but also in the presence of mental health problems and escalating violence. In half of the cases, the perpetrators were able to retrieve their service firearms while off duty without incident. Mental health problems or heavy alcohol use was a risk factor in two of the three cases.

The expectation of toughness and the reticence to seek support in policing culture may have dissuaded disclosures of struggles with mental health, emotional problems, and substance abuse. The DVDRC has noted that the link between job-related trauma and stressors and the potential to harm to self and others is not adequately addressed in training (Ontario DVDRC, 2010).

David Brame and Crystal Judson

On April 26, 2003, Tacoma, Washington police chief David Brame shot and killed his estranged wife, Crystal Judson, in front of their two children in the parking lot of a local shopping plaza. Brame then killed himself using his service weapon. The day before Mr. Brame murdered his wife, a local newspaper released a news story chronicling the couple's divorce, including charges against Mr. Brame for threatening Ms. Judson with his service weapon.

Mr. Brame began a career in policing in 1981 when the Tacoma Police Department hired him. He came from a family of police officers and was well-connected to local city leaders through his work with the police union. Concerns raised during the hiring process led to three psychological evaluations before he was deemed eligible. The first psychologist found Mr. Brame to be a danger to himself, other officers, and the community. The second examiner, hired by Mr. Brame, deemed him suitable for the career, while a third, appointed by the department recommended against his hiring. Ultimately Mr. Brame was hired. Early in Mr. Brame's career, a woman reported to internal affairs that Mr. Brame raped her after a date and left a gun on the nightstand to threaten her. The allegation was investigated through internal affairs. Court documents reveal that the investigating detective believed the woman's allegations but lacked sufficient evidence to prove the allegation. Despite reported allegations of abuse, he was permitted to rise through the ranks of the Tacoma Police Department.

Ms. Judson and Mr. Brame married in 1991. The couple had two children, Haley and David Jr., born in 1994 and 1997, respectively. A long history of DV was documented in divorce proceedings and reported by Ms. Judson's parents, Lane and Patty Judson. Mr. Brame controlled many of Ms. Judson's daily activities. He marked the time she left home and returned, checked her odometer, and forced her to weigh herself every day. She was seldom allowed privacy, with Mr. Brame frequently watching her, even when she went to the bathroom. Mr. Brame was psychologically abusive with Ms. Judson, calling her mentally unstable and telling others the same. Mr. Brame made threats to take their children away if she left and reminded her that if she reported him, he would lose his job, leaving her without financial stability. Mr. Brame reported to police three times in 1996 that he and Ms. Judson had an intense argument and later that his wife abused him. In fact many bureaucrats within the local government were aware of Mr. Brame's abusive behaviors and failed to heed warning signs or take preventative action. Known allegations were ignored by the city manager even when he promoted Mr. Brame to the police chief.

In 1998 Ms. Judson tried to meet with a divorce attorney secretly. However, Mr. Brame hijacked the meeting and put an end to Ms. Judson's attempt to separate. Mr. Brame involved several officers in the surveillance of that attorney's office. Ms. Judson's father found another attorney for her, but Ms. Judson decided not to proceed. During the course of the marriage, Mr. Brame brought Ms. Judson to a marriage counseling session with the police chaplain.

Ms. Judson lived in fear for herself and the couple's two children. In November 2002 reports showed that Mr. Brame choked Ms. Judson and threatened to snap her neck. On February 15, 2003 Mr. Brame pointed his police-issued handgun at Ms. Judson and threatened her, stating "accidents happen." While Ms. Judson did not formally report these incidents to the police, she did tell the assistant police chief, Catherine Woodard. Ms. Woodard made notes and gave them to Mr. Brame. Reports from coworkers indicated that Mr. Brame made demands that Ms. Judson have a sexual threesome with a female Tacoma Police Department detective.

On February 21, 2003, Ms. Judson and the children moved out of the family home to stay with her parents in a gated community. Three days later, Ms. Judson filed for divorce after enduring years of physical and psychological abuse. She filed the papers in a different county, and despite her lawyer's advice, she decided not to file a restraining order to minimize publicity that could harm Mr. Brame's career. She stated in a March 2003 declaration, "I went to great lengths to try to not upset my husband initially because I was so afraid of his reaction." (Associate Press, 2003). In divorce proceedings, Mr. Brame accused his wife of scratching and bruising him in 1996 and said she threatened to hurt his career. Reports indicate that Mr. Brame consulted city attorneys on his divorce and was preoccupied by it, distracting him from his job.

Mr. Brame continued to blur work and personal boundaries when he brought three uniformed officers to one of his divorce hearings to facilitate moving the trial to his local county. He continued to seek legal advice from city attorneys. On April 11, 2003, Mr. Brame attended his in-laws' home with an officer to pick up his children. A few hours later, Ms. Judson reported to the police that Mr. Brame and the officer reentered this gated community under false pretenses. Around this time, several police officers anonymously requested an internal affairs investigation of this incident, threatening to go to the news media if the matter was ignored. The police department did not comment on whether an investigation was started.

Less than 2 weeks later, a local blog writer published a post on Mr. Brame's abusive behavior after receiving a copy of court papers anonymously detailing the couple's divorce proceedings. On April 25, 2003, the Seattle Post-Intelligencer published an article on Mr. Brame, outlining the allegations of abuse found in his divorce papers. Following the article, senior human resource officials recommended taking away Mr. Brame's gun and badge. City attorneys rebuffed the recommendation. Tacoma's Mayor and city manager told news media that they would not investigate because the issue was a private matter. The following day, Mr. Brame shot and killed his wife and then himself.

This murder—suicide, perpetrated in a public space in broad daylight by the chief of a major police department, sparked public demands for accountability. Ms. Judson's family became advocates for improving policy and resources for OIDV both locally and statewide. As a result of their work, the Tacoma Police Department consulted experts throughout the country and developed a policy for dealing with OIDV. In 2004 the state of

Washington passed legislation that mandated every law enforcement agency in the state to adopt and implement a written policy on DV committed or allegedly committed by sworn employees of the agency. The state association of sheriffs and police chiefs was also tasked with developing a model policy, to address staff training, reporting requirements, and procedures for investigating OIDV. On the national level, the family was successful in convincing Congress to vote to create the David Judson Domestic Violence Protocol Program as part of legislation to extend the Violence Against Women Act. The measure gave law enforcement agencies access to grant funds that can be used to develop and implement programs to prevent OIDV, sexual assault, and other crimes and to support survivors of such crimes.

This case contains a number of risk factors commonly identified in domestic homicides and not specific to police-perpetrated domestic homicides. They include the history of DV, the controlling behavior of Mr. Brame, Ms. Judson's extreme fear of her husband, and the separation. It also highlights some risk factors that are specific to policing. Although Mr. Brame was identified as a potential risk to himself and others from the moment, he applied to become a police officer, a poor screening process overrode those concerns, and he was not only hired but promoted all the way to chief of police. Mr. Brame involved other officers in the monitoring and intimidation of Ms. Judson. And Mr. Brame used his service weapon in the murder—suicide. Ms. Judson experienced the victim vulnerability factors of not being believed and of having her concerns minimized by officers who stood in solidarity with Mr. Brame. She was stalked by an abusive husband who used the authority and the resources of the police department to keep tabs on her when she tried to separate. All of this made it difficult for her to seek safety and support.

Conclusions and recommendations

The case studies summarized earlier as well as the research reviewed on DV and homicide within the military and policing point to some common themes need to be addressed to prevent these tragedies.

Selection and preparation for difficult careers

The recruitment phase is fundamental to establishing a positive work culture in a police service or a military unit.

Researchers agree that current procedures and standards need to be improved to identify recruits who hold prosocial attitudes and values (Arrigo & Claussen, 2003; Roslin, 2017; Wilham, 2012). The widespread hostility to women in both policing and the military (Deschamps, 2015; Gillis, 2017) points to the need to specifically test for misogynistic attitudes and beliefs and to prevent these applicants from becoming police officers and soldiers. Stricter recruitment practices could improve internal police cultures by addressing the higher risk of DV perpetration associated with misogynistic attitudes. It is also a time when those who may be at higher risk for developing long-term behavioral or psychological health issues can be identified (Wilham, 2012). Given the strong links between mental health problems and DV perpetration, especially PTSD among soldiers, this could be an effective preventative measure.

Addressing the workplace culture

The recent external review of the Canadian Armed Forces (Deschamps, 2015) has identified a positive and supportive workplace culture as, "[o]ne of the most important factors in preventing and dealing with harassment" (Deschamps, 2015, p. 81). Because the problems of sexual misconduct and DV are rooted in the same realities of gender inequality and dynamics of power and control, many of the recommendations intended to address sexual misconduct have the potential to prevent police and military-perpetrated DV and to ensure more supportive responses to victims.

Leadership is a critical factor in building a supportive workplace culture. Leaders in both police and military institutions need to start by acknowledging that the misogynistic values and social norms that have shaped the traditionally male-dominated, patriarchal work cultures are problematic. They need to go a step further to make it clear that violence toward intimate partners is unacceptable. They can do this through modeling respectful behavior and appropriate self-care, encouraging members to seek psychological supports regularly and especially when they are showing signs of psychological distress; ensuring appropriate policies, procedures, and training are in place; demanding accountability from their members; and collaborating with external experts to develop appropriate prevention measures and supportive responses to victims. Both police and military organizations need to take action to reach greater gender parity in their workforces and to integrate women into leadership roles better. When adequately resourced and supported by leadership, good training is a tool for culture change. Workplace prevention and awareness starts with a strong policy and is reinforced by high-quality training (see Chapter 10: Domestic violence and homicide in the workplace).

Prevention and early intervention

It is critically important to overcome the reluctance to seek help that exists in both the military and police. Death review committees have made recommendations to address this, including providing access to an anonymous helpline for police officers, military members, and their families as well as referral to specialized counseling services (Ontario DVDRC, 2012; Ontario DVDRC, 2017). Recommendations also emphasize enhancing support for the mental health and wellness of members by building liaisons with community services or employee assistance networks to provide access to experts familiar with the challenges emergency responders face, vicarious trauma, PTSD, and the subcultures of policing and the military (Ontario DVDRC, 2010; Ontario DVDRC, 2017). Peer support programs can play an important role in providing mental health supports if they are adequately resourced, with those providing peer support receiving recognition and accommodations for their roles.

In the military, chaplains, nurses, social workers, and physicians are present on every base and should be able to offer support to victims. In reality, they often lack the understanding and training that would enable them to provide appropriate care (Deschamps, 2015). Ensure that internal service providers and professionals are adequately prepared to respond effectively to warning signs and risk factors of DV.

Both police officers and members of the military are at higher risk of developing substance use problems. Zero-tolerance policies, stigma, and a lack of confidentiality may deter those who need treatment from seeking it. Providing confidential support to high-quality mental health services promotes prevention and early intervention. Breaking down the stigma associated with accepting mental health supports and providing options and easy access to supports can encourage early intervention in situations that have the potential to escalate. Once a situation escalates to physical violence, a police officer or member of the military cannot ask for help without being charged. This makes perpetrators highly unlikely to seek help, pushing the problem underground.

Perpetrator access to firearms can be the difference between life and death for a victim of DV. Death review committees have recommended, "that where feasible and practical, police services should consider supervised control of issue firearms when officers are off duty" (Ontario DVDRC, 2005, p. 96). Restricting access to firearms in periods of high risk, without causing long-term negative implications for careers would increase the likelihood of police officers or military members reaching out for psychological support when they need it.

Reporting and investigating

Victims have lost confidence in police and military chains of command and are not reporting DV assaults. This must be remedied. In a context where women are objectified and devalued, victims do not come forward when they experience DV because they are concerned that they will not be believed. Victims are also reluctant to report to military tribunals or police services where complaints may be taken by coworkers or friends of the abusive partner and where investigations all too often result in cover-ups and no consequences for the perpetrator (Heal, 2019; Muriel McQueen Ferguson Centre & RESOLVE, 2000; Roslin, 2016; Wetendorf, 2000). Women who are police officers or members of the military and who are abused by their partners who are also police officers or members of the military report concerns about negative consequences for their careers if they report the violence (Deschamps, 2015; Roslin, 2017).

The external review of the Canadian Armed Forces recommends creating an independent, outside center for reporting, prevention, and victim support for those who experience sexual misconduct in the military (Deschamps, 2015). This model could also meet the needs of DV victims assaulted by members of the military. Police services can ensure that DV complaints about an officer are not investigated by the officer's peers, but by another police service or a specially appointed unit. If police officers or members of the military have training and tools to track internet use, phone calls, and travels, their victims require specialized support to ensure their safety. More research is needed to understand workplace climate and incidence rates to better inform interventions/supports. Specific surveys of victims and perpetrators can help to determine what supports are required and will best respond to the unique needs of DV in policing and the military.

References

Ammons, J. (2004). Batterers with badges: Officer-involved domestic violence. *Women Lawyers. The Journal, 90,* 28.

Arrigo, B. A., & Claussen, N. (2003). Police corruption and psychological testing: A strategy for preemployment screening. *International Journal of Offender Therapy and Comparative Criminology, 47*(3), 272–290. Available from https://doi.org/10.1177/0306624X03047003003.

Associate Press. (2003). *Crystal Brame avoided embarrassing restraining order.* Retrieved from <https://products.kitsapsun.com/archive/2003/0609/170763_crystal_brame_avoided_embarrass.html>.

Blosnich, J. R., Dichter, M. E., Cerulli, C., Batten, S. V., & Bossarte, R. M. (2014). Disparities in adverse childhood experiences among individuals with a history of military service. *JAMA Psychiatry, 71*(9), 1041–1048. Available from https://doi.org/10.1001/jamapsychiatry.2014.724.

Blumenstein, L., Fridell, L., & Jones, S. (2012). The link between traditional police sub-culture and police intimate partner violence. *Policing: An International Journal of Police Strategies & Management, 35*(1), 147–164. Available from https://doi.org/10.1108/13639511211215496.

Bostock, D. J., & Daley, J. G. (2007). Lifetime and current sexual assault and harassment victimization rates of active-duty United States Air Force women. *Violence Against Women, 13*(9), 927–944.

Clever, M., & Segal, D. R. (2013). The demographics of military children and families. *The Future of Children, 23*(2), 13–39.

Deschamps, M. (2015). *External review into sexual misconduct and sexual harassment in the Canadian Armed Forces.* Retrieved from National Defence and the Canadian Armed Forces <http://www.forces.gc.ca/assets/FORCES_Internet/docs/en/caf-community-support-services-harassment/erafinal-report-(april-20-2015)-eng. pdf>.

Garvey, T. M. (2015). The highly trained batterer: Prevention, investigation, and prosecution of officer-involved domestic violence. *Strategies, 14,* 1–12. Retrieved from <https://www.evawintl.org/Library/DocumentLibraryHandler.ashx?id = 622>.

Gershon, R. (1999). *Domestic violence in police families.* Baltimore, MD: Mid-Atlantic Regional Community Policing Institute.

Gershon, R. (2000). *Police stress and domestic violence in police families in Baltimore, Maryland, 1997-1999 (2000-08-28 ed.).* Ann Arbor, MI: Inter-university Consortium for Political and Social Research [distributor].

Gierisch, J. M., Shapiro, A., Grant, N. N., King, H. A., McDuffie, J. R., & Williams, J. W. (2013). *Intimate partner violence: Prevalence among U.S. military veterans and active duty service members and a review of intervention approaches.* Retrieved from <https://www.ncbi.nlm.nih.gov/books/NBK241595/pdf/Bookshelf_NBK241595.pdf/>.

Gillis, W. (October 23, 2017). Canadian female police band together to change 'intolerable' working conditions. *The Star.* Retrieved from <https://www.thestar.com/news/crime/2017/10/23/canadian-female-police-band-together-to-change-intolerable-working-conditions.html>.

Haddock, V. (August 13, 2006). The science of creating killers/human reluctance to take a life can be reversed through training in the method known as killology. *SF Gate.* Retrieved from <https://www.sfgate.com/science/article/THE-SCIENCE-OF-CREATING-KILLERS-Human-2514123.php>.

Harrison, D., & Laliberte, L. (1994). *No life like it: Military wives in Canada.* Toronto: James Lorimer & Company.

Heal, A. (2019). The bureau of investigative journalism. Nowhere to turn: Women say domestic abuse by police officers goes unpunished. Retrieved from <https://www.thebureauinvestigates.com/stories/2019-05-01/police-perpetrators-domestic-violence>.

Johnson, L. B., Todd, M., & Subramanian, G. (2005). Violence in police families: Work-family spillover. *Journal of Family Violence, 20*(1), 3–12. Available from https://doi.org/10.1007/s10896-005-1504-4.

Johnson, R. R. (2010). Making domestic violence arrests: A test of expectancy theory. *Policing: An International Journal of Police Strategies & Management, 33*(3), 531–547. Available from https://doi.org/10.1108/13639511011066890.

Langhinrichsen-Rohling, J., Neidig, P., & Thorn, G. (1995). Violent marriages: Gender differences in levels of current violence and past abuse. *Journal of Family Violence, 10*(2), 159–176.

Lonsway, K. A. (2006). Policies on police officer domestic violence: Prevalence and specific provisions within large police agencies. *Police Quarterly, 9*(4), 397–422. Available from https://doi.org/10.1177/1098611104268884.

MacDonald, M. (January 9, 2017). 'We can't ignore the role of family violence' in N.S. murder-suicide, professor says. *The Star*. Retrieved from <https://www.thestar.com/news/canada/2017/01/09/we-cant-ignore-the-role-of-family-violence-in-ns-murder-suicide-professor-says.html>.

MacManus, D., & Wessely, S. (2012). Trauma, psychopathology and violence in recent combat veterans. In C. S. Widom (Ed.), *Trauma, psychopathology, and violence: Causes, consequences, or correlates* (pp. 267–287). New York: Oxford University Press.

Marshall, A. D., Panuzio, J., & Taft, C. T. (2005). Intimate partner violence among military veterans and active duty servicemen. *Clinical Psychology Review, 25* (7), 862–876. Available from https://doi.org/10.1016/j.cpr.2005.05.009.

Marshall, P. F., Vaillancourt, M. A., & Canadian Panel on Violence Against Women. (1993). *Changing the landscape: Ending violence-achieving equality.* Ottawa, ON: Minister of Supply and Services.

Mazzola, J. M. (2013). Honey, I'm home: Addressing the problem of officer domestic violence. *Journal of Civil Rights & Economic Development, 27,* 347–368. Retrieved from <https://heinonline.org/HOL/Page?collection = journals&handle = hein.journals/sjjlc27&id = 371&men_tab = srchresults>.

Milliken, C. S., Auchterlonie, J. L., & Hoge, C. W. (2007). Longitudinal assessment of mental health problems among active and reserve component soldiers returning from the Iraq war. *The Journal of the American Medical Association, 298*(18), 2141. Available from https://doi.org/10.1001/jama.298.18.2141.

Muriel McQueen Fergusson Centre for Family Violence Research & RESOLVE Violence and Abuse Research Centre. (2000). *Report on the Canadian forces' response to woman abuse in military families.* Retrieved from <https://www.springtideresources.org/sites/all/files/Woman-abuse-in-military-families.pdf>.

Neidig, P. H., Russell, H. E., & Seng, A. F. (1992). Interspousal aggression in law enforcement families: A preliminary investigation. *Police Studies: The International Review of Police Development, 15,* 30–38. Retrieved from <https://heinonline.org/HOL/Page?handle = hein.journals/polic15&div = 12&g_sent = 1&casa_token = &collection = journals#>.

The National Center on Women and Policing. (2013). *Police family violence fact sheet.* Retrieved from National Center for Women & Policing: <http://womenandpolicing.com/violencefs.asp>.

Oehme, K., Prost, S. G., & Saunders, D. G. (2016). Police responses to cases of officer-involved domestic violence: The effects of a brief web-based training.

Policing: A Journal of Policy and Practice, 10(4), 391–407. Available from https://doi.org/10.1093/police/paw039.

Ontario Domestic Violence Death Review Committee (DVDRC). (2005). *Domestic Violence Death Review Committee 2004 annual report.* Toronto: Office of the Chief Coroner.

Ontario Domestic Violence Death Review Committee (DVDRC). (2010). *Domestic Violence Death Review Committee 2009 annual report.* Toronto: Office of the Chief Coroner.

Ontario Domestic Violence Death Review Committee (DVDRC). (2012). *Domestic Violence Death Review Committee 2011 annual report.* Toronto: Office of the Chief Coroner.

Ontario Domestic Violence Death Review Committee (DVDRC). (2017). *Domestic Violence Death Review Committee 2016 annual report.* Toronto: Office of the Chief Coroner.

Orcutt, H. K., King, L. A., & King, D. W. (2003). Male-perpetrated violence among Vietnam veteran couples: Relationships with veteran's early life characteristics, trauma history, and PTSD symptomatology. *Journal of Traumatic Stress, 16*(4), 381–390.

Patton, C. L., McNally, M. R., & Fremouw, W. J. (2015). Military versus civilian murder suicide. *Journal of Interpersonal Violence,* 1–25. Available from https://doi.org/10.1177/0886260515593299.

Renzetti, E. (January 6, 2017). Women killed by their spouses are not casualties in someone else's story. *The Globe and Mail.* Retrieved from <https://www.theglobeandmail.com/opinion/women-killed-by-their-spouses-are-not-casualties-in-someone-elses-story/article33535098/>.

Rosen, L. N., Knudson, K. H., & Fancher, P. (2003). Cohesion and the culture of hypermasculinity in US Army units. *Armed Forces & Society, 29*(3), 325–351. Available from https://doi.org/10.1177/0095327X0302900302.

Roslin, A. (2016). The secret epidemic of police domestic violence: How it affects us all. *Family & Intimate Partner Violence Quarterly, 8*(4), 319–329.

Roslin, A. (2017). *Police wife: The secret epidemic of police domestic violence.* Quebec: Sugar Hill Publishing.

Russell, B. L., & Pappas, N. (2018). Officer involved domestic violence: A future of uniform response and transparency. *International Journal of Police Science & Management, 20*(2), 134–142. Available from https://doi.org/10.1177/1461355718774579.

Saunders, D. G., Prost, S. G., & Oehme, K. (2016). Responses of police officers to cases of officer domestic violence: Effects of demographic and professional factors. *Journal of Family Violence, 31*(6), 771–784. Available from https://doi.org/10.1007/s10896-016-9822-2.

Semiatin, J. N., Torres, S., LaMotte, A. D., Portnoy, G. A., & Murphy, C. M. (2017). Trauma exposure, PTSD symptoms, and presenting clinical problems among male perpetrators of intimate partner violence. *Psychology of Violence, 7*(1), 91–100. Available from https://doi.org/10.1037/vio0000041.

Shaller, B. R. (2012). *Veterans on trial: The coming court battles over PTSD.* Virginia: Potomac Books.

Sparrow, K., Kwan, J., Howard, L., Fear, N., & MacManus, D. (2017). Systematic review of mental health disorders and intimate partner violence victimisation among military populations. *Social Psychiatry and Psychiatric Epidemiology, 52*(9), 1059–1080. Available from https://doi.org/10.1007/s00127-017-1423-8.

Statistics Canada. (2018). *Survey on sexual misconduct in the Canadian armed forces.* Statistics Canada Catalogue no. 85-603-X. Ottawa. Version updated

May 22, 2019. Ottawa. Retrieved from <https://www150.statcan.gc.ca/n1/en/pub/85-603-x/85-603-x2019002-eng.pdf?st = GlEkdEHD>.

Stinson, P. M., Sr, & Liederbach, J. (2013). Fox in the henhouse: A study of police officers arrested for crimes associated with domestic and/or family violence. *Criminal Justice Policy Review, 24*(5), 601−625. Available from https://doi.org/10.1177/0887403412453837.

The Canadian Press. (2017). *Nova Scotia murder-suicides sparks difficult conversation.* Retrieved from <https://www.macleans.ca/news/canada/nova-scotia-murder-suicides-sparks-difficult-conversation/>.

Trevillion, K., Williamson, E., Thandi, G., Borschmann, R., Oram, S., & Howard, L. M. (2015). A systematic review of mental disorders and perpetration of domestic violence among military populations. *Social Psychiatry and Psychiatric Epidemiology, 50*(9), 1329−1346. Available from https://doi.org/10.1007/s00127-015-1084-4.

Turchik, J. A., & Wilson, S. M. (2010). Sexual assault in the US military: A review of the literature and recommendations for the future. *Aggression and Violent Behavior, 15*(4), 267−277. Available from https://doi.org/10.1016/j.avb.2010.01.005.

Wetendorf, D. (2000). The impact of police-perpetrated domestic violence. In D. C. Sheehan (Ed.), *Domestic violence by police officers* (pp. 375−382). Washington, DC: Department of Justice.

Wilham, C. L. W. (2012). *An ounce of prevention: Accessions screening to prevent PTSD.* Retrieved from <https://apps.dtic.mil/dtic/tr/fulltext/u2/a562077.pdf>.

Further reading

Ballenger, J. F., Best, S. R., Metzler, T. J., Wasserman, D. A., Mohr, D. C., Liberman, A., . . . Marmar, C. R. (2011). Patterns and predictors of alcohol use in male and female urban police officers. *The American Journal on Addictions, 20*(1), 21−29. Available from https://doi.org/10.1111/j.1521-0391.2010.00092.x.

10

Domestic violence and homicide in the workplace

Barbara MacQuarrie, Margaret MacPherson, Laura Olszowy and Michael Saxton

Centre for Research & Education on Violence Against Women & Children, Faculty of Education, Western University, London, ON, Canada

Domestic violence (DV) impacts the safety and productivity of workers and by extension, the operation, reputation, and success of organizations (Krug, Dahlberg, & Mercy, 2002; Rothman & Perry, 2004; Swanberg, Logan, & Macke, 2005; Taylor, 2016; Wathen, MacGregor, & MacQuarrie, 2014; Wathen et al., 2014). This chapter charts the emergence of DV as a global workplace issue and highlights how, tragically, workplace domestic homicides have often been drivers of change. We review the evidence of prevalence as well as the impacts of victimization and perpetration on workers and workplaces and present case studies as examples. We conclude with recommendations and promising approaches.

How common is domestic violence at work?

A series of national surveys on the impacts of DV on workers and the workplace conducted in collaboration with labor movements have provided estimates on prevalence. Results find that one-third of Canadian workers reported experiencing DV in their lifetime and 54% said the violence followed them to work (Wathen et al., 2014). Surveys from Australia, New Zealand, Philippines, Taiwan, Mongolia, and Belgium found comparable rates (Fos-Tuvera, 2015; McFerran, 2011; Olszowy, Saxton, & MacQuarrie, 2017a, 2017b; Rayner-Thomas, 2013; Saxton, Olszowy, & MacQuarrie, 2017). The boundary between home and work is permeable in many ways. Survivors receive abusive phone calls and text messages and emails while they are at work. They are sometimes stalked and harassed at or near work, and abusive partners contact coworkers and or employers

Preventing Domestic Homicides. DOI: https://doi.org/10.1016/B978-0-12-819463-8.00010-1

and physically show up at work (Fos-Tuvera, 2015; McFerran, 2011; Olszowy et al., 2017a, 2017b; Rayner-Thomas, 2013; Saxton et al., 2017). Such behaviors can cause difficulties in relationships with coworkers, supervisors, and/or customers, clients, or patients (LaVan, Lopez, Katz, & Martin, 2012; Swanberg et al., 2005; Swanberg, Macke, & Logan, 2006; Wathen et al., 2014). Not surprisingly the vast majority of survivors report a negative impact of DV on their work performance, usually due to being distracted, tired and/or unwell (McFerran, 2011; Rayner-Thomas, 2013; Wathen et al., 2014). While work may be difficult, it is also often seen as a place of refuge and stability. As one woman explained:

> There's no doubt it had impact, but I took pride in my ability to stay focussed and on task with a professional presentation. However, those were very difficult times.
>
> **Wathen et al. (2014)**

DV can impede a survivor's ability to get to work or arrive on time. Reasons range from being physically and mentally exhausted to being physically restrained, having car keys hidden, uniforms or work identification hidden, stolen, or destroyed or the perpetrator failing to show up for child or elder care (Galvez, Mankowski, McGlade, Ruiz, & Glass, 2011; McFerran, 2011; Trades Union Congress, 2014; Wathen, MacGregor, & MacQuarrie, 2015).

When both partners work at the same organization, abusive partners often take advantage of the physical proximity to monitor and harass survivors, subjecting them to ongoing abuse that undermines psychological and sometimes physical safety at work (Dupont Inquest, 2007; Wathen et al., 2015).

Whether because it causes poor performance and high absenteeism, or because perpetrators deliberately set out to get a survivor fired by harassing, stalking, and threatening them at work, survivors' experiences of DV at work can affect career advancement, and it is common for survivors to lose their jobs due to DV (Corporate Governance Forum of Turkey, 2019; MacGregor, Wathen, & MacQuarrie, 2017; Mighty, 1997; O'Leary-Kelly, Lean, Reeves, & Randal, 2008; Swanberg et al., 2005; Wathen et al., 2015). Although partner violence does not consistently affect a woman's overall probability of being employed, it does appear to influence a woman's earnings and her ability to keep a job. A study in Chicago, IL, United States, found that women with a history of partner violence were more likely to have experienced spells of unemployment, to have had a high turnover of jobs, and to have suffered more physical and mental health problems that could affect job performance. They also had lower personal incomes and were significantly more likely to receive welfare assistance than women who did not report a history of partner violence (Showalter, 2016).

Few studies have focused on the impacts of DV perpetration in the workplace, but some pioneering studies provide critical insights into impacts for workers and workplaces (Galvez et al., 2011; Lim, Rioux, & Ridley, 2004; Mankowski, Galvez, & Perrin, 2013; Rothman & Perry, 2004; Schmidt & Barnett, 2011; Scott et al., 2017). Consistent with findings from the studies investigating the experience of victims, DV is associated with substantial negative impacts on productivity and safety for the perpetrator and their workplace (Lim et al., 2004; Schmidt & Barnett, 2011; Scott et al., 2017). Perpetrators use workplace resources including time, telephones, computers, and vehicles to make contact with their (ex)partner during work hours to engage in emotionally abusive behaviors (Lim et al., 2004; Schmidt & Barnett, 2011; Scott et al., 2017).

Perpetrators have self-reported negative impacts on their job performance. As one man explained, "anxiety, depression resulted from conflicts and I was unable to focus/concentrate on my work. When I did work, much of my work was substandard." (Scott et al., 2017). Of additional concern were reports that perpetrators caused or almost caused a work accident as a result of being distracted or preoccupied by DV issues (Lim et al., 2004; Schmidt & Barnett, 2011; Scott et al., 2017). Again, similar to survivors, perpetrators indicated that DV issues led to difficulties getting to and staying at work and many reported taking time off as a result of DV (Scott et al., 2017).

Some perpetrators also lost their job either directly or indirectly (too many missed days, low productivity) as a result of DV perpetration. For those who did lose their jobs, many reported substantial difficulties getting new work; sometimes because they had a charge on their record, and other times because information spread informally about their DV perpetration (Lim et al., 2004; Schmidt & Barnett, 2011; Scott et al., 2017).

Coworkers may also become involved when DV spills over to the workplace. They may experience harassment from a perpetrator seeking information about their partner; they may be lied to, or they may even be threatened or harmed. Knowing about or suspecting the abuse is happening causes many coworkers to worry and feel stress (Logan, Shannon, Cole, & Swanberg, 2007; MacGregor et al., 2017; Swanberg, Macke, & Logan, 2007; Wathen et al., 2015). In addition to the direct impacts, coworkers may have to cope with unexplained absences or changes to their workload without knowing that

DV is at the root of the problem (MacGregor et al., 2017; Wathen et al., 2015). While DV is a cause of concern and stress for some coworkers, they can also be complicit in the behaviors. Some of the men who admitted to engaging in abusive behavior within the workplace reported that someone at work covered for them while they engaged in harassing abusive behavior (Scott et al., 2017).

Warning signs at work

The inclination to separate home and work and to see DV as a private matter means that situations are often hidden in plain view. Estimates of workplace awareness of DV victimization vary. Earlier American surveys found that 58% of CEOs and 41% of employees were aware of victims of DV in their workplaces (CAEPV, 2007). A more recent Canadian study found that 71% of employers had found it necessary to intervene to protect a worker experiencing DV (Stewart, 2015). A Canadian study focusing on workers found nearly 40% of workers believed that they recognized a DV victim or perpetrator in their workplace (MacGregor et al., 2017). Commonly recognized warning signs were depression, changes in work performance, signs of anxiety and fear, and missing work or being late (Corporate Governance Forum of Turkey, 2019; MacGregor et al., 2017).

Little is known about exactly how supervisors or coworkers respond when they recognize the warning signs of DV. In Canada we know that 71% of managers intervened to protect a worker, but we do not know if they did that safely and with appropriate support. Some studies suggest that many times supervisors say or do nothing in response to the DV, and many times responses by both supervisors and coworkers are harmful because they blame the victim, joke about the situation, or collude with the perpetrator (MacGregor et al., 2017). In workplaces that are well prepared, warning signs are opportunities to intervene and to avert potential tragedies.

Domestic homicide at work

In the United States, DV has been reported as a leading cause of death for women in the workplace (LaVan et al., 2012; Tiesman, Gurka, Konda, Coben, & Amandus, 2012). On average, two women have been killed at work every month by an intimate partner in the United States since 1997 (Futures Without

Violence, 2017a, 2017,b). Fewer women are murdered at work in Canada, but when the tragedies happen, they are deeply felt and they leave a wake of devastation (Mitchell, 2007; Star Staff Reporter, 2006; Tobin, 2018).

Understanding that coercive control is the central dynamic of DV helps to explain why victims are at risk at work. For a perpetrator who needs to control every aspect of their partner's life, a job can be a reminder of the survivor's financial independence. Perpetrators who extend their abuse to the work setting are increasing the number of domains in which they control their partners (O'Leary-Kelly et al., 2008). Risk factors for a victim to be killed in the workplace are consistent with known risk factors for domestic homicide. They commonly include a history of violence, an escalation of violence, stalking behaviors, separation, threats to kill, and a perpetrator with mental health problems (DVDRC, 2017; Hellwege, 1995).

When a perpetrator begins to monitor their partner at work they are extending the domains in which they control their partner beyond the home and social settings to the workplace. DV showing up in the workplace is a risk factor as it indicates violence escalation. This is equally true whether the means are electronic (calls and messages), indirect (contact with coworkers or supervisors) or direct (physically showing up) (O'Leary-Kelly et al., 2008).

While the workplace can be a place of safety and escape from the violence, it can also be the place where a perpetrator can find their (ex)partner. This becomes particularly important if the victim is attempting a separation (ILO, 2006; DVDRC, 2005). Parking lots and publicly accessible buildings are particularly dangerous locations for victims who are being stalked and one study found that over half of workplace homicides perpetrated by intimate partners occurred in parking lots and public buildings (Tiesman et al., 2012).

Coworkers, managers, and others who are in the workplace can be traumatized by witnessing the event or just by being in the vicinity when it happens (Dupont Inquest, 2007). Healthcare settings and schools are among the workplaces where domestic homicides have taken place, shattering sense of safety, and ethos of care usually associated with these institutions (The Canadian Press, 2012; Channel 4 & Associated Press, 2017; Seitz & Babwin, 2018). Coworkers, managers, and others who are present in the workplace may themselves be injured or even killed while trying to intervene, or just because they were present (Channel 4 & Associated Press, 2017; Seitz & Babwin, 2018).

Employers may find themselves exposed to liability due to their failure to protect the murdered worker and sometimes other victims as well. US lawyers have opined that by paying attention to warning signs and taking preventative action, companies can help to prevent homicides (Hellwege, 1995). Jurisdictions in Canada are beginning to lay out legal obligations for employers to prevent and respond to DV that enters the workplace through new Occupational Health and Safety (OHS) obligations (Canada. Government of Alberta. Occupational Health & Safety, 2018; Canada. New Brunswick Occupational Health & Safety, 2018).

Quite aside from legal liability is the profound regret that coworkers experience if they realize in retrospect that they had been witnessing the escalation of a deadly situation. Workplaces where domestic homicides happen remain associated with the tragic events for years after they happen, disrupting individual careers and general operations of the organization (Thompson, 2015). The following three case studies outline some of the tragedies in the workplace that seem so predictable and preventable after the fact.

Case studies

Windsor, ON, Canada: the case of Lori Dupont

Many of the details outlined in this case can be retrieved from:
https://www.cbc.ca/news/canada/toronto/slain-windsor-nurse-often-harrassed-by-doctor-colleague-testifies-1.664590 (CBC News, 2007).

https://www.pressreader.com/canada/windsor-star/20061111/281956013285655 (Star Staff Reporter, 2006).

Ms. Lori Dupont was a 37-year-old registered nurse and mother living in Windsor, ON, Canada. Dr. Marc Daniel was an anesthesiologist who worked at the same hospital as her. Ms. Dupont and Mr. Daniel started dating in 2002. Although married, Mr. Daniels pursued Ms. Dupont "relentlessly" and within 6 months of starting the relationship, had moved out of his home and rented an apartment in the small town near where Ms. Dupont lived with her parents.

The relationship lasted 2 years, and friends and family said that it was not one in which she thrived. On a number of occasions through 2003−2004, Ms. Dupont tried to end the relationship. Each time she tried to terminate the relationship, Mr. Daniel threatened to kill himself.

Mr. Daniel was described by some colleagues as controlling and possessive. Some hospital staff reported that they found him difficult to work with. Colleagues reportedly observed his aggression toward Ms. Dupont and other nurses. One nurse reported her concerns to her supervisor on a number of occasions and was informed that the hospital administration was aware. Upon further inquiry, she was told that "Dupont and Daniel were grown adults and could deal with their own problems" (CBC News, 2007).

In the early months of 2005, Mr. Daniel was placed on probation and threatened with suspension following a nurse manager's complaint. He was also required to enroll in an anger management course. At the same time, Ms. Dupont was in the processes of leaving Mr. Daniel for the last time. In late February of that year, Mr. Daniel attempted to take his life in front of Ms. Dupont over the relationship ending. Daniel was given a provisional diagnosis of bipolar affective disorder, spent 2 weeks in the psychiatric unit, and was placed on medical leave from work. Ms. Dupont also took a leave of absence. At the end of her leave, Ms. Dupont returned to work and discovered a letter from Mr. Daniel. He had been looking for her at the hospital despite being on leave and under review.

In April Ms. Dupont met with Mr. Daniel to repeat their relationship had ended. Mr. Daniel was enraged and over the next week his behavior became increasingly erratic and threatening. The day after their meeting, Mr. Daniel went to the hospital and physically blocked Ms. Dupont's path as she tried to avoid him. Soon after Ms. Dupont found a compromising photo of herself, left on her car, parked in the hospital lot. The next day Mr. Daniel called and threatened Ms. Dupont's father that he would release pictures of Ms. Dupont. He continued to follow her to work.

Fearing for her safety, Ms. Dupont met with her managers as well as hospital security and informed them of Mr. Daniel's threats and his capacity for violence. Ms. Dupont was provided with a reserved parking spot close to security and a security escort to her vehicle. Hospital security was instructed to remove Mr. Daniel from the hospital grounds if he caused issues. Ms. Dupont applied for a peace bond to limit Mr. Daniel's access to her. Daniel refused to agree to a peace bond and a hearing to decide the matter was set for December 2005.

Around the same time, the hospital administration met to discuss Mr. Daniel. They deactivated his access card to the operating room. Then, in late April, the chief of staff suggested Mr. Daniel to take a leave of absence. However, clinicians working with Mr. Daniel determined that he was clinically stable and ready to work. Mr. Daniel returned to work at the end of May under supervision. Soon thereafter nurses expressed concerns over his return and his behavior. In spite of the history and documented complaints, Mr. Daniel was permitted to continue working in the same areas as Ms. Dupont. This decision prompted coworkers to work extra shifts to ensure that Ms. Dupont and Mr. Daniel worked on separate scheduled shifts.

In June Ms. Dupont advised the hospital administration that she was no longer needed an escort to her vehicle. By the end of July, Mr. Daniel's full hospital privileges were reinstated despite continued concerns by staff, who noted his obsession with Ms. Dupont. These concerns continued to go unaddressed over the next few months. Then on the morning of Sunday, November 12, 2005, Mr. Daniel walked into the hospital and stabbed Ms. Dupont to death while she worked her shift in the recovery room. Mr. Daniel was found unconscious in his car hours later—he died 2 days later from a drug overdose in an apparent suicide.

Themes and recommendations

There were many risk factors for lethality in this situation. Mr. Daniel's obsessive behavior, suicide attempts, mental health problems, and the recent separation all pointed to a dangerous situation. In 2007 the Chief Corner of Ontario held an inquest into the deaths of Lori Dupont and Marc Daniel resulting in comprehensive recommendations. The findings highlight multiple warning signs and missed opportunities where the workplace failed to effectively intervene. Mr. Daniel used the workplace to access and to monitor and harass Ms. Dupont. He had a lengthy history of control, abuse, and violence directed at Ms. Dupont as well as other staff. Yet discipline for his behavior was minimal. A culture that enforced physicians' power and privilege made it difficult to for staff to file complaints and for administration to take action. This was further complicated by a lack of policies and procedures to address DV in the workplace. The inquest underscored the importance of the workplace and its role in identifying, monitoring, and aiding in the management of DV. The inquest also recommended legislative changes to enhance protections against workplace violence and harassment, including DV. Those changes came into effect in ON, Canada in 2010, when Bill 168 was passed, amending the Occupational Health and Safety Act and requiring employers across Ontario to develop policies, programs, and procedures that prevent and protect employees from workplace violence and harassment, including DV.

De Grau, NL, Canada: the case of Stephanie Chaisson

Many of the details outlined in this case can be retrieved from: https://globalnews.ca/news/228034/police-say-man-involved-in-double-fatal-shooting-in-newfoundland-killed-himself/ (The Canadian Press, 2012).

https://www.cbc.ca/news/canada/newfoundland-labrador/Dupont-chaffey-nurse-workplace-violence-1.4895163 (Tobin, 2018).

Stephanie Chaisson, 49 years, worked as a receptionist at a medical clinic in the rural community of De Grau. She was estranged from her husband, 54-year-old Luke Chaisson. Ms. Chaisson confided to her coworker, Lori Chaffey, a nurse working at the same clinic, that she was in a difficult situation with Mr. Chaisson because he would show up wherever she went. She also told her coworker that she slept with a bat. Ms. Chaffey confirmed that if they ever went out socially, Mr. Chaisson would easily find them. Ms. Chaffey said that Ms. Chaisson had considered finding a different job in another place, but she loved her home, her job, and the community where her family was. She did not want to leave.

Mr. Chaisson was ordered to stay away from Ms. Chaisson after he was arrested in January 2012 for allegedly criminally harassing her. He was released on conditions, including a no-contact order. He was due to appear in court on April 2, 2012.

On March 26, 2012, Ms. Chaisson and Ms. Chaffey were working alone in the clinic. After working through the morning, they locked up for lunch and ate together. Afterward, Ms. Chaffey left the reception area and went to the washroom toward the back of the building. Ms. Chaisson unlocked the door for the afternoon appointments. Mr. Chaisson entered the clinic and told a patient to leave. After the patient left, Ms. Chaffey heard shots. When she heard the first shot, she looked out the door and could see her friend on the floor in front of her office door. Ms. Chaisson was not moving. She could also see the barrel of a rifle pointed over Ms. Chaisson's body. Ms. Chaffey retreated and closed the door, terrified that Mr. Chaisson would find her. She was trapped in the bathroom with no way out of the building. She could hear him pacing and yelling at Ms. Chaisson. Then she heard a second shot followed by more pacing and finally a third shot. When she heard

Mr. Chaisson moan, she looked again and could see his body on the floor. She took her chance and fled the building to get help. The ambulance arrived right away but could not enter the clinic until the police arrived. It took over an hour for police coming from the detachment in Stephenville, to arrive in the rural community. Ms. Chaisson was found deceased at the scene and Mr. Chaisson was taken to hospital where he died from his injuries.

After the murder, Ms. Chaffey spoke out about unsafe working conditions, including the physical environment of the building. Prior to the murder did everything she could to let those around her at the clinic know that she needed help. She told managers and coworkers. She asked for cameras to be installed. She asked for support for Ms. Chaisson to get to and from work. She complained about only having one exit and no lock on the bathroom door. With support from Ms. Chaisson, she sent emails about the general safety of the building, especially that you could not see who was approaching the building at the main entrance. Nothing was done.

Themes and recommendations

Risk factors for lethality in this situation include stalking, extreme fear expressed by the victim, access to a gun, and separation. It is not clear in the news reports that followed the murder—suicide how informed the employer was of the situation; but at least one coworker was aware that the couple was separated, that there had been multiple stalking events, and that Ms. Chaisson was afraid of Mr. Chaisson. It is common for victims tell their coworkers about their experiences of DV (Swanberg et al., 2006; Wathen et al., 2014). These disclosures provide a strategic point of intervention, provided workers are prepared to recognize warning signs and risk factors and respond appropriately. It is not unusual that the significance of risk factors as indicators of an escalating situation is not understood. Without training and the support of workplace policies and procedures, they are unprepared to respond and may fear making the situation worse or drawing the risk to themselves. There may also be a tendency to minimize what is happening because the person behaving abusively is known.

Once a situation of DV is known to a workplace, safety planning, risk assessment, and ongoing monitoring need to be part of a risk management strategy. Police can also be called upon to assist with an assessment of the physical building and its surroundings to enhance security. As a receptionist, Ms. Chaisson was exposed to the public. When employers understand the risk, they are better positioned to work with the person being targeted to explore options for safety that may include removing her from view or resituating her at another location.

Chicago, IL, United States: the case of Tamara O'Neal

Many of the details outlined in this case can be retrieved from: https://www.nbcchicago.com/news/local/doctor-killed-in-mercy-hospital-shooting-identified-500885211.html (NBC Staff Report, 2018).

https://www.theguardian.com/us-news/2018/nov/21/chicago-doctor-killed-by-ex-fiance-called-police-feared-for-her-life (Durkin, 2018). https://www.theglobeandmail.com/world/article-four-dead-including-gunman-after-argument-at-chicago-hospital-erupts/ (Seitz & Babwin, 2018).

https://www.huffingtonpost.ca/entry/tamara-oneal-chicago-shooting-domestic-violence_n_5bf576a6e4b0771fb6b4ceef (Jeltsen, 2018).

Dr. Tamara O'Neal was a 38-year-old emergency room physician at a Chicago hospital. She met 32-year-old Juan Lopez who was working as a security guard while she was doing her residency. Mr. Lopez went on to become an associate program specialist for the Chicago Housing Authority in the customer care center. The two knew each other for about 3 years but were engaged for only a short time before Ms. O'Neal called off the wedding in September 2018. Ms. O'Neal broke off the relationship but tried to stay friendly with Mr. Lopez. Her family reported, however, that Mr. Lopez would not let go of the relationship. Ms. O'Neal had told an acquaintance that she was afraid of her ex.

Mr. Lopez appears to have had a history of violence with coworkers and an ex-partner. In 2014 he was accused of threatening a female cadet at the city's fire department. When the fire department learned of the threats, Mr. Lopez was told he would be disciplined. Instead of returning to the academy to meet with department officials, Mr. Lopez went absent without leave and was fired. The same year his then-wife sought an emergency order of protection against him, saying that she was afraid for her safety because he was acting erratically with his gun and had threatened to go to her job and cause a scene. Mr. Lopez was not criminally charged. Mr. Lopez had a permit to possess a concealed firearm and had legally purchased four guns in the last 5 years. It was unclear if officials knew about the 2014 complaint when the permit was granted.

On November 20, 2018, Mr. Lopez called the hospital to talk to Ms. O'Neal on the phone, but she refused to take his call. Later in the day, Mr. Lopez came to the hospital. Ms. O'Neal called 911 as soon as she saw him outside the hospital to say that he was armed, and she feared for her life. Mr. Lopez confronted Ms. O'Neal, arguing about her calling off the engagement and demanding that she return the ring. When a friend who was with Ms. O'Neal attempted to intervene, Mr. Lopez lifted his shirt to show a handgun. The friend fled inside to call 911 where she reported that there had been an assault and two gunshots. Mr. Lopez shot Ms. O'Neal repeatedly as he stood over her. When police arrived, Mr. Lopez started shooting at them while they were still in the car. He ran into the hospital where he killed one officer and one hospital employee who got caught in the gunfire as she exited an elevator. Mr. Lopez fired the gun randomly. One witness said that he reloaded the gun twice, which meant 32 shots were fired. Mr. Lopez eventually shot himself in the head and died in a stairwell.

Themes and recommendations

Risk factors for lethality in this situation include a recent separation, obsession with the victim, a past history of DV, and a past history of other criminal behavior and gun ownership. The fact that Ms. O'Neal called 911 when she saw Ms. Lopez in the parking lot and told police she was afraid for her life indicates that she understood the risk he posed to her. There is no indication, however, that she conveyed her concerns to the hospital or that the hospital had a program with policies and procedures in place that would have helped to manage those risks. This is a situation that shows how bystanders can be put at risk when a DV victim is targeted at the workplace.

Workplace programs to educate coworkers and supervisors how to recognize, respond, and refer to DV can help to prevent this kind of deadly escalation. Workplace programs and policies to address DV make it easier for victims to seek help and protection before a crisis arises. Perpetrators often access victims in parking lots and public buildings. Prior knowledge of the situation makes it possible to put safety measures in place for employees who are being threatened by DV.

Responding to workplace DV

The three case studies highlight the presence of warning signs and show workplaces can miss opportunities to help survivors of DV. Responding to DV in the workplace can help to prevent the escalation of DV situations and thereby prevent homicides. Some research indicates that the type of support survivors of DV want from their workplace is dependent on their stage of behavior in the abusive relationship. All three cases reviewed were similar in they involved women who were separating, or had separated, from their partners. The closer a survivor is to deciding to leave an abusive partner the more likely they are to seek support from their workplace (Tiesman et al., 2012). Given that separation is a time when DV is likely to escalate (DVDRC, 2005, 2017) and given that the workplace may become the easiest place to find a survivor after separation, it is in the interests of both survivors and employers to have workplace supports in place. The following examples show that survivors are more likely to disclose what is happening when a supervisor notices that their work performance is suffering.

Polaroid Corporation was one of the first companies to recognize a link between DV and performance problems. In 1984 the performance of an excellent female employee was in steady decline. One evening her supervisor confronted her about her consistent lateness and days missed. The employee revealed that her husband was becoming increasingly abusive and controlling toward her. Rather than turning away from what was commonly considered a "private issue" the supervisor enlisted the help of Human Resources. Polaroid continued on to offer support to other employees experiencing DV. Then in 1994 the company faced a crisis when five employees were taken hostage by their coworker who was the abusive husband of another employee. It became clear to Human Resources that DV was prevalent and was directly impacting workplace safety and productivity. Polaroid would go on to be a best-practice study for the Harvard School of Public Health Injury Control Center as an organization that responded to the needs of workers (Meier, 1996; Solomon, 1998). Liz Claiborne is another company known for pioneering work to address DV in the workplace. Their interest in DV started as a Corporate Social Responsibility issue managed by the marketing department. But following employee disclosures, shifted their focus inward and rather than being about public relations or sales, support to DV victims became about employee well-being and retention (O'Leary-Kelly et al., 2008).

The Corporate Alliance to End Partner Violence (CAEPV) was founded in 1995 as a result of experiences of companies like Polaroid and Liz Claiborne (O'Leary-Kelly et al., 2008). The CAEPV grew to include a long list of companies headquartered in the United States, formed a sister alliance in the United Kingdom (Corporate Alliance Against Domestic Abuse, UK), and included the Hurriyet Newspaper Group as a Corporate member in Turkey (Wells, 1995). Companies involved in the CAEPV offered a range of support, including flex time, short-term paid leave, and extended leave without pay to seek protection and legal recourse against DV. Many also provided an employee-assistance program and supported education programs outside as well as inside the workplace. The CAEPV developed the *Recognize, Respond and Refer* framework to guide workplace intervention efforts in DV situations, widely adapted and still used in many initiatives today (Centre for Research & Education on Violence Against Women and Children, 2014; McMurray, 1995; Wells, 1995; O'Leary-Kelly et al., 2008).

Other initiatives and collaborative efforts followed. Workplaces Respond formed in 2005, spearheaded by the nonprofit advocacy group, Futures Without Violence (2017a, 2017,b), in partnership with the US Department of Justice Office on Violence Against Women. It educates, trains, and empowers employers, survivors, coworkers, advocates, labor unions, and worker centers to prevent and appropriately respond to domestic and sexual violence, trafficking, and stalking impacting workers and the workplace. No More (2019) represents a further development in building alliances with experts and corporations. Launched in 2013 this organization brings together nonprofits, corporations, government agencies, media, schools, and individuals to join efforts to end DV and sexual assault. It aims to end DV and sexual assault by increasing awareness, inspiring action, and fueling culture change. While many members are based in the United States, it has a global membership (https://nomore.org/about/our-story/). In Australia the White Ribbon Workplace Accreditation Program has been operating since 2012 with 15 criteria for companies to meet to be accredited (White Ribbon Australia, 2019). Also in Australia, Male Champions of Change (2019) brought together 30 business and federal government leaders, collectively employing 600,000 people to release the report, *Playing Our Part: Workplace Responses to Domestic and Family Violence*. Developed with input from experts, it suggests how workplaces can help to reduce the prevalence and impact of domestic and family violence.

In Europe, the CEASE project, cofunded by the Rights, Equality and Citizenship Programme of the European Commission and managed by a partnership of groups working for equality and social justice, is working to create the first European Corporate Network working to stop DV. They are building and facilitating a training module for Human Resource departments and managers, developing a European map representing organizations supporting victims and raising awareness on this issue on a European scale (CEASE, 2019).

In Canada the Centre for Research and Education on Violence Against Women and Children (CREVAWC, 2014) developed the Make It Our Business workplace education program in response to recommendations from the Ontario Domestic Violence Death Review Committee. The committee often highlights the fact that people close to the victims of domestic homicide knew that DV was happening, but neither know how serious the situation was nor know what to do about it. They repeatedly recommend teaching everyone how to recognize warning signs and risk factors, how to intervene safely with the victim and, if possible, perpetrators, and how to refer to supportive services (DVDRC, 2005, 2017).

In addition to these collaborative corporate and not-for-profit efforts, the labor movement has taken a significant leadership role in efforts to address DV in the workplace. This work started in Australia in 2010 with the *Safe at Home, Safe at Work* initiative which launched a national survey about the impact of DV on workers and workplaces. The Australian Council of Trade Unions promoted the survey to their members and when findings showed that DV is a significant problem for workers, they promoted collective bargaining as a means to gain entitlements such as paid leave, safety planning, and protection from reprisals for workers experiencing DV (McFerran, 2011). At the same time, unions began lobbying the Australian government to provide paid leave for victims of DV through a modern award.[1] In 2018 the Fair Work Commission of Australia agreed to provide 5 days of unpaid leave annually to workers experiencing family violence or DV (Australian Government Fair Work, 2009).

Unions in New Zealand and the United Kingdom followed Australia's lead and collaborated to implement similar surveys (Trades Union Congress, 2014; Rayner-Thomas, 2013). In New Zealand, which has one of the highest rates of DV in the world, MP Jan Logie, a former women's shelter worker, took up the fight to pass a law at the national level to grant DV victims 10 days of paid leave. When the law was passed in 2018 she said,

"Part of this initiative is getting a whole-of-society response. We don't just leave it to police but realise we all have a role in helping victims. It is also about changing the cultural norms

---

[1]Modern awards are legal documents that outline the minimum pay rates and conditions of employment.

and saying 'we all have a stake in this and it is not OK'." (Ainge Roy, 2018)

Other countries have followed suit, with surveys completed in Canada, the Philippines, Mongolia, Taiwan, and Belgium (Fos-Tuvera, 2015; Olszowy et al., 2017a, 2017b; Saxton et al., 2017; Wathen et al., 2014). Labor unions used the growing body of evidence to advance collective bargaining, to build partnerships with employers to address the issue, and to lobby for legislative changes to provide paid leave (Canadian Labour Congress, 2019; Australian Council of Trade Unions; Pillinger, 2017). Canada now provides 5 days of paid leave for federally regulated workers experiencing DV (Young & Butler, 2019). Other jurisdictions including, Argentina, France, Italy, the Philippines, Spain, and many states in the United states also provide legislated leaves of absence from work for DV victims (Pillinger, 2019).

We are beginning to see changes to OHS legislation in several Canadian jurisdictions. British Columbia, motivated by the murder of a Vancouver Starbucks manager who died defending an employee from an attack by her husband, was the first province to recognize DV in OHS regulations (Work Safe BC, 2012). Ontario changed its OHS legislation in 2010 to include DV as a workplace hazard in response to pressure from women's advocates, unions, and recommendations from the inquest into the death of Lori Dupont (Canada. Government of Ontario Consolidated Laws, 2009; Dupont Inquest, 2007). Alberta amended its OHS legislation in 2018 to include DV as a form of workplace violence that employers are responsible for preventing and responding to in an effective manner (Schmidt, 2018). New Brunswick and Newfoundland are the latest jurisdictions to address violence, including DV in its OHS regulations (Canada. Newfoundland & Labrador Regulation, 2019; Work Safe NB, 2019).

Federal and regional governments across the globe continue to build on the work of advocates, unions, and pioneering employers by requiring employers to take steps to protect employees when DV spills over into the workplace (International Labour Conference, 2018; Pillinger, 2019). Across several Canadian jurisdictions, for example, changes have been made to OHS legislation to include DV as a form of workplace violence that employers are responsible for preventing and responding to in an effective manner. In other places, obligations around protection and leave associated with DV experiences are integrated into laws on DV, gender equality law, and labor law/labor codes. They might contain provisions for prohibition of discrimination or retaliation against employees based on their status as a victim, paid or unpaid DV leave, security of employment and guarantee of a job following paid or unpaid leave, support for victims in the workplace, and/or obligations for employers to take steps to ensure women's safety in the workplace (Pillinger, 2016).

Legislative and policy reform will be significantly strengthened by the recent adoption of a new convention by the International Labour Organization. Countries that ratify the new international treaty will have to develop laws that prohibit workplace violence and take preventative actions such as addressing violence and harassment through their OHS management and requiring companies to have policies on violence. The convention sets out standards for how governments should mitigate the effects of DV in the world of work, including by having flexible working arrangements and leave for DV survivors (International Labour Conference, 2019).

Finally it is worth noting that research in this area is continuing. While the surveys discussed earlier are beginning to provide data about the impacts of DV on workers and workplaces, when governments or researchers collect epidemiological data about DV, they have not traditionally asked questions about experiences at work. The Canadian government may begin to fill that gap with the launch of two new surveys. The Survey of Safety in Public and Private Spaces, focusing on the incidence and consequences of gender-based violence (GBV), implemented in 2018–2019, released results in December 2019 (Canada. Status of Women Canada, 2018).

Conclusion

Many of the risk factors for domestic homicides that occur in the workplace are disconcertingly similar. Usually there has been a recent separation, a history of DV, the perpetrator has demonstrated obsessive behavior toward the victim and/or has been stalking the victim, including at the workplace. Frequently the murders occur in parking lots or in buildings that allow public access. Usually the victim has disclosed DV to someone at work, most likely a coworker, but possibly a supervisor as well. Tragedy strikes when, despite the clear indications of growing risk, the workplace has not conducted a risk assessment, put in place a safety plan for potential victims and a risk management, and progressive discipline plan for those perpetrating violence within the workplace. Also often lacking is collaboration of community-based experts to assist with those lifesaving measures. DV is a complex issue. A generic approach to workplace violence will not prepare workers or organizations to respond to dynamic risk in situations that can escalate suddenly. Instead workers need to learn about the underlying issues of coercion, power, and control so that they can identify warning signs and risk factors and respond supportively to disclosures. Supervisors, human resource managers, and OHS experts who might be called upon to intervene in a situation need additional training that also involves skill building. But employers and other workplace stakeholders do not need to become experts in DV prevention and response. As very early programs realized, the key is to build relationships with DV experts and to call on them when a problem arises.

Sometimes it is not just the victim who dies but others who are present in the workplace, supervisors, coworkers, patients, students, customers, or clients. Victims do not die at work because workplaces are uncaring. They die because workplaces are unprepared. Despite having model programs that date back to the 1980s, we seem bound to learn the same lesson over and over. DV is not a private problem.

Undoubtedly there has been progress. The labor movement and advocates working to end GBV have raised awareness and pushed for changes. Governments have responded with legislation to provide paid and unpaid leave and protection under OHS laws. Unions have secured entitlements for victims through collective bargaining. Academics are building a body of evidence to better understand the problem. Employers are partnering with experts to create policies and programs to raise awareness and to build capacity and confidence to respond when they become aware of situations of DV. Still, more remains to be done.

References

Ainge Roy, E. (July 26, 2018). 'A huge win': New Zealand brings in paid domestic violence leave. *The Guardian*. Retrieved from <https://www.theguardian.com/world/2018/jul/26/new-zealand-paid-domestic-violence-leave-jan-logie>.

Australian Government Fair Work. (2009). *Family & domestic violence leave*. Retrieved from Australian Government Fair Work Website <https://www.fairwork.gov.au/leave/family-and-domestic-violence-leave>.

Canada. Government of Alberta. Occupational Health and Safety. (2018). *Harassment and violence in the workplace OHS requirements for workers and employers*. Edmonton: Occupational Health and Safety. Retrieved from <https://open.alberta.ca/dataset/e04784c3-6779-41b5-97ae-183a092e5d93/resource/871d63c7-0525-4378-a876-39266ac96880/download/ohs-workplace-violence-harassment.pdf>.

Canada. Government of Ontario Consolidated Laws. (2009). *Occupational Health and Safety Amendment Act (violence and harassment in the workplace), 2009, S. O. 2009, c.23-Bill 168.* Toronto, ON: Queen's Printer for Ontario.

Canada. New Brunswick Occupational Health & Safety. (2018). *Occupational Health and Safety Act, 2018.* Saint John, NB: Queen's Printer for New Brunswick. Retrieved from <https://www.gnb.ca/0062/acts/BBR-2018/2018-82.pdf>.

Canada. Newfoundland and Labrador Regulation. (2019). The Newfoundland and Labrador Gazette Extraordinary Part II. Saint John, NB: Authority. Retrieved from <https://www.servicenl.gov.nl.ca/printer/gazette/extraordinary_issues/2019/NLG190515_EXTRA.pdf>.

Canada. Status of Women Canada. (2018). *2018–19 Departmental plan.* Retrieved from <https://cfc-swc.gc.ca/trans/account-resp/pr/dp-pm/1819/dp-pm-en.html>.

Canadian Labour Congress. (2019). Retrieved from <https://canadianlabour.ca/issues-research/domestic-violence-work/>.

CBC News. (September 27, 2007). Slain Windsor nurse often harassed by doctor, colleague testifies. *CBC News.* Retrieved from <https://www.cbc.ca/news/canada/toronto/slain-windsor-nurse-often-harrassed-by-doctor-colleague-testifies-1.664590>.

CEASE. (2019). Retrieved from <https://cease-project.eu/about/>.

Centre for Research and Education on Violence Against Women and Children. (Producer). (2014). *Domestic violence in the workplace: Recognize, respond, refer* (Video webinar). Retrieved from <https://beta.otffeo.on.ca/en/learning/otf-connects/resources/domestic-violence-workplace-recognize-respond-refer/>.

Channel 4 & Associated Press. (April 11, 2017). Brief marriage precedes fatal San Bernardino school shooting. *NBC LosAngeles.* Retrieved from <https://www.nbclosangeles.com/news/local/Man-Who-Killed-Wife-at-San-Bernardino-School-Called-Her-Angel-419097884.html>.

Corporate Alliance to End Partner Violence, *Corporate leaders and America's workforce on domestic violence. Summary of findings*, 2007, Bloomington: Liz Claiborne Inc, Corporate Alliance to End Partner Violence, Safe Horizon, Retrieved, December 13, 2019, from < http://www.ncdsv.org/images/Corporate%20Leaders%20and%20America%27s%20Workforce%20on%20DV%20Summary_9-25-07.pdf >

Corporate Governance Forum of Turkey. (2019). Retrieved from <http://cgft.sabanciuniv.edu/>.

Dupont Inquest: Coroner's Jury Recommendations. (2007). Retrieved from Ontario Association of Interval and Transition Housing (OAITH) website <http://www.oaith.ca/assets/files/Publications/Coroners-Jury-Recommendations-Dupont.pdf>.

Durkin, E. (November 21, 2018). Chicago doctor called 911 to report fears of ex-fiance moments before he killed her. *The Guardian.* Retrieved from <https://www.theguardian.com/us-news/2018/nov/21/chicago-doctor-killed-by-ex-fiance-called-police-feared-for-her-life>.

Fos-Tuvera, A. L. (2015). *Key findings of national survey on the impact of domestic violence on workers and in workplaces in the Philippines: Joint ITUC-AP/Philippine Aliates' report.* Retrieved from <http://dvatworknet.org/sites/dvatworknet.org/files/Philippine_Domestic_Violence_survey_key%20findings_September%202015.pdf>.

Futures Without Violence. (2017a). *Futures without violence unveils re-designed workplaces respond website. Futures without violence.* Retrieved from <https://www.futureswithoutviolence.org/futures-without-violence-workplaces-respond-website/>.

Futures Without Violence. (2017b). *The facts on gender-based workplace violence. Workplaces respond to domestic and sexual violence.* Retrieved from <https://www.workplacesrespond.org/resource-library/facts-gender-based-workplace-violence/>.

Galvez, G., Mankowski, E. S., McGlade, M. S., Ruiz, M. E., & Glass, N. (2011). Work-related intimate partner violence among employed immigrants from Mexico. *Psychology of Men & Masculinity, 12*(3), 230–246. Available from https://doi.org/10.1037/a0022690.

Hellwege, J. (1995). Claims for domestic violence in the workplace may be on the rise (n.d.). *The Free Library.* Retrieved from <https://www.thefreelibrary.com/Claims + for + domestic + violence + in + the + workplace + may + be + on + the + rise.-a0168084849>.

International Labour Conference. (2018). *Ending violence and harassment against women and men in the world of work.* Retrieved from International Labour Office <https://www.ilo.org/wcmsp5/groups/public/---ed_norm/---relconf/documents/meetingdocument/wcms_553577.pdf>.

International Labour Conference. (June 2019). *Convention 190. Concerning the elimination of violence and harassment in the world of work at the meeting of the International Labour Organization.*

Jeltsen, M. (November 21, 2018). Tamara O'Neal was almost erased from the story of her own murder. *Huffpost US.* Retrieved from <https://www.huffingtonpost.ca/entry/tamara-oneal-chicago-shooting-domestic-violence_n_5bf576a6e4b0771fb6b4ceef>.

Krug, E. G., Dahlberg, L. L., & Mercy, J. A. (2002). *World report on violence and health.* Retrieved from World Health Organization <https://www.who.int/violence_injury_prevention/violence/world_report/en/introduction.pdf>.

LaVan, H., Lopez, Y., Katz, M., & Martin, M. (2012). The impact of domestic violence in the workplace. *Employment Relations Today Wiley Online Library.* Available from https://doi.org/10.1002/ert.21377.

Lim, K. C., Rioux, J., & Ridley, E. (2004). *Impact of domestic violence offenders on occupational safety & health: A pilot study.* Augusta, ME: Maine Department of Labor, Family Crisis Services.

Logan, T. K., Shannon, L., Cole, J., & Swanberg, J. (2007). Partner stalking and implications for women's employment. *Journal of Interpersonal Violence, 22* (3), 268. Available from https://doi.org/10.1177/0886260506295380.

MacGregor, J. C. D., Wathen, C. N., & MacQuarrie, B. J. (2017). Resources for domestic violence in the Canadian workplace: Results of a pan-Canadian survey. *Journal of Workplace Behavioral Health, 32*(3), 190–205. Available from https://doi.org/10.1080/15555240.2017.1349612.

Male Champions of Change. (2019). Retrieved from <https://malechampionsofchange.com/domestic-violence-is-a-workplace-issue-male-champiosns-of-change-call-on-all-leaders-to-step-up-together/>.

Mankowski, E. S., Galvez, G., & Perrin, N. A. (2013). Patterns of work-related intimate partner violence and job performance among abusive men. *Journal of Interpersonal Violence, 28*(15). Available from https://doi.org/10.1177/0886260513488681.

McFerran, L. (2011). *Safe at home, safe at work? National domestic violence and the workplace survey.* Retrieved from University of New South Wales, Sydney, NSW <https://www.arts.unsw.edu.au/media/FASSFile/National_Domestic_Violence_and_the_Workplace_Survey_2011_Full_Report.pdf>.

McMurray, K. (1995). Workplace violence: Can it be prevented? *The Free Library.* Retrieved from <https://www.thefreelibrary.com/Workplace + violence%3a + can + it + be + prevented%3f-a017920796>.

Meier, B. (March 10, 1996). EARNING IT; when abuse follows women to work. *The New York Times.* Retrieved from <https://www.nytimes.com/1996/03/10/business/earning-it-when-abuse-follows-women-to-work.html>.

Mighty, E. J. (1997). Conceptualizing family violence as a workplace issue: A framework for research and practice. *Employee Responsibilities and Rights Journal, 10*(4), 249–262.

Mitchell, B. (January 23, 2007). Wife lived in fear, murder trail told. *The Star.* Retrieved from <https://www.thestar.com/news/2007/01/23/wife_lived_in_fear_murder_trial_told.html>.

NBC Staff Report. (November 19, 2018). Chicago Doctor killed in Mercy Hospital shooting had 'heart of gold'. *NBC Chicago 5.* Retrieved from <https://www.nbcchicago.com/news/local/doctor-killed-in-mercy-hospital-shooting-identified-500885211.html>.

No More. (2019). Retrieved from <https://nomore.org/about/our-story/>.

O'Leary-Kelly, A., Lean, E., Reeves, C., & Randal, J. (2008). Coming into the light: Intimate partner violence and its effects at work. *Academy of Management Perspectives, 22*(2), 57–72. Retrieved from <https://www.jstor.org/stable/27747445?seq = 1#metadata_info_tab_contents>.

Olszowy, L., Saxton, M. D., & MacQuarrie, B. J. (2017a). *National results survey on the impact of domestic violence on work, workers and workplaces in Taiwan: Joint CFL and ITUC-AP report.* London, ON: Centre for Research & Education on Violence against Women and Children. Retrieved from <http://dvatworknet.org/sites/dvatworknet.org/files/dvatwork-taiwanese-surveyresults.pdf>.

Olszowy, L., Saxton, M. D., & MacQuarrie, B. J. (2017b). *National survey results on the impact of domestic violence on workers and workplaces in Mongolia: Joint CMTU and ITUC-AP report.* London, ON: Centre for Research & Education on Violence against Women and Children. Retrieved from<http://dvatworknet.org/sites/dvatworknet.org/files/dvatwork-mongolian-surveyresults.pdf>.

Ontario Domestic Violence Death Review Committee (DVDRC). (2005). *Domestic Violence Death Review Committee 2004 annual report.* Toronto, ON: Office of the Chief Coroner.

Ontario Domestic Violence Death Review Committee (DVDRC). (2017). *Domestic Violence Death Review Committee 2016 annual report.* Toronto, ON: Office of the Chief Coroner.

Pillinger, J. (2016). Psychosocial risks and violence in the world of work: A trade union perspective. *International Journal of Labour Research, 8*(1/2), 35. Retrieved from <https://www.ilo.org/wcmsp5/groups/public/---ed_dialogue/---actrav/documents/publication/wcms_551796.pdf>.

Pillinger, J. (2017). *Safe at home, safe at work trade unions strategy to prevent, manage and eliminate work-place harassment violence against women.* Retrieved from Syndicat European Trade Union <https://www.etuc.org/sites/default/files/document/files/en_-_brochure_-_safe_at_home_1.pdf>.

Pillinger, J. (2019). *Handbook on violence and harassment against women in the world of work.* Retrieved from UN Women <http://www.unwomen.org/en/digital-library/publications/2019/03/handbook-addressing-violence-and-harassment-against-women-in-the-world-of-work#view>.

Rayner-Thomas, M. M. (2013). The impacts of domestic violence on workers and the workplace. *The University of Auckland,* 1–137). Retrieved from <http://dvatworknet.org/sites/dvatworknet.org/files/New%20Zealand_survey_report_2013.pdf>.

Rothman, E. F., & Perry, M. J. (2004). Intimate partner abuse perpetrated by employees. *Journal of Occupational Health Psychology, 9*(3), 238–246. Available from https://doi.org/10.1037/1076-8998.9.3.238.

Saxton, M. D., Olszowy, L., & MacQuarrie, B. J. (2017). *National Survey results on the impact of domestic violence on work, workers and workplaces in Belgium: Joint UWO and IEWM Report.* London, ON: Centre for Research & Education on Violence Against Women and Children. Retrieved from <http://dvatworknet.org/sites/dvatworknet.org/files/dvatwork-belgium-surveyresults-Sept18-2017.pdf>.

Schmidt, D. (June 4, 2018). *Alberta now regulates harassment & violence in the workplace* (Web log post). Retrieved from <https://www.stringam.ca/ab-now-regulates-workplace-harassment-and-violence/>.

Schmidt, M. C., & Barnett, A. (2011). *How does domestic violence affect the Vermont workplace? A survey of male offenders enrolled in batterer intervention programs in Vermont.* Montpelier, VT: Vermont Council on Domestic Violence.

Scott, K. L., Lim, D. B., Kelly, T., Holmes, M., MacQuarrie, B. J., Wathen, C. N., & MacGregor, J. C. D. (2017). *Domestic violence at the workplace: Investigating the impact of domestic violence perpetration on workers and workplaces.* Toronto, ON: University of Toronto. Retrieved from <http://dvatworknet.org/sites/dvatworknet.org/files/PAR_Partner_report-Oct-23-2017dl.pdf>.

Seitz, A. & Babwin, D. (November 20, 2018). Gunman in Chicago hospital shooting was kicked out of firefighting academy. *The Globe and Mail.* Retrieved from <https://www.theglobeandmail.com/world/article-four-dead-including-gunman-after-argument-at-chicago-hospital-erupts/>.

Showalter, K. (2016). Women's employment and domestic violence: A review of the literature. *Aggression and Violent Behavior, 31*, 37–47. Available from https://doi.org/10.1016/j.avb.2016.06.017.

Solomon, C. (February 1998). 1998 Vision Optimas Award Profile Polaroid Corp. *Workforce, 77*(2), 82–86. Retrieved from <https://www.workforce.com/1998/02/01/1998-vision-optimas-award-profile-polaroid-corp/>.

Star Staff Reporter. (November 6, 2006). Murder stunned family, friends. *Windsor Star.* Retrieved from <https://www.pressreader.com/canada/windsor-star/20061106/281526516554314>.

Stewart, N. (2015). *Benefits benchmarking 2015.* Retrieved from The Conference Board of Canada <https://www.conferenceboard.ca/e-library/abstract.aspx?did=7364&AspxAutoDetectCookieSupport=1>.

Swanberg, J., Macke, C., & Logan, T. K. (2007). Working women making it work: Intimate partner violence, employment, and workplace support. *Journal of Interpersonal Violence, 22*(3), 292–311.

Swanberg, J. E., Logan, T., & Macke, C. (2005). Intimate partner violence, employment and the workplace: Consequences and future directions. *Trauma, violence & abuse, 6*(4), 286–312.

Swanberg, J. E., Macke, C., & Logan, T. (2006). Intimate partner violence, women, and work: Coping on the job. *Violence and Victims, 21*(5), 561–578.

Taylor, G. (2016). *The Chief Public Health Officer's Report on the State of Public Health in Canada 2016: A Focus on Family Violence in Canada.* Public Health Agency of Canada.

Tiesman, H. M., Gurka, K. K., Konda, S., Coben, J. H., & Amandus, H. E. (2012). Workplace homicides among U.S. women: The role of intimate partner violence. *Annals of Epidemiology, 22*(4), 277–284. Available from https://doi.org/10.1016/j.annepidem.2012.02.009.

Canadian Press. (March 29, 2012). Police say man involved in double fatal shooting in Newfoundland killed himself. *Global News.* Retrieved from <https://globalnews.ca/news/228034/police-say-man-involved-in-double-fatal-shooting-in-newfoundland-killed-himself/>.

Thompson, C. (November 12, 2015). Nurses say little has changed since Dupont death. *Windsor Star*. Retrieved from <https://windsorstar.com/news/local-news/nurses-say-little-has-changed-since-dupont-death>.

Tobin, S. (November 7, 2018). Nurse who witnessed murder-suicide speaks out about domestic, workplace violence. *CBC news*. Retrieved from <https://www.cbc.ca/news/canada/newfoundland-labrador/lori-chaffey-nurse-workplace-violence-1.4895163>.

Trades Union Congress. (2014). *Domestic violence and the workplace: A TUC survey report*. London, UK: Trades Union Congress. Retrieved from <http://dvatworknet.org/sites/dvatworknet.org/files/Britain_survey_report_2014.pdf>.

Wathen, C. N., MacGregor, J. C. D., & MacQuarrie, B. J. (2014). *Can work be safe, when home isn't? Initial findings of a pan-Canadian survey on domestic violence and the workplace*. London, ON: Centre for Research & Education on Violence Against Women and Children and Canadian Labour Congress. Available from <http://dvatworknet.org/sites/dvatworknet.org/files/Canada_survey_report_2014_EN_0.pdf>.

Wathen, C. N., MacGregor, J. C. D., & MacQuarrie, B. J. (2015). The impact of domestic violence in the workplace: Results from a pan-Canadian survey. *Journal of Occupational and Environmental Medicine, 57*(7), 65–71.

Wells, K. (1995). *Corporate alliance to end partner violence. GuideStar by Candid*. Retrieved from <https://www.guidestar.org/profile/37-1347657>.

White Ribbon Australia. (2019). Retrieved from <https://www.whiteribbon.org.au/stop-violence-against-women/get-workplace-involved/workplace-accreditation/>.

Work Safe BC. (2012). Retrieved from <https://www.worksafebc.com/en/health-safety/hazards-exposures/violence/domestic-violence>.

Work Safe NB. (2019). *Workplace violence and harassment*. Retrieved from <https://www.worksafenb.ca/safety-topics/workplace-violence-and-harassment/>.

Young, J. & Butler, A. (2019). *Overhaul of the Canada Labour Code and the implications for federally-regulated employers. Burnet, Duckworth, & Palmer LLP Law Firm*. Retrieved from <https://www.bdplaw.com/publications/%E2%80%8Boverhaul-of-the-canada-labour-code-and-the-implications-for-federally-regulated-employers/>.

Further reading

Green, P. (2018). *Domestic violence. Australian Council of Trade Unions*. Retrieved from <https://www.actu.org.au/our-work/policy-issues/domestic-violence>.

US Department of Labour. (2017). *Injuries, illnesses and fatalities. Bureau of Labour Statistics*. Retrieved from <https://www.bls.gov/iif/oshwc/cfoi/workplace-homicides.htm>, <https://www.bls.gov/iif/oshwc/cfoi/cfoi-chart-data-2017.htm>.

11

Domestic homicide within Indigenous communities: examining violence in the context of historical oppression

Catherine Richardson/Kinewesquao[1], Elizabeth Fast[2], Vicky Boldo[3], Janie Dolan-Cake[3], Kristina Giacobbe[4] and Jackie Salas[5,6]

[1]Concordia University, Montreal, QC, Canada [2]Department of Applied Human Sciences, Concordia University, Montreal, QC, Canada [3]L'Université de Montréal Concordia University, Montreal, QC, Canada [4]Faculty of Education, Western University, London, ON, Canada [5]Dr. Jeffrey Wong & Associates, CA, United States [6]Faculty of Education, Western University, London, ON, Canada

Dedication

We dedicate this chapter to the women and their families who have been harmed by violence in Canada, particularly the Indigenous women who have been named "murdered and missing." This includes all the ones who were taken or who disappeared in conjunction with state violence, including residential school or foster care internment. Our liberation and empowerment is joined with yours. All our relations!

We begin this chapter by acknowledging the traditional Indigenous lands upon which we live and the genocidal violence that was witnessed on these lands. Particularly, we acknowledge the Kanien'kehá: ka, the Anishinaabek, the Haudenosaunee, the Lūnaapéewak, and the Attawandaron, the peoples upon whose land the authors reside. We acknowledge the ancestors, the departed ones, and the seven generations to come, with the hope and intention that this research will help make Turtle Island safe for Indigenous women, men, children, and families. Canada should be a home where individuals and families from all nations may live together in peace and justice, where past wrongs are repaired and where the cultures, rights, and nations of the First Peoples are respected.

Preventing Domestic Homicides. DOI: https://doi.org/10.1016/B978-0-12-819463-8.00011-3

Historical origins of violence against Indigenous women

Indigenous teachings hold that life is sacred and that women are to be honored as the givers of life. Women figure centrally in almost all Aboriginal creation legends. In Ojibway and Cree legends, it was a woman who came to Earth through a hole in the sky to care for the Earth. It was a woman, Nokomis (grandmother), who taught Original Man, Anishinabe, an Ojibway word meaning "human being," about the medicines of Earth and about technology. When a traditional Ojibway person prays, thanks is given and the pipe is raised first in each of the four directions, then to the Mother Earth and to Grandfather, Mishomis, in the sky.

European colonialism was designed to destroy Indigenous culture and worldview, and to take over the land and seize its wealth for monarchs in Europe and the local colonial regime. Invading colonial governments were intent on making the First Peoples subservient to the new colonial rulers, to creating a servile class of racially inferior laborers who would put their own needs aside for the well-being of colony and empire (Berkhofer, 1978; Lutz, 2008; Mackie, 1997). But Indigenous labor was only one thing taken by force in the colonial invasion. Indigenous women, too, were commodified in a number of ways for European use. The Indian Act was used to validate and legitimize genocidal violence in the newly formed country of Canada.

Prior to colonization, worldviews and the value of land, Earth, and the natural world differed across cultures. Since the Industrial Revolution, European capitalists exploited the land and human labor, for profit. The ways in which "resources" were extracted by many Europeans seemed violent to Indigenous people who held a certain reverence in their interaction with living beings and the natural world—their relatives. Because Indigenous people were relegated to the status of wards of the state and were not recognized as full citizens of their own sovereign nations, they faced ongoing dehumanization and disrespect; Earth was equated with resources and Indigenous people became commodities to be exploited by the settler society (Razack, 2002).

In order for the dehumanization process to succeed, the colonizers had to turn Indigenous people against each other; this they did using divide-and-conquer strategies which facilitated violence in all forms—by the state against Indigenous people, by men against women, and by adults against children. The Indian Act created conditions in which Indigenous men began to denigrate and violate Indigenous women:

Once the Indian Act was passed, the responsibilities of our men and women changed drastically. As a result of being confined to a reserve, our traditional men and women lost their responsibilities in using their strengths, either physically or mentally. Women were thought of as property by our O:gwe ho:we men who became acculturated into believing that they had to think like white men. The entitlement to status under the Indian Act itself enabled that to happen, wherein the male would gain status and his wife, and his children would gain his status.

Jacobs (2000, p. 108)

Thus was violence against Indigenous women, even at the hands of Indigenous men, induced by the Canadian state.

Even missionaries undertook projects to teach Indigenous men how to control and dominate women, in a European fashion (Anderson, 2000; National Inquiry into Missing and Murdered Indigenous Women and Girls, 2019). The Missing and Murdered Indigenous Women and Girls (MMIWG) report, "Reclaiming Power and Place: The Final Report of the National Inquiry into Missing and Murdered Indigenous Women and Girls (2019)," documents how "Jesuit priests held public gatherings to teach Indigenous men how to beat Indigenous women and children" (2019, p. 24). Some accounts tell of women being "deprived of food, humiliated, tied to posts in the centre of the village and publicly whipped" (p. 25); many priests forbade Indigenous women to continue in their role as healers and midwives, saying they were "evil and superstitious" (p. 26). Such controlling and harnessing of Indigenous women was a parallel project to gaining access to land. Seldom were state actions designed to benefit Indigenous communities, either in process or outcome. Apologies and present-day decolonization efforts have not yet helped to restore the practices, beliefs, medicines, knowledge, and roles that Indigenous women held proudly in the past.

Authors

Authors Boldo, Fast, and Richardson identify as Métis and have ancestral connections to various First Nations and Métis communities across Canada. Quebec-based researchers, educators, and community activists (Boldo, Dolan-Cake, Fast, and

Richardson) have worked in areas of violence prevention for a number of years, including addressing structural violence affecting women, youth, and Indigenous communities. They are connected in community to a number of agencies mandated to stop violence and support women. Ontario researchers Giacobbi and Salas, graduate students in Counselling Psychology at Western University, have been actively involved in research on domestic homicide. As a visible minority, Giacobbi believes strongly in the importance of advocating for women who have been made vulnerable. Research and writing inform her work in psychotherapy. As a Latina Canadian from Alberta, Salas understands processes of migration, assimilation, and acculturation, as well as concerns of Indigenous people in relation to settlement, sovereignty, and cohabitation in Canada.

Our focus, our stance

This chapter focuses on the context of neglect and harm that Indigenous women experience, on how violence against Indigenous women is perceived, managed, and dealt with in Canada, and on how the women themselves respond to and resist violence.

We write with OCAP principles in mind—Ownership, Control, Access, and Possession—and with a commitment to accountability to Indigenous people and communities. The OCAP principles guide researchers on how to interact with Indigenous knowledge and experience (First Nations Information Governance Centre, n.d.). Indigenous communities have cultural and intellectual ownership of knowledge related to themselves, and it is important to avoid doing harm through mishandling that information. Further, rather than use a case study methodology where distressing details about a loved one's killing would be detailed, we have created two composite scenarios, partially fictionalized, to demonstrate some of the interactive details related to understanding violence in context.

We believe that ethical research requires us to challenge colonial discourse in psychology and, in particular, to challenge the notion that either colonial research or psychology can be objective. We draw from a literary and scholarly canon that positions Indigenous women as competent and worthy, and which contests victim-blaming and colonial discourses. We believe in supporting Indigenous initiatives to create safety based on Indigenous principles and the esteeming of Indigenous women (Anderson, 2000; Lavell Harvard & Corbiere Lavell, 2006; Maracle, Anderson, & Lawrence, 2003;

Richardson & Wade, 2008; Simpson, 2013). We end the chapter with recommendations concerning how to increase safety and care for Indigenous women, their children, and their families.

Terms and definitions

Three key words

Indigenous refers to status and nonstatus First Nations people, both urban and rural, and both on- and off-reserve. It includes the Inuit and the Métis populations, even though some national Métis organizations and the Quebec government deny the presence, and rights, of the Métis in Quebec. The acronym "SPVM" is used for the Montreal police—Service de Police de la Ville de Montréal (Montreal City Police); the S.Q. is the Sûreté du Quebec, and RCMP stands for Royal Canadian Mounted Police.

Violence relates to a person's decision to use power over another, often for some gain. It refers to a unilateral act where one person acts against the will and well-being of another (Coates, 1997; Richardson & Wade, 2008; Wade, 1997). It is social, in that it occurs in a social interaction between at least two people, but the positioning of victim and perpetrator is largely horizontal, with the perpetrator having access to more social power when violence is enacted.

Resistance refers to the way in which victims push back to try to preserve themselves, and their dignity, in the face of risk and danger. The fact that victims resist in a myriad of ways, some of which are observable and others of which are not detectable from the outside, does not make them coaggressors to the violence. It is important to acknowledge the difference between violence and self-defense. Resistance is one of many responses to violence, in the moment and afterward. In working with victims of violence, it is important to help them articulate the ways they tried to preserve their dignity and maximize their safety in times of violence. Doing so helps them to recover more quickly and to have success in court when the details of the violent interaction are clarified. When accounts of resistance are omitted, courts may not understand the victim's depth of resistance to violence and her lack of options before her murder.

Terms of interaction

Victim and *perpetrator* describe temporary and situational positions in social interaction; a person can be a victim in one situation and a perpetrator in another. The term *survivor* is sometimes preferred to *victim*, often in cases in which a victim did not die in a residential school or in an attack. The term, however, may be interpreted as dishonoring those who, though no fault of their own, did not survive the violence. The terms *sexual violence, sex trafficking*, and *sex tourism* are misleading terms because they actually refer to rape. Sex, as Coates (1997) reminds us, is mutual and consensual, between adults. Sexualized violence or "sexual assault" is not consensual, often involves women under 18 (Wesley, 2012) attacked by men over 18, and constitutes a unilateral and deliberate violation of power, not a mutual agreement.

Issues

Distorted views of Indigenous women

Indigenous women have been both eroticized and romanticized in colonial discourse and in the courts (Coates & Wade, 2007; Gilman, 1985; Lewis, 1996; Sharpley-Whiting, 1999; Stoler, 1990), and during times of missionization (Anderson, 2000; Lavell Harvard & Corbiere Lavell, 2006; Razack, 2000). Eroticization exaggerates the women's sexuality and suggests a false availability that commodifies Indigenous women as products for purchase or for the taking. Missionization refers to church-based attempts to "tame" Indigenous women through state-sanctioned marriage, monogamy, and nuclear family life (Anderson, 2000; Lavell Harvard & Corbiere Lavell, 2006; Smith, 2007). Both eroticization and missionization create imposed identities, falsehoods that diminish the power, leadership, and multifaceted roles of Indigenous women. Nevertheless, the false identities continue to exist as part of media discourses concerning Indigenous women, particularly after they have been murdered. When the victims are Indigenous women, there is seldom an outcry about the need to find the perpetrator and get to the racist, sexist, and colonial roots of the problem. The fact that Indigenous women have been made poor through colonial and capitalist systems is typically missing from the analysis.

Residential schools were designed to create a class of Indigenous girls and boys who would form a servant class for white settlers (Lutz, 1992). They would do domestic and farm work, and work in factories and mines. The schools never envisioned Indigenous people being in charge of the country and guiding its political future. Most Indigenous people perceive that the 2019 dismissal of Jody Wilson-Raybould from Canada's federal cabinet illustrates Indigenous women leaders being punished for challenging potential systemic corruption and that they may not be welcome in governance unless they follow the agenda of the governing party. Colonial and missionary ideas about limiting the power and participation of women persist and statistics show that those women who challenge traditional and male power are often killed for it.

The systemic devaluing of Indigenous women is not adequately challenged in Canada. The MMIWG report recommends that Canada, and the RCMP, create public awareness campaigns that address issues critical to the protection of Indigenous women, girls, and people of nontraditional gender. Current campaigns "feed bias and stereotyping, encouraging racism, without addressing violence perpetrated by non-Indigenous people" (National Inquiry into Murdered and Missing Indigenous Women 1b, p. 250). One challenge, however, in a society where racism is prevalent, is that violence against the targeted group can increase in the aftermath of sensitization campaigns, largely because dominant groups do not like to be told what to do or how to think, especially when it comes to cross-racial issues. The MMIWG report reiterates the fact that many perpetrators of violence have accepted the media's stereotyping and view the victims as people that no one cares about. Consequently, they believe they won't get caught or prosecuted (p. 391). Misinformation abounds, and little accurate information of what it means to be an Indigenous woman or man in Canada today exists.

Indigenous women's special need for safety

Planning for the safety and protection of Indigenous women must take place with full recognition that violence against Indigenous women is commonly justified by racist, sexist, and gender/sexual-prescriptive constructs. These constructs make Indigenous women's needs different from those of other groups who experience violence. Indigenous women's needs and situations cannot be understood if these women are subsumed in a larger category of women and if their particular cultural and spiritual needs are not acknowledged. Even within the category of Indigenous women, attention must be paid to their diversity, and to understanding definitions of Métis, Inuit, and the various cultures and status of First Nations women.

The incidence and type of violence against Indigenous women in rural and isolated settings can be particularly brutal. Indigenous women have been kidnapped, held by force in a cabin for an extended period of time, and, in a society with liberal views of gun safety (Banman, 2015; Doherty & Hornosty, 2008) and strong traditions around hunting and target practice, faced firearms as weapons of fear, control, and violence (Banman, 2015; Doherty, 2006; Doherty & Hornosty, 2008). Standard responses to domestic violence safety planning are ineffective (Gordon, Hallahan, & Henry, 2002). Leaving an abusive man is not always a viable option in rural and isolated communities, and safety planning should be done with sensitivity and an understanding of the rural context. While plans should always focus on the woman's preference, they should also focus on minimizing potential harm to women rather than encouraging them to end the relationship (Doherty & Hornosty, 2004). Rural and isolated women report that strategies such as developing an escape plan and a code so that others know she is in danger, hiding important papers from the abuser, staying in a shelter, and sending children to stay with family or friends are helpful (Anderson, Renner, & Bloom, 2014; Riddell, Ford-Gilboe, & Leipert, 2009). For further discussion of women living in rural communities, see Chapter 3, Domestic homicides in rural communities: challenges in accessing resources.

While there is debate about who kills Indigenous women, society has little reliable data. We know that many women make a calculated choice not to report violence to police, and RCMP statistics are often inaccurate and based on a very small sample size. "Problem is, there's no published research that supports the figure. It's based on years of sloppily collected RCMP data that doesn't examine the actual problems underlying violence against Indigenous women, and is grounded in racist assumptions about Indigenous people" (McIntosh, 2019, n.p.).

State neglect

Discourse characteristic of colonial times still exist in Canada. Currently, the federal government nurtures a dichotomy—those in favor of "progress" (e.g., pipelines and industry) and those standing in its way. When Canada's first Prime Minister, John A. MacDonald, sought support for a transnational railway, Indigenous people seeking to protect the land, their homes, and the water were seen as obstacles. So it is with today's Prime Minister Trudeau as he seeks support for pipelines. Within such contexts, violence against Indigenous women and girls cannot be considered one-off acts of random violence caused by unfortunate circumstances or bad luck. Violence has been used to shape, punish, and correct the behavior of Indigenous women for centuries, as church and state both sought to harness women's labor and life force for their own benefit.

In some contexts, Indigenous men have apologized to their women and avowed better treatment. Conditions of abject poverty and food and water insecurity have created ongoing conditions of despair where violence still exists, including suicide as a means of escaping life's brutality. And while Bill C-31 was supposed to remedy past inequalities and reinstate fairness, Pamela Palmater says, "Canada continues to deny sex equality to First Nations women and children" (Palmater, 2019). On August 16, 2019 Crown-Indigenous Relations Minister Carolyn Bennett announced changes to the Indian Act aimed to address these gender and race-based inequalities (Brake, 2019). However, the Indian Act only applies to "status Indians" and does not address the situation for non-Status, for Métis and for Inuit women. While Indigenous communities are left to restore and recuperate from colonial violence, the federal government remains responsible for addressing ongoing inequality and systemic violence. A number of the rights of Indigenous peoples are still being violated in Canada, including the right to security for women and access to food security and clean water.

The state's ineffectiveness and neglect in ensuring safety for women, and justice and rehabilitation for male perpetrators, creates the conditions for continued violence. Critics of the justice system talk of rape cultures and cultures of impunity (Johnson, 2012, 2017; Reynolds, 2014). These critics report that out of the 33% of cases in which women report sexualized assault, fewer than 1% of the perpetrators are sentenced and jailed. Antiviolence advocate and therapist Allan Wade, when speaking about gendered and racialized violence in the Yukon, stated that such low sentencing rates suggest an "open season on violence against Indian women!" (Wade, 2015, public communication, Mind the Gap Congress, Cowichan Bay, B.C.). The MMIWG report indicates that non-Indigenous men's violence toward Indigenous women is motivated, in part, by the Canadian public's indifference to the deaths and disappearances of Indigenous women and girls (p. 391).

Blaming the victim

What tends to happen in cases of violence against Indigenous women in Canada is a shift in focus from the actions of the perpetrator to the dysfunction of the victim (Coates & Wade, 2004, 2007), confusing the victim's means of dealing with emotional pain and economic insecurity with who they are as a whole person, and how their human rights are being violated. The perpetrator is often cut out of the picture. Sometimes trauma discourse is used—to blame women for the violence perpetrated against them—as when a battered mother is seen as too traumatized to parent her children and they are removed from her by the state (Strega, 2006; Strega, Krane, LaPierre, Richardson, & Carleton, 2013)—and at the same time to excuse the perpetrator—as in he lost control, he did it because he was also a victim, he is an alcoholic, he had a bad childhood, and so on. Replacing discussions of violence with discussions of trauma does not advance human rights (Reynolds, 2018). Seeing the victim as vulnerable rather than targeted situates the problem within her, usually with deficit-based or pathologizing discourses (Richardson & Wade, 2008). The issue is recast as individual and psychiatric rather than social and colonial. Dr. Bruce Lavallee reminds us that "Indigenous women are not vulnerable, Indigenous women are targeted in secular society for violence" (National Inquiry into Missing and Murdered Indigenous Women and Girls, 2019, p. 129).

Sometimes, when a woman is trying to leave a very dangerous man, she needs an escort. In such cases, she may find a powerful but slightly less violent man to serve as a "bodyguard" while she leaves her violent partner. Outsiders do not always understand her actions and may pathologize her, judging her for "going from one violent man to another." Women are often criticized for staying with a violent man (Nixon, Tutty, & Radke, 2017). These women tend to know that, statistically, women are more likely to be murdered by their partners after they leave the relationship. Separation creates significant tension and worries for children as well. Women survivors know they can better keep an eye on the man and plan for their child's safety when they can see him and monitor his actions.

It is important to keep a woman's actions in context. On the path to pathologizing women, actions are typically decontextualized, including in the psychological diagnostic process (de Certeau, 1984; Goffman, 1963; Wade, 1997). Others can support her plan but must be careful to avoid offering actions and strategies that seem sensible generally but may not fit into the woman's particular context (Richardson & Wade, 2008).

Indigenous communities view the topic of violence against women and mothers from two perspectives. One perspective is that violence is a family issue and the other that violence is a feminist issue, part of a global issue that sees men's violence against women as rooted in gender inequality and in patriarchy. The choice of perspective influences how treatment is delivered. Our view is that a perpetrator's violence should not be seen as a family issue; it should not be seen as a mutual responsibility, as in it-takes-two-to-tango matter. Seeing it thus inhibits the healing and recovery of the victim (Coates & Wade, 2007) and increases the likelihood of her not feeling empowered in her decision-making (Richardson & Wade, 2012). It is for these reasons that some violence-cessation activists do not recommend using restorative justice or family group conferencing in cases of violence against women in intimate partner settings.

Excusing the perpetrator

Attacks by individual males against Indigenous women and girls take place within a colonial context. This is true whether the perpetrator is Indigenous or of European descent, or other cultural background. Certainly the background and informing aspects of the perpetrator are important, especially related to the needed treatment of the offender.

Those adults who use violence toward their intimate partners often experienced violence themselves earlier in life (Malinosky-Rummell & Hansen, 1993; Murrell, Christoff, & Henning, 2007). This we know to be true. However, just because one experienced violence in childhood does not mean that they will go on to become a perpetrator. Whether or not one is likely to perpetuate violence is linked to the quality of the social responses and the messages one received at the time, rather than the single fact of having experienced violence (Andrews & Brewin, 1990; Richardson & Wade, 2008). While deterministic perspectives are often applied in psychology, the reality of the matter is actually based on a number of concomitant factors. If the notion of mere repetition of past experience in relation to Bandura's social learning theory, copying without mindful decision-making or values, or Sigmund Freud's notion of catharsis and the power of the unconscious mind (McLeod, 2019) were accurate, we would see many more women perpetrating violence, given the frequency with which women are themselves targets of violence. We believe that values and the level of social supports are mediating factors in deciding to use violence.

While colonial and structural violence created conditions where men such as those described in our scenarios might use violence, one can see typical linguistic functions at work to minimize his responsibility. When he is not held responsible for his actions, it is more likely he will go on to harm other women. Whatever the explanation for his violence, in the court process he is often characterized as the victim of his own psychological forces (bad childhood, out of control, normalization, etc.). The more he is excused, the more the victim will suffer, if still living, because responsibility and blame tends to be passed on to her. Research has shown that when courts minimize the responsibility of the perpetrator, or use minimizing language, the victim tends to be blamed for at least part of the crime, often accused of having poor discernment and choosing "bad men"[1] (Coates & Wade, 2007). When perpetrators are excused for their violence, victims, as well as the community in general, tend to become less safe. When victims are blamed, their suffering is compounded and they are more likely to experience sadness and despair, and to be given a mental diagnosis (Andrews & Brewin, 1990).

Scenarios

In discussions of issues of violence in society at large, and violence against Indigenous women in particular, the *individual*—the *person*—can get pushed to the background, lost, and forgotten within the complexity of issues that surround violence. This is particularly true in regards to the justice system where courts focus on assessing the actions of the perpetrator. Before we move on to discuss courses of action against violence, let us remind ourselves that violence always involves *real, individual people*, with real, individual lives, women and men, and, often, children, in the context of their family, their community, and their society. To that end, we have created two scenarios, composites of real women and events only partially fictionalized, to represent the issues we address in this chapter.

Darcy

Darcy McDonald was a 28-year-old woman living with various disabilities. She was a sociable and friendly person who sometimes invited unhoused people into her Toronto apartment. On one occasion, she invited a man, "Roger," into her

---

[1]If you ask a woman what the man was like in the beginning, it becomes clear that she generally chose a kind, respectful, well-behaved man, not a violent and degrading man.

home after he presented himself as "a friend of her boyfriend." During the middle of the night, he attacked and killed her. Despite the fact that he had strangled and brutalized her, Roger served only 6 years in jail. He was released back into the community despite concerns by a judge of his ongoing danger to the public. After his release, he began dating another woman in her 30s named Becky. Because she was not duly warned, Becky was placed in harm's way in her relationship with Roger.

Becky had previously been involved with an older man, "Dave." Dave and Roger had interacted from time to time. After a series of events, Roger decided to kill Dave. He attacked him and then left him to die without calling for help. Due to his actions, both he and Becky were charged with murder.

When the Judge discovered that the Roger was Indigenous, he began to see Roger as a victim as well as a perpetrator. The lawyer alluded to Roger's history of colonial violence and the fact that he had been deemed to have a number of mental disorders by psychiatrists. Roger was a victim of colonial violence, probably undiagnosed and untreated, and a two-time murderer within the space of a decade. Both these murders were characterized as "domestic homicides." While it is important to consider the contextual background in sentencing, as Gladue Principles would advise, the real threat posed by Roger remains. Advocates for Roger would hope that he would receive cultural and therapeutic services in prison, delivered by Elders and teachers of his cultural background, in order to help him restore his values and his traditions. For Becky, and for Dave, Roger was a violent assailant who brought death and destruction into their respective lives.

Deborah

In this second case study, Deborah, a 28-year-old mother of two children was found dead in her home in one of Canada's Prairie Provinces. The murderer, "Joel," had befriended Deborah in a community program under the pretext of offering peer support for her life issues and in the parenting of her children.

One day, a few months after this initial contact, Deborah's brother called emergency services. He told them that he had found his sister that she was not breathing and did not appear to be alive. Upon arrival, emergency service workers found blood all over the apartment as well as all over Joel's clothes. Deborah's body was badly beaten and harmed in various ways. Even though the pair was not a romantic couple, it was treated as a domestic homicide because the couple was said to have become close.

Before the murder, Deborah had been seen in the community with numerous bruises. When asked about this, Joel blamed another man for the violence and no one followed up on his claims. Upon investigation, Joel was found to have had a history of violence toward women and was still on probation. No one warned Deborah or the community about this. The man who committed this violence was also said to be Indigenous, a residential school survivor, and a victim of childhood abuse.

Courses of action

Responding to a violent incident

Coates and Wade (2007) identify "Four operations of discourse" that should occur in response to cases such as Darcy's and Deborah's.

1. *Describe accurately the actions of the perpetrator*: The full extent of the past and current violence by the perpetrator was never fully captured in the investigations described earlier.

2. *Describe accurately the victim's resistance*: In self-defense and extreme fear of their abusers, Indigenous women often attack their abusers (Balfour, 2013; Reitmanova & Henderson, 2016) and consequently are counter-charged by police with committing violent crimes (Comack, Chopyk, & Wood, 2000). This is one reason so many Indigenous women never report their abusers to police (Hydén, Gadd, & Wade, 2016; Moorecroft, 2011), and why so many are incarcerated or eventually end up homeless (Lambertus, 2007).

3. *Hold the perpetrator responsible*: The perpetrators in both Darcy's and Deborah's cases appear to have been to some degree pathologized; the deliberateness of their actions appear to have been somewhat minimized and their behavior somewhat excused as repeating their own historical experience of violence. Given the judge's observations that several risk factors were present, Darcy's attacker should not have been released from prison, and a comprehensive assessment and intervention plan should have been prepared.

4. *Align with the victim and support her*: We can assist Indigenous women in their safety planning and avoid the

urge to tell them what to do. We can create safe housing for women, even some which are men-free, where they can live in security with the support of other women residents. But although approaches to domestic violence cessation and recovery are scattered across the country, many are not desirable for Indigenous women because they do not assist the whole family. Understanding and addressing support for Indigenous women and their families requires attention to a number of issues that we address in the following sections.

Social services reform

Colonial systems of policing, child welfare, justice, criminology, and health and education have all played a role in creating dependency and servility in Indigenous populations. It is important that non-Indigenous professionals, whether researchers, social workers, professors, or professionals, receive training in how to work alongside Indigenous people and to avoid replicating dominance, stereotypes, and falsehoods (Dupuis-Rossi & Reynolds, 2019; Jiwani & Young, 2006). Cross-sectorial workplace and institutional Indigenous and antiracist training is important because most Canadians did not receive the accurate and appropriate information in the education system and possess large gaps in their learning around Indigenous peoples and truthful history. Studies of whiteness in social service provision (Jeffry, 2005) are also relevant here. Providing dignified and culturally appropriate services to Indigenous families necessitates ensuring that non-Indigenous workers understand their own location, privilege, and history in relation to colonization. Theories of traumatization and victimization are often applied to Indigenous and marginalized communities and are seldom examined in the community of the colonizers. Intergenerational experiences of war, male violence, and gender socialization, within the settler community, are all relevant to the issue at hand.

Culture and community

Bopp, Bopp, Lane, and Four Worlds Centre for Development Learning (2003) report that mainstream responses to domestic violence often emphasize the individual or a specific family rather than the whole community. Failing to consider the role of the community in domestic violence research and interventions is an important reason why Indigenous communities cannot be approached with mainstream models of service.

Strategies to address domestic violence must be community-specific and developed with local knowledge and an understanding of community dynamics (Bopp et al., 2003). Intervention programs for family violence in Indigenous communities should focus on healing for the whole community (Burkhardt, 2004).

Restoring missing elements of Indigenous culture is an important step toward addressing the problem of domestic violence (Blagg, Bluett-Boyd, & Williams, 2015; Brownridge, 2003). Today, many Indigenous women, youth, and children leave communities where violent or dangerous behavior is prolific (Lamontagne, 2011), thus weakening their connections to cultural experiences. Many Indigenous women would prefer to remain in their home community but find it difficult to do so when they face harm or stigmatization in relation to violence. Strategies to address domestic violence should be holistic in nature and consider the victim's family and community, what Bopp et al. (2003) call the "community dimension." Community-based Indigenous safety-planning models, such as the Islands of Safety (Richardson & Wade, 2012), can help to empower families by attempting to rebalance the power dynamics between the state and the family and insisting that all participants, including professionals, treat the family with dignity. Any man can be asked to leave if he disrespects his wife/partner. Tribal police may be more safe, or less safe, depending on their relationship to the family and the perpetrator, but they do not practice racism in the same way as found in mainstream Canadian policing.

Indigenous communities organized along traditional matriarchal lines offer more protective factors for women. When women own their homes, they pass their homes down to their daughters. This creates safety for women and children across generational lines.

Indigenous men often feel better in programs that are facilitated by other Indigenous people, including Elders (Burkhardt, 2004). This is due to the fear of rejection, misunderstanding, and condescension which Indigenous perpetrators of domestic violence report experiencing in mainstream programs. When non-Indigenous facilitators have demonstrated awareness and sensitivity and employed decolonizing approaches, they may be seen as helpful interventionists.

Many, if not most, Indigenous people would say that the justice system is broken, that the prison system is corrupt and harmful to Indigenous men. From an Indigenous governance perspective, the goal is not only system decolonization but also a transfer of legal and governing power, and land, back to Indigenous communities. There, the community can decide how they want to serve their people and what services they will offer. There may be traditional ways of peacekeeping and social responsibility that could be revived. The Elders talk about wanting culturally based programs of rehabilitation for Indigenous people who are suffering and who are harmful to others or themselves. In a few cases, these types of cultural programs are offered through prisons, but mostly not. From an antioppressive social work perspective, programs could be offered in the mainstream, as well as in Indigenous communities, where the social worker would accompany the individual or family, without imposing solutions or telling them what to do. This would involve practice that transcends the "colonial code of the helping professions" (Todd & Wade, 1994).

Risk assessment

Although very few risk assessment tools have been developed for Indigenous peoples, those that do exist are often specific to the community. For example, in Alberta a risk assessment has been developed called the Walking the Path Together POP TARTS tool: Protection, Options, Planning: Taking Action Related to Safety (Alberta Council of Women's Shelters, 2012). This tool, developed specifically for women living on-reserve, is an alternative to standard safety planning available on-reserve. It provides guidelines for assessing risk, helps women and their children to recognize dangerous situations and behavior, and encourages women to trust their own feelings, body sensations, and intuitions (Alberta Council of Women's Shelters, 2012). Buchanan (2009) found that the predictive accuracy of the Ontario Domestic Assault Risk Assessment and DVSI-R is comparatively weak with Indigenous populations, likely due to a lack of culturally specific risk factors.

Other forms of risk assessments are also helpful in planning for the safety of Indigenous women who seek help. While tools can be helpful, we have found that the most effective way to plan for safety is to listen to the voices of those most targeted and follow their suggestions. Sometimes interaction with state institutions—child protection services, police, the courts, medical systems, psychologists—can actually make life less safe for Indigenous women. Those institutions are often still bound by their own colonial mandates and timelines, and are unable to attend to the knowledge about safety that Indigenous women, families, and communities themselves possess. The need for decolonization and recontextualizing with Indigenous cultural values at all systemic levels is urgent. Safety needs to come first, but safety can be generated both in mainstream and in Indigenous-centered process and assessment. Many Indigenous organizations have developed their own process for safety planning within an Indigenous cultural context. Indigenous communities can choose whether or not to work in collaboration with mainstream services in the safety-planning process. At times, the police and mainstream services can be helpful for creating safety and restraining violent men; at other times, these services are colonial and make life less safe for Indigenous women. The Together for Justice project, for example, facilitated in the Yukon, was identified as a "promising practice" in the United Nations Report of the Working Group on the Issue of Discrimination Against Women in Law and in Practice (2017, p. 16). This violence- and racism-cessation initiative created space and relationships for Yukon Kaska women to address violence in collaboration with local RCMP, in an ongoing partnership.

Web- and computer-based safety decision aids for women are also beginning to emerge (Glass, Eden, Bloom, & Perrin, 2010; Koziol-McLain et al., 2015). These automated tools guide women through risk assessment, help them consider safety-related priorities (e.g., child's well-being, having resources, maintaining privacy, or feelings for partner), and develop tailored safety plans (Bloom et al., 2014). These cost-effective tools can be used in diverse settings, including welfare offices, community agencies, libraries, and women's own homes when safe and convenient (Glass et al., 2010; Koziol-McLain et al., 2015). One study found that women who used an online safety decision aid felt less decisional conflict and more support about their safety than women who engaged in the usual safety planning for domestic violence (Eden et al., 2015). The process of analyzing various options for safety may help women feel empowered and proactive.

One aspect that contributes to safety is when others follow the woman's guidance when planning for safety. The targeted woman holds safety knowledge from having lived with, or interacted with, the violent man. Her knowledge, together with her "inner radar," and "situational logic" (de Certeau, 1984) help her maximize safety.

However, one-size-fits-all approaches should not be recommended over analyzing the situational and contextual

particularities in the life of each individual woman. The importance of providing services for Indigenous women that are culturally centered cannot be overstated (Klingspohn, 2018). Racist
and state policy—driven child protection services and justice
services tend to overlook what the Indigenous mother has
already been doing to create safety and to see only her deficits
(Strega et al., 2013). Child protection workers misinterpret a
woman's decision to not leave her situation as a sign of failure
to protect, even when it has been established that women (and
her children) are more likely to be murdered after she leaves.

Perpetrator rehabilitation

One important part of addressing violence is understanding
that it is deliberate and that perpetrators could choose to act in
nonviolent ways. One important understanding, which can be
applied to both states and to individuals, is that because perpetrators know victims will resist, they seek to suppress that resistance in advance with a myriad of strategies for silencing and
discrediting. This is why men use date rape drugs, bank robbers
bring guns to the robbery, and governments put laws in place to
arrest environmental or Indigenous rights protesters before
beginning a pipeline project. Such strategies are deliberate and
often created to serve a larger desire to dominate or control the
victim. "Terror" is used to socialize people into compliance and
deliberate violence is often recast as involuntary by psychologists, attributing it to anger, alcohol, or a bad childhood, removing any deliberation or agency. This is a problematic view. If
perpetrators can choose violence, they can also choose to
desist. If they have no control, then we do not believe they can
change. Mechanical and steam metaphors are applied, which
minimize perpetrator's responsibility, with explanations like "he
just lost it," "he was so angry he lost control," often ignoring
acts that contradict this passive representation (Coates & Wade,
2007, p. 513). For example, men who "lose it" and beat women
often stop when the pizza delivery man rings the doorbell, open
the door with composure, and then return to the beating when
he leaves (Wade, 2015, Mind the Gap, personal communication,
Cowichan Bay, B.C.).

Indigenous men would benefit from a violence-cessation
treatment program, which is holistic in nature, related to
culture, identity, and reclaiming one's self from the harm of
colonial violence. For Euro-Canadian perpetrators a violence-
cessation treatment option would need to be linked to

addressing power, issues of Euro-cultural supremacy and entitlement as well as childhood wounds, and male socialization into violence. Intergenerational treatment for men whose fathers were terrorized by war could be important to help men recover from their past and commitment to a nonviolent future as well as gender equality. Prisons need to include therapeutic treatment for male perpetrators of violence, not simply allow men to become hardened and forgotten in prison. If we cannot apprehend men who harm or kill Indigenous women, then the problem will continue.

Holding the perpetrator responsible helps to decrease the likelihood that the victim will be blamed. As well, it is important to understand men as being human beings who can change, and who can decide to desist from violence. Theories of socialization that view men as merely copying the violence they have experienced or witnessed do not take into account the fact that many who have been harmed, who drink, or who get angry never hurt other people. They could be helped with the kind of men's treatment program offered at the Calgary Women's Emergency Shelter—a treatment program that holds men responsible while offering options for change (see https://www.calgarywomensshelter.com/index.php/shelter-programs/men-s-counselling-service).

Conclusion

In this chapter, we have explored the various and multiple forces that have created the conditions where Indigenous women and girls are harmed. Within the colonial context, we have outlined a number of destructive, and favorable, approaches to offering dignity-based and culturally centered services for Indigenous women. In order to address this problem, a Canada-wide overhaul of attitudes and practices is required. We must create the conditions where violence against Indigenous women and girls would never be tolerated. Further, we must ensure that violence would never be enacted by police or in Canada's justice or helping systems. We must end racism and create opportunities for Indigenous people to thrive in Canadian society, alongside non-Indigenous Canadians. From the perspective of Indigenous women, resistance is ubiquitous and will not end until the violence stops. In the words of the Cheyenne proverb, "A nation is not conquered until the hearts of its women are on the ground."

References

Alberta Council of Women's Shelters. (2012). *Walking the path together tools: Danger Assessment.*

Anderson, K. (2000). *A recognition of being: Reconstructing Native womanhood.* Toronto, ON: Canadian Scholar's Press.

Anderson, K. M., Renner, L. M., & Bloom, T. S. (2014). Rural women's strategic responses to intimate partner violence. *Health Care for Women International, 35*(4), 423–441.

Andrews, B., & Brewin, C. R. (1990). Attribution of blame for marital violence: A study of antecedents and consequences. *Journal of Marriage and Family Therapy, 52.*

Balfour, G. (2013). Do law reforms matter? Exploring the victimization-criminalization continuum in the sentencing of Aboriginal women in Canada. *International Review of Victimology, 19*(85), 85–102.

Banman, V. L. (2015). *Domestic homicide risk factors: Rural and urban considerations* (Electronic thesis and dissertation repository). 2767. <https://ir.lib.uwo.ca/etd/2767>.

Berkhofer, J. (1978). *The white man's Indian. Images of the North American Indian from Columbia to the present.* York: Vintage Press.

Blagg, H., Bluett-Boyd, N., & Williams, E. (2015). Innovative models in addressing violence against Indigenous women: state of knowledge paper. Sydney: ANROWS.

Bloom, T. L., Glass, N. E., Case, J., Wright, C., Nolte, K., & Parsons, L. (2014). Feasibility of an online safety planning intervention for rural and urban pregnant abused women. *Nursing Research, 63*(4), 243–251.

Bopp, J., Bopp, M., Lane, P., & Four Worlds Centre for Development Learning. (2003). *Aboriginal domestic violence in Canada.* Ottawa, ON: Aboriginal Healing Foundation.

Brake, J. (August 19, 2019). First Nations women finally to be treated equally under the Indian Act: Bennett. *APTN National News.* Retrieved from <https://aptnnews.ca/2019/08/16/first-nations-women-finally-to-be-treated-equally-under-indian-act-bennett/>.

Brownridge, D. A. (2003). Male partner violence against Aboriginal women in Canada: An empirical analysis. *Journal of Interpersonal Violence, 18*(1), 65–83.

Buchanan, K. (2009). *Risk assessment and spousal violence: Predictive validity and cultural applicability* (Doctoral dissertation). University of Regina.

Burkhardt, K. J. (2004). *Crime, cultural reintegration and community healing: Narratives of an Inuit community (Nunavut)* (Electronic Theses and Dissertations). 1581. <https://scholar.uwindsor.ca/etd/1581>.

Coates, L., & Wade, A. (2004). Telling it like it isn't: Obscuring perpetrator responsibility for violent crime. *Discourse & Society, 15*(5), 499–526.

Coates, L., & Wade, A. (2007). Language and violence: Four discursive operation. *Journal of Family Violence, 22*(7), 511–522.

Coates, L. (1997). Causal attributions in sexual assault trial judgements. *Journal of Language and Social Psychology, 16*(3), 278–296.

Comack, E., Chopyk, V., & Wood, L. (2000). *Mean streets? The social locations, gender dynamics, and patterns of violent crime in Winnipeg.* Winnipeg, MB: Canadian Centre for Policy Alternatives. Retrieved from <https://www.policyalternatives.ca/sites/default/files/uploads/publications/Manitoba_Pubs/meanstreets.pdf>.

de Certeau, M. (1984). *The practice of everyday life*. Oakland, CA: University of California Press.

Doherty, D. (2006). Domestic homicide in New Brunswick: An overview of some contributing factors. *Atlantis: Critical Studies in Gender, Culture & Social Justice, 30*(3), 4–14.

Doherty, D., & Hornosty, J. (2004). Abuse in a rural and farm context. In M. Stirling, C. Cameron, N. Nason-Clark, & B. Miedema (Eds.), Understanding Abuse: Partnering for Change. Toronto: University of Toronto Press. (pp. 55–81).

Doherty, D., & Hornosty, J. (2008). La culture des armes a feu en mileu rural: Impact sur la violence contres les femme (Trans. by the editors). In S. Arcand, D. Damaant, S. Gravel, & E. Harper (Eds.), *Violences Faites aux Femmes* (pp. 17–37). Quebec: Les presses de l'Universite.

Dupuis-Rossi, R., & Reynolds, V. (2019). Indigenizing and decoloniozing therapeutic responses to trauma-related dissociation. In *Counselling in cultural contexts* (pp. 293–315). International and Cultural Psychology. Springer, Cham.

Eden, K. B., Perrin, N. A., Hanson, G. C., Messing, J. T., Bloom, T. L., Campbell, J. C., . . . Glass, N. E. (2015). Use of online safety decision aid by abused women: Effect on decisional conflict in a randomized controlled trial. *American Journal of Preventive Medicine, 48*(4), 372–383.

First Nations Information Governance Centre. (n.d.). *The First Nations principles of OCAP*. Retrieved on January 29, 2020 from <www.fnigc.ca/OCAP>.

Gilman, S. (1985). *Difference and pathology: Stereotypes of sexuality, race and madness*. Ithaca, NY: Cornell University Press.

Glass, N., Eden, K. B., Bloom, T., & Perrin, N. (2010). Computerized aid improves safety decision process for survivors of intimate partner violence. *Journal of Interpersonal Violence, 25*(11), 1947–1964.

Goffman, E. (1963). *Stigma: Notes on the management of a spoiled identity*. London: Penguin Books.

Gordon, S., Hallahan, K., & Henry, D. (2002). *Interim report: Inquiry into response by government agencies to complaints of family violence and child abuse in Aboriginal communities*. Government of Western Australia.

Hydén, M., Gadd, D., & Wade, A. (2016). *Introduction to response based approaches to the study of interpersonal violence. Response based approaches to the study of interpersonal violence* (pp. 1–16). London: Palgrave Macmillan.

Jacobs, B. (2000). *International law/the great law of peace* (LL.M. thesis). University of Saskatchewan.

Jeffry, D. (2005). What good is anti-racist social work if you can't master it?: Exploring a paradox in anti-racist social work education. *Journal of Race, Ethnicity and Education, 8*(4), 409–425.

Jiwani, Y., & Young, M. L. (2006). Missing and murdered women: Reproducing marginality in news discourse. *Canadian Journal of Communication, 31*(4), 895–918.

Johnson, H. (2017). Why doesn't she just report it? Apprehensions and contradictions for women who report sexual violence to the police. *Canadian Journal of Women and the Law, 29*(1).

Johnson, H. (2012). Limits of a criminal justice response: Trends in police and court processing of sexual assault. In E. Sheehy (Ed.), *Sexual assault in Canada: Law, legal practice and women's activism* (pp. 613–634). Ottawa, ON: University of Ottawa Press.

Klingspohn, D. (2018). The importance of culture in addressing domestic violence for First Nations women. *Frontiers in Psychology, 9*, 872.

Koziol-McLain, J., Vandal, A. C., Nada-Raja, S., Wilson, D., Glass, N. E., Eden, K. B., . . . Case, J. (2015). A web-based intervention for abused women: the

New Zealand is safe randomised controlled trial protocol. *BMC Public Health, 15*(1), 56.

Lambertus, S. (2007). *Addressing violence perpetrated against Aboriginal women in Alberta violence. Project lifeline. Final report.* Retrieved from <www.acjnet. org/abresources/research.aspx>.

Lamontagne, M. (2011). *Violence against aboriginal women: Scan and report* (p. 36). Canadian Women's Foundation.

Lavell Harvard, D., & Corbiere Lavell, J. (2006). *Until our hearts are on the ground: Aboriginal mothering, oppression, resistance and rebirth.* Bradford, ON: Demeter Press.

Lewis, R. (1996). *Gendering orientalism, race, femininity and representation.* London: Routledge.

Lutz, J. (1992). After the fur trade: The Aboriginal laboring class of British Columbia, 1849–1890. *The Journal of the Canadian Historical Association, 3* (69).

Lutz, C. (2008). Selling our independence? The perils of Pentagon funding for anthropology. *Anthropology Today, 24*(5), 1–3.

Malinosky-Rummell, R., & Hansen, D. J. (1993). Long-term consequences of childhood physical abuse. *Psychological Bulletin, 114*, 68–79.

Mackie, R. (1997). *Trading beyond the mountains: The British fur trade on the pacific, 1793–1843.* Vancouver, BC: UBC Press.

Maracle, S. (2003). The Eagle Has Landed: Native women, leadership and community development. In K. Anderson, & B. Lawrence (Eds.), *Strong women stories: Native vision and community survival* (pp. 70–80). Toronto, ON: Sumach Press.

McIntosh, E. (2019). We fact-checked a viral claim about who's killing MMIWG. It was wrong. *Analysis, Politics.* Republished in Canada's National Observer, June 7. Retrieved from <https://www.mmiwg-ffada.ca/wp-content/uploads/2019/06/Final_Report_Vol_1a.pdf>.

McLeod, S. (2019). Psychoanalysis. In *Simply psychology.* Retrieved from <https://www.simplypsychology.org/psychoanalysis.html> on August 24, 2019.

Moorecroft, L. (2011). *If my life depended on it: Yukon women and the RCMP.* (Submission to Review of Yukon's police force on behalf of Yukon women's groups 2010).

Murrell, A. R., Christoff, K. A., & Henning, K. R. (2007). Characteristics of domestic violence offenders: Associations with childhood exposure to violence. *Journal of Family Violence, 22*(7), 523–532.

Nixon, K., Tutty, L., & Radke, L. (2017). Protective strategies of mothers abused by intimate partners: Rethinking the deficit model. *Violence Against Women, 23*, 1271–1292.

National Inquiry into Missing and Murdered Indigenous Women and Girls. (2019). *Reclaiming power and place. The final report of the National Inquiry into Missing and Murdered Indigenous Women and Girls.* Government of Canada. Retrieved from <https://www.mmiwg-ffada.ca/wp-content/uploads/2019/06/Final_Report_Vol_1a-1.pdf>.

Palmater, P. (January 23, 2019). Canada continues to deny sex equality to First Nation women and children. *Rabble.ca.* Retrieved from <http://www.rabble.ca/blogs/bloggers/indigenous-nationhood/2019/01/canada-continues-deny-sex-equality-first-nation-women>.

Razack, S. (2002). *Race, space and the law: Unmapping white settler society.* Toronto, ON: Between the Lines Publishers.

Razack, S. (2000). Gendered racial violence and spatialized justice: The murder of Pamela George. *Canadian Journal of Law and Society, 15*(2), 91–130.

Reitmanova, S., & Henderson, R. (2016). Aboriginal women and the Canadian Criminal Justice System: Examining the Aboriginal Justice Strategy through the lens of Structural Social Work. *Critical Social Work, 17*(2).

Reynolds, V. (2014). Resisting & restructuring rape culture: An activist stance for therapeutic work with me who have used violence. *The No To Violence Journal, Spring*, 29–49.

Reynolds, V. (2018). Harm reduction as dignity-driven practice. In *Presentation at Dignity 2018 conference*. September 29, 2018, Stockholm.

Richardson, C., & Wade, A. (2008). Chapter 12: Taking resistance seriously: A response-based approach to social work in cases of violence against Indigenous women. In S. Strega, & J. Carriere (Eds.), *Walking this path together: Anti-racist and anti-oppressive child welfare practice*. Winnipeg, MB: Fernwood.

Richardson, C., & Wade, A. (2012). Creating islands of safety: Contesting failure to protect and mother-blaming in child protection cases of paternal violence against children and mothers. In S. Strega, J. Krane, S. LaPierre, C. Richardson, & R. Carlton (Eds.), *Failure to protect: Moving beyond gendered responses to violence*. Winnipeg, MB: Fernwood.

Riddell, T., Ford-Gilboe, M., & Leipert, B. (2009). Strategies used by rural women to stop, avoid, or escape from intimate partner violence. *Health Care for Women International, 30*(1–2), 134–159.

Sharpley-Whiting, T. (1999). *Black venus, sexualized savages, primal fears and primitive narratives in French*. Durham: Duke University Press.

Simpson, L. (2013). *Islands of decolonial love*. Winnipeg, MB: ARP Books.

Smith, A. (2007). *Conquest: Sexual violence and the American Indian*. Durham, NC: Duke University Press.

Stoler, L. A. (1990). Making empire respectable. The politics of race and sexual morality in 20th century colonial cultures. In J. Breman (Ed.), *Imperial monkeys business. Racial supremacy in social Darwinist theory and colonial practice (CASA monographs)*. London: Paul & Co. Publishers Consortium.

Strega, S. (2006). Failure to protect. Child welfare interventions when men beat mothers. In R. Alaggia & C. Vine (Eds.), *Cruel but not unusual: Violence in Canadian families* (pp. 237–266). Waterloo: Wilfrid Laurier University Press.

Strega, S., Krane, J., LaPierre, S., Richardson, C., & Carleton, R. (2013). *Failure to protect: Moving beyond gendered responses*. Winnipeg, MB: Fernwood Press.

Todd, N., & Wade, A. (1994). *Domination, deficiency and psychotherapy*. Calgary, AB: The Calgary Participator.

United Nations Working Group on the Issue of Discrimination against Women in Law and Practice. (April 19, 2017). *Report of the working group in the issue of discrimination against women in law and practice. A/HRC/35/29*. Retrieved from <https://documents-dds-ny.un.org/doc/UNDOC/GEN/G17/095/46/PDF/G1709546.pdf?OpenElement>.

Wade, A. (1997). Small acts of living: Everyday resistance to violence and other forms of oppression. *Journal of Contemporary Family Therapy, 19*(l), 23–40.

Wade, A. (May 6–8, 2015). Public communication. *Mind the gap – Annual Congress on response-based practice*. Cowichan Bay, BC.

Wesley, M. (2012). *Marginalized: The Aboriginal women's experience in federal corrections APC 33 CA*. Ottawa, ON: Public Safety Canada.

12

Domestic homicide involving female perpetrators and male victims

Alexandra Lysova[1] and Jackie Salas[2,3]
[1]*School of Criminology, Simon Fraser University, BC, Canada* [2]*Dr. Jeffrey Wong & Associates, CA, United States* [3]*Faculty of Education, Western University, London, ON, Canada*

This chapter considers cases of domestic homicide perpetrated by women against their intimate partners. In many cases, such deaths are a result of self-defensive actions or violent resistance by women who have endured years of victimization. In others, there is a complex history of violence perpetration and victimization in the relationship that may include a pattern of abuse and control perpetrated primarily by a woman against her partner. Recommendations are given for policy and practice relevant to prevention for each of these forms of domestic homicide.

Although women are substantially overrepresented as victims of domestic homicide, about one in five individuals killed by an intimate partner are men (Burczycka, 2018b). Specifically between 2007 and 2017, there were 197 domestic homicides of men in Canada (Burczycka, 2018b) with the majority killed by current or former legally married or common-law wives (59%) or girlfriends (27%) and a notable proportion killed by same-sex spouses or dating partners (14%). Analysis of data from the National Violent Death Reporting System in the United States similarly suggests that 21% of victims of homicide perpetrated by a heterosexual intimate partner were male victims of a female suspect (Velopulos, Carmichael, Zakrison, & Crandall, 2019).

The major difference between domestic homicides perpetrated by men and women is history of victimization (Browne, Williams, & Dutton, 1999; Caman, Howner, Kristiansson, & Sturup, 2016; Jurik & Winn, 1990). Male victims are more likely to have been perpetrators of domestic violence prior to their death in comparison to female victims, or stated another way,

Preventing Domestic Homicides. DOI: https://doi.org/10.1016/B978-0-12-819463-8.00012-5

257

women who kill their partners are more likely to do so following a history of domestic violence victimization (Caman et al., 2016; Häkkänen-Nyholm, 2012; Peterson, 1999; Weizmann-Henelius et al., 2012). Ironically resources to address violence against women (e.g., shelters, advocacy services) have allowed female victims to get help before the violence escalates and thereby contributed to reducing domestic homicide of men to a greater degree (proportionally) than the domestic homicide of women (Dugan, Nagin, & Rosenfeld, 1999; Reckdenwald & Parker, 2012). Thus part of the answer to reducing male victims of homicide is to continue to invest in services for women victims. There are also some domestic homicides that involve men who had not been perpetrators or who are in relationships where patterns of victimization and perpetration are multiple and complex. Although lower in prevalence, these cases also deserve attention in policies and programs directed at prevention, early intervention, and risk management.

This chapter focuses on female perpetrators and male victims of domestic homicide in heterosexual relationships. First a number of perspectives on female-perpetrated domestic homicide are discussed including domestic homicide as self-defense, violent resistance, and as a situational transaction. Exceptional circumstances of coercive control by a female against a male intimate partner are also considered. Case studies that illustrate main themes in domestic homicide involving male victims are presented and lessons learned are reviewed.

Perspectives and examples of female-perpetrated domestic homicide of men

Understanding cases of domestic homicide perpetrated by women against men requires consideration of a continuum from predominant perpetration by men against women to bidirectional perpetration to predominant perpetration by women against men. Different theoretical perspectives apply at different points along that continuum.

Self-defense

Domestic violence death review processes have identified that a large proportion of female homicides against male intimate partners occur in relationships that fall at the far end of the continuum of sole or predominant male perpetration—

where women's lethal actions against their partners were self-defensive, following significant victimization at the hands of their male partners (Black, 1983; Browne, 2008; Caman et al., 2016; Carmichael et al., 2018; Häkkänen-Nyholm, 2012; Peterson, 1999; Weizmann-Henelius et al., 2012). In lay conception, self-defense tends to be fairly narrowly and situationally defined as immediate acts of self-protection against imminent danger. However, as has been recognized legally, in the context of domestic violence, self-defense must be understood more broadly.

The term "battered woman syndrome" was coined by Lenore Walker in 1979 to explain the psychological impact of experiencing years of coercive control and victimization in intimate relationships (Ono, 2017). Applied in landmark rulings in court (e.g., R. v. Lavallee, Supreme Court of Canada, see Tang, 2003), this work has helped triers of fact understand the dynamics of abusive relationships and the experiences and context within which some abused women resort to lethal force. Subsequent commentators have argued that women's reactions should not be characterized as pathological (i.e., part of a syndrome) but as rational and reasonable reactions to the traumatic events they have experienced and to their limited choice of actions (Shaffer, 1997). Women's experiences of social isolation, fear, and limited access to legal forms of social control are emphasized as important in understanding female-perpetrated domestic homicide (White-Mair, 2000). Overall this work has helped increase recognition of how women in violent relationships may reasonably perceive themselves to be in imminent danger in situations when this may not be apparent to others and thereby allow understanding that acts of preemptive violence may be self-defensive (Kim, 2013; Ono, 2017). An example is the case of Ms. Dixon and Mr. Omar in the United States. In this case, Ms. Omar was at Ms. Dixon's home in violation of a protection order (https://www.care2.com/causes/success-grand-jury-drops-charges-against-woman-who-shot-abuser-in-self-defense.html). Upon finding a condom in the outside garbage, he allegedly assumed that Ms. Dixon was cheating on him and started charging toward her at which point Ms. Dixon shot him. Following Alabama's "Stand Your Ground" statute that justifies use of physical force on another person in order to defend oneself against what is he or she reasonably believes in the imminent use of unlawful force against them, Ms. Dixon was able to testify as to the circumstances of the event in front of a grand jury. The jury ultimately decided against indicting her and dropped the charges.

Violent resistance

Moving down the continuum of understanding women's violence against intimate partners who abuse and control them is the concept of violent resistance (also called resistance violence, Johnson, 1995). Violent resistance is defined as the use of violence to resist, or fight against, an intimate partner who is abusive and controlling (Kelly & Johnson, 2008) and is recognized as one of a range of resistance strategies that a victim of domestic violence may use (Hayes, 2013). The concept of violent resistance incorporates actions that would fall into a legal definition of self-defense, as described earlier, but also encompasses forms of physical resistance that are not preemptively or immediately self-defensive but rather, are strategies that women may use to regain sense of control, autonomy, and safety (Ferraro, 2006; Rajah, 2007). An example may be the case of a women who, after experiencing many years of severe victimization, kills her partner while he is asleep or passed out.

Theories of resistance violence emphasize that women victims of domestic violence will not only fight against their victimization and oppression, often using physical means (e.g., hitting or throwing things at their partner), but also point out that such actions may ironically increase women's risk of future victimization (Charles, Whitaker, Le, Swahn, & DiClemente, 2011; Hamberger & Larsen, 2015; Holmes et al., 2019; Langhinrichsen-Rohling, Misra, Selwyn, & Rohling, 2012; Palmetto, Davidson, & Rickert, 2013; Park & Dadou, 2017). In a recent study of violent resistance, Holmes et al. (2019) surveyed 227 women survivors of domestic violence residing in shelters, the vast majority of who reported minor and severe physical victimization at the hands of their partners. They found that 55% endorsed *perpetrating* minor physical violence and a third reported perpetrating severe physical violence against their partners. Women's perpetration occurred almost exclusively in the context of mutual violence and was predicted by experiences of victimization. The authors suggest that results support a cyclical pattern of domestic violence in which women respond to victimization both with self-defensive actions and by fighting back—in other words, resistant violence.

Domestic homicide as a situated transaction

A major challenge in research, policy, and practice is making distinctions between violence perpetration that is resistant and self-defensive in nature as compared to abuse perpetration that is mutual and bidirectional. One important means of clarifying and interpreting specific incidents is to consider the severity, pervasiveness, impact, and patterns over time (Jaffe, Johnston, Crooks, & Bala, 2008). An additional perspective that is helpful for understanding violent acts by both members of a couple is "situated transaction" (Swatt & He, 2006). This perspective focuses on the moment to moment, event to event components of conflict—how did the conflict start? What actions, by whom, escalated or deescalated the situation? Who could end the interaction? According to situational-level perspectives, people engage in violence to gain compliance, redress grievances, or defend their identity and it is through the unfolding of the event that victim−offender roles become clear (Felson & Tedeschi, 1993; Wolfgang, 1957). Situational analyses have helped to clarify that women who experience coercive control and end up using the same tactics themselves place themselves in greater danger of harm (Dichter, Thomas, Crits-Christoph, Ogden, & Rhodes, 2018).

Situational analyses can also help to identify the range of motives that lead to female-perpetrated domestic violence and homicide, some of which are situational and some associated with violent resistance. Conflicts over substance use, in particular, might be an important situational factor in women's use of violence. The national study of domestic homicide offenders in Finland found that the likelihood of homicide perpetration among females (but not males) increased due to the (male) victim being intoxicated at the time of the offense and quarrels due to intoxication, as well as self-defense (Weizmann-Henelius et al., 2012). Similarly analyzing US homicide data, Carmichael and colleagues (2018) found that significantly more cases with male victims had evidence of an argument preceding the homicide (42% vs 31%) and that these cases were more than twice as likely to have a positive alcohol result on toxicology of the victim. Regardless the most significant challenge for research in this area is balancing situational understandings of the role of each partner in a specific interaction with the broader context of abuse and control within the relationships in way that both contributions can be reflected in efforts to prevent and change domestic violence.

Controlling and violent women

At the farthest end of the continuum are cases of domestic violence perpetrated by women who are generally violent, coercive, and abusive toward their male intimate partners, who are primarily victims of this abuse. These cases are considerably rarer than female-perpetrated domestic homicides that are self-defensive or resistant, but they do occur. Scholars conducting research on women's use of violence in intimate relationships have characterized women into at least two types: partner-only and generally violent women (Babcock, Miller, & Siard, 2003; Swan & Snow, 2002). Partner-only women were those who used violence only in the context of an intimate relationship, whose violence tends to be less severe and less likely to cause injury and who have learnt through their adult relationships that violence was an acceptable and effective way to deal with conflict in intimate relationships. Generally violent women, on the other hand, were likely to use violence in a variety of situations, including intimate relationships, mostly for the purposes of retribution, gaining compliance or control, and demonstrate many traumatic symptoms (e.g., memory problems, a desire to hurt themselves) (Babcock et al., 2003). Henning, Renauer, and Holdford (2006) study of women convicted of domestic violence identified a small group of women (9%) who were primary aggressors in the relationship, which is close to the proportion of generally violent women in other classifications. These women used coercive control and severe violence with their partners more often than other women. As is the case for women, male victims of such violence are severely impacted. For example, a recent study comparing men who report being victims of noncoercive, physical aggression by their partners (often called situational couple violence) to those who report experiencing severe and coercive violence at the hands of their female intimate partners found that men experiencing coercive violence report substantially more mental health symptoms (depression, posttraumatic stress disorder) and more physical health problems (Hines & Douglas, 2018).

As follows from the discussion above, men who are likely to become victims of female-perpetrated domestic homicide are in relationships that fall somewhere on this continuum of sole perpetrator to sole victim. Many are perpetrators of violence against their female partners, sometimes with mostly nonviolent female partners but sometimes whose partners are engaging in violent resistance (Burczycka, 2018b; Weizmann-Henelius et al., 2012). A few are victims of the unidirectional severe violence perpetrated mostly by generally violent women. There are also many for whom a close analysis of violent actions by both partners is needed to clarify the pattern, pervasiveness, impact, and motive for domestic homicide. The following case studies illustrate these various forms of domestic homicide involving male victims and make recommendations for prevention of future deaths.

Case studies

The three homicide cases presented in this section illustrate the various forms of domestic homicide involving male victims killed by their female intimate partners. Each has been described in detail by the media. All provide valuable messages for professionals and academics aiming to prevent similar deaths in the future.

The case of Jeffrey Brown, Bridgeport, Connecticut, USA

Many of the details outlined in this case can be retrieved from:

https://www.democracynow.org/2016/3/31/the_price_of_fighting_back_how and

https://www.huffingtonpost.ca/entry/cherelle-baldwin-acquitted_n_570d48dbe4b0836057a2a311.

On May 18, 2013, Mr. Jeffrey Brown was found dead, pinned against a cinder-block garage wall by Ms. Cherelle Baldwin's car. Ms. Baldwin was found in the car with a broken leg and barely conscious. Their 19-month-old son was found unharmed inside the house. Ms. Baldwin was charged of first-degree murder, with bail set at $1 million, which effectively prevented her release. Ms. Baldwin maintained that Mr. Brown's death was an accident and that she had acted to defend herself against a man who had been abusive and who was trying to kill her.

Mr. Brown and Ms. Baldwin met and started a relationship in 2010 when Ms. Baldwin was 19 years old. They had a baby together about a year later. Reports from police and court documents reveal that Mr. Brown was abusive and controlling throughout their relationship. Ms. Baldwin's family reported that she started to pull away from family, be absent from family gatherings, and that she frequently had to check in with Mr. Brown before making decisions. Ms. Baldwin got a job at the Yale-New Haven Hospital, and Mr. Brown, who was unemployed, was supposed to be in charge of child care. Instead he would frequently take Ms. Baldwin's car keys and disappear for hours. With no one to care for the baby and often without transportation, Ms. Baldwin was regularly late for work and eventually she was fired.

By 2013 Mr. Brown and Ms. Baldwin has split up. Although Mr. Brown moved out, he continued to harass and abuse Ms. Baldwin. In February 2013 Ms. Baldwin came home to find Mr. Brown throwing all her clothes out the window. While she was calling 911, he ripped the phone out of her hand and smashed it to the ground. The police arrived on scene, arrested Mr. Brown, and gave Ms. Baldwin an order of protection. Despite this protection order, Mr. Brown continued to stalk, harass, and threaten Ms. Baldwin, regularly putting her in the position of capitulating to his demands in concern for the safety of herself and their child. In May 2013, 10 days prior to the incident that led to his death, Mr. Brown was convicted of a breach of peace for his ongoing contact. This event reportedly angered him and resulted in escalating harassment of Ms. Baldwin. Ms. Baldwin, at this point, confided to her cousin that she was very scared of Mr. Brown and what he might do and that she suspected that he was following her.

On the morning of May 18, Mr. Brown sent a series of threatening text messages stating that she should be ready to "call the cops cuz it over today" and because of how "crazy shit will get today" (Huffington Post). He then showed up at the house, attacked Ms. Baldwin, and tried to choke her with his belt. She escaped out a window and managed to get into her car, where Mr. Brown again attempted to choke her. Details from this point are unclear; however, when police arrived they found Baldwin on the ground with a broken leg and Brown dead in front of the car, pinned against the garage wall.

Ms. Baldwin was charged with first-degree murder. She faced trial in early 2015. After a six-week trial and five days of deliberation, 11 jurors wanted to acquit her of charges and there was one who disagreed and would not shift position. The judge declared a mistrial. To the surprise of many, the prosecution decided to retry Ms. Baldwin on the first-degree murder charge. The second trial took place in 2016. At the end of March 2016, Ms. Baldwin was acquitted of all charges in the death of Mr. Brown. At that point, Ms. Baldwin had lost nearly three years of her life behind the bars. She was financially bankrupt. While incarcerated, she was granted twice-monthly visits with her son Jeffrey who was 19-months-old when she went to prison and 4 and a half when she came home.

Themes and recommendations

The death of Mr. Brown exemplifies cases where men who become victims of female-perpetrated domestic homicide are primary perpetrators of domestic violence. In this case, the most significant theme is the lack of support and protection in place for Ms. Baldwin who was continuously assaulted despite her efforts to physically separate from her abuser and reach out for help. Ms. Baldwin took various measures to try and stop the violence, including separating from Mr. Brown, calling police, and getting a protection order. As a result of Mr. Brown's abusive actions, Ms. Baldwin lost her job, which is unfortunately a reality for many women and speaks to the need for workplaces to better recognize and respond to domestic violence concerns (see Chapter 10: Domestic violence and homicide in the workplace). In this case, as in others, application of legal consequences resulted in an escalation of violence which was not recognized or responded to by the justice system. Despite continuing to violate a protection order, there seemed to have been no risk assessment or risk management plan put in place for Mr. Brown and no safety planning with Ms. Baldwin. Instead, she was left alone to deal with her rising level of alarm. Ultimately and unfortunately, for Ms. Baldwin, protecting herself involved taking matters into her own hands.

Ms. Baldwin was eventually deemed innocent and cleared of charges, though only after having spent years in jail and missing many years of her child's life. Other women in the same situation face even worse consequences. Academics and legal commentators have identified that, although the law clearly makes provision for domestic homicide in self-defense and recognizes the importance of past victimization in making this determination, inaccessibility of strong representation and expert testimony makes it unusual for women to be able to successfully raise and argue self-defense (Ono, 2017). Sheehy, Stubbs, and Tolmie (2012), for example, studied 67 homicide cases between 2000 and 2010 that specifically involved battered women defendants found that 64% of battered women pleaded guilty and only 16% secured an acquittal. They lament that pleading guilty to manslaughter in exchange for dropping murder charges seems to have emerged as the most common defense strategy (Kim, 2013). Abuse victims who kill need proper legal representation and often an expert witness who can explain the homicide in the context of the prior violence. Even in those cases, women who kill who have been in custody pending the trial, have difficulty turning down a plea bargain for manslaughter and time served rather than gamble on an understanding judge and/or jury (Kim, 2013; Ono, 2017).

Padstow, Sydney: the case of David Walsh

Many of the details outlined in this case can be retrieved from:

https://www.kidspot.com.au/news/cathrina-cahill-reveals-hidden-abuse-in-trial-over-death-of-david-walsh/news-story/44d850c2be4282687065eb8ec0616a73,

https://www.news.com.au/national/nsw-act/courts-law/young-girl-tells-killer-i-hope-you-rot-in-hell/news-story/4c6f02ff23d09f5ca0ca7c1db9e035c5, and

https://www.independent.ie/irish-news/tina-cahill-sentenced-to-eight-years-for-killing-controlling-fianc-37618597.html.

On February 18, 2017, Ms. Cathrina "Tina" Cahill, 27 years, killed her fiancé Mr. David Walsh in southwest Sydney. The homicide occurred during an argument while both parties were inebriated. According to court documents, the couple had gone out drinking with others. Mr. Walsh went home, and Ms. Cahill, two female, and one male friend (Mr. Matthew Hyde) continued to socialize in a pub until they later all returned to Mr. Walsh's home where he was asleep on the couch. Mr. Walsh awoke and initiated an unprovoked attack toward Mr. Hyde, demanding to know who he was. According to witness report, Mr. Walsh punched Mr. Hyde repeatedly, bit his face, grabbed his hair, and attempted to smash Mr. Hyde's face into the floor. Ms. Cahill screamed, tried to clarify that Mr. Hyde was partnered with one of her friends, and attempted to physically intervene. Ms. Cahill punched Mr. Walsh in the face and he retaliated. Ms. Cahill then grabbed a knife and stabbed Mr. Walsh in the neck, killing him. A witnessing friend reported that Ms. Cahill said that, "He needs to be taught a lesson. It is not fair." (news.com.au)

In review of this case, Justice Peter Johnson described Mr. Walsh and Ms. Cahill's relationship as violent and degrading and characterized it as a "two-way domestic violent relationship" noting that there were repeated episodes of violence and mutual protection orders (called Apprehended Violence Orders in the jurisdiction in which the couple resided). Ms. Cahill described Mr. Walsh as violent, controlling, and extremely jealous. She explained that he would show up at her work and make threatening gestures, such as tracing his finger across his throat so to intimidate her. Often he would grab and scratch her face and bite her. Ms. Cahill also explained how he would often break things in their home, punch walls, and throw things. Ms. Cahill also described Mr. Walsh as jealous, reporting that he repeatedly accused her of having affairs. After the killing, it also emerged Mr. Walsh was on the run from police in Ireland where he was facing five prior charges of assault.

There was also evidence of violence perpetrated by Ms. Cahill against Mr. Walsh. During court proceedings, it was reported that Ms. Cahill had stabbed Mr. Walsh in the back of the head causing minor injuries in October 2015, 18 months before killing him. There was conflicting testimony on whether this assault was unprovoked and accompanied by threats by Ms. Cahill against Mr. Walsh or was done in response to Mr. Walsh's attempts to block Ms. Cahill's exit. In April 2016 as a result of another incident, Ms. Cahill was convicted of reckless wounding for injuring Mr. Walsh by throwing a large candlestick at him. She was subsequently placed on a two-year peace bond. A protection order was in place to protect Mr. Walsh from Ms. Cahill at the time of his death.

In sentencing, the judge drew on this history in making a determination, deciding that the relationship was more accurately characterized as one of mutual violence rather than one where the actions of Ms. Cahill could be understood as violent resistance. However, the judge also acknowledged the impact of Mr. Walsh's abuse on Ms. Cahill during sentencing, stating that "I am satisfied the psychiatric evidence supports the existence of significant depression on the part of the offender at the time of the killing which arose from the unusual and abusive relationship with Mr. Walsh" (i.e., independent) which informed his decision to downgrade the charge from murder to manslaughter. Ms. Cahill plead guilty to manslaughter and was sentenced to eight years in prison.

Themes and recommendations

The case of Walsh and Cahill illustrates domestic violence involving male victims in the context of a relationship in which there is evidence of violence perpetration by both partners. It also illustrates the complexities of determining when violence is best characterized as violent resistance and when it is farther down the continuum, with both members of the couple engaging in acts that are abusive, fear provoking, and injurious. Examined as a situational transaction, it is clear that given the history and risk factors in this case, if it were not Mr. Walsh who was killed, then it could easily have been Ms. Cahill who was killed by her partner. In highly volatile and dangerous relationships such as the one that had developed between Ms. Cahill and Mr. Walsh, the outcome may depend substantially on situational factors, including alcohol/substance use by one or both partners, presence of a weapon, and incidents of anger or jealousy.

As in the majority of domestic homicides, this case had numerous lethality risk indicators that could have prompted justice and social service to act in ways that might have prevented this death. Speaking briefly to risk factors related to Mr. Walsh's abuse, there was evidence of a criminal history, prior domestic violence, and of intersection with the workplace (see Chapter 10: Domestic violence and homicide in the workplace) as a location for abuse perpetration. Mr. Walsh was also facing numerous charges in another jurisdiction where he was a father to three young children and presumably had some level of responsibility for them.

Justice and social service response to the domestic violence perpetrated by Ms. Cahill was also insufficient. Ms. Cahill had one previous conviction for which she received a peace bond. There was also a previous assault of Mr. Walsh eight months before the murder that was not reported to police. A protection order issued to protect Mr. Walsh from Ms. Cahill at the time of his death was not enforced. Although professionals, friends, and work colleagues were aware of problems in the relationship, there was no current social service or justice involvement with Ms. Cahill or Mr. Walsh to assess or manage ongoing risk.

This case also highlights broader issues and concerns about dealing with women's use of violence (Swan, Gambone, Caldwell, Sullivan, & Snow, 2008) and specifically about how to deal with abusive relationships in which there are allegations of abuse perpetration and victimization for both partners. All too often, within domestic violence services, there is a lack of opportunity, time, and resources to identify, clarify, and differentiate mutual and bidirectional violence from broader patterns of abuse in the relationship that tilt more clearly to a predominant perpetrator and victim (i.e., resistance violence) and/or to manage the complexities of cases where there is evidence of both victimization and perpetration. Judgments around mutuality, or lack of mutuality, typically begin with police responders to domestic incidents. Following a period in the early 1990s when the number of dual charges for domestic violence skyrocketed, police developed protocols requiring them to identify the "primary perpetrator" at the scene and to lay charges only against this member of the couple (e.g., see Chewter, 2003). Although this was a good step in preventing downstream complications that result from inappropriate charges, this immediate and primarily incident-based judgment is, of course, fallible (Finn & Bettis, 2006). Strong critiques and many examples can be provided of judgments that were, in retrospect, inappropriate both to women and men (Hirschel & Buzawa, 2002; McMahon & Pence, 2003). The inevitable fallibility of this initial judgment would be less problematic if there were later opportunities to revisit it by assessors with expertise in domestic violence; however, such opportunities are extremely hard to access. Court processes around domestic violence are lengthy, expensive, and time consuming. For many accused, and especially accused that are socially disadvantaged, the most prudent route through the system is to take a plea bargain, perhaps taking diversion or deferred prosecution offers that link a guilty plea with justice-linked intervention and, upon completion of such intervention, with reduced sentencing (Scott, Heslop, David, & Kelly, 2017). Although efficient, this route means that the court does not hear or consider arguments about the case.

Family court is another point where a more detailed assessment could, and likely should, be done. Within many jurisdictions however, the first major task for reform is for recognition of domestic violence and sharing of information across criminal and family court. Recommendations abound for family court systems and services to better recognize and assess domestic violence and to have domestic violence appropriately considered as part of assessing the best interests of the child. High quality, comprehensive assessment of the nature, severity, and primary perpetrator of domestic violence with family court would be helpful for all (see Chapter 8: Child homicides in the context of domestic violence: when the plight of children is overlooked, for more discussion of this issue). Such assessments are available, in theory, in jurisdictions including Canada, the United States, and Australia; however, in practice, these assessments are not readily accessible and affordable and they are very seldom initiated. As a result, full assessment of patterns of coercion, violence, risk and response, and careful consideration of parenting plans that might be appropriate given different contexts are not typically not available (Jaffe et al., 2008).

Finally intervention programs designed to work with perpetrators of domestic violence may be a location where there is sufficient expertise, and sound clinical rationale, to conduct a more comprehensive assessment of the nature, severity, and directionality of abuse. Such assessments would be helpful, not only for revisiting the question of mutuality but also for gaining a better understanding of the context, risk factors, risk management, and intervention needs of each individual. Intervention programs that best recognize the complexities of mutuality, violent resistance, self-defense, and associated safety and risk management needs are those designed for women arrested for domestic violence perpetration (Larance, 2006). These intervention groups typically include women who are primarily victims and who have used force in self-defense or resistance, women in bidirectionally violent partnerships, and a few women who are best described a primary perpetrators of abuse. In recognition of this heterogeneity, intervention is famed ecologically, concentrates on contextualizing women's experiences, and is tailored to meet the needs of women in the group (Larance & Miller, 2015; Larance, 2006). Models of intervention for male perpetrators of domestic violence, in contrast, are geared toward men who are primary perpetrators of domestic violence within their relationships. These programs often have insufficient funding for individual assessment and, within group processes, deliberately limit exploration of individual needs and context in favor of psychoeducation and group-based work (Scott et al., 2017). Many programs have a strong focus on the agency and choices of male offenders and on the need for men to admit the use of the control and power in the relationships and focus on changing their own attitudes and behavior. Although this focus might be appropriate for a majority of offenders for whom countering of minimization and blame is a central component of intervention, it does limit exploration of the relational and couple context and often precludes discussion of patterns of mutuality and of women's use of violence.

In summary, in cases where there is evidence of violence perpetration by both members of a couple, there is a need for more in depth assessment in justice, family court, and intervention services. Such assessments would have multiple benefits, one of which is to better identify cases of mutual abuse, but also for more effectively delineating the risk management and intervention needs of both members of a couple.

Chorley, Lancashire, England: the case of David Edwards

Many of the details outlined in this case can be retrieved from:

https://www.bbc.com/news/uk-england-lancashire-45277554;https://www.dailymail.co.uk/news/article-3482122/Bullying-violent-new-bride-jailed-life-convicted-murdering-solicitor-husband-two-months-married-Las-Vegas.html.

Ms. Sharon Edwards, 44, described as "bullying wife" killed her husband, Mr. David Edwards, 51, on August 23, 2015, just two months after they married in Las Vegas. It was the culmination of months of violence from the time their relationships developed in 2014. According to media accounts, Ms. Edwards, murdered Mr. Edwards, a solicitor, out of rage because he was "made redundant" at work. Jurors involved in the case were told that Ms. Edwards liked the idea of being a solicitor's wife and that, when her husband lost his job, their already rocky relationship deteriorated further. The jurors heard that Ms. Edwards' lethal attack of Mr. Edwards followed multiple instances of abuse by Ms. Edwards toward her husband. He died following an argument during which Ms. Edward used a knife to stab Mr. Edwards in the heart. When Mr. Edwards's body was found, he was bruised and cut with 60 external injuries revealing the degree of the consistent assaults he suffered.

During the trial, it was revealed that friends and colleagues were concerned about a decline in his Mr. Edward's professionalism as a solicitor, and in his self-respect following his involvement with Ms. Edwards. They warned Mr. Edwards to leave after they began noticing black eyes, scratches, and bite marks. In the beginning, Mr. Edwards reportedly played down his injuries stating that he had fallen down or walked into a door but in the last weeks of his life, he appeared to care less about the visibility of his injuries and told more people about his situation. For her part, Ms. Edwards reported that Mr. Edwards was an alcoholic and explained that his injuries were a result of her husband falling over while drunk.

During the trial, jurors heard about a long history of abuse. In one instance, Ms. Edwards hit Mr. Edwards with an ashtray and a coffee table. On another occasion, Mr. Edwards was seen at a local pub where he was bleeding from injuries to his head and chest. It was suspected that Ms. Edwards inflicted these injuries. After the couple left the pub, a police officer noticed Ms. Edwards screaming and shouting at Mr. Edwards. The officer had a body camera and the footage recorded Ms. Edwards saying "I'm gonna fucking kill ya... I swear Mr. Edwards, when I wake up tomorrow I don't know what mood I'm going to be in" (Daily Mail). The officer responded by instructing Ms. Edwards to calm down. A domestic homicide review by Chorley further found that in the year prior to his death, two GPs and a hospital emergency room had treated Mr. Edwards' but failed to ask him about how he was injured (BBC). On the evening before his death, after coming back from holiday, Ms. Edwards's 19-year-old daughter found Mr. Edwards in the bathroom bleeding from cuts on his chest and leg. She confronted Ms. Edwards who denied abusive actions. It was also revealed that Ms. Edwards had previous convictions and cautions related to domestic violence dating back to 2004.

During the court case, Ms. Edwards' claims that Mr. Edwards walked into her knife were disbelieved by jurors who unanimously convicted her of murder. The judge found Ms. Edwards to have a "bullying and violent nature." He continued to state that: "this deadly attack was the culmination of long-term bullying by you on this respected member of the community" (Daily Mail). Mr. Edwards is remembered as a successful solicitor and loving father to his daughter. Ms. Edwards was sentenced to life with a minimum of 20 years in prison.

Themes and recommendations

There are several important themes and areas for recommendations from this tragedy. One is for heightened awareness about men who are abused by their female intimate partners (Dutton & White, 2013; Lysova, Dim, & Dutton, 2019). Since these are exceptional cases, it is more difficult for friends, family, and professionals within the community to be open to possibility of male victimization. Male victims may be more reluctant to disclose violence and seek help. Women, who are typically smaller in size and physically weaker, often appear incapable of seriously hurting their male partners. Although it is the case that women are less likely to perpetrate violence that is fear provoking, injurious, and potentially lethal, there are cases in which women are primary abusers, causing significant harm to their male partners. Experiences of domestic violence for male victims are exacerbated by the embarrassment, shame, and stigmatization that men feel about being abused by a woman (Morgan & Wells, 2016). This often prevents male victims from acknowledging their victimization to their friends, family, police, and to themselves, and, as a result, holds them back from reporting the experiences of victimization to the authorities (Walker et al., 2019). Senior investigating officer Detective Chief Inspector Dean Holden reflected, as well, that Mr. Edwards case demonstrated how domestic violence is not "exclusive to age, sex, status, or profession" (Daily Mail). Even though some of Mr. Edward's friends and colleagues knew about the ongoing serious violence, stereotypes, and generalizations about domestic violence victims (i.e., being female and of lower socioeconomic status) may have contributed to the fact that no one stepped in to report, get professionals involved, or assess risk.

Also relevant in Mr. Edwards' case is the role of police. There was at least one instance that police might have intervened in this case—the night Ms. Edwards was observed threatening Mr.

Edwards. Studies of police charging in cases of domestic violence consistently find the assault severity, injury, and the presence of weapons increase the likelihood of arrest (Durfee, 2012; Hamilton & Worthen, 2011; Hirschel, Hutchison, & Shaw, 2010; Lee, Zhang, & Hoover, 2013). Over and above these factors though, charges are more likely to be laid in cases where the victim was female (Dawson & Hotton, 2014), and potentially as a result, in cases of domestic violence reported to police involving male victims, a higher proportion involve severe assaults including assaults with weapon, threats to use a weapon, or causing bodily harm (Burczycka, 2018a). It is important to acknowledge that there may be multiple explanations for these findings, including the possibility that some violence was deemed to be resistance or self-defensive; however, profession adherence to traditional gender stereotypes that see women as nonviolent and more in need of protection compared to men also play a role (Dawson & Hotton, 2014; Felson & Ackerman, 2001; Felson & Pare, 2007).

Health workers, as well, had an opportunity to intervene in Mr. Edwards' case. There are very few studies of the experience of male victims of domestic violence with the medical and mental health service system, though those that have been completed generally find that male victims find these services to be more helpful than ones specifically focused on domestic violence (Douglas & Hines, 2011). More attention needs to be paid to this issue especially given the association of men's depression and risk for lethal domestic violence perpetration and identified gaps in communication and collaboration between the medical and mental health systems and specialist domestic violence services (see Chapter 7: Perpetrator mental health: depression and suicidality as risk factors for domestic homicide).

Finally it is worth noting that for the men who are victims of controlling and abusive women and who do reach out for help, this help may be difficult to find. Most resources for preventing domestic violence homicide focus on women victims and many have gender-specific service policies (Douglas & Hines, 2011). However, there are a growing number of shelters for men (Mail Online, 2009) and transitional housing services, which are part of a traditionally women-centered domestic violence response, increasingly serve a range of clients including both women and men who are survivors of domestic violence; still availability of these services is very limited. In Canada, for example, only between 6% and 8% of domestic violence shelters serve male victims (Beattie & Hutchins, 2015; Burczycha & Cotter, 2011). Other housing supports, such as the YMCA, that primarily serve emergency shelter needs of men would do well to integrate supports and services for domestic violence risk management, be it around victimization or perpetration. Such developments would be in line with broader recommendations in this, and other, chapters for greater awareness of domestic violence within social services in general and for more availability of high quality, comprehensive assessments to clarify patterns of abuse and the safety and risk management needs of those involved.

Conclusion

The research on domestic homicide involving male victims raises important themes regarding prevention, early intervention, and management of high-risk cases, and there are many lessons to be learned from these cases. Whether the victim of domestic homicide is a woman or a man, human life is lost, and many people are deeply affected. Despite substantial improvements in the treatment of female victims of domestic violence since the earlier 1970s, it is alarming that there are still many women who cannot get help with stopping their male abuser and have to take justice in their own hands by murdering a perpetrator as the last resort. This strongly indicates that intervention programs should continue to prioritize female victims of domestic violence. Moreover there is an optimistic observation that resources and policies available for female victims of domestic violence do work and prevent violence escalation. When opportunities are in place for abused women to exit violent relationships or inhibit the development of such relationships in the first place, there is a reduction in a number of male victims of domestic homicide (Dawson, Bunge, & Balde, 2009; Dugan et al., 1999). In other words, female victims may feel that they have more viable options than killing a partner to end their victimization. However, given the pressing issue of disproportional domestic homicide of women, continuing efforts should be applied to help female victims and deal with male perpetrators. Intervention resources need to be available to provide safety and manage risk so that women are not forced to kill their partner as the only escape from violence.

At the same time, there are also complex relationships where both members of a couple are engaging in abusive and potentially injurious violence. This violence may be a form of resistance against severe victimization, or it may be more situationally and bidirectionally motivated. Professionals with expertise in domestic violence, access to history, and ability to interview both partners are needed to properly assess these complex cases, and such assessments are currently very difficult to come by. Although a minority, there are also some men in relationships where they are the primary victims of domestic violence, subject to severe abuse and potentially lethal violence. As documented in domestic violence death review processes, family, friends, colleagues, and professionals often only recognize risk factors for domestic homicide in retrospect. This problem may be intensified in cases in which the victim of abuse is a man. Men who are victims of generally violent women may also be less likely to tell people about what is happening and/or seek help, which is consistent with general patterns of male help seeking (Campbell, Neil, Jaffe, & Kelly, 2010; Mansfield, Addis, & Mahalik, 2003). Universal prevention programs in the media and educational settings directed at boys and girls, men and women should challenge the minimization of domestic violence and educate people about the harms of any violence in relationships. Continuing research and efforts to improve policy responses to domestic violence of both men and women will challenge the societal culture of violence, prevent future deaths, and reduce a degree of secondary victimization of family members and friends involved in these tragedies.

References

Babcock, J. C., Miller, S. A., & Siard, C. (2003). Toward a typology of abusive women: Differences between partner-only and generally violent women in the use of violence. *Psychology of Women Quarterly, 27*, 153–161.

Beattie, S., & Hutchins, H. (2015). *Shelters for abused women in Canada, 2014. Statistics Canada.* Government of Canada. Retrieved August 20, 2019 from <https://www150.statcan.gc.ca/n1/pub/85-002-x/2015001/article/14207-eng.htm#n03>.

Black, D. (1983). Crime as social control. *American Sociological Review, 48*, 34–45.

Browne, A. (2008). *When battered women kill.* Simon and Schuster.

Browne, A., Williams, K. R., & Dutton, D. G. (1999). Homicide between intimate partners. *Studying and Preventing Homicide: Issues and challenges*, 55–78.

Burczycka, M. (2018a). *Police-reported intimate partner violence. Family violence in Canada: A statistical profile, 2016* (pp. 56–69). Ottawa: Juristat. Statistics Canada.

Burczycka, M. (2018b). *Police-reported intimate partner violence in Canada, 2017. Family violence in Canada: A statistical profile, 2017* (pp. 22–39). Ottawa: Juristat. Statistics Canada.

Burczycha, M., & Cotter, C. (2011). *Shelters for abused women in Canada, 2010. Statistics Canada.* Government of Canada. Retrieved August 20, 2019 from <https://www150.statcan.gc.ca/n1/pub/85-002-x/2011001/article/11495-eng.htm>.

Caman, S., Howner, K., Kristiansson, M., & Sturup, J. (2016). Differentiating male and female intimate partner homicide perpetrators: A study of social, criminological and clinical factors. *International Journal of Forensic Mental Health*, *15*, 26–34.

Campbell, M., Neil, J. A., Jaffe, P. G., & Kelly, T. (2010). Engaging abusive men in seeking community intervention: A critical research & practice priority. *Journal of Family Violence*, *25*, 413–422.

Carmichael, H., Jamison, E., Bol, K. A., McIntyre Jr, R., & Velopulos, C. G. (2018). Premeditated versus "passionate": patterns of homicide related to intimate partner violence. *Journal of surgical research*, *230*, 87–93.

Charles, D., Whitaker, D. J., Le, B., Swahn, M., & DiClemente, R. J. (2011). Differences between perpetrators of bidirectional and unidirectional physical intimate partner violence. *Partner Abuse*, *2*, 344–364.

Chewter, C. L. (2003). Violence against women and children: Some legal issues. *Canadian Journal of Family Law*, *20*, 99–178.

Dawson, M., Bunge, V. P., & Balde, T. (2009). National trends in intimate partner homicides: Explaining declines in Canada, 1976 to 2001. *Violence Against Women*, *15*, 276–306.

Dawson, M., & Hotton, T. (2014). Police charging practices for incidents of intimate partner violence in Canada. *Journal of Research in Crime and Delinquency*, *51*, 655–683.

Dichter, M. E., Thomas, K. A., Crits-Christoph, P., Ogden, S. N., & Rhodes, K. V. (2018). Coercive control in intimate partner violence: Relationship with women's experience of violence, use of violence, and danger. *Psychology of Violence*, *8*, 596.

Douglas, E. M., & Hines, D. A. (2011). The helpseeking experiences of men who sustain intimate partner violence: An overlooked population and implications for practice. *Journal of Family Violence*, *26*, 473–485.

Dugan, L., Nagin, D. S., & Rosenfeld, R. (1999). Explaining the decline in intimate partner homicide: The effects of changing domesticity, women's status, and domestic violence resources. *Homicide Studies*, *3*, 187–214.

Durfee, A. (2012). Situational ambiguity and gendered patterns of arrest for intimate partner violence. *Violence Against Women*, *18*, 64–84.

Dutton, D. G., & White, K. R. (2013). Male victims of domestic violence. *New Male Studies: An International Journal*, *2*, 5–17.

Felson, R. B., & Ackerman, J. (2001). Arrest for domestic and other assaults. *Criminology*, *39*, 655–676.

Felson, R. B., & Pare, P. P. (2007). Does the criminal justice system treat domestic violence and sexual assault offenders leniently? *Justice Quarterly*, *24*, 435–459.

Felson, R. B., & Tedeschi, J. T. (1993). *Aggression and violence: Social interactionist perspectives*. American Psychological Association.

Ferraro, K. J. (2006). *Neither angels nor demons: Women, crime and victimization*. Lebanon, NH: Northeastern University Press.

Finn, M. A., & Bettis, P. (2006). Punitive action or gentle persuasion: Exploring police officers' justifications for using dual arrest in domestic violence cases. *Violence Against Women*, *12*, 268–287.

First refuges for battered husbands offer support to male victims". *Mail Online*. February 16, 2009. Retrieved August 29, 2019 from <https://www.dailymail.co.uk/femail/article-1146783/First-refuges-battered-husbands-offer-support-male-victims.html>.

Häkkänen-Nyholm, H. (2012). Gender-specific risk factors for intimate partner homicide: A nationwide register-based study. *Journal of Interpersonal Violence, 27,* 1519–1539.

Hamberger, L. K., & Larsen, S. E. (2015). Men's and women's experience of intimate partner violence: A review of ten years of comparative studies in clinical samples; part I. *Journal of Family Violence, 30,* 699–717.

Hamilton, M., & Worthen, M. G. (2011). Sex disparities in arrest outcomes for domestic violence. *Journal of Interpersonal Violence, 26,* 1559–1578.

Hayes, B. E. (2013). Women's resistance strategies in abusive relationships: An alternative framework. *Sage Open, 3*(3), 2158244013501154.

Henning, K., Renauer, B., & Holdford, R. (2006). Victim or offender? Heterogeneity among women arrested for intimate partner violence. *Journal of Family Violence, 21,* 351–368.

Hines, D. A., & Douglas, E. M. (2018). Influence of intimate terrorism, situational couple violence, and mutual violent control on male victims. *Psychology of Men & Masculinity, 19,* 612–623.

Hirschel, D., & Buzawa, E. (2002). Understanding the context of dual arrest with directions for future research. *Violence Against Women, 8,* 1449–1473.

Hirschel, D., Hutchison, I. W., & Shaw, M. (2010). The interrelationship between substance abuse and the likelihood of arrest, conviction, and re-offending in cases of intimate partner violence. *Journal of Family Violence, 25,* 81–90.

Holmes, S. C., Johnson, N. L., Rojas-Ashe, E. E., Ceroni, T. L., Fedele, K. M., & Johnson, D. M. (2019). Prevalence and predictors of bidirectional violence in survivors of intimate partner violence residing at shelters. *Journal of Interpersonal Violence, 34,* 3492–3515.

Jaffe, P. G., Johnston, J. R., Crooks, C. V., & Bala, N. (2008). Custody disputes involving allegations of domestic violence: Toward a differentiated approach to parenting plans. *Family Court Review, 46,* 500–522.

Johnson, M. P. (1995). Patriarchal terrorism and common couple violence: Two forms of violence against women. *Journal of Marriage and the Family,* 283–294.

Jurik, N. C., & Winn, R. (1990). Gender and homicide: A comparison of men and women who kill. *Violence and Victims, 5,* 227–242.

Kelly, J. B., & Johnson, M. P. (2008). Differentiation among types of intimate partner violence: Research update and implications for interventions. *Family Court Review, 46,* 476–499.

Kim, S. (2013). *Looking at the invisible: When battered women are acquitted by successfully raising self-defence.* UNSWLJ Student Series, No. 13-04.

Langhinrichsen-Rohling, J., Misra, T. A., Selwyn, C., & Rohling, M. L. (2012). Rates of bidirectional versus unidirectional intimate partner violence across samples, sexual orientations, and race/ethnicities: A comprehensive review. *Partner Abuse, 3,* 199–230.

Larance, L. Y. (2006). Serving women who use force in their intimate heterosexual relationships: An extended view. *Violence Against Women, 12,* 622–640.

Larance, L. Y., & Miller, S. L. (2015). Finding the middle ground: Reimagining responses to women's use of force. *University of Miami Race & Social Justice Law Review, 5,* 437–443.

Lee, J., Zhang, Y., & Hoover, L. T. (2013). Police response to domestic violence: Multilevel factors of arrest decision. *Policing: An International Journal of Police Strategies & Management, 36,* 157–174.

Lysova, A., Dim, E., & Dutton, D. (2019). Prevalence and consequences of intimate partner violence in Canada as measured by the national victimization survey. *Partner Abuse, 10*, 199–221.

Mansfield, A. K., Addis, M. E., & Mahalik, J. R. (2003). Why won't he go to the doctor?: The psychology of men's help seeking. *International Journal of Men's Health, 2*, 93–110.

McMahon, M., & Pence, E. (2003). Making social change: Reflections on individual and institutional advocacy with women arrested for domestic violence. *Violence Against Women, 9*, 47–74.

Morgan, W., & Wells, M. (2016). 'It's deemed unmanly': Men's experiences of intimate partner violence (IPV). *The Journal of Forensic Psychiatry & Psychology*, 1–15.

Ono, E. (2017). Reformulating the use of battered woman syndrome testimonies in Canadian law: Implications for social work practice. *Affilia, 32*, 24–36.

Palmetto, N., Davidson, L. L., & Rickert, V. I. (2013). Predictors of physical intimate partner violence in the lives of young women: Victimization, perpetration, and bidirectional violence. *Violence and Victims, 28*, 103–121.

Park, S., & Dadou, S. H., Ms. (2017). Who are the victims and who are the perpetrators in dating violence? Sharing the role of victim and perpetrator. *Trauma, Violence, & Abuse*, 1524838017730648.

Peterson, E. S. (1999). Murder as self-help: Women and intimate partner homicide. *Homicide studies, 3*, 30–46.

Rajah, V. (2007). Resistance as edgework in violent intimate relationships of drug-involved women. *British Journal of Criminology, 47*, 196–213.

Reckdenwald, A., & Parker, K. F. (2012). Understanding the change in male and female intimate partner homicide over time: A policy-and theory-relevant investigation. *Feminist Criminology, 7*, 167–195.

Scott, K. L., Heslop, L., David, R., & Kelly, T. (2017). Justice-linked domestic violence intervention services: Description and analysis of practices across Canada. In T. Augusta-Scott, K. L. Scott, & L. Tutty (Eds.), *Innovations in interventions to address intimate partner violence: Research and practice.* Routledge.

Shaffer, M. (1997). *The battered women syndrome revisited: Some complicating thoughts five years after R. v. Lavallee, . University of Toronto Law Journal* (47, pp. 1–33). .

Sheehy, E., Stubbs, J., & Tolmie, J. (2012). Battered women charged with homicide in Australia, Canada and New Zealand: How do they fare? *Australian & New Zealand Journal of Criminology, 45*, 383–399.

Swan, S. C., Gambone, L. J., Caldwell, J. E., Sullivan, T. P., & Snow, D. L. (2008). A review of research on women's use of violence with male intimate partners. *Violence and Victims, 23*(3), 301–314.

Swan, S. C., & Snow, D. L. (2002). A typology of women's use of violence in intimate relationships. *Violence Against Women, 8*, 286–319.

Swatt, M. L., & He, N. P. (2006). Exploring the difference between male and female intimate partner homicides: Revisiting the concept of situated transactions. *Homicide Studies, 10*, 279–292.

Tang, K. L. (2003). Battered woman syndrome testimony in Canada: Its development and lingering issues. *International Journal of Offender Therapy and Comparative Criminology, 47*, 618–629.

Velopulos, C. G., Carmichael, H., Zakrison, T. L., & Crandall, M. (2019). Comparison of male and female victims of intimate partner homicide and bidirectionality—An analysis of the national violent death reporting system. *Journal of Trauma and Acute Care Surgery, 87*, 331–336.

Walker, A., Lyall, K., Silva, D., Craigie, G., Mayshak, R., Costa, B., . . . Bentley, A. (2019). *Male victims of female-perpetrated intimate partner violence, help-seeking, and reporting behaviors: A qualitative study. Psychology of Men & Masculinities.* Advance online publication.

Weizmann-Henelius, G., Matti Grönroos, L., Putkonen, H., Eronen, M., Lindberg, N., & Häkkänen-Nyholm, H. (2012). Gender-specific risk factors for intimate partner homicide: A nationwide register-based study. *Journal of Interpersonal Violence, 27,* 1519–1539.

White-Mair, K. (2000). Experts and ordinary men: Locating R. v. Lavallee, battered woman syndrome, and the "new" psychiatric expertise on women within Canadian legal history. *Canadian Journal of Women and the Law, 12,* 406–438.

Wolfgang, M. E. (1957). Victim precipitated criminal homicide. *The Journal of Criminal Law, Criminology, and Police Science, 48,* 1–11.

13

Future directions on promoting domestic homicide prevention in diverse populations

Peter Jaffe[1], Katreena Scott[2] and Anna-Lee Straatman[1]

[1]*Centre for Research & Education on Violence against Women & Children, Faculty of Education, Western University, London, ON, Canada* [2]*Department of Applied Psychology and Human Development, University of Toronto, Toronto, ON, Canada*

Introduction

This final chapter provides an overview of the major themes identified throughout the book on preventing domestic homicide. While there is no doubt that domestic violence (DV) and domestic homicide are recognized as a major health problem across the globe and a leading cause of death for women (World Health Organization, 2016), there is a debate about the extent to which these deaths are preventable. Even picking the title for this edited book was difficult in trying to be realistic about the significant challenges in preventing homicide. We came down on the side of being hopeful that careful review of past tragedies with collective efforts across the globe could reduce the number of DV deaths and serious injuries as well as the trauma for friends and family. We often forget the number of lives destroyed by this violence and the profound aftermath for survivors. The individual case studies in every chapter are a reminder of the individuals behind the statistics.

Throughout this book, we have utilized well publicized cases to illustrate the extent to which domestic homicides appear predictable and preventable with hindsight. Although there is a minority of times when a homicide is unexpected, most domestic homicide reviews suggest that friends, family, coworkers, and/or professionals who had contact with the victim and/or perpetrator saw warning signs that had concerned them. The signs were often noted but either no action followed or the action that followed was insufficient to prevent homicide,

Preventing Domestic Homicides. DOI: https://doi.org/10.1016/B978-0-12-819463-8.00013-7

notwithstanding the complexity of a victim's autonomy to make choices for themselves (e.g., Anderson, 2015). There is significant evidence that frontline professionals may have lacked awareness or training about these warning signs when they were providing services to victims. There is also reason to be concerned that professionals are too often unable to act efficiently and effectively to manage and contain the risk posed by the perpetrator. In many too many cases, no-contact orders or reprimands by the justice system represent the limit of strategies used to manage risk of those at risk of perpetrating harm. The chapters in this book represent homicides within diverse cultures, contexts, and social locations. It is difficult to do justice to all the vulnerable groups who suffer from DV and have difficulty accessing support. We wanted to highlight the major issues identified in the current literature. Although the individual chapter's title suggests one dimension of vulnerability, the reality is that most of the cases reflect multiple intersecting challenges and obstacles to finding safety and support.

A significant development in the field has been the number of DV death review committees and public inquiries into domestic homicide in the past decade. Years ago, few people aside from family members and advocates would ask critical questions about who knew what, when and what professionals or agencies did about the prior reports of DV. As of 2019 there are dozens of multidisciplinary review teams that examine these homicides in detail. There are websites reflecting national initiatives in the United States (https://ndvfri.org/) and Canada (www.cdhpi.ca) as well as jurisdictional review committees in Australia, United Kingdom, and New Zealand (Bugeja, Dawson, McIntyre, & Walsh, 2015). The review process most often identifies gaps in training and service delivery as well as potential strategies to prevent a homicide in similar circumstances in the future. Many of the themes that appear repeatedly in the work of review committees and the preceding chapters are summarized in this concluding chapter. We begin with some of the important theoretical frameworks that help us understand the challenges to prevent homicide and the solutions to reducing DV in the first place.

Major themes

Intersectionality

Women who experience DV have multiple identities which may determine their options in seeking safety and support. The early work in the field focused primarily on a gender analysis and the recognition that women were more likely than men to be injured or killed by DV (Sokoloff & Dupont, 2005). Intersectionality means identifying many different contexts and conditions that are particularly advantageous or disadvantageous and work over the past decade has increasingly focused on the importance of these intersections for DV (Tutty et al., 2017). For example, in Chapter 2, Older women and domestic homicide, there are clear indications that older women's risks of domestic homicide are further compounded by the added challenges of ageism. Older women's experiences of ageism, sexism, and other forms of oppression across their lifespan may be ignored in considering the possibility of intimate partner violence. At the other end of the lifespan, there may be a tendency to ignore youth and dating violence as being too minor to consider as high-risk circumstances. From the cases presented in Chapter 5, Domestic homicides in teens and young adult dating relationships: ignoring the dangers of dangerous relationships, the abuse escalated after the relationship ended and often family, friends, and frontline professionals did not fully appreciate the volatility of the situation and lurking danger. Youth dating relationships and "breakups" may be trivialized by older adults in positions of authority. Youth relationships also open the door to the negative context of social media through digital harassment and enhanced stalking mechanisms.

In a similar vein, viewing intersectionality through the lens of LGBTQ2S+ DV survivors is critical. This vulnerable group may face numerous barriers to support and safety. There is a lack of LGBTQ-specific DV programs and LGBTQ individuals often have to deal with a lack of knowledge among mainstream DV service providers, and discrimination when accessing social service, health, and justice services. These barriers may contribute to increased risk of further violence and homicide. Governments often do not prioritize and allocate resources to programs for LGBTQ2S+ survivors and perpetrators. There is a lack of research funding to identify the incidence of the problem and effective intervention programs to address this issue.

Cultural and historic context

Consideration of cultural and historical context is another critical aspect of intersectionality. A critical analysis of domestic homicide research related to culture is of particular importance for understanding the vulnerability and resilience of Indigenous peoples. Chapter 11, Domestic homicide within Indigenous communities: examining violence in the context of historical oppression, stresses the importance of the historical context of colonization and oppression that account for high levels of victimization in

Indigenous peoples, and being mindful of what a deep understanding of Indigenous culture can bring to addressing the problem of DV (Blagg, Bluett-Boyd, & Williams, 2015; Brownridge, 2003). Mainstream responses to DV often emphasize the individual or a specific family rather than the whole community (Bopp, Bopp, & Lane, 2003). Strategies to address DV must be community specific and developed with local knowledge and an understanding of community dynamics (Bopp et al., 2003).

Careful consideration of political and cultural context is also critical in understanding the experiences of immigrant and refugee women who may face multiple barriers that interfere with help seeking in postmigration contexts. This group is often not made aware of information about the existing services for women experiencing DV (Erez, Adelman, & Gregory, 2009; Guruge & Humphreys, 2009). They may be overwhelmed and reluctant to enter the legal and justice system, which can be discriminatory. Many of the available services are not culturally safe and responsive (Guruge & Humphreys, 2009). Immigrant women face the additional threat that their immigration status or their partner's may be revoked. Calling the police may cause victims concern about losing whatever social network and support they have in the country because of stigma and shame that may follow (Guruge & Humphreys, 2009; Guruge, Khanlou, & Gastaldo, 2010).

Availability of resources for victims of domestic violence

Another important theme across chapters and cases presented in this book is the unavailability and/or inaccessibility of critical and effective resources to help victims of DV. Reductions in domestic homicide are associated with increases in methods that support intimate partner victims leaving abusive relationships, having resources and skills to manage day-to-day risks, and preventing the development of violent relationships in the first place (Dawson, Bunge, & Balde, 2009). The increased accessibility of DV prevention resources and lethality risk assessment tools that aid in safety planning are two such methods (Dawson, 2001; Dugan, Nagin, & Rosenfeld, 1999, 2001, 2003), as long as such resources are culturally and contextually accessible and appropriate to women's unique situations.

Many of these issues are explored in Chapter 3, Domestic homicides in rural communities: challenges in accessing resources, on women experiencing DV in rural and remote communities. These women may face increased dangers in seeking help and leaving a relationship. Calling a distant police service that may take hours to respond may make retaliation more likely. Qualitative studies dealing with DV in rural communities speak to the importance of creating innovative solutions that recognize the social and cultural experience of violence including location (DeKeseredy & Schwartz, 2009; Doherty, 2017; Logan, Walker, & Leukefeld, 2001). Rural is more than a demographic descriptor — it creates the social and cultural location in which women may experience violence and need interventions that are accessible and responsive to this reality.

Another place this theme is illustrated is in Chapter 12, Domestic homicide involving female perpetrators and male victims, on domestic homicide involving female perpetrators and male victims. In many cases, such homicides are a result of self-defense or violence resistance by women who have endured years of victimization and for whom intervention by justice, health, and social services has been absent or ineffective. In such cases, it is the availability of resources to victims of DV, including shelters, effective policing, and strong women's advocates, that are likely to prevent male deaths.

Finally, the military and police contexts (Chapter 9: Domestic homicides with police and military: understanding the risks enhanced by trauma and workplace culture) are ones with heightened risk and in which it is particularly challenging to provide effective safety planning and supports to victims of DV. Within police and military professions, use of power-to-gain compliance is routine and part of training. Personnel have ready access to firearms. Reporting DV is tremendously difficult not only due to the possible presence of a "code of silence" that discourages reporting of misconduct but also because of concerns about confidentiality (i.e., how do you report police to police) and fears that reporting will lead to the perpetrator losing his job. The importance of prevention via selection and training of officers and by changing workplace cultures is emphasized.

Risk management for abuse perpetrators

Support for those experiencing DV is a critical component of our response—but it is only half of what is needed to prevent tragedies. Equally important are interventions to manage the ongoing and dynamic risk posed by those with potential to perpetrate serious and potentially lethal DV. Another theme discussed in many chapters has to do with the insufficiency of response to perpetrators—who is working with him to assess and contain risk? How is this information being communicated? Beyond applying criminal justice sanctions, how is risk being tracked and monitored and what interventions are being used to promote change?

The importance of better recognition and support of potential perpetrators of severe and lethal violence is emphasized in Chapter 7, Perpetrator mental health: depression and suicidality as risk factors for domestic homicide, on depression, suicidality, and mental health of perpetrators. Homicide−suicide, although a rare form of crime, is common in the context of domestic homicide. Between one quarter and one half of DV homicides involving male perpetrators and female victims also include a suicide or suicide attempt. This chapter emphasizes that better recognition of risks in potential perpetrators by health and mental health service providers and correspondingly improved coordination with DV specialist services to adequately assess, monitor, contain and change his risk are likely important to preventing future tragedies.

In circumstances that involve children, exposure reducing mechanisms may increase the likelihood of a domestic homicide through a backlash or retaliation effect (Dugan et al., 2003; Reckdenwald & Parker, 2010). In these cases, "backlash" arises when interventions anger the perpetrator without providing an effective safety plan or risk management strategy (Dugan et al., 2003). Chapter 8, Child homicides in the context of domestic violence: when the plight of children is overlooked, on children killed in the context of domestic homicide illustrates this point because it is more difficult for a victim with children to break off contact with the abuser. When children are involved, there is added pressure for contact with the perpetrator as both parents are presumed to be equal parents until any risk they pose is determined in criminal or family court (Dugan et al., 2003). Intervention to monitor, manage and change risk posed by perpetrators is again essential.

Public awareness

A recurring theme in almost all of the chapters is the critical role of neighbors, friends, family, and coworkers as informal supports required to respond to DV. These informal supports around DV victims and perpetrators may be the first to recognize warning signs and encourage help seeking. Public education campaigns are critical to raise awareness and have these informal supports be aware that DV can become lethal. For example, New Zealand has had a broad public education for over a decade with a message that family violence is "not OK and it is OK to get help or help." The campaign has had positive results showing increased awareness and willingness to discuss family violence, as well as reports to police (Roguski, 2015). There are unique challenges with each unique population discussed in this book. Youth in dating relationships are more likely to turn to their peers and therefore require education campaigns through schools and colleges. With older woman, gender socialization can be a barrier to help seeking and can be further exacerbated by feelings of fear and shame by these victims (Salari, 2007; Sutton & Dawson, 2017). Public awareness campaigns have to highlight the plight of senior citizens who may be dealing with various forms of abuse and include DV as one of those realities (see It is not right campaign http://itsnotright.ca/).

There is also a need for culturally informed public education programs to raise the awareness of diverse communities and help them understand DV and its effects on individuals, families, and communities (Du Mont, Hyman, O'Brien, White, Odette, & Tyysa, 2012; Guruge, Tiwari, & Lucea, 2010). Programs are needed to provide information to immigrant communities and their service providers about risk factors to facilitate effective responses to DV (Du Mont et al., 2012; Rana, 2012). The Ontario Council of Agency Serving Immigrants (OCASI) has developed the Immigrant and Refugee Communities Neighbours Friends and Families (IRCNFF) Campaign, a province-wide campaign to promote an understanding about the signs of woman abuse in immigrant and refugee communities. OCASI coordinates the campaign and engages the community directly through educational events. The IRCNFF Campaign website has information about DV, how to support victims, and agencies available in the province. (See http://www.immigrantandrefugeenff.ca/.) Unique programs are also available to support Francophone communities within Ontario that recognize the unique needs of this minority group in Ontario (see https://aocvf.ca/).

Public awareness campaigns need to connect the concepts and context to the cultural groups being addressed. For example, in Ontario, Canada, there is a specific campaign designed for Indigenous communities. The Ontario Federation of Indian Friendship Centers has developed a campaign entitled "Kanawayhitowin - Taking care of each other's spirit" (see http://www.kanawayhitowin.ca/). "Kanawayhitowin" is a Cree word, which translates to "taking care of each other's spirit". The website states that people are born with "spirits are pure and whole - as we journey through our time on earth, our spirit may encounter abuse and neglect. Everyone has the right to have their spirit protected and the responsibility to take care of the sacredness of life." The campaign is geared to people who are close to abuse victims or the abusive man who can provide support. A traditional and cultural approach to community healing are promoted. The program has resources such as public service announcements and training videos as well as guidelines on how to implement the initiative in individual communities. Another Canadian grass roots initiative developed by Indigenous people is the Moose Hide Campaign which calls on men to stand up against violence against women and children (see www.moosehidecampaign.ca).

Aside from public education directed at friends and family, there are also campaigns directed at the workplace which recognizes the extent to which DV follows victims to work. As Chapter 10, Domestic violence and homicide in the workplace, outlines, there is a growing awareness in workplace legislation and policies across the globe that DV is a workplace health and safety issues. Education of supervisors and coworkers on DV is now seen in many jurisdictions as essential. Campaigns in Canada (http://makeitourbusiness.ca/), the United States (Corporate Alliance to End Partner Violence), and the United Kingdom (http://thecorporatealliance.co.uk/) have all emphasized the critical role of the workplace in addressing DV. These initiatives are born out tragedies when violence at home came to work.

Professional training

Beyond the need for broad public awareness, professionals across all service sectors such as justice, health, social services, and education require the most up-to-date training on DV as well as risk assessment, safety planning, and risk management. Some frontline professionals need to understand the basics on screening cases that have allegations of DV and know how to refer to experts who may specialize in the field such as advocates for abuse victims, and police or forensic mental health professionals. It may be beneficial to enhance awareness among healthcare professionals who might be the first to see the sense of hopelessness from prolonged physical and mental disorders. Most domestic homicides are preceded by warning signs that are often overlooked by frontline professionals which underlines the importance of training. Many of the recommendations from DV death review committees point to the importance of better training at the preservice level as well as ongoing professional training in regard to screening and risk assessment for DV cases.

Beyond training on the knowledge and skills required to assess and intervene in DV cases is the importance of cultural competence. As the Chapter 6, Domestic homicide in immigrant communities: lessons learned, authors point out, practitioners working with immigrant and refugee women need to meaningfully apply cultural humility within their practice. Cultural humility can improve practitioner awareness of the diverse and intersecting factors that affect one's lived experiences and evolving notion of the self. The relationships between practitioners and immigrant and refugee women and families should be based on respect through acknowledgment that cultures are fluid, recognition of the inherent power imbalance in client—professional relationships, ongoing critical self-reflection, continuous learning, and working in conjunction with immigrant and refugee populations (Fisher-Borne, Cain, & Martin, 2015; Foronda, Baptiste, Reinholdt, & Ousman, 2016).

Chapter 4, Domestic homicides within LGBTQ2S+ communities: barriers in disclosing relationships and violence, outlines how the needs of LGBTQ2S+ DV survivors have not been adequately addressed. LGBTQ2S+ communities have often had to choose between accessing mainstream DV services where they may be met by untrained and/or discriminatory staff, or staying with an abusive partner. LGBTQ-specific DV programs are few and far between. To serve LGBTQ2S+ survivors of DV, many mainstream DV services have been working to expand their services to be inclusive of queer, trans, and nonbinary survivors. Training for service providers in the DV, health, justice, child protection, and social services sectors is desperately needed. All service providers should be offered mandatory agency-wide antioppression/antidiscrimination training as well as training on the unique and varied circumstances, contexts, and needs of LGBTQ2S+ DV survivors (Messinger, 2017; Ristock, 2011).

Multiple chapters highlight the importance of educating a broad range of professionals about risk factors related to domestic homicide. The history of DV and a pending separation should demand as many questions about risks to intimate partners as risks for self-harm. Concerning incidents in the workplace should result in conversations about abuse that might be experienced at home.

Interagency collaboration

A consistent theme from DV death review committees is the importance of interagency collaboration. Effective responses to high-risk DV cases require multiple agencies and systems to respond. The chain of action required may only be as strong as its weakest link. In many case examples in this book, an individual professional may have recognized the dangers presented by the perpetrator but fell short in engaging other agencies and the justice system. For example, Chapter 6, Domestic homicide in immigrant: lessons learned, stressed the importance of culturally informed integrative and collaborative services to assess and manage risk and enhance safety. Collaboration among and across diverse organizations promotes collective responses to abused immigrant and refugee women and provides them access to diverse service providers. Service providers can coordinate efforts to assess risk, share information, undertake safety planning, and tailor interventions that meet the needs of immigrant and refugee women as well as services for abusers (Baobaid & Ashbourne, 2017; Whitaker, Haileyesus, Swahn, & Saltzman, 2007).

Chapter 8, Child homicides in the context of domestic violence: when the plight of children is overlooked, highlighted the many systems that must plan for the victim parent and child safety in navigating the family and criminal court after allegations of DV. Without a coordinated plan, the criminal and family court can create long delays and uncertainty before any meaningful safety plans and risk management strategies are put in place. In a similar vein, Chapter 7, Perpetrator mental health: depression and suicidality as risk factors for domestic homicide, highlights the need for collaboration between mental health and justice agencies when the perpetrator presents with both mental health disorders and a pattern of DV. The Oklahoma Domestic Violence Fatality Review Board recommended promoting awareness of the relationships between mental health, substance abuse, and DV (Oklahoma Domestic Violence Fatality Review Board, 2014). This work resulted in DV liaison positions within mental health and substance abuse agencies across the state (Oklahoma Domestic Violence Fatality Review Board, 2014). Such collaborative relationships are a starting point in training professionals on the assessment and management of cooccurring mental health and violence concerns. Mental health agencies should ensure that they provide adequate training to ensure staff have the skills to work with perpetrators of DV and coordinate their efforts with the justice system.

Future research

This book outlines diverse populations whose needs could be readily overlooked in any study on domestic homicide without careful attention to the subpopulations. Average scores for risk factors or frequency of individual risk factors would disguise the unique population being examined. Often studies have limited sample sizes to explore these differences which emphasizes the need for national and crossjurisdictional studies.

Chapter 8, Child homicides in the context of domestic violence: when the plight of children is overlooked, makes the point that often children's deaths are not considered in domestic homicide research. In some jurisdictions, child homicides in the context of DV are not counted or seen as collateral causalities, as if in a war. Aside from the pejorative nature of the label "collateral" victim, in many cases, the children are an intentional target of the perpetrator (Jaffe et al., 2017). Inconsistencies in definitions about who died and how they died takes away the possibility for more in-depth analyses. Similarly, Chapter 4, Domestic homicides within LGBTQ2S+ communities: barriers in disclosing relationships and violence, and Chapter 5, Domestic homicides in teens and young adult dating relationships: ignoring the dangers of dangerous relationships, underline that DV and homicide research among young dating and LGBTQ2S+ communities will be strengthened by common definitions of these communities that reflect a wide range of identities and relationship types, including one-time sexual encounters, short-term dating relationships, and long-term monogamous partnerships, and polyamorous relationships, regardless of cohabitation or marital status. Researchers must also apply an intersectional framework when seeking to better understand the unique vulnerabilities of LGBTQ2S+ survivors and barriers to accessing support and protection.

A critical analysis required in domestic homicide research is related to culture. For example, Chapter 11, Domestic homicide within Indigenous communities: examining violence in the context of historical oppression, stresses the importance of deeper understanding of Indigenous culture and the historical context of colonization and oppression that account for high levels of victimization and unique perspectives to address the problem of DV (Blagg et al., 2015; Brownridge, 2003). Mainstream responses to DV often emphasize the individual or a specific family rather than the whole community (Bopp et al., 2003). Strategies to address DV must be community specific and developed with local knowledge and an understanding of community dynamics (Bopp et al., 2003).

Research on risk assessment tools needs to consider culture. The predictive accuracy of popular risk assessment tools is comparatively weak with Indigenous populations due to a lack of culturally specific risk factors (Buchanan, 2009). Risk assessment tools such as the Walking the Path Together: Protection, Options, Planning: Taking Action Related to Safety tool that have been developed for Indigenous peoples still require validity studies to see the extent they can be helpful across diverse Indigenous communities on reserve and in urban centers (Hoffart, 2014).

Chapter 9, Domestic homicides with police and military: understanding the risks enhanced by trauma and workplace culture, and Chapter 10, Domestic violence and homicide in the workplace, underscore the need for more research on the role of workplaces in preventing domestic homicide. On the broader workplace issue, it would be important to evaluate workplace programs to see if there is a shift in help seeking and a potential reduction in high-risk incidents. The police and military require more accurate information on the incidence of DV compared to other professions. There is a need for research on the recruitment phase for people becoming police officers or members of the military. The widespread hostility to women often reported in both policing and the military (Deschamps, 2015; Gillis, 2017) points to the need to specifically test for misogynistic attitudes and beliefs and to prevent these applicants from becoming police officers and soldiers.

Stricter recruitment practices could also help to identify those who may have higher risk factors for developing long-term behavioral or mental health issues, including posttraumatic stress disorder (PTSD) (Wilham, 2012). Given the strong links between mental health problems and DV perpetration, especially PTSD among soldiers (Taft, Walling, Howard, & Monson, 2011), this could be an effective preventative measure. It is critically important to understand workplace cultural changes that can prevent situations from escalating into DV. Key to this work will be overcoming the culture of reluctance to seek help that exists in both the military and policing. Death review committees have made several recommendations in this regard. These include providing access to an anonymous helpline for police officers, military members, and their families where they would have contact with immediate assistance and crisis intervention as well as referral to specialized counseling services (Ontario DVDRC, 2011, 2016). Currently, there is a lack of empirically validated DV intervention programs for military service members or veterans (Taft et al., 2011). DV interventions may be more successful and have increased efficacy if they address trauma experiences. The Strength at Home Men's Program is an example of a program designed specifically for military veterans and service members that considers how trauma influences social information processing leading to DV. The program has been found to be effective in reducing use of physical and psychological DVs (Taft, Macdonald, Creech, Monson, & Murphy, 2016).

Many of the case studies in this book have been reviewed by criminal courts, inquests, and/or DV death review committees. Many of the domestic homicides have been followed by specific recommendations for changes to professional training, policies, service delivery, and collaboration. What is often missing is the tracking of these recommendations to make sure they are implemented and evaluated. This issue represents a needed area of research (Dawson, 2017). Storer, Lindhorst, and Starr (2013) emphasized this need in their analysis of the implementation of recommendations from the Washington State Domestic Violence Fatality Review Committee. They found that there was a high level of endorsement for recommendations but limited implementation. For example, almost 90% of community officials surveyed endorsed the prioritization of enhanced training on teen dating violence but only 16% indicated any actual movement toward implementation. In a similar vein, over 80% said it was a priority for custody evaluators to recognize victim and child safety planning but only a quarter acknowledged any implementation of this idea (Storer et al., 2013).

Conclusion

This book was written in the hopes that raising awareness may help save lives. Domestic homicides appear predictable and preventable with hindsight. The hindsight is made clear by the fact that the vast majority of domestic homicides have multiple warning signs known to friends, family, coworkers, and/or frontline professionals. Saving lives requires greater public awareness, professional training and enhanced collaboration across justice and community agencies. Saving lives also depends on the recognition that domestic homicides occur across diverse communities, populations and social contexts. Understanding that there is not a "one size fits all" solution is an important starting point in the search for solutions.

There are many factors associated with DV and domestic homicide. A central factor is gender and the extent to which domestic homicide is fundamentally a gender-based crime. Ultimately our collective goal has to be dedicated to the effective prevention of gender-based violence that is directed toward women and girls. The high prevalence and negative impact of violence against women and girls is seen more and more as a public health issue. A public health approach and an ecological framework can help us understand why some girls and women are at higher risk of violence, while others may be more protected from it. Violence is viewed as the outcome of many interacting factors, including the role of the individual, relationships, the community, and the broader societal influences.

The case studies throughout this book are a call to action to not only recognize warning signs much earlier but also to work toward preventing DV that is embedded within interpersonal relationships, and larger institutional and societal contexts. There should be a greater focus on interventions and research with diverse and vulnerable populations. There are encouraging signs of a growing commitment to DV prevention across the globe (Crooks, Jaffe, Dunlop, Kerry, & Exner-Cortens, 2019). Much more needs to be done to examine effective implementation and sustainability of these efforts—and how these efforts can save lives. Some scholars have called this violence on the most critical public health crises:

> In this age of dwindling resources, programs against violence are apt to be dismissed as an unaffordable luxury. But it is precisely now, when the survival of many families hinges on the mother's emotional and physical strength, that anti-violence programs are most desperately needed. More importantly, it is time that the international community recognizes that women have a right to live free from physical and psychological abuse. Gender violence is crippling, both physically and emotionally. A health agenda that values women as women could not ignore this all-too common reality of women's lives.

Heise (2018, p. 185).

References

Anderson, K. L. (2015). Victims' voices and victims' choices in three IPV courts. *Violence Against Women*, 21(1), 105–124.

Baobaid, M., & Ashbourne, L. M. (2017). *Enhancing culturally integrative family safety response in Muslim communities*. New York: Taylor & Francis.

Blagg, H., Bluett-Boyd, N., & Williams, E. (2015). Innovative models in addressing violence against Indigenous women: State of knowledge paper. *(ANROWS Landscape series)*. Australia: ANROWS.

Bopp, M., Bopp, J., & Lane, P. (2003). *Aboriginal domestic violence in Canada.* Ottawa: Aboriginal Healing Foundation.

Brownridge, D. (2003). Male partner violence against Aboriginal women in Canada. *Journal of Interpersonal Violence, 18*(1), 65–83.

Buchanan, K. (2009). Risk assessment and spousal violence: Predictive validity and cultural applicability *(Unpublished doctoral dissertation).* Saskatchewan, Canada: University of Regina.

Bugeja, L., Dawson, M., McIntyre, S. J., & Walsh, C. (2015). Domestic/family violence death reviews: An international comparison. *Trauma, Violence & Abuse, 16*(2), 179–187.

Crooks, C. V., Jaffe, P., Dunlop, C., Kerry, A., & Exner-Cortens, D. (2019). Preventing gender-based violence among adolescents and young adults: Lessons from 25 years of program development and evaluation. *Violence Against Women, 25*(1), 29–55.

Dawson, M. (2001). *Examination of declining intimate partner homicide rates: A literature review.* Department of Justice Canada, Research & Statistics Canada.

Dawson, M. (2017). *Domestic homicides and death reviews: An international perspective.* New York: Palgrave.

Dawson, M., Bunge, V. P., & Balde, T. (2009). National trends in intimate partner homicides: Explaining declines in Canada, 1976 to 2001. *Violence Against Women, 15*(3), 276–306.

DeKeseredy, W., & Schwartz, M. (2009). *Dangerous exits: Escaping abusive relationships in rural America.* Rutgers University Press.

Deschamps, M. (2015). *External review into sexual misconduct and sexual harassment in the Canadian Armed Forces.* Retrieved from National Defence and the Canadian Armed Forces <http://www.forces.gc.ca/assets/FORCES_Internet/docs/en/caf-community-support-services-harassment/erafinal-report-(april-20-2015)-eng. pdf>.

Doherty, D. (2017). *Rethinking safety planning: A self-directed tool for rural women who are abused. In* Innovations in Interventions to Address Intimate Partner Violence (pp. 18–32). Routledge.

Dugan, L., Nagin, D. S., & Rosenfeld, R. (1999). Explaining the decline in intimate partner homicide: The effects of changing domesticity, women's status, and domestic violence resources. *Homicide Studies, 3*(3), 187–214.

Dugan, L., Nagin, D., & Rosenfeld, R. (2001). *Exposure reduction or backlash? The effects of domestic violence resources on intimate partner homicide: Final report.* National Criminal Justice Reference Service. Retrieved from the United States Department of Justice on December, 19, 2011.

Dugan, L., Nagin, D. S., & Rosenfeld, R. (2003). Exposure reduction or retaliation? The effects of domestic violence resources on intimate-partner homicide. *Law & Society Review, 37*(1), 169–198.

DuMont, J., Hyman, I., O'Brien, K., White, M. E., Odette, F., & Tyyska, V. (2012). Factors associated with intimate partner violence by a former partner by immigration status and length of residence in Canada. *Annals of Epidemiology, 22*(11), 772–777.

Erez, E., Adelman, M., & Gregory, C. (2009). Intersections of immigration and domestic violence: Voices of battered immigrant women. *Feminist Criminology, 4*(1), 32–56.

Fisher-Borne, M., Cain, J. M., & Martin, S. L. (2015). From mastery to accountability: Cultural humility as an alternative to cultural competence. *Social Work Education, 34*(2), 165–181.

Foronda, C., Baptiste, D. L., Reinholdt, M., & Ousman, K. (2016). Cultural humility: A concept analysis. *Journal of Transcultural Nursing*. Available from https://doi.org/10.1177/1043659615592677.

Gillis, W. (October 23, 2017). Canadian female police band together to change 'intolerable' working conditions. *The Star*. Retrieved from: <https://www.thestar.com/news/crime/2017/10/23/canadian-female-police-band-together-to-change-intolerable-working-conditions.html>.

Guruge, S., & Humphreys, J. (2009). Barriers affecting access to and use of formal social supports among abused immigrant women. *Canadian Journal of Nursing Research*, *41*(3), 64−84.

Guruge, S., Khanlou, N., & Gastaldo, D. (2010). Intimate male partner violence in the migration process: Intersections of gender, race and class. *Journal of Advanced Nursing*, *66*(1), 103−113.

Guruge, S., Tiwari, A., & Lucea, M. (2010). In J. Humphreys, & J. C. Campbell (Eds.), *International perspectives on family violence. In* Family violence and nursing practice. New York: Springer.

Heise, L. (2018). *Violence against women: The missing agenda. The health of women* (pp. 171−196). Routledge.

Hoffart, I. (2014). *Walking the path together evaluation − Phases I and II*. The Alberta Council of Women's Shelters. Retrieved from <https://acws.ca/collaborate-document/2595/view>.

Jaffe, P.G., Fairbairn, J., & Reif, K. (2017). Children at risk of homicide in the context of intimate partner violence. In J. Campbell, & J. Messing (Eds.), *Assessing dangerousness, Third Edition: domestic violence offenders and child abusers*. New York: Springer.

Logan, T. K., Walker, R., & Leukefeld, C. G. (2001). Rural, urban influenced, and urban differences among domestic violence arrestees. *Journal of Interpersonal Violence*, *16*(3), 266−283.

Messinger, A. M. (2017). *LGBTQ intimate partner violence: Lessons for policy, practice, and research*. Oakland, CA: University of California Press. Available from https://doi.org/10.1525/california/9780520286054.001.0001.

Oklahoma Domestic Violence Fatality Review Board. (2014). *Domestic violence homicide in Oklahoma: A report of the Oklahoma Domestic Violence Fatality Review Board*. Retrieved from <https://ndvfri.org/download/oklahoma-statewide-annualreport-2014/?wpdmdl = 971&ind = 1QV4YFOq76Wnq8wpEgjfCkBNjY3Dh BdCaX1sGPPA9j0HYBZ5NwLVtCF2UpvR7tU7oLZBBu-8EcA7RxZN2fvzsA>.

Ontario Domestic Violence Death Review Committee (DVDRC). (2011). *Domestic Violence Death Review Committee 2010 annual report*. Toronto, ON: Office of the Chief Coroner.

Ontario Domestic Violence Death Review Committee (DVDRC). (2016). *Domestic Violence Death Review Committee 2015 annual report*. Toronto, ON: Office of the Chief Coroner.

Rana, S. (2012). *Addressing domestic violence in immigrant communities: Critical issues for culturally competent services*. National Resource Center on Domestic Violence.

Reckdenwald, A., & Parker, K. F. (2010). Understanding gender-specific intimate partner homicide: A theoretical and domestic service-oriented approach. *Journal of Criminal Justice*, *38*(5), 951−958.

Ristock, J. (2011). *Intimate partner violence in LGBTQ lives*. New York: Routledge.

Roguski, M. (2015). *It's not OK Campaign community evaluation project*. New Zealand: Prepared for Ministry of Social Development.

Salari, S. (2007). Patterns of intimate partner homicide suicide in later life: Strategies for prevention. *Clinical Interventions in Aging*, *2*(3), 441.

Sokoloff, N. J., & Dupont, I. (2005). Domestic violence at the intersections of race, class, and gender: Challenges and contributions to understanding violence against marginalized women in diverse communities. *Violence Against Women, 11*(1), 38–64.

Storer, H. L., Lindhorst, T., & Starr, K. (2013). The domestic violence fatality review: Can it mobilize community-level change? *Homicide Studies, 17*(4), 418–435.

Sutton, D., & Dawson, M. (2017). *Femicide of older women. Learning network brief 31.* London, ON: Learning Network, Centre for Research and Education on Violence Against Women and Children.

Taft, C. T., Macdonald, A., Creech, S., Monson, C. M., & Murphy, C. M. (2016). A randomized controlled clinical trial of the strength at home men's program for partner violence in military veterans. *Journal of Clinical Psychiatry, 77*(9), 1168–1175. Available from https://doi.org/10.4088/JCP.15m10020.

Taft, C. T., Walling, S. M., Howard, J. M., & Monson, C. (2011). Trauma, PTSD, and partner violence in military families. In S. Wadsworth, & D. Riggs (Eds.), *Risk and resilience in U.S. military families.* New York, NY: Springer.

Tutty, L. M., Radtke, H. L., Ateah, C. A., Ursel, E. J., Thurston, W. E., Hampton, M., & Nixon, K. (2017). The complexities of intimate partner violence: Mental health, disabilities, and child abuse history for White, Indigenous, and other visible minority Canadian women. *Journal of Interpersonal Violence,* 0886260517741210.

Whitaker, D. J., Haileyesus, T., Swahn, M., & Saltzman, L. S. (2007). Differences in frequency of violence and reported injury between relationships with reciprocal and nonreciprocal intimate partner violence. *American Journal of Public Health, 97*, 941–947. Available from https://doi.org/10.2105/AJPH.2005.079020.

Wilham, C. L. W. (2012). *An ounce of prevention: Accessions screening to prevent PTSD.* Retrieved from <https://apps.dtic.mil/dtic/tr/fulltext/u2/a562077.pdf>.

World Health Organization (WHO). (2016). *Global plan of action to strengthen the role of the health system within a national multisectoral response to address interpersonal violence, in particular against women and girls, and against children.* Retrieved from <https://apps.who.int/iris/bitstream/handle/10665/252276/9789241511537-eng.pdf?sequence = 1>.

Further reading

Michau, L., Horn, J., Bank, A., Dutt, M., & Zimmerman, C. (2015). Prevention of violence against women and girls: Lessons from practice. *The Lancet, 385* (9978), 1672–1684.

Moose Hide Campaign. (2019). Victoria BC: Moose Hide Campaign Development Society.

Index

Stereotypes, 21–22
Strength at Home Men's
    Program, 292–293
Structural violence, 19–21,
    243–244
Structured professional
    judgement, 126
Suicidal ideation, 24
Suicidality, 137, 286, 290
    Jeanne Cathleen Heard case,
        146–147
    Jeannette Goodwin case,
        149–150
    in perpetrators of domestic
        homicide, 138
    recommendations for
        addressing, 144–146
Survivor, 237–238

T
Teens dating relationships, 8
Toxic masculinity, 76
Traditional risk assessment
    tools, 126, 249–250
Transgender women, 74
Two-spirit, 64

U
Universal prevention, 102–103,
    274–275

V
VAIW. *See* Violence against
    Indigenous women
    (VAIW)

VAW. *See* Violence against
    women (VAW)
Victimization, 209, 212, 247, 257
Victoria Police Department,
    122–123
Violence, 65–66, 72, 234–235,
    237. *See also* Domestic
    violence (DV)
    in Adolescents' Dating
        Relationships Inventory,
        101
    perpetration, 257, 267,
        269–270
    prevention programming,
        101–102
    resistance, 260
Violence against Indigenous
    women, 234–235,
    240–242, 244
Violence against women (VAW),
    16, 18
Violent women, 261–262

W
Walking the Path Together:
    Protection, Options,
    Planning: Taking Action
    Related to Safety tool,
    291–292
Warning signs at work, 212
Web-based safety decision, 250
White Ribbon Workplace
    Accreditation Program,
    222
Women

controlling and violent,
    261–262
cyclical pattern of domestic
    violence in, 260
experiences of social
    isolation, 259
survivors of domestic
    violence, 169
victims, 257
Work
    domestic homicide at,
        212–214
    domestic violence at,
        209–212
    warning signs at, 212
Workplace
    dynamics, 119–120
    responding to Workplace DV,
        220–225
World Health Organization
    (WHO), 18

Y
Young adult dating
    relationships, 8
Youth
    dating relationships
        domestic violence in, 87
        as high-risk cases, 100–101
    defining, 88
    relationships, 282–283
Youth-specific prevention, 101

Made in the USA
Las Vegas, NV
08 January 2024

84078369R00181